Date Due

~~OCT 2 3 1989~~		ILL# 7[illegible]	2
~~#4474777~~		[illegible]	

Due

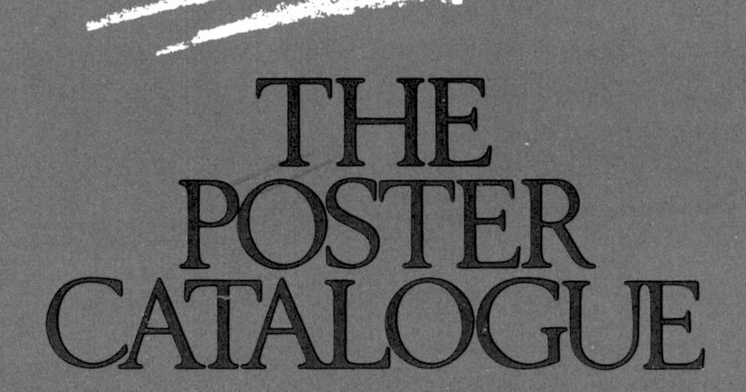

THE POSTER CATALOGUE

Art & Creative Director
Bruce McGaw

Editor-in-Chief
Nancy McGaw

Director of Production
Dennis Gaskin

Production Manager
Diana M. Jones

Layout and Design
Marion Manber Fine
Joann Jablonski

Copy
Vicki Wray

Acquisitions Coordinator
Paul Liptak

Printing
Kordet Graphics, Inc.

ISBN 0-9613932-0-3

TABLE OF CONTENTS

Artists whose subjects were too eclectic to be classified have their own sections in this Catalogue. For other artists, refer to the sections that best pertain to their work or look in the Index for specific page numbers.

I N T R O D

You are holding the embodiment of our ultimate quest for excellence—THE POSTER CATALOGUE. Thi Catalogue is the most comprehensive look ever taken at the young and dynamic poster industry, a industry that truly reflects the style of our times. Posters from the major publishers and the major artist who have contributed to the success of the medium are represented here, along with posters fro major galleries and museums, in what is surely the definitive book on contemporary poster

Milton Glaser, preeminent graphic artist has said, "Every time I make a poster I hope its function goe beyond the immediate objective to inform; that it clearly reflects my point of view and that it has an afterli that permits it to endure past its original intention. Curiously, the audience for posters is also responsive these non-essential elements. What is not essential becomes the place where the imagination is capture and where these ephemeral works produce their deepest effects. In this regard poste share with other truly poetic works the ability to illuminate the obvious.

The principal use of posters is no longer to impart information about events, but to impart impressio about ourselves. Once primarily a means of mass communication, posters have evolved into an art form their own with an audience that seems to be insatiabl

The poster industry has experienced monumental growth in the past decade. Prior to that time, a poster main function was to announce a gallery or museum exhibit, hence the name fine art exhibition poste Occasionally, a strong image might sell in a handful of shop

Today, the situation has turned itself around. Posters are produced primarily to be sold in shops and on occasionally to announce exhibitions. The "exhibition" has been dropped from their nam and they are now known simply as fine art poster

In 1979, there were probably less than 100 shops in major cities which specialized in posters. Toda countless establishments located everywhere from Chicago to Anchorage, from Los Angeles Laramie, thrive on the sale of posters while publishers are busy producing new pieces to me the demands of the poster consume

Although posters were barely an option for the consumer or retailer ten years ago, today they are a accepted and influential part of the art industry. According to a recent random sampling of readers of leading magazine for the art industry, the market for posters has almost doubled in the past two years. 1981, 36% of those polled sold posters. As of 1983, that figure had risen to 67% with 44 stating that posters were their most popular selling ite

Interest in posters has spread to the international market as well. One can find busy poster shops aroun the world from London to Tokyo; from Sydney to Singapor

It is interesting to note that although European posters launched the business, American posters no dominate the market. The industry has, in a sense, turned full cycle. The success generated by posters

U C T I O N

:e United States caused international marketers to look at the poster industry with renewed interest. An itial resistance on their part to the more expensive American posters was overcome by the indisputable gh quality and graphic appeal of the images the best American publishers produce.

ɔt a day can go by without seeing a poster. The media, a barometer of public tastes, has embraced the ɔster medium enthusiastically. Notice how often posters are used to decorate television and movie sets. ɿeir high visibility in magazines also underscores the popularity of the poster.

ɔsters are everywhere in our contemporary environment. They are appreciated mainly for the quality of ɿage rather than the message, if any, that they convey. They are, in fact, one medium where the image is r more important than the name of the artist who has created the image. The public buys what appeals them whether the creator is well known or unknown.

ɿree elements go into the making of a successful poster: image, design, and printing quality. The image is, course, the central focus of the poster. A dynamic image, however, also needs a strong design before it can ecome an aesthetically viable poster. And even with these two elements in sync, poor printing can still :in the overall effect. While not a formula for success, it is the happy marriage of these three elements that akes a poster special.

reation of a poster begins with the careful selection of the art work. Poster publishers, in their quest for esh, new images, find art work in several ways. Sometimes, they have a group of artists with whom they ave established continual working relationships. In addition, publishers review work submitted by hopeful tists. They also seek work from artists who are successful in other media. For every image that is ublished, hundreds of works of art have been reviewed.

ɿce an image is chosen, equal heed must be paid to the composition of an appropriate poster design. This cludes selection of type, positioning of the various elements and choosing background or border colors.

inting technology is then pushed to its limits to ensure accurate reproduction of the original image. Laser anning is utilized for color separation of the image. Utilizing this incredible technological development lows colors to be manipulated for absolute fidelity to the original image.

typical poster is printed in four colors, using offset lithography. After the initial run through the press, wever, much more work is likely to be done before arriving at the final printed image.

ɿe border or background colors may be an additional three colors. More work might include touch plates ed to augment a color already on the paper. Perhaps red flower petals need to be still brighter. A touch ate could be used to accomplish this.

pe may be still another color and varnishes might be applied to create contrast etween different elements of the poster.

INTRODUCTION

Using matte and glossy varnish side by side adds a richness to the poster surface and gives a distir punch to certain elements of the desig

Special inks can be used to reproduce a unique effect of the original or to highlight the type or other desi element. Posters can also be foil stamped, where a thin layer of metallic foil is stamped or various areas of the image, or even printed on foil coated pap

The paper on which a poster is printed is also of the utmost importance. A fine poster is printed on hi quality, heavy stock paper. Technically, this paper provides a printing surface that holds the ink well wh aesthetically yielding an attractive surface quality in the resulting printed image. Paper quality is a important to avoid crimping and insure a long life for the post

Some posters are silkscreened rather than offset. This is a particularly expensive process better suited some work than others. It might be noted that there is very little difference between a silkscreen poster a an original silkscreen other than edition size and artist's signatu Silkscreening can also be used in conjunction with offs

Today's typical poster is vastly different from the four color poster of ten years ago. The difference is subt but dramatic when you add all these other elements. These improvements have been fostered by industry experiencing prosperity and subsequent evolution. Today's discriminating poster consum demands greater sophistication and higher quality in their poster imag

"When we first entered the business some six years ago, the industry was yet to be born as we know today," says Bruce McGaw, a leading poster publisher/distributor. "The few images that existed were 'fi art exhibition' posters and had to be culled from European museums and galleri

"Interest in these works was steadily growing, but with the introduction of the 'generic' poster, the indust really took off. Here were images with a more widespread appeal. They were the sar kinds of images , design-wise, the public saw on a daily basis in the various med

"The poster business is still in its infancy stages," he continues. "We believe the audience for posters w continue to grow as long as publishers strive for quality and produce those special pieces that not or epitomize, but are on the forefront, of contemporary desig

It is, after all, quality that distinguishes a fine art poster from the rest. Well produced, artistically design posters speak eloquently to a large audience and hold the key to the industry's future. Carefully chos carefully printed, quality images will carry the poster indust

Posters are an art form that keeps pace with the times in which we live. As you go through the pages of t book, we are sure that the images you see will affirm th

'Although the poster is at its heart a medium for advertising an event or service, it has by virtue of its historical development remained the form among the applied arts most receptive to imaginative or artistic content."

Milton Glaser

A B S T R

M165 MEYER HAWTHORNE I 23 × 39

DAVID MEYER / HAWTHORNE I / MCGAW EDITIONS

DAVID MEYER / HAWTHORNE II / MCGAW EDITIONS

M166 MEYER HAWTHORNE II 23 × 39

A C T S

The aim of art is to represent not the outward appearance of things, but their inward significance."
This is not Jackson Pollock or Pablo Picasso talking, but the ancient Greek philosopher Aristotle.

uccessful poster speaks to the viewer immediately; it either communicates or it does not. Quality of
age and directness of composition make an instantaneous powerful impression or the poster has visually
led. Because abstract art shares some of these same qualities, it is enjoying a recent success in the poster
dium. With no recognizable references to fall back on, these images rely on purity of composition to
ate aesthetic impact.

nsider the abstract illusionist Michael Gallagher. His use of simple, direct composition and bold colors
kes his work easy to relate to at first glance. Other layers of artistic interpretation wait to be unravelled,
vever, giving his work the depth that makes him an important contributor to the contemporary art scene.

here's an acknowledged analogy between my work and a one room schoolhouse in that there is
nething to respond to for the elementary as well as the more advanced, enlightened students," says
llagher. "My work is a mad house of contradictions."

llagher's Greek Mouth *and* Night Fire By The River *are alive with color. Tactile brush strokes coalesce on*
illusionary three dimensional surface. A strength of these and other abstract posters lies in their ability
remain aesthetically viable long after that first powerful encounter with the image.

obvious, yet important, thing to note about abstract art is that it leaves the meaning of any image up to
viewer making it very adaptable to a multitude of environments. Look at The Arc, *by artist Jurgen*
ers. What one sees is color, form and movement. If these elements appeal to the viewer, the piece can be
lized as easily in home design as in corporate design.

re and more designers, in fact, are turning to abstract art to enrich public spaces. A piece like Peter
chell's diptych, Shasta A *and* Shasta B, *in a corporate environment, for example, makes a contemporary*
istic statement while adding warmth to what might otherwise be an impersonal space. Abstract images
ke just the right statement; there is never cause for concern about the inappropriateness of the subject
tter.

stract art takes on many guises. It can be hard edged and geometrical like the work of Agam or loose and
wing like Paul Jenkins' pieces. It can be the subtlely colored posters of Sonny Zoback or the bright palette
lized by Arthur Secunda.

asso once said, "There is no abstract art. You must always start with something." For abstract art
rrors the forms and colors found in the world around us, elements we live comfortably with each day.

GALLAGER
LOUIS K. MEISEL GALLERY / NEW YORK, NEW YORK

G75 GREEK MOUTH ☆ 34 × 24

GALLAGHER
LOUIS K MEISEL GALLERY
©1984 GALLAGHER / PUBLISHED & DISTRIBUTED BY BRUCE MCGAW GRAPHICS INC. NEW YORK, AND JUDITH L POSNER ASSOCIATES

G77 NIGHT FIRE BY THE RIVER ☆ 30 × 26

A7 AGAM BIRTH OF A FLAG 29 × 21 1/2

AGAM
AN AMERICAN PORTRAIT
1776-1976

Art 10'79
INTERNATIONAL ART FAIR
AGAM
GOLDMAN'S ART GALLERY HAIFA-ISRAEL
Stand 11-325

A12 AGAM GOLDMAN 32 1/2 × 21 5/8

MALKE · SAGE GALLERY

M31 McKINLEY SUN 30 × 16

G119 GRAMS LUNAR ASCENT 25 × 31

B158 BLOCK CURTAIN 25 × 39

AMANDA BLOCK AT EDITIONS LIMITED GALLERIES

一九八一年 セカンダ(米国)
東京国際美術展

S177 SECUNDA A CLEAR SPACE 35 × 22½

JAMES BYRD · PAINTINGS
ADI Gallery · San Francisco

B120 BYRD PINK WEDGE 32½ × 24½

A49 ALVAREZ ART EXPO '82 38 × 24

Elya Alvarez
at ART EXPO 1982

A54 ALVAREZ ART EXPO '84 24 × 32

Elya Alvarez OFFICIAL POSTER Art expo NY
NEW YORK COLISEUM · APRIL 5-9, 1984

"SOBRE LAS OLAS"

A52 ALVAREZ SOBRE LAS OLAS 24 × 32

OFFICIAL POSTER
Artexpo NY

A50 ALVAREZ ART EXPO '83 38 × 24

A C T S

K38 KITCHELL QUECHUA POT 25 × 39

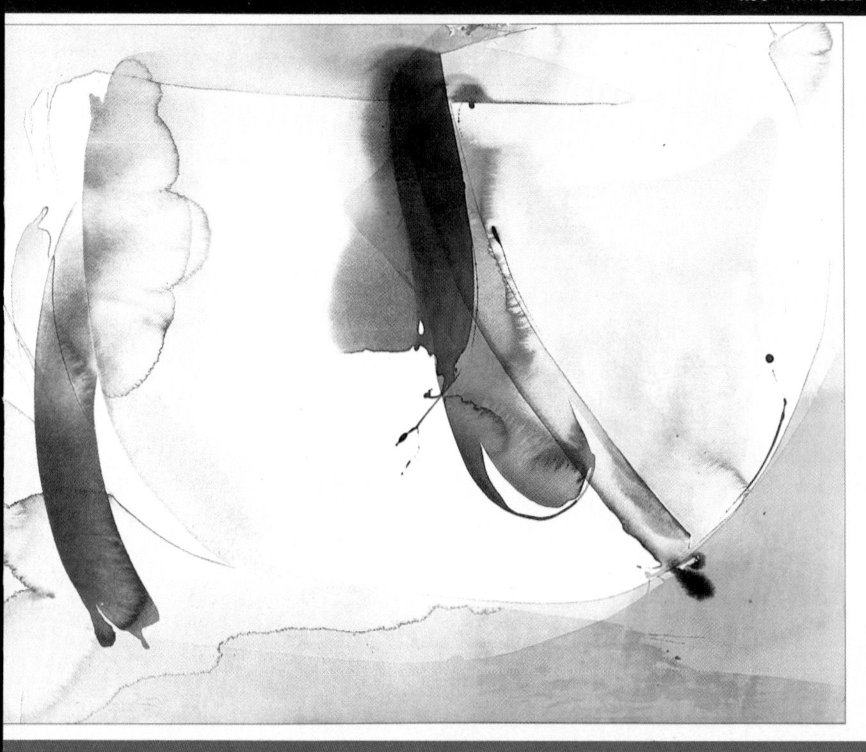
E D I T I O N S L I M I T E D

R O O K T E M P L E
A L L W E T

T30 TEMPLE ALL WET 36× 24

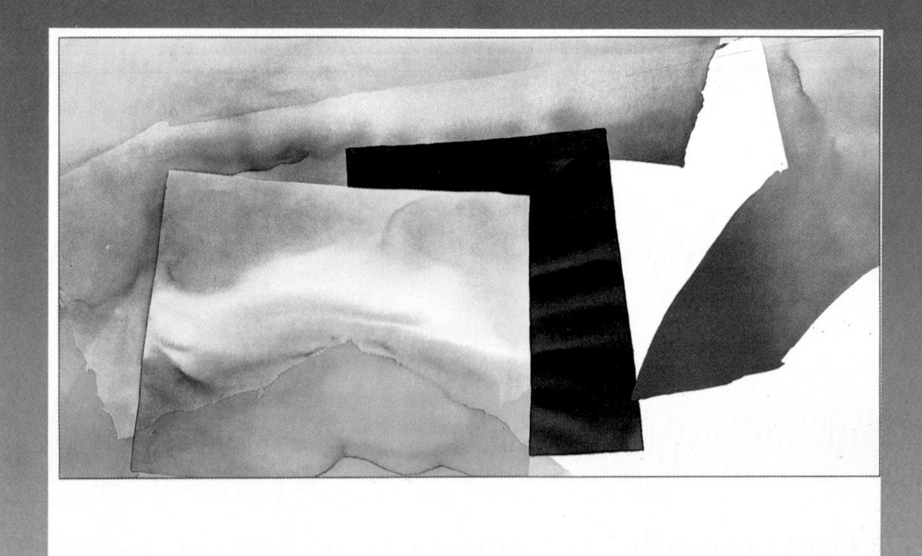

K51 KITCHELL SOLID PAST 24 × 38 1/2

K I T C

K54A SHASTA "A" 25×39

EDITIONS
LIMITED

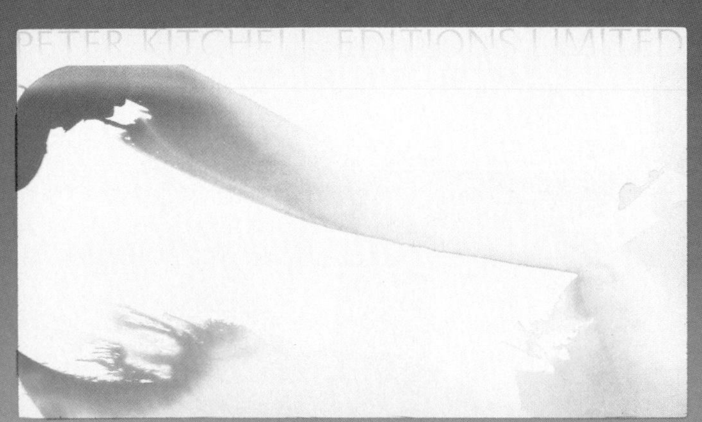
PETER KITCHELL EDITIONS LIMITED

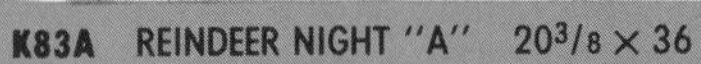

K83A REINDEER NIGHT "A" $20^3/_8 \times 36$

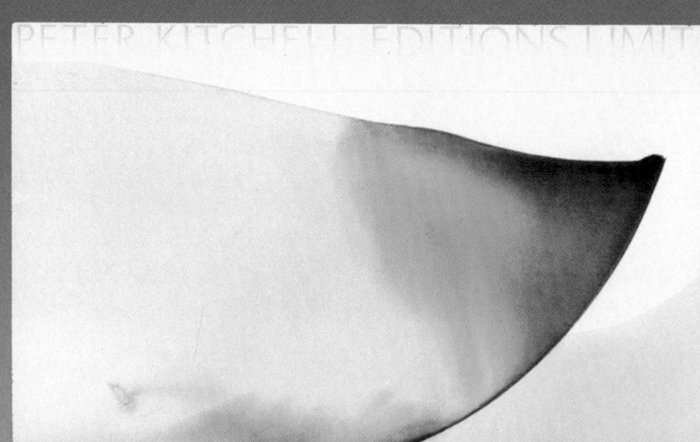
PETER KITCHELL EDITIONS LIMITE

K83B REINDEER NIGHT "B" $20^3/_8 \times 36$

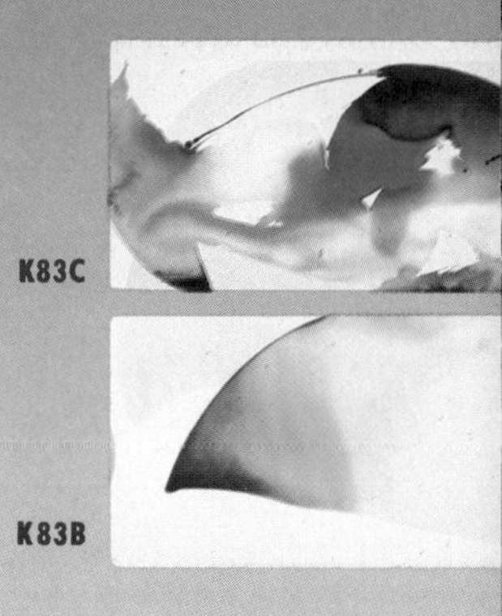

K83C

K83B

H E L L

K54B SHASTA "B" 25 × 39

EDITIONS
LIMITED

K83C REINDEER NIGHT "C" $20^{3}/_{8} \times 36$

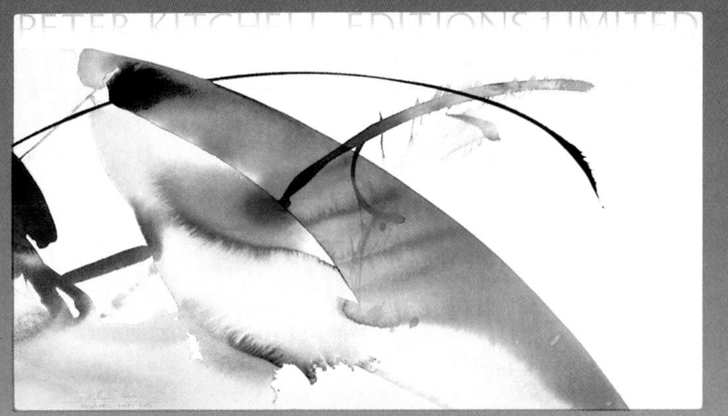

K83D REINDEER NIGHT "D" $20^{3}/_{8} \times 36$

K83D

K83A

PLEASE NOTE THAT *REINDEER NIGHT A, B, C, and D* SHOWN ABOVE, CAN ALSO BE HUNG IN THE CONFIGURATION SHOWN TO THE LEFT.

A B S T R

J20A JONES DIPTYCH "A" $38^{1}/_{8} \times 27^{1}/_{4}$

J20B JONES DIPTYCH "B" $38^{1}/_{8} \times 27^{1}/_{4}$

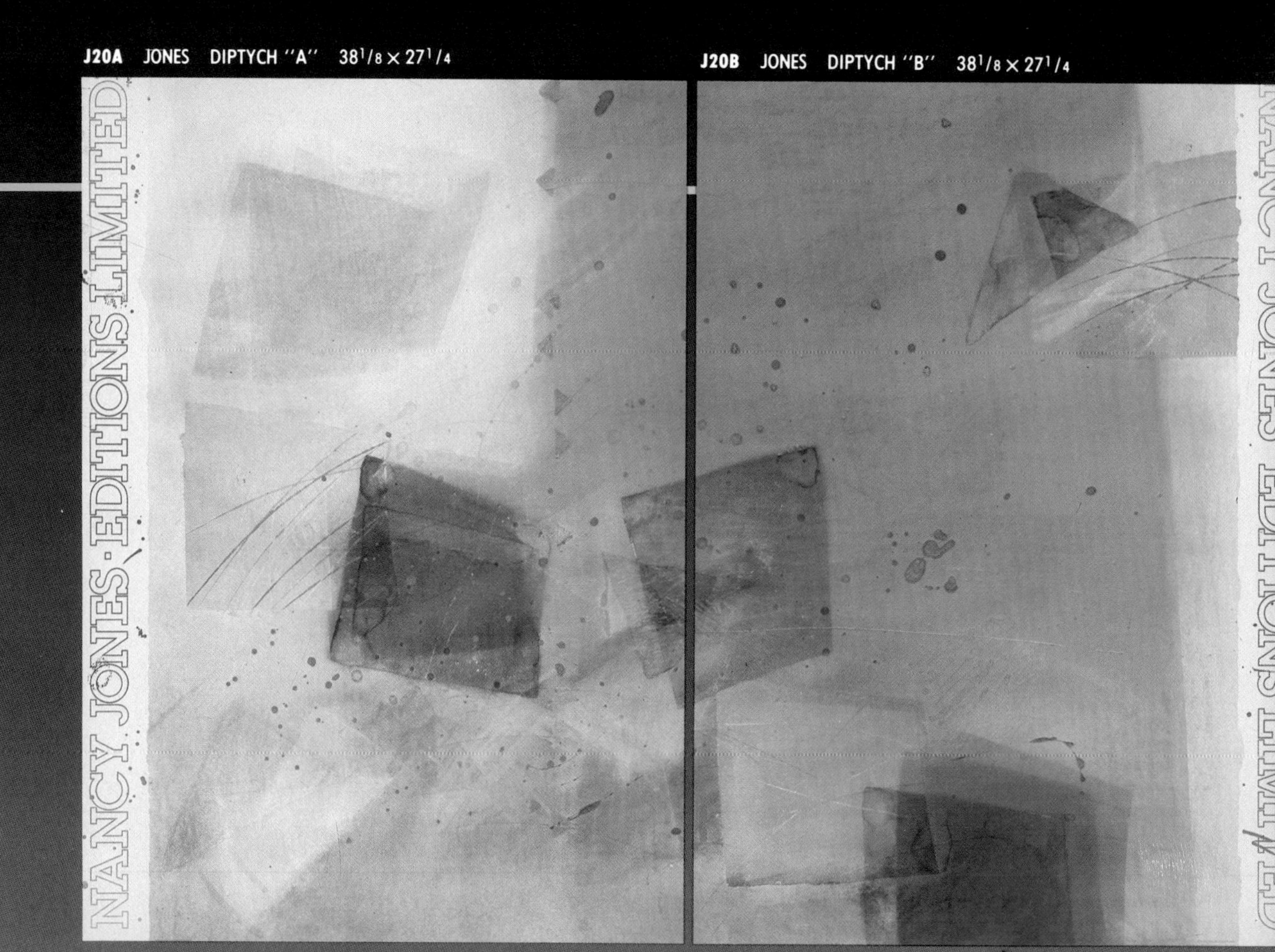
NANCY JONES · EDITIONS LIMITED

KOZO

IMPRESSIONS
46 RUE DE SEINE 75006 PARIS
JUIN-SEPTEMBRE 8

K66 KOZO IMPRESSIONS $22^{1}/_{2} \times 30^{1}/_{4}$

B44 BRIGGS BLUE CERVES II $24^{5}/_{8} \times 30$

LAMAR BRIGGS
FEBRUARY 20-MARCH 22, 1981 THE ART COLLECTOR SAN DIEGO, CALIFORNIA

B112 BRIGGS SPIRIT OF COAS VIII 38×25

Lamar
briggs
Ankrum Gallery Los Angeles January 23-February 17, 1979

LAMAR BRIGGS
ART EXPO 1981 NEW YORK CITY

B53 BRIGGS #9 $35^{1}/_{2} \times 24^{1}/_{4}$

LAMAR BRIGGS
PAINTINGS AND WORKS ON PAPER AUGUST 2-AUGUST 23, 1981
THE PUTNEY GALLERY ASPEN, COLORADO

B45 BRIGGS VEDRA / IBIZA #2 24×31

J3 GREEN BARRYMORE $24^1/_8 \times 35^5/_8$

PAUL JENKINS
watercolors
ELAINE HORWITCH GALLERIES July 12-31, 1979

PAUL JENKINS
American Music Theater
FESTIVAL

TRANSWORLD ART 1970-1980 / ALEX ROSENBERG GALLERY / APRIL 10-MAY 24 1980 / 20 W 57 NYC

J5 JENKINS VERMILLION BARAKA LITHOGRAPH $21^1/_2 \times 32$

PAUL JENKINS
American Music Theater
FESTIVAL
1985 SEASON · PHILADELPHI

J27 DURANGO WEDGE 23×39

J7 PALM SPRINGS $24^{1}/_{2} \times 38^{1}/_{8}$

PAUL JENKINS
PALM SPRINGS DESERT MUSEUM
9 DEC 1980 — 15 FEB 1981

THE DALLAS OPERA
1983 SEASON
IN CELEBRATION OF CARMEN BY PAUL JENKINS

J25 CELEBRATION OF CARMEN 36×24

FRIENDS of the EARTH

J9 RAIN PALACE $25 \times 26^{1}/_{4}$

W21 WOLTERS #101 $38^{7}/_{8} \times 18^{5}/_{8}$

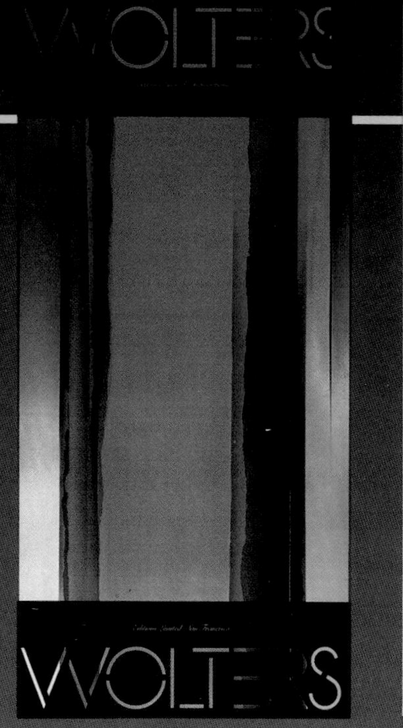
WOLTERS
WOLTERS

Z3 ZOBACK DAYBREAK 38 × 25

Zoback/Daybreak

Z2 ZOBACK SOLITUDE 38 × 25

Zoback
at the
Galerie Cote

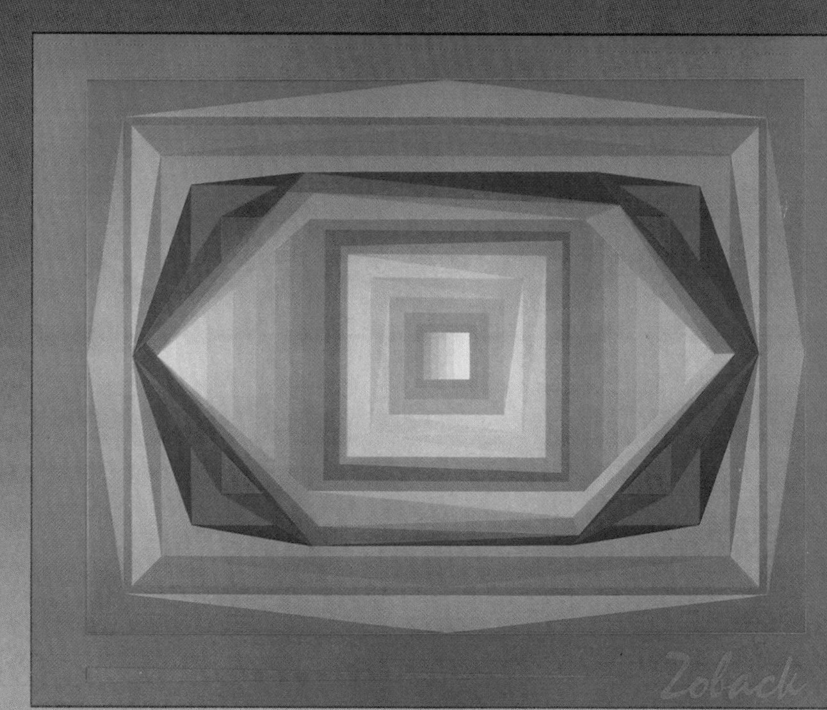
Zoback

Z9 ZOBACK SPECTRUM 24 × 36

M143 MOROSS NEW WAVES 36 × 24

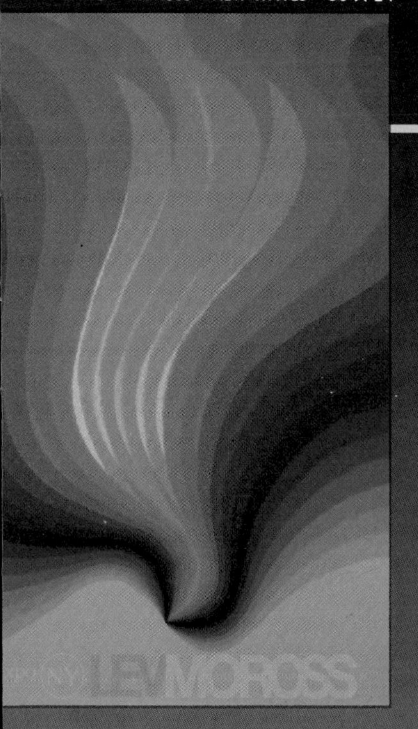
LEV MOROSS

M23 MOROSS RENE 36 × 24

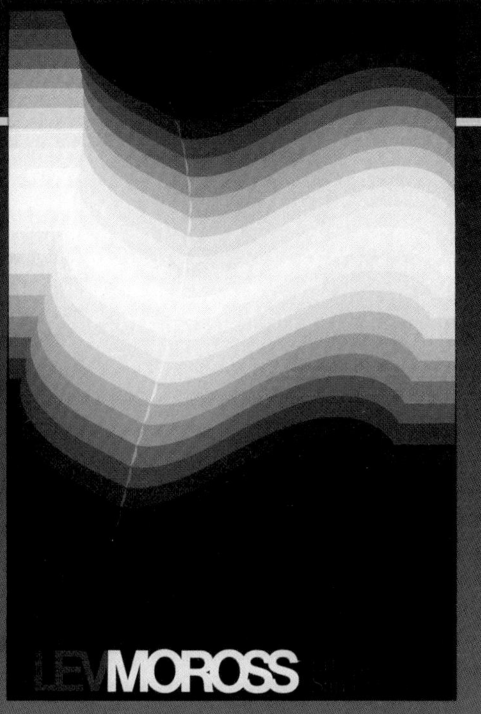
LEV MOROSS

M27 MOROSS FANS $35\frac{7}{8} \times 24\frac{3}{8}$

LEV MOROSS

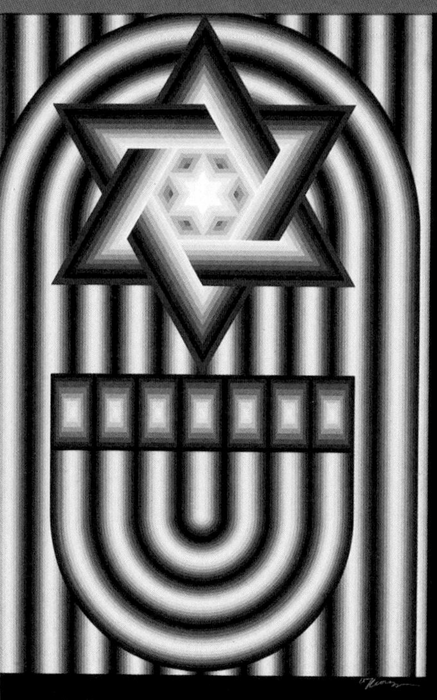
LEV MOROSS

M142 MOROSS STAR OF DAVID 36 × 24

M25 MOROSS ALIVENESS 36 × 24

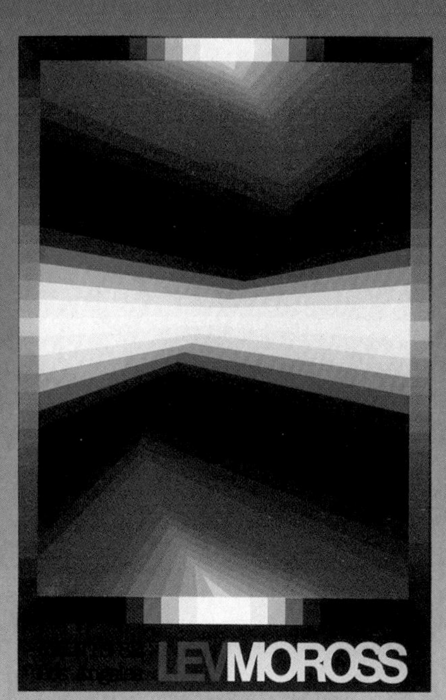
LEV MOROSS

M47 MOROSS NAIF INTERNATIONAL 36 × 24

ALL POSTERS ON THIS PAGE ARE SERIGRAPHS.

P E T

P2 BROWN & BEIGE *SERIGRAPH* 40 × 30

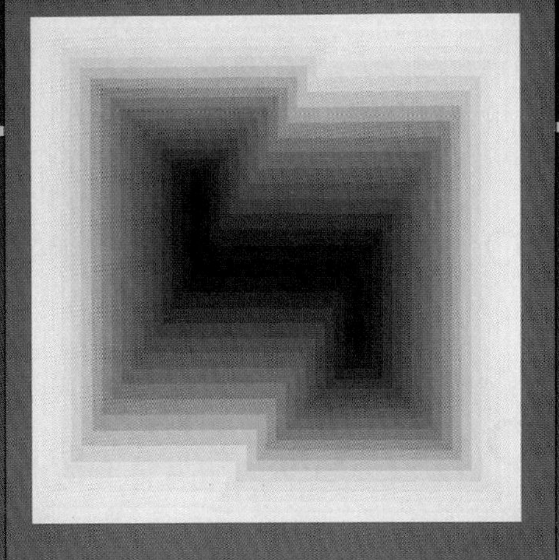
jurgen peters
editions limited
indianapolis san francisco

P6 ARC *SERIGRAPH* 40 × 30

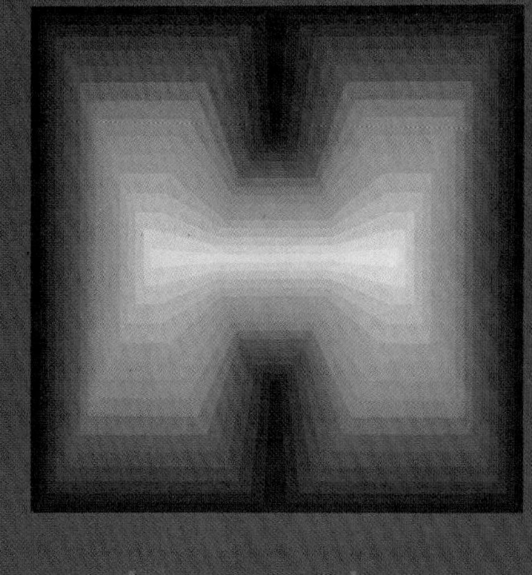
jurgen peters
editions limited
indianapolis san francisco

P21 FALTUNG *SERIGRAPH* $40^{7}/_{8}$ × $29^{7}/_{8}$

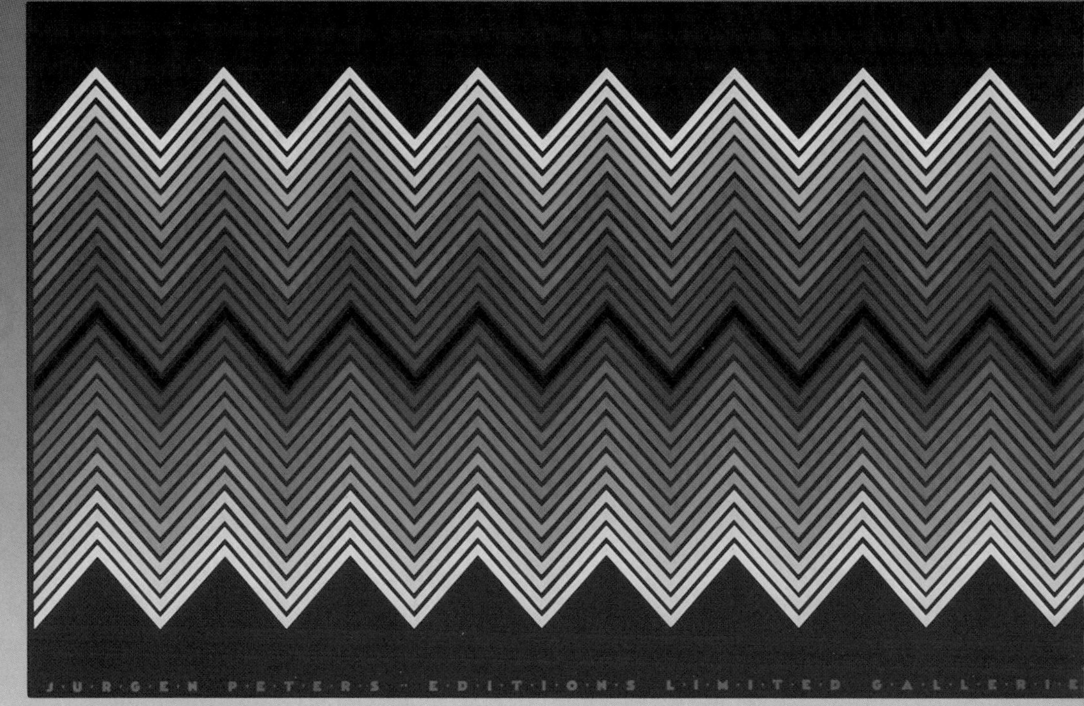

P44 HORIZON *SERIGRAPH* $24^{1}/_{2}$ × $38^{1}/_{2}$

P8 OCTAGON *SERIGRAPH* 40 × 30

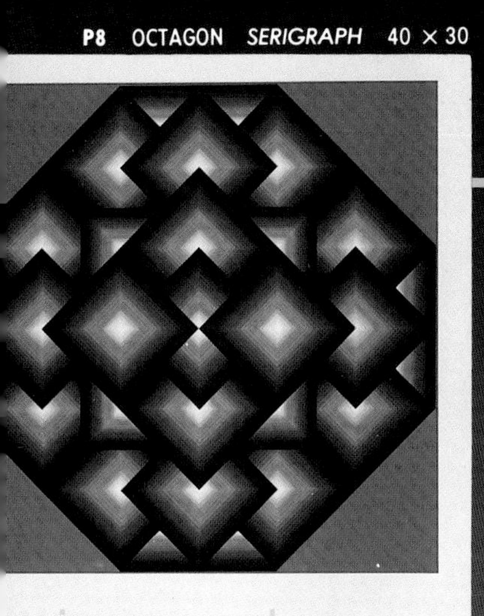
jurgen peters
editions limited
ndianapolis san francisco

P7 ILLUMINATION *SERIGRAPH* 40 × 30

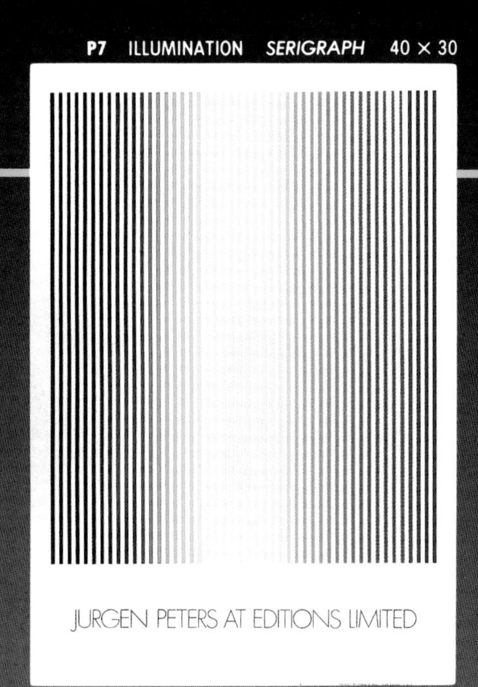
JURGEN PETERS AT EDITIONS LIMITED

P62 MATRIX 39 × 25

jurgen peters – editions limited

R·G·E·N P·E·T·E·R·S - E·D·I·T·I·O·N·S L·I·M·I·T·E·D G·A·L·L·E·R·I·E·S

P63 LIGHT HORIZONS *SERIGRAPH* $24^{3}/_{4} \times 37^{1}/_{2}$

P E T E R S

P84 SIMULTANEOUS II *SERIGRAPH* 25 × 40

JURGEN PETERS/EDITIONS LIMITED

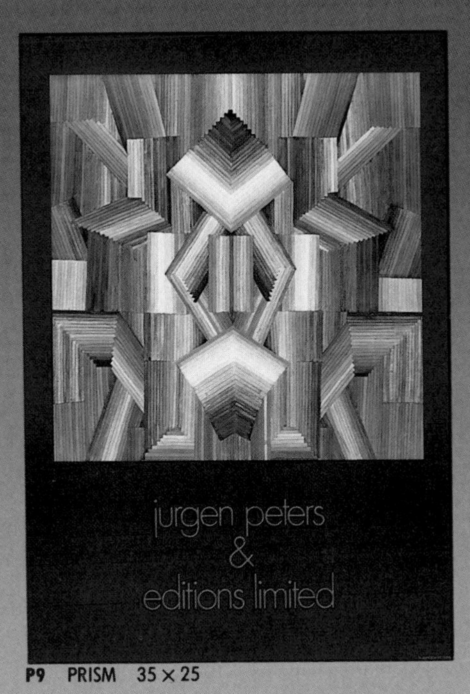
jurgen peters
&
editions limited

P9 PRISM 35 × 25

RAINBOW SPACE LIGHT
JURGEN PETERS - EDITIONS LTD.

P19 SPACE LIGHT 30 × 22

RAINBOW
JURGEN PETERS - EDITIONS LTD.

P20 SPACE DARK 30 × 22

L E P A R C

L43 WAVE/BURGUNDY *SERIGRAPH* 24 × 30

LE PARC
JUDITH L. POSNER & ASSOC. INC.

LE PARC
JUDITH L. POSNER & ASSOC. INC.

L45 WAVE/GREY *SERIGRAPH* 24 × 30

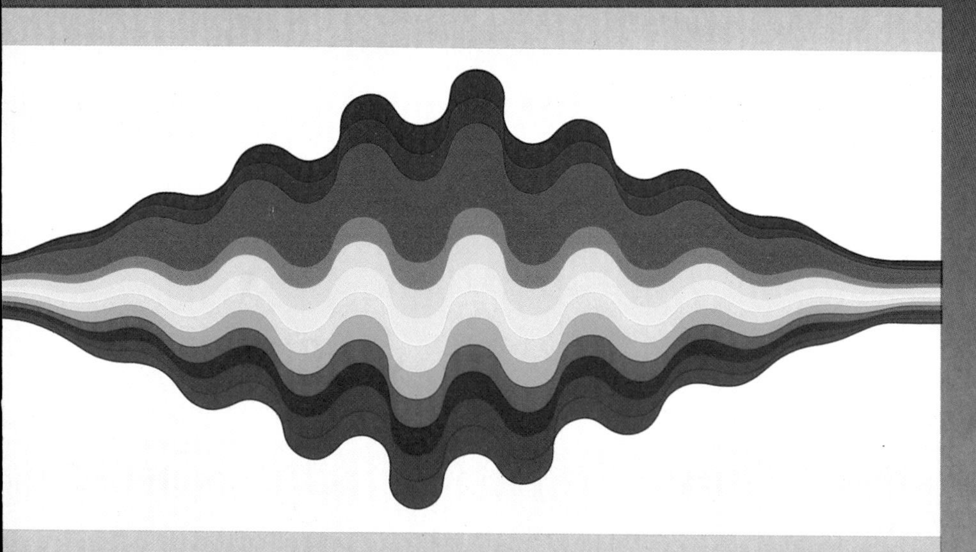
LE PARC
JUDITH L. POSNER & ASSOC. INC.

L44 WAVE/BEIGE *SERIGRAPH* 24 × 30

S E C

S68 LE CHAPITRE 34 5/8 × 21

ARTHUR SECUNDA
Fiac 79 - Le Chapitre - Paris

S2 HELLO CALIFORNIA 37 1/8 × 19 1/2

Secunda
HELLO CALIFORNIA
20th
ANNIVERSARY
HADDAD'S
FINE ARTS

S145 COLINA D'ORO 29 × 22 1/4

Secunda
25th
ANNIVERSARY
HADDAD'S FINE ART

Secunda
Owl 57 Galleries
Woodmere, New York
December 1978 - January 1979

S3 NEW DAWN 25 × 29

Secunda
JOHN & LYNNE BOLEN GALLERY, IN
ART EXPO NY

S77 MASSIF CENTRAL 37 1/4 × 23 3/4

U N D A

S5 VOLCANO 38 × 20

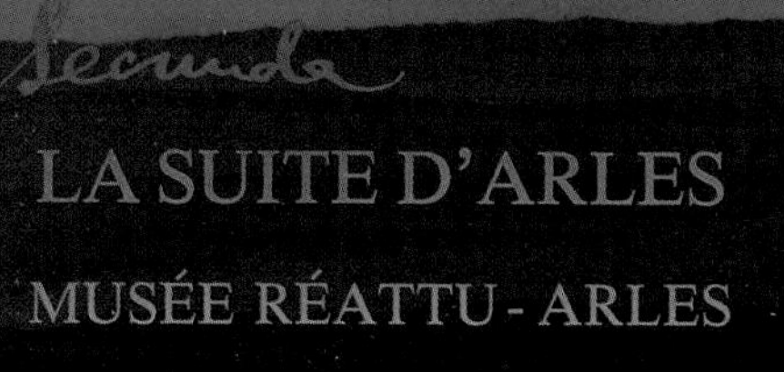
Secunda
LA SUITE D'ARLES
MUSÉE RÉATTU - ARLES

S28 BLUE OCEAN $37^{3}/_{4} \times 21^{7}/_{8}$

Secunda
ART 80

S21 SPACE WARP 31 × 18

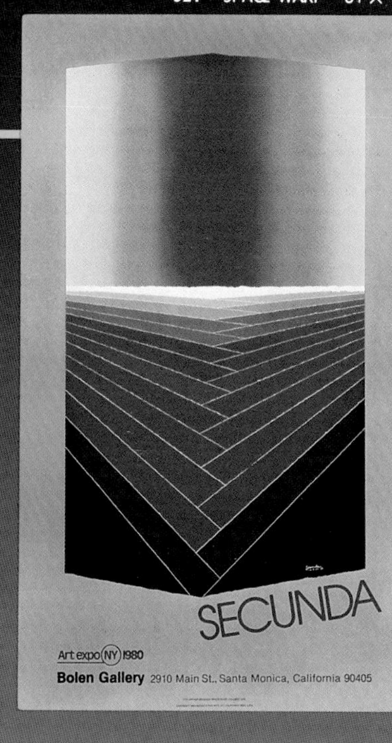
SECUNDA
Art expo NY 1980
Bolen Gallery 2910 Main St., Santa Monica, California 90405

K E L L E R

K17 NEVADA BURGUNDY *OFFSET & SERIGRAPH* ☆ 19½ × 39½

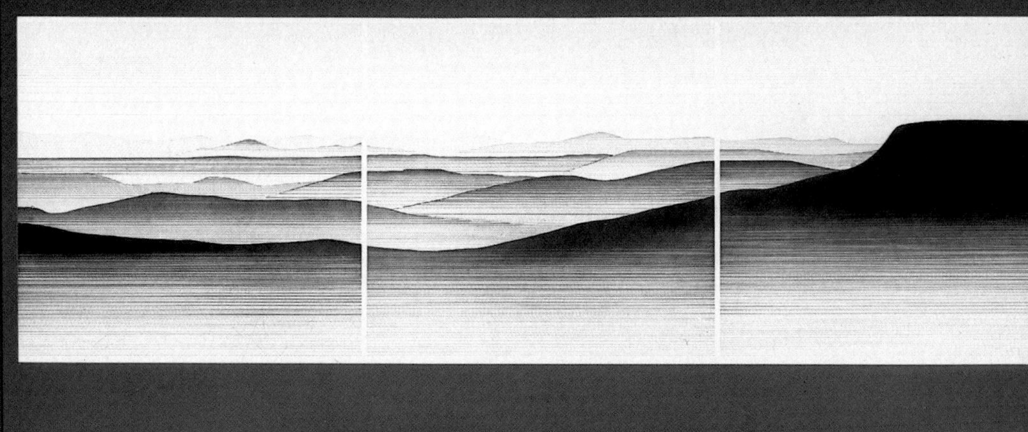
CLAUDIA KELLER · NEVADA · JOHN SZOKE GRAPHIC

CLAUDIA KELLER · NEVADA · JOHN SZOKE GRAPHIC

K18 NEVADA BEIGE *OFFSET & SERIGRAPH* ☆ 19½ × 39½

CLAUDIA KELLER · NEVADA · JOHN SZOKE GRAPHIC

K19 NEVADA GREY *OFFSET & SERIGRAPH* ☆ 19½ × 39½

D50 BEIGE ROUND *SERIGRAPH* 35 × 23

doug danz
JUDITH L. POSNER & ASSOC., INC.

D49 BROWN ROUND *SERIGRAPH* 34 × 23

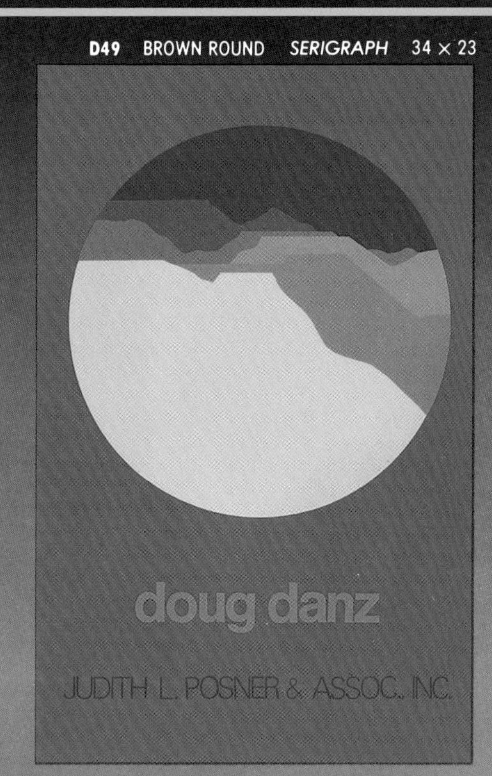
doug danz
JUDITH L. POSNER & ASSOC., INC.

DOUG DANZ POSNER GALLERY MILWAUKEE

D78 WAY OUT WEST 24 × 31 7/8

PEGASUS
CARMELA EMERSON

E46 EMERSON PEGASUS 24 × 30 ☆

M A L S

hen early man picked up the original drawing implement, the very first thing to appear on the walls of his cave were pictures of animals. From that day onward, people have continued to adorn their s with images of animals making the popularity of animal posters only natural.

nals can represent many things to different people. They can be perceived as friendly or majestic; cute owerful; sleek or lovable. These posters are the visualizations of these many qualities and, so, fulfill a ety of design needs.

most popular animal poster in the collection is Bob Talbot's Orca. *The subtle textures of the water, the ssive graceful forms of the whales, and the intriguing play of lights against darks make this image slate into a poster with terrific impact.*

ais image, Bob Talbot says: "When you're photographing whales you have to get a lot of things coming ther at the same time—the weather, the water conditions, the light; you have to be ready, your pment has to be working and the whales have to be doing something. To me, this image is the epitome l those things being right. It's that one moment when everything comes together that makes this poster pecial."

r since the "Save the Whales" movement brought this endangered species to the forefront of our ntion, there has been tremendous interest in this spectacular creature. This also contributes to the cial success of Orca.

lovers are notorious for their devotion to the feline species. Cats are beautiful and their different lities lend well to a number of design options. Artist Liz Shepherd, for example, uses the sleek lines of to create clean, elegant imagery in her posters. Major Felten uses another member of the cat family, panther, to create dramatic, very modern poster images. Carlos Sanchez also uses the panther, but his ges have an art deco feel. Other posters such as Ms. Muffet *or* The Favorite Cat *emphasize the lovable ect of cats.*

s create engaging poster imagery because of their often unusual shapes and vibrant coloration. cocks, flamingoes, and birds of fortune lend their vivid plumage to create colorful posters that would hten any environment.

kind has always respected and loved animals. We have depended on animals for our transportation, for sport, and for companionship. We recognize the beauty and strength and vulnerability of these atures. Animal posters convey all this while decorating our interiors with dynamic images.

M45 MENDELSOHN WHITE CRANES 35 × 26

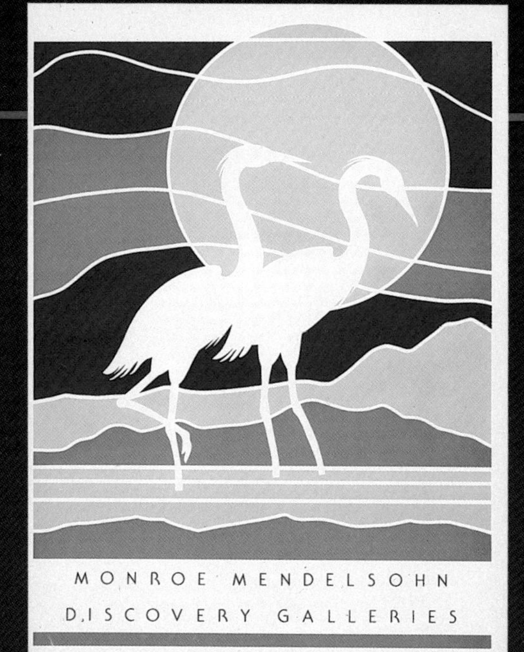
MONROE MENDELSOHN
DISCOVERY GALLERIES

S38 SHOUSON CRANES 25 7/8 × 18

SHOUSON

S39 SHOUSON PHEASANTS 25 7/8 × 18

SHOUSON

MONROE MENDELSOHN/DISCOVERY GALLERIES/CENTURY CITY/LOS ANGELES

M38 MENDELSOHN SWANS *OFFSET WITH EMBOSSING* 17 × 38

S163 SPAFFORD FLAMINGOS 36 × 24

B150 BROWN CRANE 30 × 22 1/4

FRESHMAN · BROWN
ESMAÑARTS

B154 BROWN KING FISHER 30 × 22 1/4

38 1/2 × 19

123 HOITSU IRIS & MANDARIN DUCKS

DEBORAH HOWARD
GALERIE MICHAEL
CENTURY CITY · LOS ANGELES
PAINTINGS AND SERIGRAPHS
AUG. 8, 1982 THRU AUG. 31, 1982

H109 HOWARD COCKATOO 36 × 24

BRIAN DAVIS
GALERIE MICHAEL
CENTURY CITY / LOS ANGELES
DEC. 1, 1981 THROUGH JAN. 1, 1982

D132 DAVIS PARROT 33 × 22

G105A GRIGG THE HERONRY "A" 24 × 28 1/2

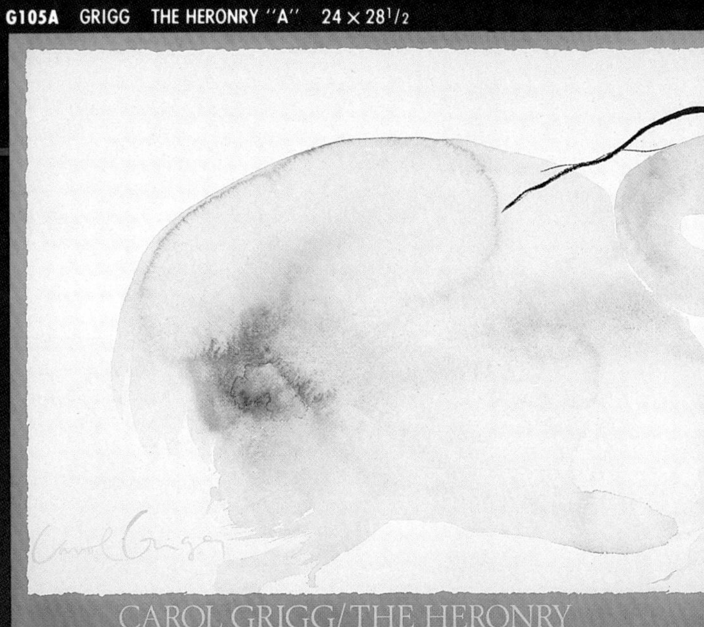
CAROL GRIGG/THE HERONRY

G105B GRIGG THE HERONRY "B" 24 × 28 1/2

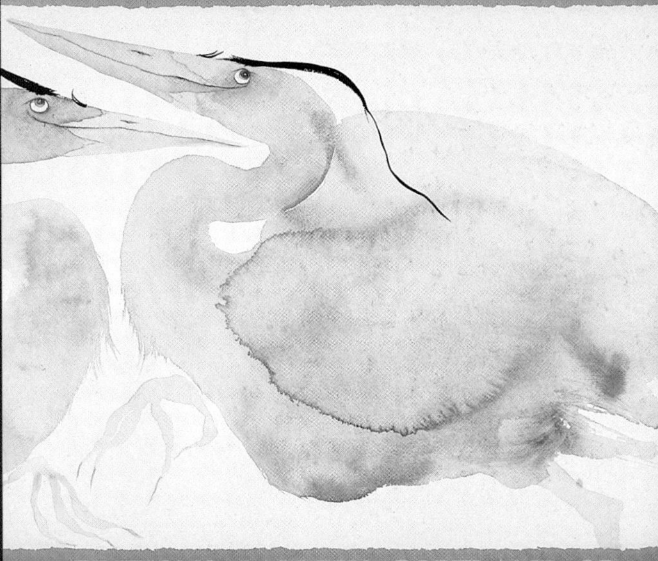
EDITIONS GALLERY/PORTLAND, OR.

Mara Abboud

A39 ABBOUD BLUE JARDINIERES 36 × 24

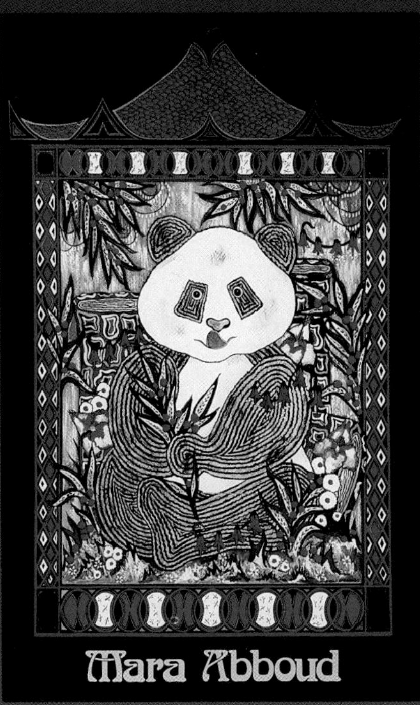
Mara Abboud

A47 ABBOUD CHINA DOLL 38 × 24

MARA ABBOUD
Edward Weston Graphics
PARIS•LOS ANGELES•LONDON•NEW YORK•MILAN

A1 ABBOUD UNICORN 34 × 22 1/4

S70 SANCHEZ COCKATOO 36 × 24

CARLOS SANCHEZ
RT EXPO NEW YORK • APRIL 22-26 1982

S71 SANCHEZ BLACK SWAN 36 × 24

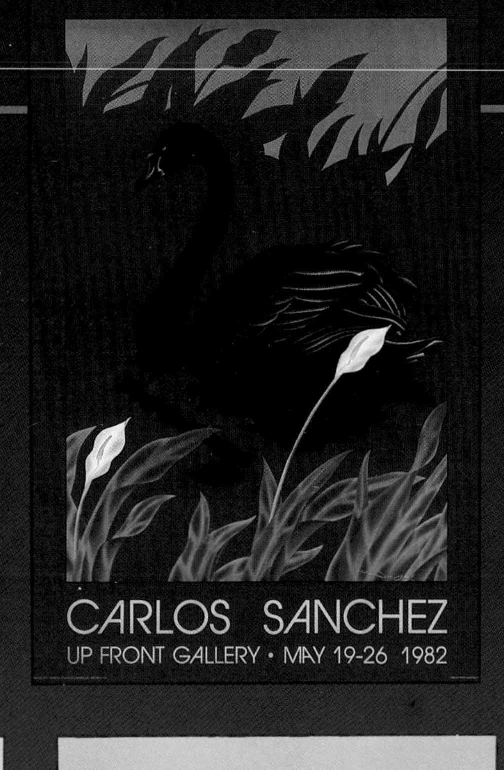
CARLOS SANCHEZ
UP FRONT GALLERY • MAY 19-26 1982

C97 CANNING PARROT $25^{5/8} \times 18^{3/4}$

KATE CANNING

L'Affiche Illustrée

Mara Abboud

A40 ABBOUD FLAMINGO WALTZ 36 × 24

Mara Abboud

A38 ABBOUD ROYAL HOUNDS 36 × 24

PHOEBE BRUNNER
BIRDS OF FORTUNE
LES BEAUX ARTS

B57 BRUNNER BIRDS OF FORTUNE $36^{1/2} \times 25$

S132 ORIENTAL EBONY ☆ 24 × 36 1/8

Liz Shepherd

Liz Shepherd 82
LIZ SHEPHERD/JANNE GALLERIE ABC ENTERTAINMENT CENTER CENTURY CITY, LOS ANGELES

S135 SIAMESE 24 × 36

Liz Shepherd '84

LIZ SHEPHERD/SHIBUNKAKU ROYAL GALLERY KYOTO, JAPAN

S141 KITTEN ☆ 24 × 36

W41 WOOD CAT IN THE WINDOW 36 × 26

Muriel Hughes-Wood
Helco Graphics
Art Expo N.Y.
April 7th to 11th '83

F45 THE FAVORITE CAT 39 × 25

THE FAVORITE CAT.
The Metropolitan Museum of Art
Department of Prints and Photographs

C158 CAT & SPIDER 38 × 25

METROPOLITAN CAT
A BOOK FROM THE METROPOLITAN MUSEUM OF

Foujita
1926
METROPOLITAN CATS A new book from The Metropolitan Museum of Art

F44 FOUJITA SMALL CAT 24 × 27

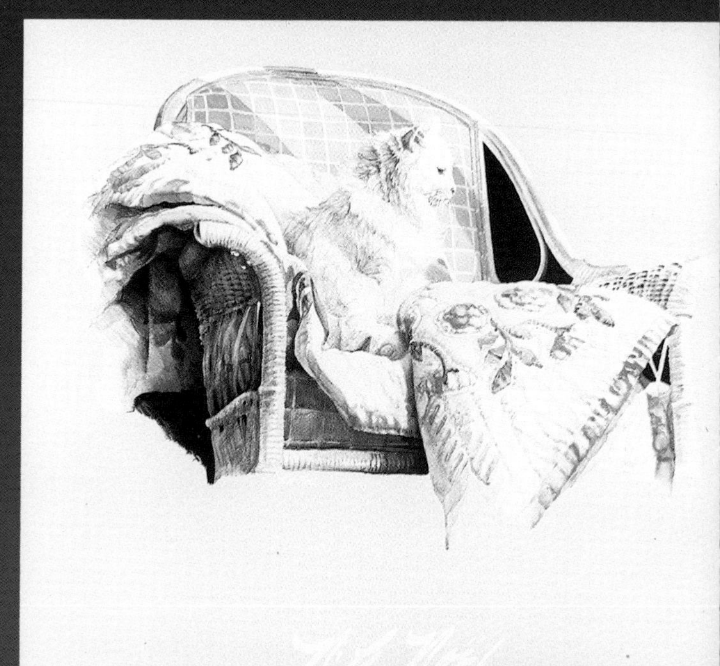

N48 NOEL CAT ON A QUILT 34 1/2 × 39

V8 VITTORIO 100 CATS AND A MOUSE $35^3/_4 \times 24^1/_4$

onehundredcatsandamouse

G87 GOLDSTROM IN THE GARDEN 26×32

G88 GOLDSTROM ORIENTAL VASE 26×32

V5 VAUX BLACK AND WHITE CAT 20×34

F70 FELTEN PANTHER 36 × 24

MAJOR FELTEN
20TH CENTURY MODERNISM A POSTER SERIES
OF INTERNATIONAL GRAPHIC ART PUBLISHED BY
DAVIS·BLUE ARTWORK

F69 FELTEN TWO PANTHERS 36 × 24

MAJOR FELTEN
DAVIS·BLUE ARTWORK

Jacquie Marie Vaux · Paintings

V6 VAUX TIGER 27 × 31

S127 SABIN CATS $31\frac{1}{2} \times 21$

RACY SABIN

E45 ELLESCAS MS. MUFFET $31\frac{7}{8} \times 26$

DICK ELLESCAS
"MS. MUFFET"
DISCOVERY GALLERIES

SHAWN RICE
This picture is from the Methuen Children's book, "Over The Moon."
This poster is published by
You can see all the pictures at
PORTAL GALLERY
16A Grafton Street, London
Nov. 14–Dec. 3.

R58 RICE OVER THE MOON 28×22

Tom Palmore

P32 PALMORE MR. D.I. $25\frac{1}{8} \times 27\frac{7}{8}$

M134 REFLECTIONS 24 × 36

SUZANNE MARIE/VIVA GRAPHICS

suzann
marie
Art Expo West 8

SUZANNE MARIE/VIVA GRAPHICS

M136 CHESHIRE CAT 24 × 30

M139 UNICORNS 36 × 24

IZANNE MARIE/VIVA GRAPHICS/ART EXPO NY 83

M138 FLAMINGOS 24 × 33

Suzanne Marie New Paintings 1981

SUZANNE MARIE NEW PAINTINGS

M135A MISTY ENCOUNTER "A" 36 × 24

M135B MISTY ENCOUNTER "B" 36 × 24

F76 FARRINGTON TIGER MOTHER WITH KITTEN 24 × 36

KITTY FARRINGTON
DISCOVERY GALLERIES

F77 FARRINGTON PANDA MOTHER WITH CUB 34 × 24

KITTY FARRINGTON
DISCOVERY GALLERIES

KITTY FARRINGTON
DISCOVERY EDITIONS

F90 FARRINGTON BLACK PANTHER 38 × 20

ENDANGERED

E34 ENDANGERED PANDA 30 × 24 1/4

T17 TALBOT ORCAS ☆ 24 × 31$^1/_2$

O R C A S
PHOTOGRAPH / BOB TALBOT

T A L B O T
ORCINUS ORCA

T35 TALBOT ORCINUS ORCAS 24 × 31$^1/_2$

S105 SANCHEZ PANTHER 24 × 36

CARLOS SANCHEZ
MARSHA MICHAELS & COMPANY

M99 MILLER FLAMINGOS 31 × 18

KIRK MILLER
M·E·I·SANTA MONICA·CALIFORNIA

FIELD GALLERY
NEW YORK

G89 GAETANO FIELD GALLERY 36 × 24

JOHN MARTINEAU
ART EXPO · 1983 · NEW YORK
American Design Ltd.

M74 MARTINEAU FLIGHT OF THE IBIS 24 × 37 1/2

R13 ROBERTS TROTTER ☆ 25 × 32

HELGA ROBERTS · BRUCE MCGAW GRAPHICS · ART EXPO · N.Y. · MARCH 5-9, 1981

S112 SANCHEZ DOG 36 × 24

CARLOS SANCHEZ
NEW YORK ART EXPO · APRIL 7-11 '83

CARLOS SANCHEZ · FRONT LINE EDITIONS · MAY 1983

S114 SANCHEZ DEER 24 × 36

N61 NEWMAN AMERICAN BISON 36 × 24

Sierra Club
WILDLIFE SERIES

N62 NEWMAN CARIBOU AT MT. DENALI 36 × 24

Sierra Club
WILDLIFE SERIES

THE NATURE COMPANY
Jeff Foott

F95 FOOTT SEA OTTER 25 × 27

W53 WEHRLI HARE & BEAR 30 × 24

MARY ELLEN WEHRLI
GEARY'S
Beverly Hills

W54 WEHRLI KITTENS 30 × 24

MARY ELLEN WEHRLI
GEARY'S
Beverly Hills

Puppies

R70 ROBYN PUPPIES 12 × 28

V10 VAN HOESEN SALLY $25^{3}/_{8} \times 19$

BETH VAN HOESEN: PRINTS, DRAWINGS, WATERCOLO

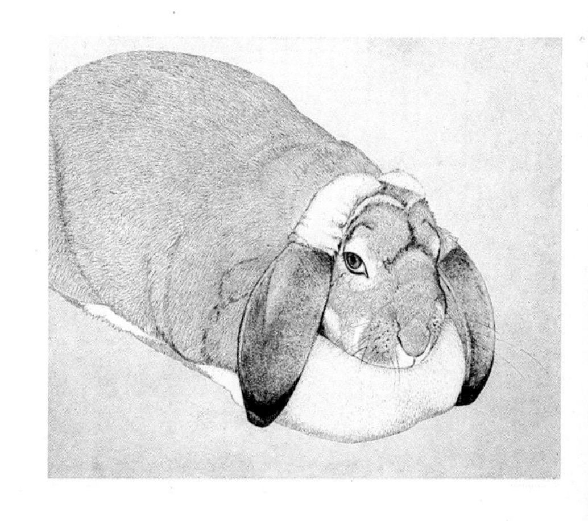

OAKLAND MUSEUM RETROSPECTIVE OAKLAND, CALIFORNIA MAY 13-JULY 6

H125 HERRERO PENGUINS 20×36

STEINHART AQUARIUM GOLDEN GATE PARK SAN FRANCISCO

FRIENDS OF THE EARTH

B107 BURLAND FRIENDS OF THE EARTH $25^{1}/_{4} \times 25^{1}/_{2}$

036 OREN KENTUCKY DERBY 30 × 21

KENTUCKY
DERBY
FESTIVAL 1984

E78 ELLIOTT BLACK PANTHERS 28 × 29 3/4

RUSS ELLIOTT

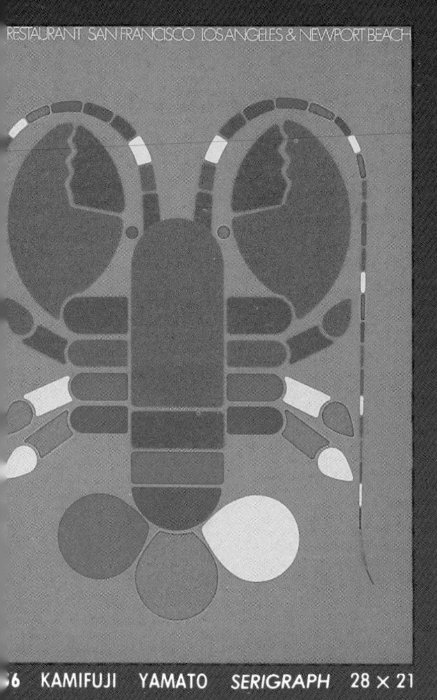
RESTAURANT SAN FRANCISCO LOS ANGELES & NEWPORT BEACH

6 KAMIFUJI YAMATO *SERIGRAPH* 28 × 21

SOHO
GALLERY

SUMMER '80
SANTA MONICA, CA

B30 BRATTON BETTA 1 24 1/4 × 34

E50 ELLIOTT REFLECTIONS ☆ 25 × 28

Reflections

John James Audubon June 1982 Douglas Kenyon, Inc, Chicago

A66 AUDUBON AMERICAN SWAN $24^3/_4$ × 33

BLOW
BUBBLE GUM
VANCE
CHICAGO USA
PAT'D
9-11-17
4-24-28

B133 GUMBALL MACHINE NO. 15 ☆ 36 × 22

"For myself," says the photo-realist Charles Bell, "choosing subjects is definitely an emotional process rather than an intellectual exercise. A large part of the process is dispassionately putting things together with disregard for what the objects are except as tools for composition, yet part of it is very much concerned with the subject. By radically changing the size of everyday objects we can get into them and more easily explore their surfaces and construction—their reality. I am also concerned with the feelings we share about familiar objects, but not in a nostalgic way. Rather it's like the feeling you get when you discover that a place you have seen in a hundred post cards really is beautiful. I'm saying, 'hey look, these everyday things really are terrific.'"

M65 McBRIDE DECISIONS, DECISIONS $31^{1}/_{2} \times 24$

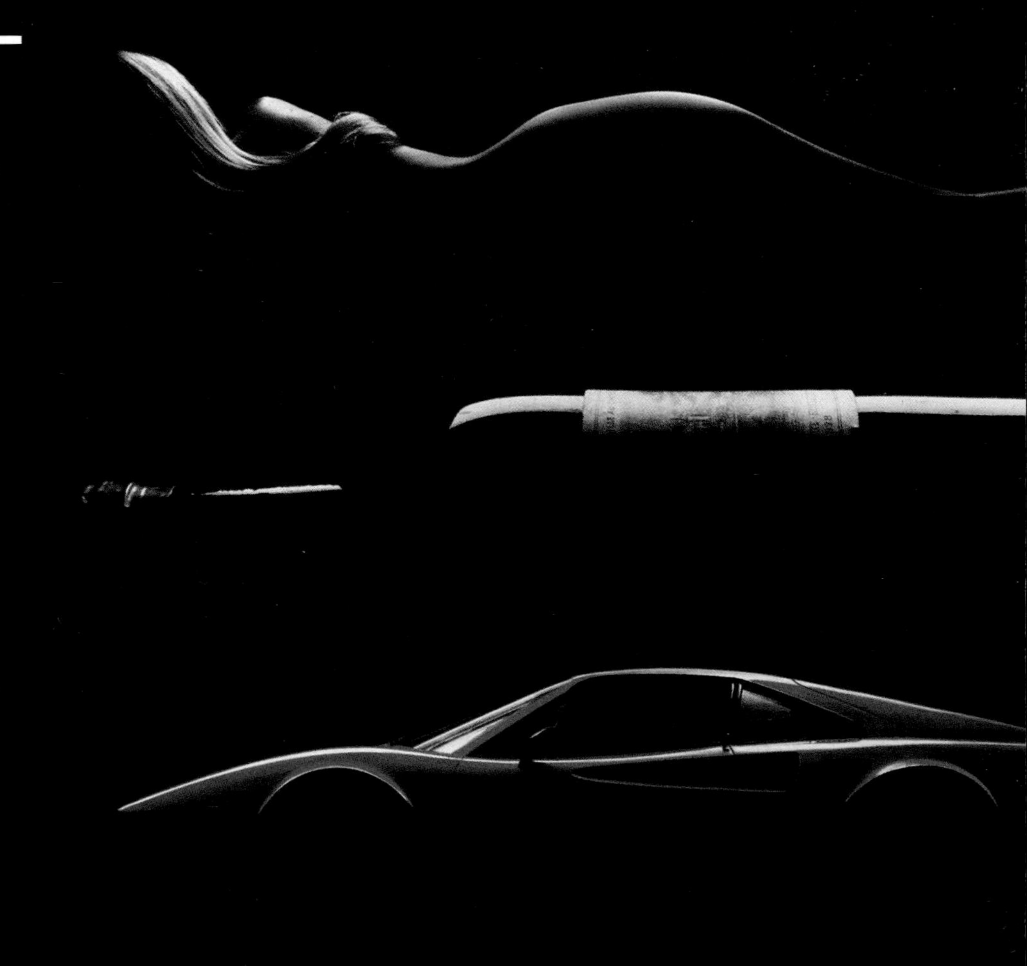

decisions, decisions

Ferrari

R S

' just happen to be a nut about cars. In fact, you could say I raise Porsches," artist Farwell Perry says jokingly. "I love to drive at high speeds and anything that can go quickly is my love. I have a lot of fast icles and even enter road rallies.

car is a very personal thing for people," he continues. "It is often the second largest investment they ever ke. People either dream about these cars I paint or they own them."

ryone who has ever dreamed of owning that shiny red Lamborghini or bright yellow Ferrari can now do Rather than coming off production lines, however, these cars are being assembled by today's poster sts on paper.

ether a person dreams about or owns the real thing, Farwell Perry's 928 Porsche is one way to enjoy the ll of this car. Hang this poster on the wall and indulge the fantasy of zooming down the road behind the eel of this sleek machine.

pping for a car poster can pose as many problems as shopping for the real car. Should one choose a fast or a classic car? Whatever the choice, it is no easy decision.

ther quandry is posed by Decisions, Decisions, today's most popular car poster, which asks the viewer to ide between wine, woman, and machine. Rick McBride, the creator of this poster has obviously touched n something universal to the man of the '80s.

Mercedes Gullwing is one of the rarest and most desired classic cars ever produced. Mercedes Benz nufactured only about 1400 of these automobiles. Poster artists such as Harold James Cleworth have duced far less limited quantities of this same Mercedes making their version available to everyone.

ybe someone is still thinking of that "beauty" they had back in '56. Nothing has ever surpassed the thrill wning that car. Though it is gone, a poster like Phyllis Krim's Yellow Chevy can be a potent reminder of glories.

sleek, high tech design of these posters has a lot to do with their popularity. The visual image of the ter is a perfect mirror of the conceptual image of the car and suits the design style of many contemporary ironments.

omotive posters are not merely pictures of transportation. Rather, these images of shiny flawless chines may represent the illusion of a faster, more exciting lifestyle or evoke nostalgia for times gone by. se racy images are steering posters onto a lot of new wall space.

P123 PADGINTON BEVERLY HILLS 36 × 24

THIRD ANNUAL
CAR SHOW
BEVERLY HILLS ANTIQUE MOTOR CAR SOCIETY

M152 MILLER EMPTY STREETS & HIGHWAYS 36 × 24

Santa Monica Juice
EMPTY STREETS & LONELY HIGHWAYS
Jack Miller
AN AMERICAN JOURNAL

PARADE

P120 PADGINTON PARADE 24 × 31

PIERRE BARRAYA
AUTOMOBILE CITROËN TRACTION AVANT TYPE "15" CARROSSÉE PAR FLAMINIO BERTONI ANNÉE 1938 © BY SPADEM 1983 IMPRIMÉ EN FRANCE

B156 BARRAYA CITROEN 31 1/2 × 23 3/4

M92 MIAD PANTERA 28 × 22

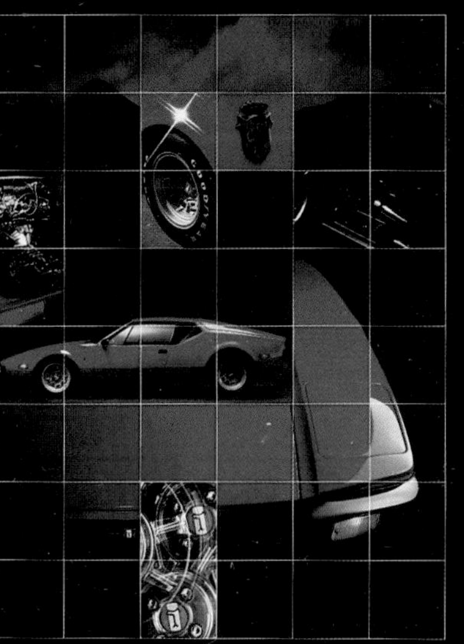

Pantera

M93 MIAD FERRARI 28 × 22

Ferrari

M94 MIAD PORSCHE 28 × 22

turbo

PORSCHE

P41 PORSCHE ☆ 25 × 36

F A R W E L L P E R R Y

9 2 8 P O R S C H E

FARWELL PERRY
ABARTH CARRERA

P73 ABARTH CARRERA ☆ 25 × 34

P65 BMW M-1 ☆ 24 × 38

F A R W E L L P E R R Y
M · 1 · B M W · T U R B O

FARWELL PERRY
L A M B O R G H I N I

P92 LAMBORGHINI III ☆ 26 × 34

C65 LAMBORGHINI 22 × 30

countach

C39 FERRARI 22 × 30

Cavallino Rampante Ltd
FERRARI RESTORATIO

LB 211

C135 ROLLS ROYCE 28 × 22

C78 PORSCHES OF BEVERLY HILLS 24 × 36

C53 SPEEDSTER $23 \times 30^1/_2$

SPEEDSTER

C136 NOMAD $22 \times 32^1/_2$

NOMAD
1GEP705
CLEWORTH

CLEWORTH
300SL 'GULLWING'

C36 GULLWING 28×22

FERRARI·CAMPIONE·DEL·MONDO

C121 FERRARI CAMPIONE $20 \times 33^1/_2$

K35 KRIM YELLOW CHEVY ☆ 30×40

904-JBP
NEW YORK
PHYLLIS KRIM

C90 CHAPLIN AFTER THE PROM $35\frac{7}{8} \times 24$

After the Prom
A. ATELIER PUBLISHING

Classics
Mercedes-Benz Typ 500K, 1936

M91 MERCEDES-BENZ 500K $24\frac{3}{8} \times 36\frac{1}{2}$

Classics
Mercedes-Benz Typ 320 Coupé, 1938

M129 MERCEDES-BENZ 320 COUPE $24\frac{1}{4} \times 36\frac{1}{2}$

K34 KRIM CORD ☆ 30 × 40

PHYLLIS KRIM

S56 SALMIERI 1939 LA SALLE ☆ 24 × 18

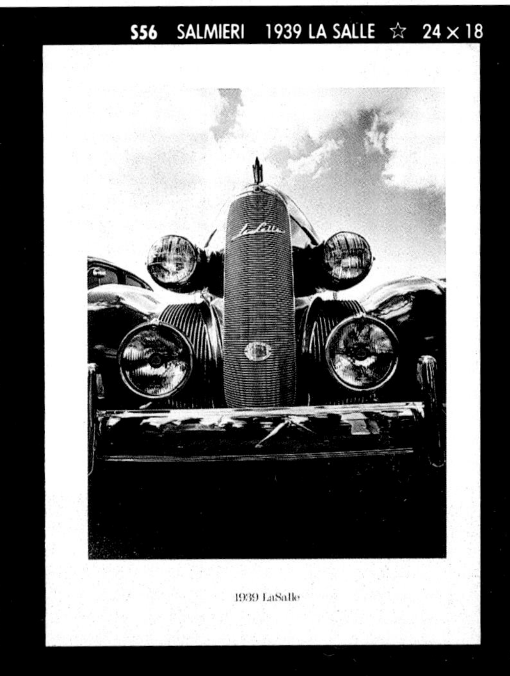
1939 LaSalle

KEITH MALLETT
FRONT LINE EDITIONS MAY 1983

M85 MALLETT TURN SOME HEADS II 20 × 36

BOB RECTOR
LASTING IMPRESSIONS · LAGUNA BEACH
I ♥ Laguna

R36 RECTOR I LOVE LAGUNA $35^{7}/_{8} \times 23^{7}/_{8}$

B130 BMW TURBO '72 $36\frac{1}{2} \times 24\frac{3}{8}$

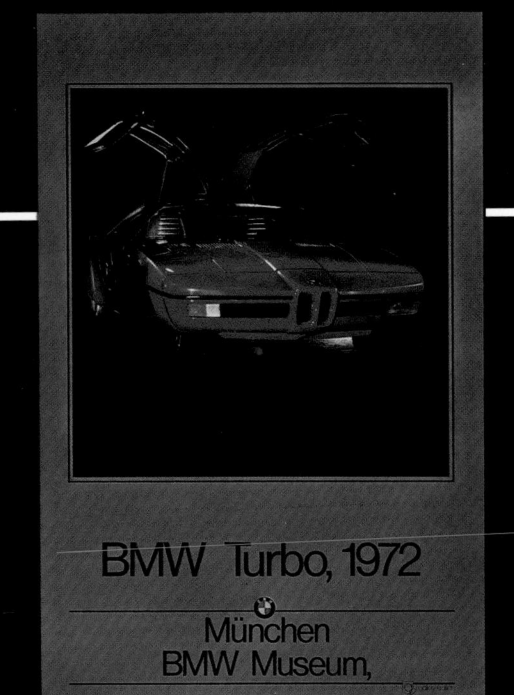
BMW Turbo, 1972
München
BMW Museum,

A43 APPEL FANTASY $24\frac{1}{2} \times 36\frac{1}{2}$

Fantasy

C L A S S I C

DMC
SNO BIRD

D E L O R E A N

L42 LAKE CLASSIC DELOREAN $22 \times 27\frac{3}{4}$

Lamborghini style... Alpine performance.
ALPINE

T36 THOMPSON LAMBORGHINI $37\frac{1}{4} \times 20$

B I K E S

030 OTLAICHR REKORD DESIGN *SERIGRAPH ON FOIL* $23^1/_2 \times 36^1/_2$

Record-design

029 OTLAICHR MILESTONE *SERIGRAPH ON FOIL* $23^1/_2 \times 36^1/_2$

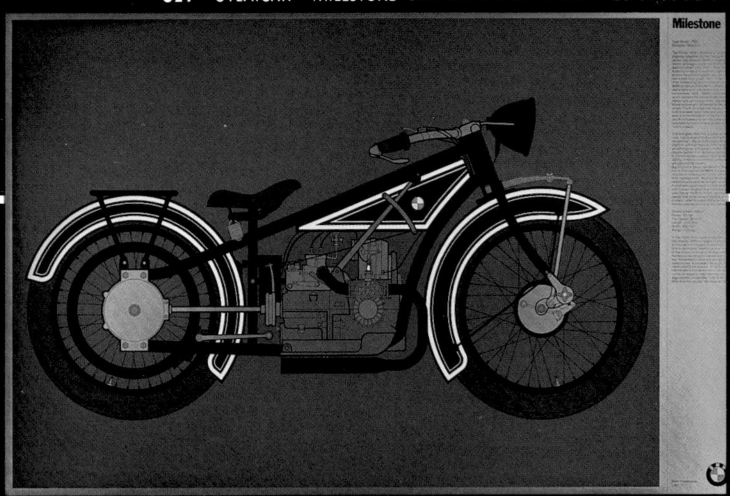
Milestone

Husqvarna
BRIAN DEINES

D61 DEINES DIRT BIKE 27×39

Birthday

B148 BMW BIRTHDAY *SERIGRAPH ON FOIL* $23^1/_2 \times 36^3/_4$

C115 CAPLAN COWS $30^1/_2 \times 25^1/_4$

N63 NOEL FINE & FANCY LEGHORN $32^1/_2 \times 36^1/_4$

N. A. N O Ë L
C.O. BOSS & SON
FINE AND FANCY
LEGHORN

PIG OF MARKET HARBO
SUZANNE RING CAPLAN

C125 CAPLAN PIG OF MARKET HARBOR $25^1/_4 \times 32$

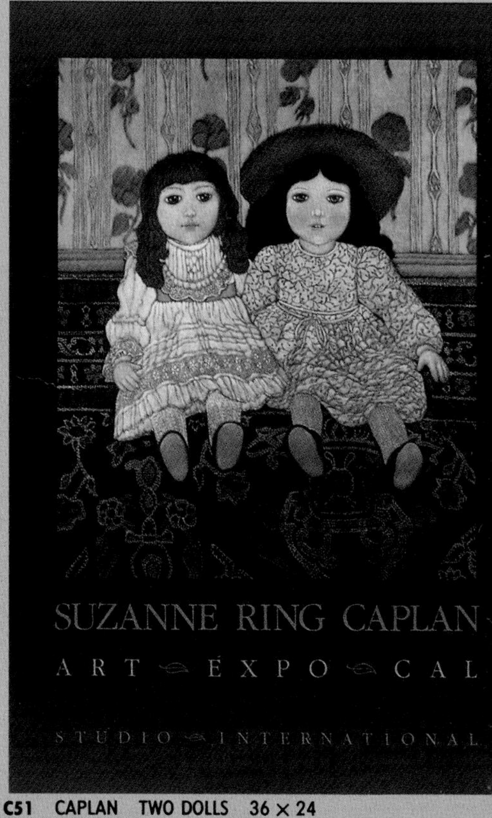
SUZANNE RING CAPLAN
ART EXPO CAL
STUDIO INTERNATIONAL

C51 CAPLAN TWO DOLLS 36×24

N42 NOEL ANTIQUE ROCKING HORSE $31^{7}/_{8} \times 38^{1}/_{4}$

S170 SIMPKINS AMERICANA 36 × 24

A·M·E·R·I·C·A·N·A

J O H N
S·I·M·P·K·I·N·S

MERICAN FOLK PAINTERS OF THREE CENTURIES
hitney Museum of American Art February 26–May 13, 1980

P71 PHILLIPS GIRL IN RED 37 × 24

Y11 YOUNG GIRL WITH FLOWERS $32^{7}/_{8} \times 21$

A Young Boy With Dog American, 19th Century
The Fine Arts Museums of San Francisco

Y10 YOUNG BOY WITH DOG $32^{7}/_{8} \times 21$

F26 FOX BROADWAY MELODY ☆ 25 × 35

FOX · GRAPHIC ORIGINALS INC. · NEW YORK

BRUNO · STIVERS · KLIMEK

K92 KLIMEK BALLET RIBBON 24 × 36

Avanti

C155 CURTIS MALE DANCER 24 × 36

N C E

tretching. Straining. Striving for perfection. Years of practice, years of study to arrive at that magical moment when the dancer steps onto the stage to perform. A member of the corps de ballet performs ry night and matinees as well. In addition, this dancer spends a minimum of two hours every day in s, two hours in rehearsals and wears out about 400 pairs of ballet slippers each year.

ce, a time honored subject for artists, is the major inspiration for Harvey Edwards, one of the most ortant contemporary poster artists. With his direct and honest photographic images of the dance world vards became the first successful, well known poster artist. Running through the imagery of his work is contrast between romance and reality, lyricism and discipline.

vards began to photograph ballet after, he says, "I went to watch the ballet class and realized in every ity there is a special drive." It is this drive that Edwards focuses on in his images showing us his version e real world of the artist.

vards' every popular original image of tattered, well-worn ballet slippers suggests the intensity of work is required to produce the beauty of dance. "Ballet Slippers is a classical form of beauty and work," vards comments. "I wanted it to capture the culmination of the motion—physical and spiritual olvement. The image speaks in general terms that I feel everyone can relate to in some form."

ays he prefers to focus on a part of the picture to illustrate what goes on backstage, the anonymous fine-ng and hard work. He believes appreciation for the final result is deeper when the viewer knows what ight about that end product of grace and refinement.

s theme runs throughout his work. Bodies are bent into graceful positions that have been achieved by rs of stretching and pushing the body. Dance is hard work and the dancers in Edwards' posters prove point. They are sweating and tired. But, they are also magnificent and using their bodies to create ges of consumate beauty.

vards uses only natural light and never has full faces in his images. When asked what differentiates a tographer from a picture taker, Edwards responds: "Being born with a sensitivity in a medium to ress emotions and a strong image."

n Duncan is one of the foremost dance photographers in the world. Duncan has photographed nearly y major dance company and principal dancer from Russia to the U.S. His posters add another spective to our appreciation of dance.

ce posters have a special appeal to anyone who studies dance, from the five-year-old in her first tutu to dedicated prima donna. These works add the graceful touch to their environment that dance adds to r lives.

ts finest, dance sublimely utilizes the human body to convey emotion and create beauty. Dance posters ture the apex of this achievement.

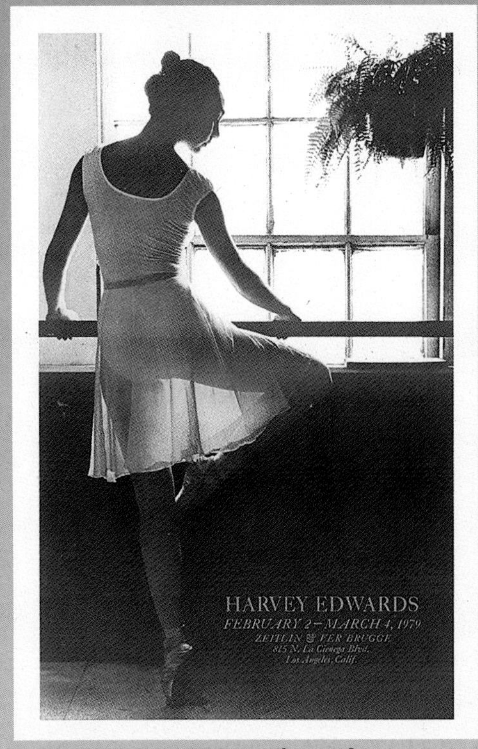
HARVEY EDWARDS
FEBRUARY 2 – MARCH 4, 1979
ZEITLIN & VER BRUGGE
815 N. La Cienega Blvd.
Los Angeles, Calif.

E2 DANCER BY THE WINDOW $39^{1}/_{8} \times 25^{5}/_{8}$

HARVEY EDWARDS
PRINTS LONG BEACH MUSEUM
OF ART MARCH 4–
MAY 6, 1979 BOOKSHOP GALLERY

E4 LEG WARMERS $36^{3}/_{4} \times 25^{1}/_{2}$

E10 TORSO $25^{3}/_{4} \times 39^{3}/_{4}$

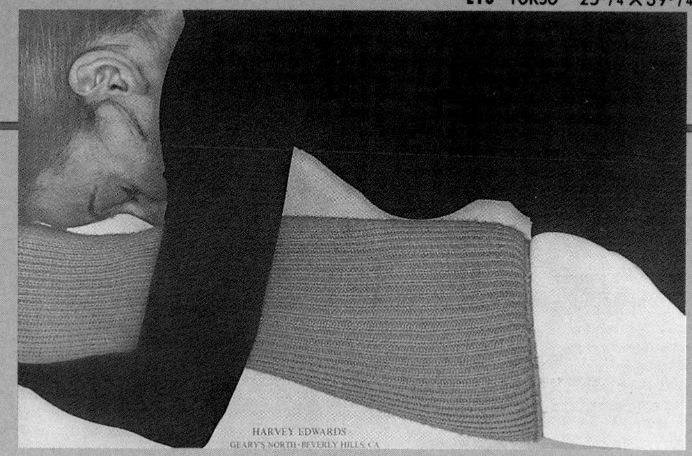
HARVEY EDWARDS
GEARY'S NORTH • BEVERLY HILLS, CA

HARVEY EDWARDS
ZEITLIN & VER BRUGGE
815 N. La Cienega Blvd.
Los Angeles, Calif.

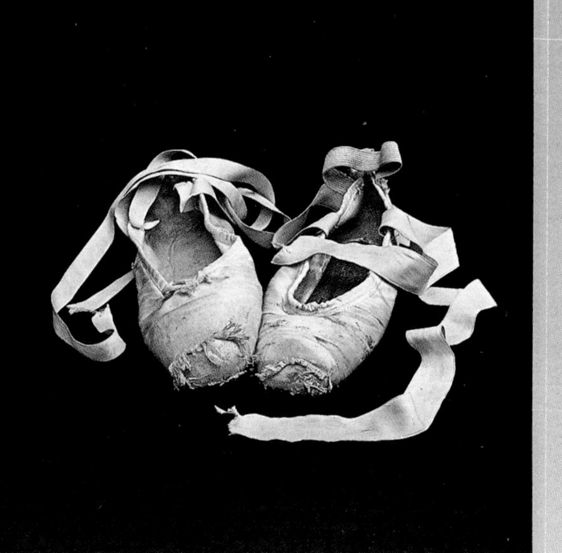

E6 SLIPPERS 36×25

HARVEY EDWARDS
ART EXPO 1982
NEW YORK

E39 WHITE LIGHT $38^{7}/_{8} \times 26$

E38 LINES OF LIFE $25^{1}/_{2} \times 38^{7}/_{8}$

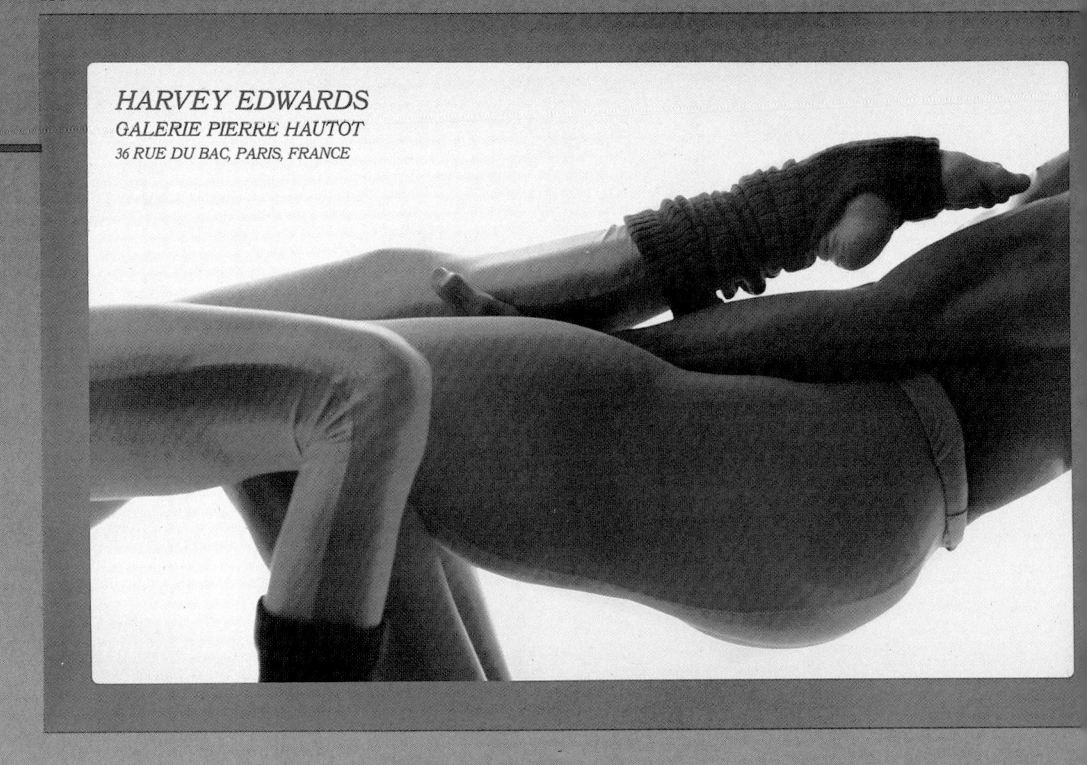
HARVEY EDWARDS
GALERIE PIERRE HAUTOT
36 RUE DU BAC, PARIS, FRANCE

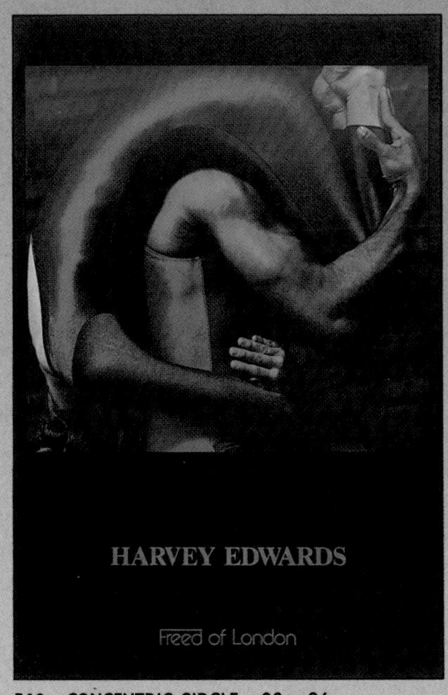
HARVEY EDWARDS
Freed of London

E40 CONCENTRIC CIRCLE 39×26

HARVEY EDWARDS — ART EXPO

E25 MIRRORED IMAGE $39^{5}/_{8} \times 25^{1}/_{2}$

E81 BLACK SWAN 27 × 39

HARVEY EDWARDS
THE BOSTON BALLET

RVEY EDWARDS
LLAS ART EXPO
MENDOLA
IBUTE TO DALLAS THEATER AND CULTURAL ARTS

E75 LA MENDOLA 36 × 24

E36 NIGHT RIDER $37^3/_4 \times 25$

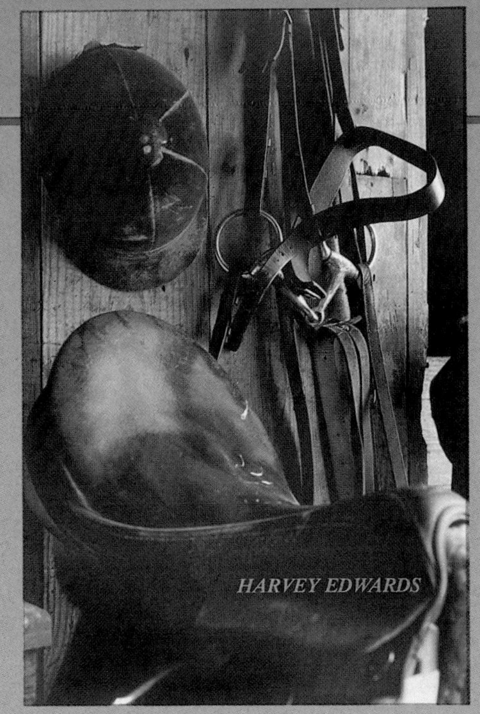
HARVEY EDWARDS

E24 VICTORIAN DOLL $38^3/_8 \times 25^3/_4$

THE
BOSTON
BALLET
W 1
HARVEY EDWARDS

E79 ON TOUR 36×24

E21 BEAM $25 \times 39^1/_4$

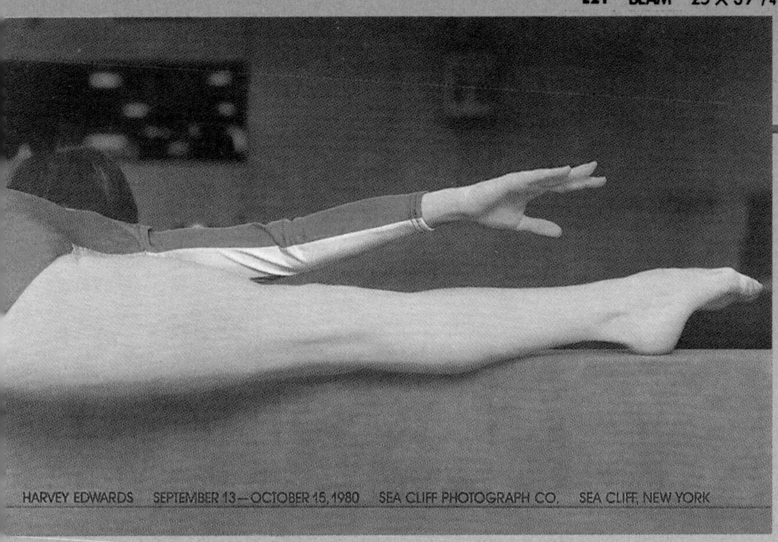
HARVEY EDWARDS SEPTEMBER 13—OCTOBER 15, 1980 SEA CLIFF PHOTOGRAPH CO. SEA CLIFF, NEW YORK

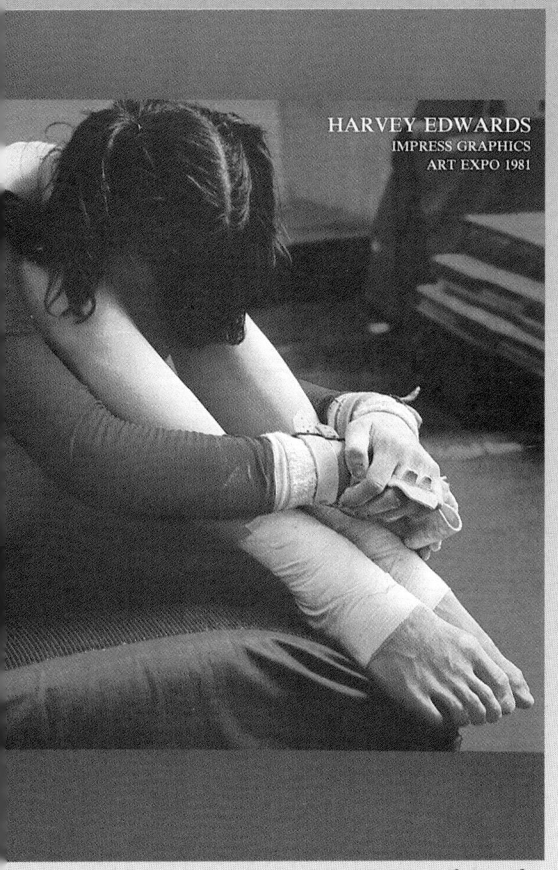
HARVEY EDWARDS
IMPRESS GRAPHICS
ART EXPO 1981

E26 REPOSE $36^3/_4 \times 25^3/_4$

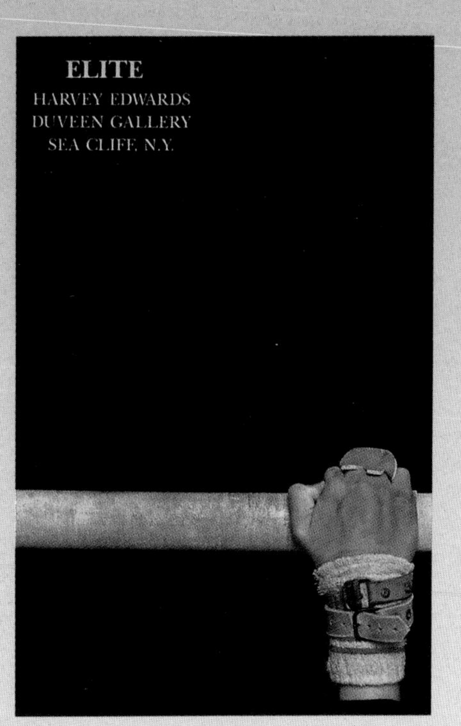
ELITE
HARVEY EDWARDS
DUVEEN GALLERY
SEA CLIFF, N.Y.

E22 ELITE $39^3/_8 \times 25^1/_2$

H A R V E Y

E3 HANDS $25^1/_2 \times 37^3/_4$

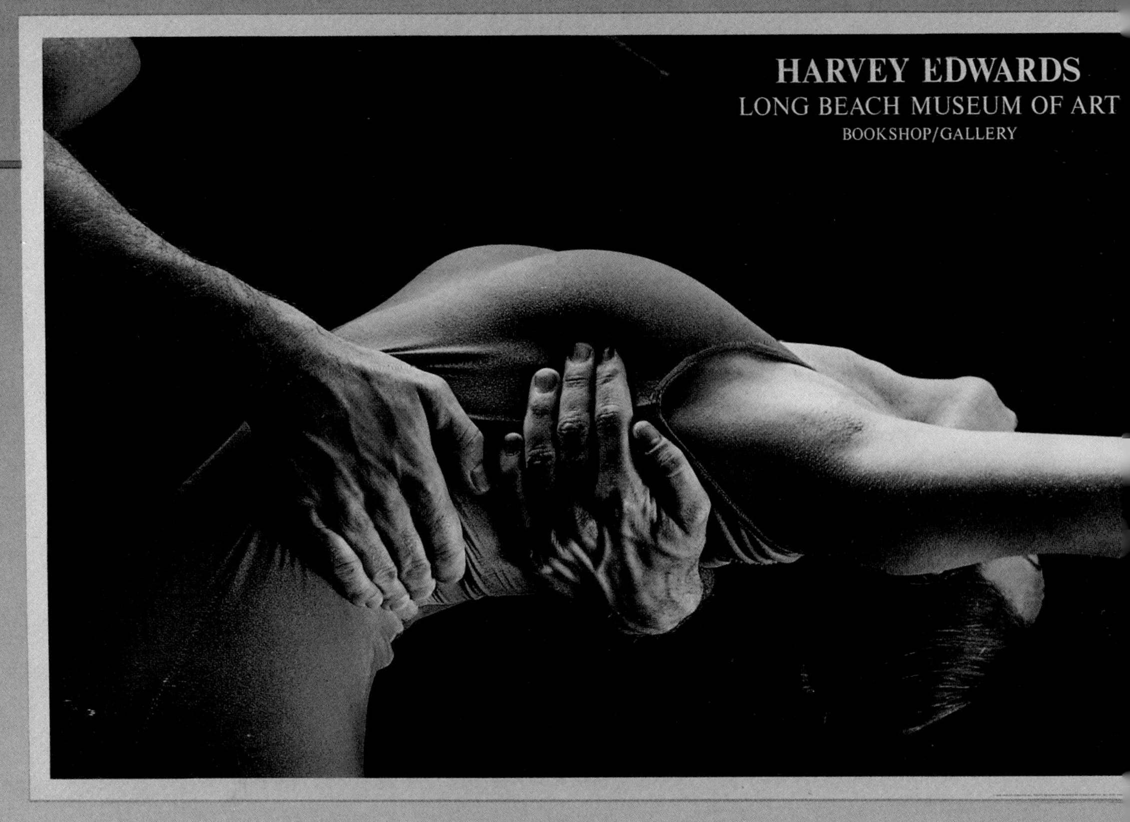
HARVEY EDWARDS
LONG BEACH MUSEUM OF ART
BOOKSHOP/GALLERY

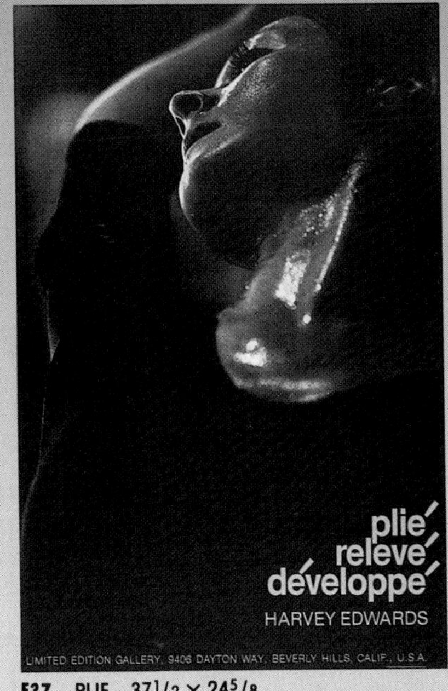
plié
relevé
développé
HARVEY EDWARDS
LIMITED EDITION GALLERY, 9406 DAYTON WAY, BEVERLY HILLS, CALIF., U.S.A.
E37 PLIE $37^1/_2 \times 24^5/_8$

HARVEY EDWARDS
SPIRIT OF DANCE
NATIONAL CORPORATE FOR DANCE
HASSELBLAD
E41 SPIRIT OF DANCE $39 \times 27^3/_8$

HARVEY EDWARDS
LINÉAIRE JOINDRE

E65 LINEAIRE JOINDRE $37^1/_2 \times 27$

HARVEY EDWARDS
THE ART OF DANCE

E76 ART OF DANCE 36×24

C87 CURTIS DANCE MAGIC 36 × 24

BRUCE CURTIS
DANCE MAGIC

C89 CURTIS ROSY TOES 24 × 36

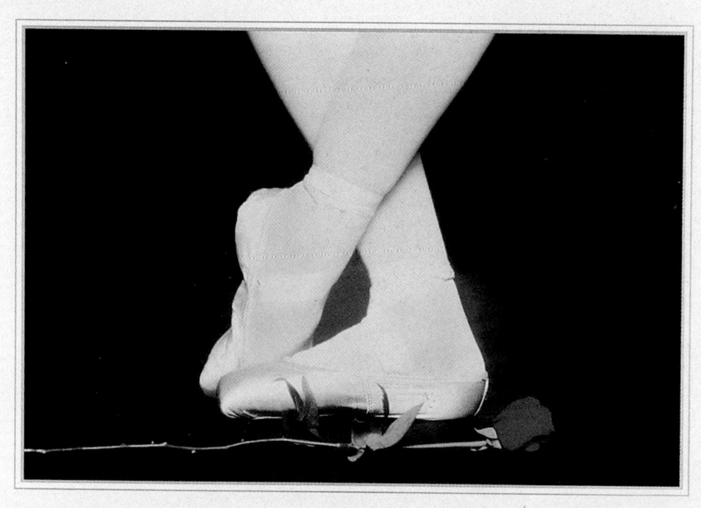

Bruce Curtis/Rosy Toes

PLAZA FRONTENAC · JANUARY 1984

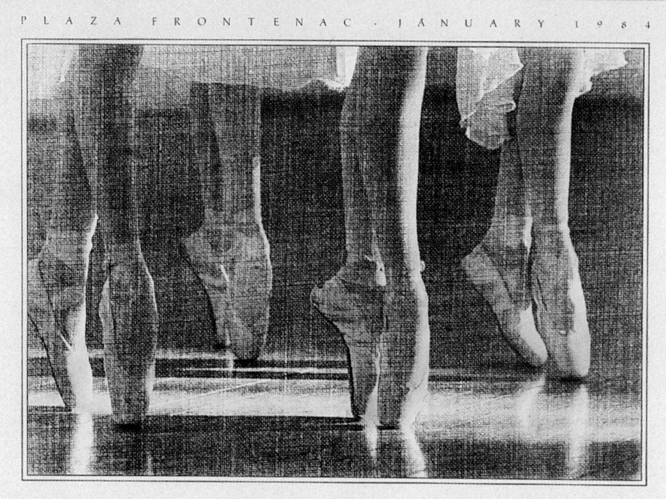

JULIE ANDERSON
Four On The Floor

HIGHGATE PUBLISHING · BOULDER COLORADO

A60 ANDERSON FOUR ON THE FLOOR $22^1/_2 \times 27^1/_2$

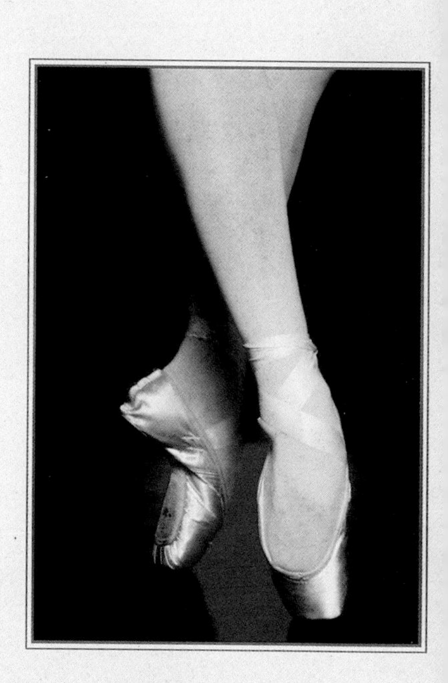

BRUCE CURTIS
ON POINT

C88 CURTIS ON POINT 36 × 24

W15 WOLK ARABESQUE ☆ 36 × 26

WILLIAM WOLK
NZ HALL FOR THE PERFORMING ARTS/ PITTSBURGH, PA.

W20 WOLK ATTITUDE ☆ $26^3/_8 \times 32^1/_2$

WILLIAM WOLK
ART EXPO N.Y. '82 BRUCE MCGAW GRAPHICS

LLIAM WOLK/ BRUCE MCGAW GRAPHICS, INC./ ART EXPO N.Y./APRIL 22–26, 1982

W16 WOLK SMOKED GLASS ☆ 25 × 40

D93 LA DANSE 20 × 30

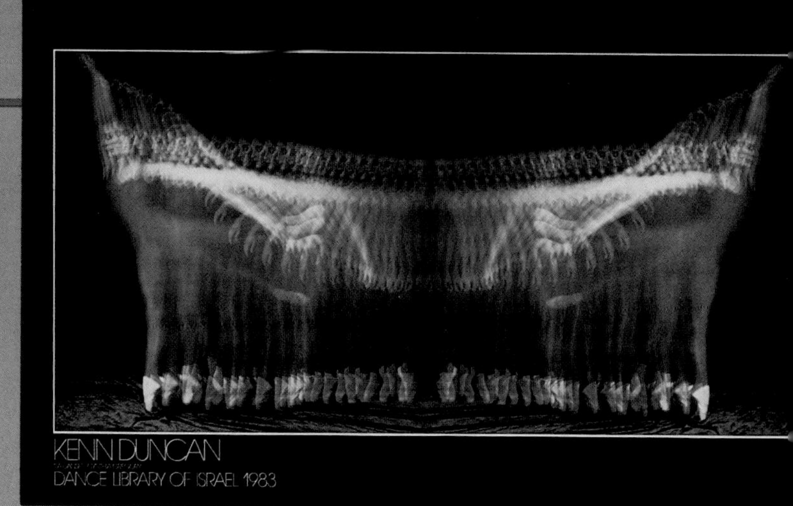
KENN DUNCAN
DANCE LIBRARY OF ISRAEL 1983

MERCE CUNNINGHAM DANCE COMPANY • SAN FRANCISCO BALLET • THE JOFFREY BALLET • THE FELD BALLET
THE PAUL TAYLOR DANCE COMPANY • AMERICAN BALLET THEATRE
ALVIN AILEY AMERICAN DANCE THEATER • TWYLA THARP DANCE
KENN DUNCAN • THE NATIONAL CORPORATE FUND FOR DANCE, INC.

D144 DANCE 24 × 36

KENN DUNCAN
W O R L D O F D A N C

D66 WORLD OF DANCE ☆ 27 × 22

Red
SHOES
ENN DUNCAN
HOTOGRAPHY

D110 RED SHOES ☆ 35 × 26

D68 DOLLARD BALLET SLIPPERS 37 × 23

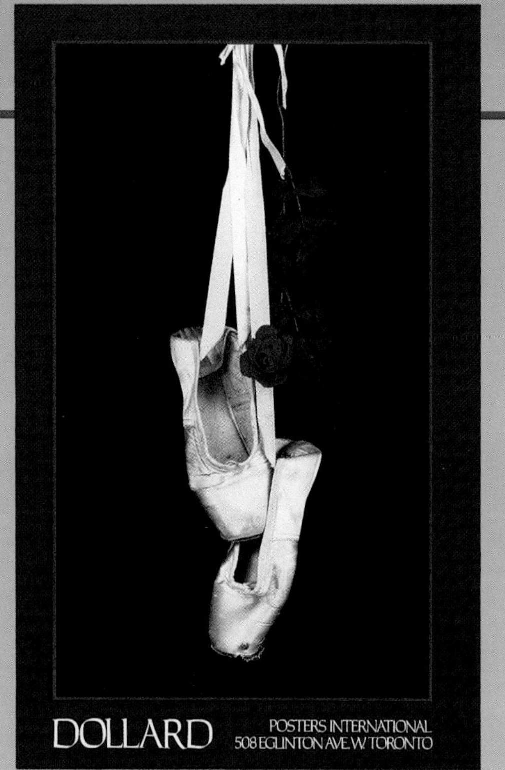
DOLLARD
POSTERS INTERNATIONAL
508 EGLINTON AVE. W. TORONTO

N40 THE NUTCRACKER 28 × 22

THE
NUTCRACKER
Ballet Metropolitan

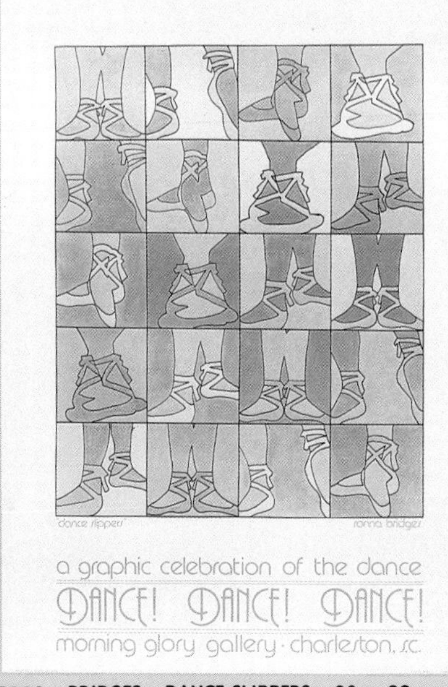
a graphic celebration of the dance
DANCE! DANCE! DANCE!
morning glory gallery · charleston, s.c.

B132 BRIDGES DANCE SLIPPERS 30 × 22

H115 HICKS BALLET BUBBLE 36 × 24

C146 CASADO DANCE, BLUE $36 \times 22\frac{1}{2}$

DANCE
ADO SERIGRAPHS MIRAGE

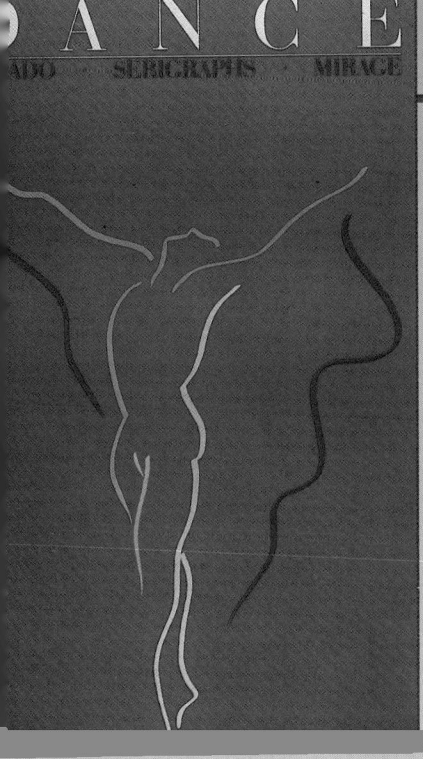

A46 ANDERSON GIRL WITH HAT 34×22

SAINT LOUIS
BALLET THEATRE

Le Jazz

S126 SCHAUB LE JAZZ 24×37

A56 ANTONIO SPRING ☆ 30 × 26

A T I V E

painter who has the feel of breasts and buttocks is saved," stated the great Auguste Renoir. This may be one reason why countless artists have turned to the human body for their inspiration.

could be more fascinating to people than people? In fact, people watching is one of our favorite nes. A sunny day finds us sitting on park benches looking not at the trees, but at other people. ative art holds this same appeal.

s one of the most important contemporary figurative artists. With the celebration of his 90th birthday al years ago, public vision was again focused on the works of this prolific creative personality. Since the public has been clamoring for his images and posters have helped fill that demand.

as had a long and varied artistic career which is well represented in his poster collection. Originally a n designer, in 1915 he began his long tenure with Harper's Bazaar magazine creating the cover ations of graceful, fashionable women that were to become his trademark. Later, he turned to theater and today is still exploring new avenues of artistic expression.

Vreeland, special consultant to the Costume Institute of the Metropolitan Museum of Art, declared o be "perhaps the major creator of the Art Deco style," which Erté describes as "an evolution from Art au in combination with geometric Cubism."

eco continues to be a strong influence in contemporary design. While Erté's figures are the very diment of this style, other artists such as Dimson, Razzia and Chrzanoska also use this highly ed imagery with success in their work. Sophisticated in design, these posters hint at an age of excess dulgence.

uman body is infinitely expressive allowing artists who use it to make a multitude of aesthetic nents. Fernando Botero chooses an extreme interpretation to achieve his wry statements about the n condition. Some of these posters are sensual such as Stephen Yeates photographic images Legs or s; others are wistful and innocent such as the Rosamond pieces. Still other artists use the figure as fiable, yet abstract parts of savvy design pieces.

Glenda Green depicts more than the visual quality of the human form. Her work is emotional and oriented. Although the imagery in a piece like Flight of Spring is from the human body, the first ssion the image gives is of happiness. A person relates to the exuberance in that piece by pulling thing similar out of their own experiences.

ative art can perhaps be best summed up by the comments of the artist Antonio who says: "A human is the most beautiful thing in the world. All my life, through my work, I have been involved with y and I have no greater hope than to continue to do so until my life has ended."

E15 SYMPHONY IN BLACK *LITHOGRAPH* 30 × 20

ERTÉ
PUBLISHED BY MIRAGE EDITIONS
SANTA MONICA, CALIFORNIA
IN ASSOCIATION WITH GROSVENOR GALLERY, LONDON, ENG. ©1980 MIRAGE EDITIONS

E86 PHOENIX REBORN *SERIGRAPH* $23^{1}/_{8} \times 31$

ERTÉ
ART EXPO NY APRIL 5-9, 1984 CHALK & VERMILION

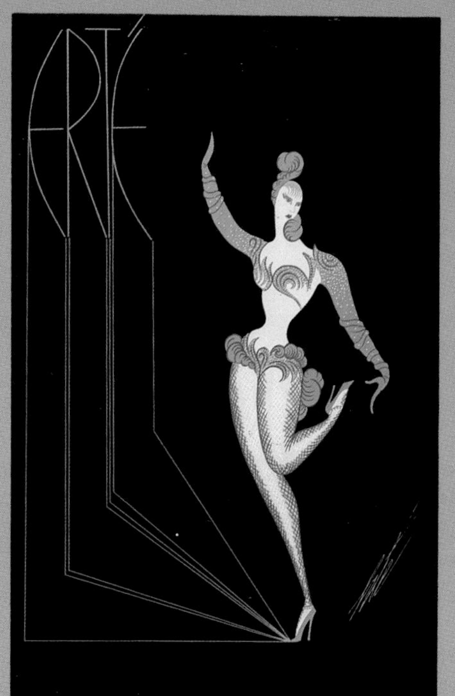
ERTÉ

E53 FANCY FREE *LITHOGRAPH* 30 × 20

ERTÉ

E57 LA ROMANCE *LITHOGRAPH* $30^{1}/_{4} \times 20^{1}/_{8}$

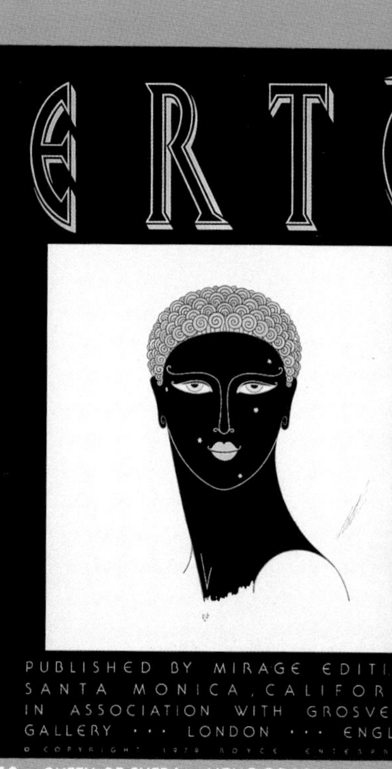
ERT
PUBLISHED BY MIRAGE EDITI
SANTA MONICA, CALIFOR
IN ASSOCIATION WITH GROSVE
GALLERY ··· LONDON ··· ENGL

E18 QUEEN OF SHEBA *LITHOGRAPH* 30 ×

SOIREE *LITHOGRAPH WITH FOIL* 30 × 20

RTE
ISHED BY MIRAGE EDITIONS

E85 FANTASIA *SERIGRAPH* $38^{1}/_{2} \times 25$

ERTÉ
CASINO DE TROUVILLE · APRIL 1984

E58 APHRODITE *LITHOGRAPH* 30 × 20

ERTE

Dyansen Gallery 90 Birthday Retrospective

E54 LACE *LITHOGRAPH* 30 × 20

30 × 20

ERTÉ
MIRAGE EDITIONS

E28 ERTE LOVE *LITHOGRAPH WITH FOIL*

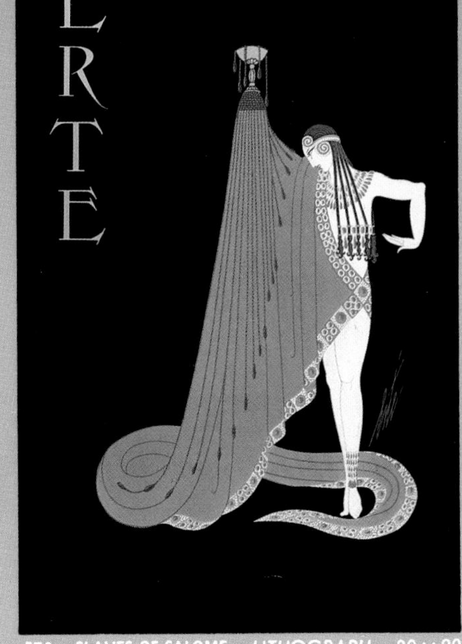
ERTE

E73 SLAVES OF SALOME *LITHOGRAPH* 30 × 20

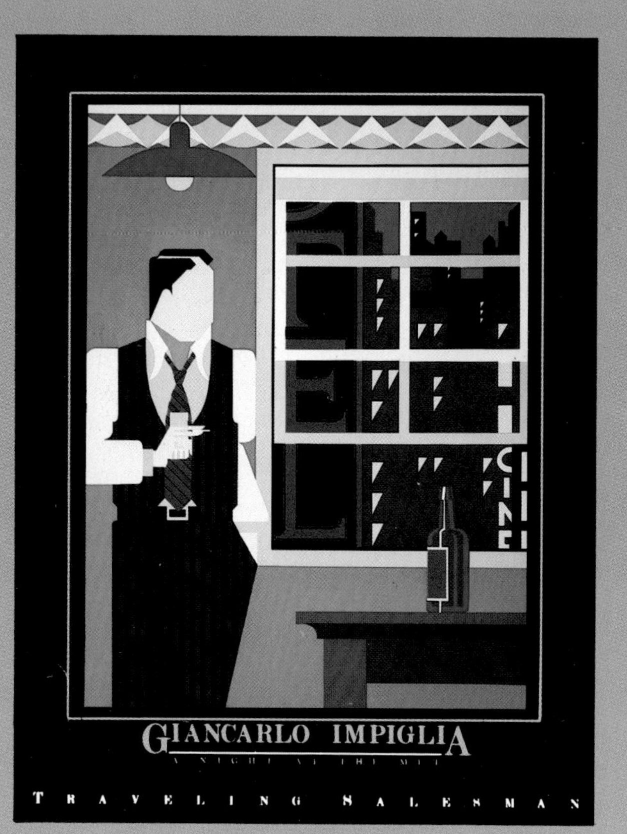
GIANCARLO IMPIGLIA
TRAVELING SALESMAN

115 TRAVELING SALESMAN ☆ 33 × 25

GIANCARLO IMPIGLIA
A NIGHT AT THE MET
THE METROPOLITAN OPER

116 FIVE ARCHES II ☆ 33 × 25

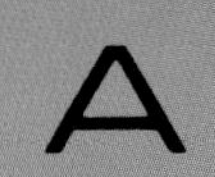

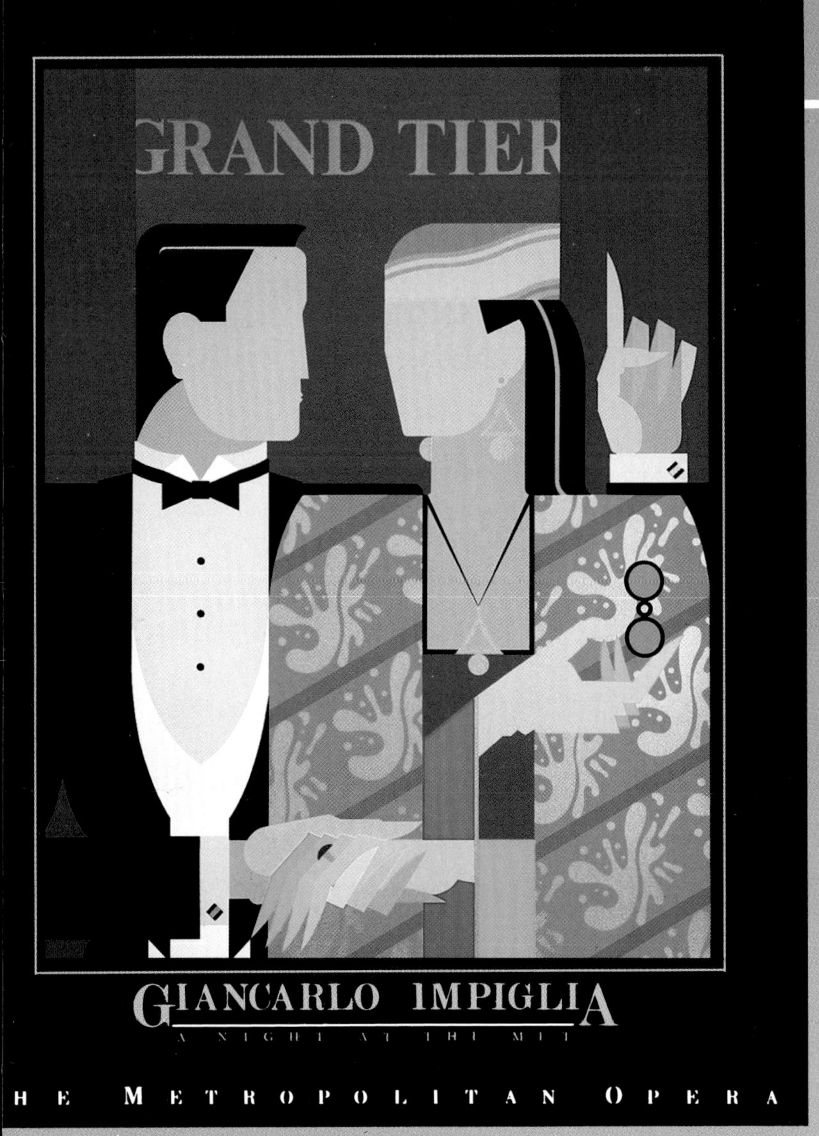
GRAND TIER
GIANCARLO IMPIGLIA
A NIGHT AT THE MET
HE METROPOLITAN OPERA

GRAND TIER ☆ 33 × 25

Giancarlo Impiglia's posters, The Arches II *and* Grand Tier, *are from a suite of silkscreens commissioned by the Metropolitan Opera Guild in honor of the Met's Centennial. According to the Guild, these images "brilliantly capture the excitement, romance, and glamour of an evening spent at the Metropolitan Opera."*

These pieces, by this important Italian artist, are the only officially sanctioned posters from this suite. Their purchase will financially benefit the Met.

B52 BRUNI EMBRACE $24^1/_2 \times 18$

BRUNO BRUNI

D82 DeJONG HOME FROM A CRUISE 22 × 28

Thom De Jong
Eva Dorog Gallery · West Hollywood

FARWELL PERRY

P116 PERRY SUNRISE $22^1/_2 \times 28^3/_4$

Bruno
Bruni

B39 BRUNI MAFIOSO 36 × 25

113 IMPIGLIA DINNER FOR TWO 36 × 24

HOTEL
DINNER FOR TWO

GIANCARLO IMPIGLIA
NEW YORK ART EXPO

P115 PERRY STATUE OF LIBERTY 34 1/8 × 23

FARWELL PERRY

M153 MONTEAUX LADY & SAX 36 × 24

MICHEL MONTEAUX · PHOTOGRAPHY · PARIS · LOS ANGELES

CADILLAC
Bar

H118 HALL CADILLAC BAR 22 1/4 × 24 1/2

THE
WINE
SPECTATOR

H117 HALL WINE SPECTATOR 19 3/4 × 28 1/2

C127 COULON PARIS PREMIERE $31^1/_2 \times 23^1/_2$

PARIS
CREATION
PREMIERE
1983

H85 HOBART TWO HEADS ARE BETTER

CATHERINE HOBART

$34^1/_2 \times 22^3/_4$

FILMEX '76
ANTHONY GOLDSCHMIDT GRAPHIC DESIGN LTD. JOHN ALVIN
THE 1976 LOS ANGELES
INTERNATIONAL FILM EXPOSITIO
MARCH 21-APRIL 4
PLITT CENTURY PLAZA THEATRES
ABC ENTERTAINMENT CENTER
CENTURY CITY

$39^7/_8 \times 13$ (G84A Available $52^1/_2 \times 18^1/_2$)

G84 GOLDSCHMIDT 1976 L.A. INT'L. FILM EXPO

PARIS
PRET A PORTER FEMININ

R45 RAZZIA PARIS $35 \times 23^1/_2$

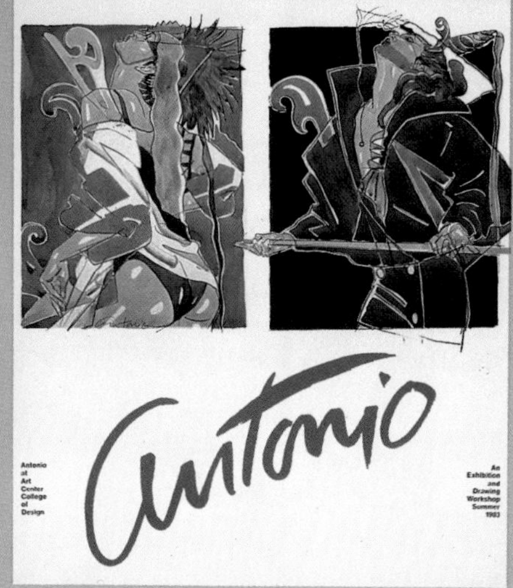
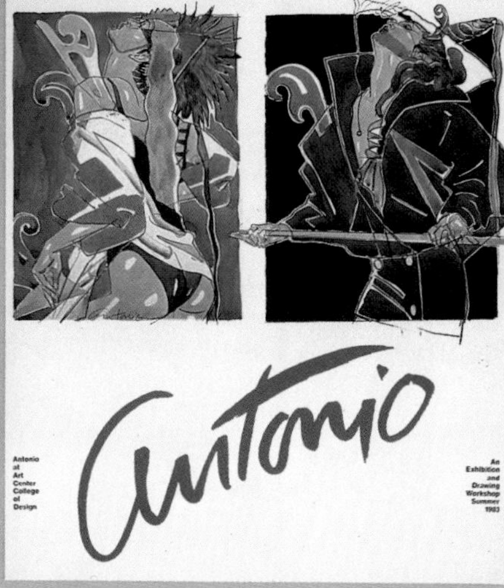
Antonio
Antonio at Art Center College of Design
An Exhibition and Drawing Workshop Summer 1983

A63 ANTONIO FASHION $35 \times 23^1/_2$

L66 LEAL DOMINIQUE 30 × 24

LEAL

L67 LEAL DESIREE 30 × 23

EDWARD WESTON GRAPHICS
LEAL

B117 BOYKO FLAMINGO WALK 35 × 21 3/4

Flamingo WALK
BILL BOYKO

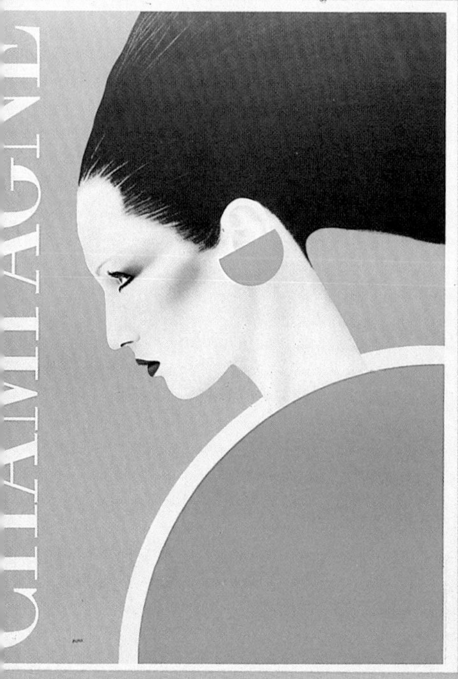
CHAMPAGNE

R46 RAZZIA CHAMPAGNE 31 × 24 1/2

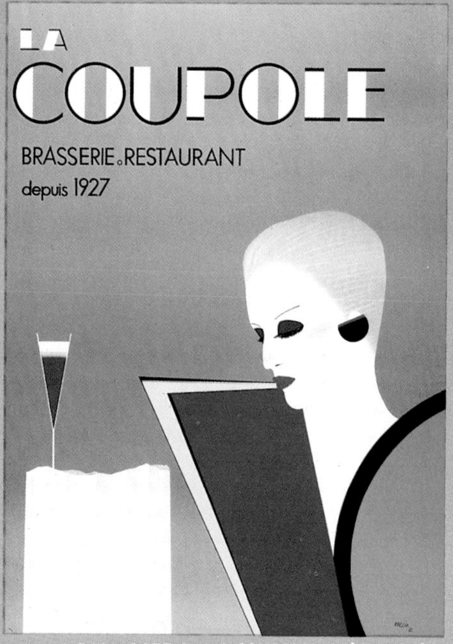
LA
COUPOLE
BRASSERIE RESTAURANT
depuis 1927

R47 RAZZIA LA COUPOLE 33 1/2 × 24 1/2

PARIS
HAUTE COUTURE

R69 RAZZIA HAUTE COUTURE 35 3/4 × 24 1/8

Y8 YEATES LEGS 36 × 15

STEPHEN YEATES PHOTOGRAPHER

Y9 YEATES SEAMS 36 × 15

STEPHEN YEATES PHOTOGRAPHE

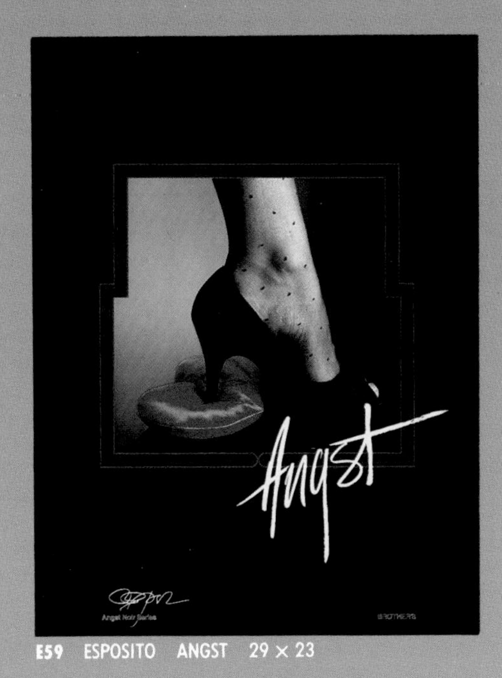
Angst
Angst Noir Series

E59 ESPOSITO ANGST 29 × 23

J15 JAWITZ MORNING LIGHT 24 × 36

M111 MEOLA FIRE EATER 36 × 24

Fire Eater
ERIC MEOLA

D70 DALLA COSTA SNAPPY GARTER 29 × 22

A.dallaCosta
Edward Weston Graphics
PARIS·LOS ANGELES·LONDON·NEW YORK·MILAN

Les Underhill/Silk Stockings

UNDERHILL SILK STOCKINGS $36^{1}/_{2} \times 24^{3}/_{8}$

UMBRELLA
COMMUNICATIONS INC.

U23 UMBRELLA COMMUNICATIONS 34 × 24

W47 WOOD PIANISSIMO 30 × 22

N14 NOYER SAMANTHA ET LE CHAT 37 × 25

PHILIPPE NOYER
ART EXPO
EDWARD WESTON GRAPHICS
PARIS·LOS ANGELES·NEW YORK·MILAN

L31 LIVINGSTON FEBRUARY ☆ $23^{1}/_{2}$ × 30

FEBRUARY
DAVID C. LIVINGSTON

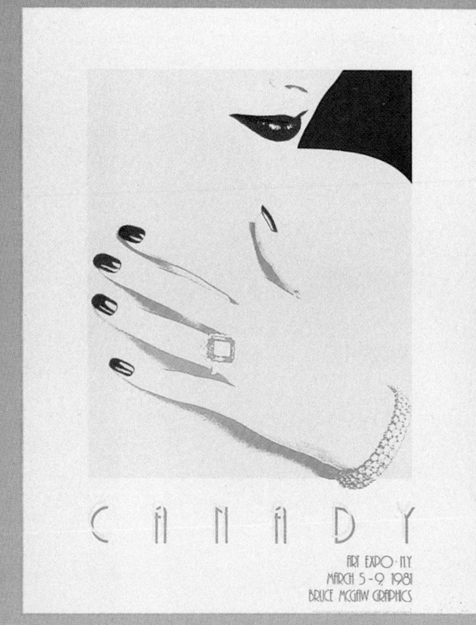
CANADY
ART EXPO·N.Y
MARCH 5-9 1981
BRUCE McGAW GRAPHICS

C34 CANADY ELEGANCE ☆ 28 × 22

Edward Weston Graphic

N20 NOYER LA DAME MONDAINE 29 × 23

A T I V E

R2 ROSAMOND GAMINE 36 × 24

ROSAMOND
lithographs, etchings, and oils
78 ONE WOMAN EXHIBITS
LOS ANGELES, HOUSTON, MEMPHIS, KANSAS CITY, DENVER, LITTLE ROCK, SAN FRANCISCO

R11 ROSAMOND DAWN 28 × 22

ROSAMOND
NINETEEN EIGHTY

OSAMOND

R34 ROSAMOND STRIPES $35^7/_8 \times 23^7/_8$

ROSAMOND
THE CROSSING

R33 ROSAMOND THE CROSSING $38 \times 25^1/_2$

G L E N D A

G22 THE KITE ☆ $33^1/_8 \times 26$

GLENDA GREEN · ART EXPO WEST 1980
bruce mcgaw graphics, inc.

G6 PREEMINENCE ☆ 38×25

GLENDA GREEN
MCGAW EDITIONS–ART EXPO CAL

GLENDA GREEN
McGAW EDITIONS
NEW YORK, NEW YORK

G11 WATERLILIES ☆ $25^1/_8 \times 28$

G R E E N

GLENDA GREEN
FLIGHT OF SPRING
MCGAW EDITIONS
NEW YORK, NEW YORK

G5 FLIGHT OF SPRING ☆ 25 × 38

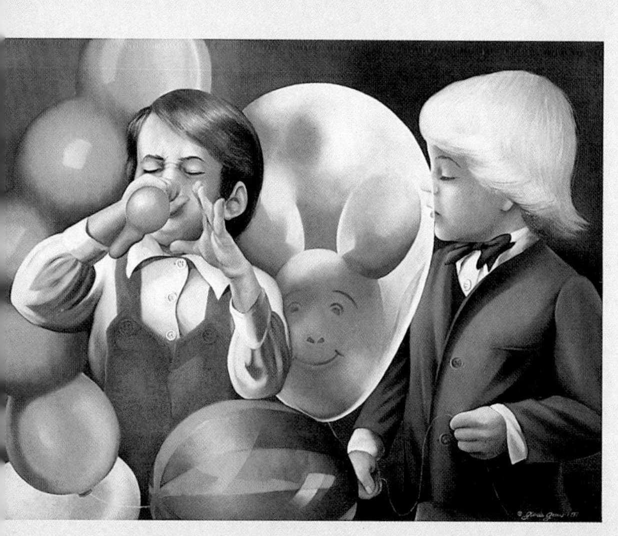
GLENDA GREEN
Q COMPANY EDITIONS · LOS ANGELES

G15 ENCHANTMENT ☆ 25 × 28

R O B I N

M147 OPENING NIGHT 36 × 24

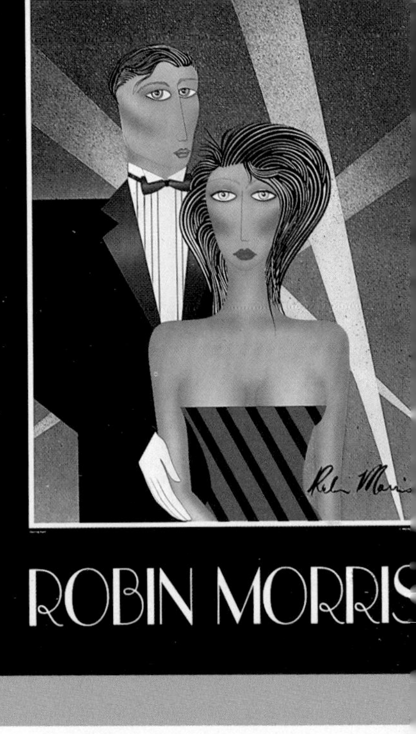
ROBIN MORRIS

ROBIN MORRIS

M148 GIRL FRIENDS 36 × 24

ROBIN MORRI

M69 THE COUPLE 36 × 24

M116 AUTUMN GIRL $36^{1}/_{4} \times 24^{1}/_{4}$

Robin Morris. 1982
robin morris

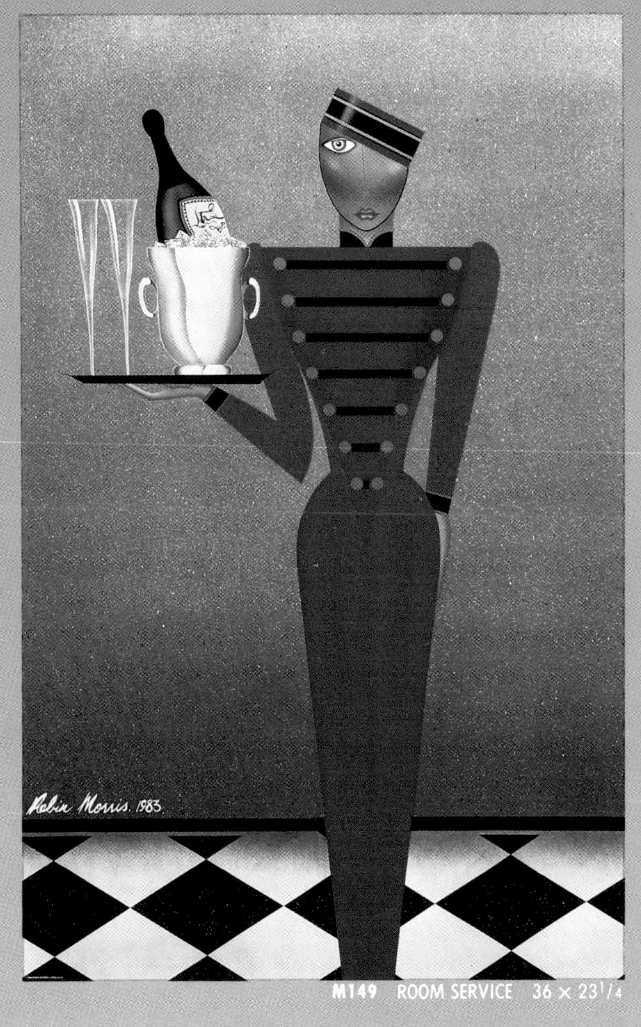
Robin Morris. 1983.

M149 ROOM SERVICE $36 \times 23^{1}/_{4}$

Robin Morris

M150 GLAMOUR GIRL $30 \times 24^{1}/_{4}$

B82 RICH CHILDREN $35^1/_8 \times 30$

BOTERO
Henie-Onstad Kunstsenter, Høvikodden 6. Mars-13. April 1980

B85 BAL EN COLOMBIE $28^3/_4 \times 40^1/_2$

June 27—August 4, 1981 The Seibu Museum of Art, Tokyo

Fernando BOTERO
June 27—August 4, 1981 The Seibu Museum of Art, Tokyo

B84 PROMENADE SUR LES COLLINES $40^3/_8 \times 26$

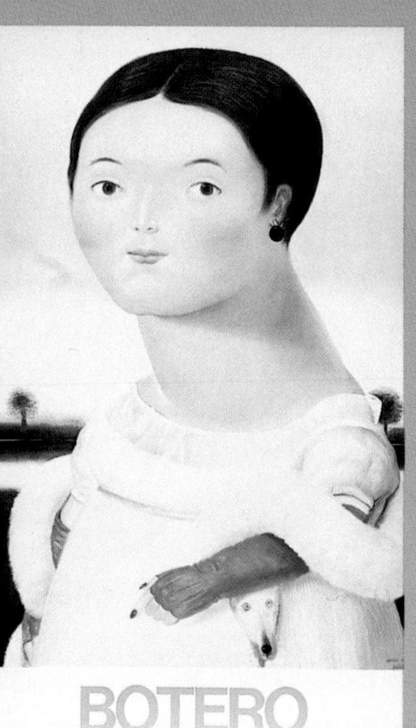
BOTERO
Musée d'Ixelles, 71 rue Jean van Volsem, 1050 Bruxelles
28 Juin-16 Septembre 1979

B83 MADEMOISELLE RIVIERE $43^3/_8 \times 25$

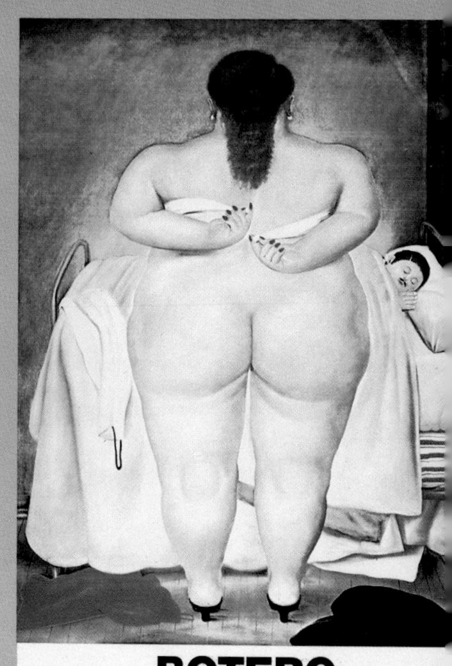
BOTERO
HENIE-ONSTAD KUNSTSENTER, HØVIKODDEN 6. MARS - 13. APRIL

B86 MORNING AFTER $38^7/_8 \times 26^7/_8$

F8 FRENCH POSTCARD ☆ 24 × 18

L'ART PHOTOGRAPHIQUE
DE LA CARTE POSTALE FRANÇAISE
C. 1925

T45 TENNISON GRAND ILLUSIONS 36 × 24

THE 1982 LOS ANGELES INTERNATIONAL FILM EXPOSITION
MARCH 16
TO APRIL
PLAZA THEATRES

C161 CHIU CHICAGO LEGS 36 × 24

Chiu

KARIN
SZÈKESSY
JOHN SZOKE GRAPHICS · NEW YORK, N.Y.

S42 SZEKESSY MADAME RECAMIER ☆ 28 × 22

MURAMASA KUDO

K97 KUDO RAIN 24 × 28

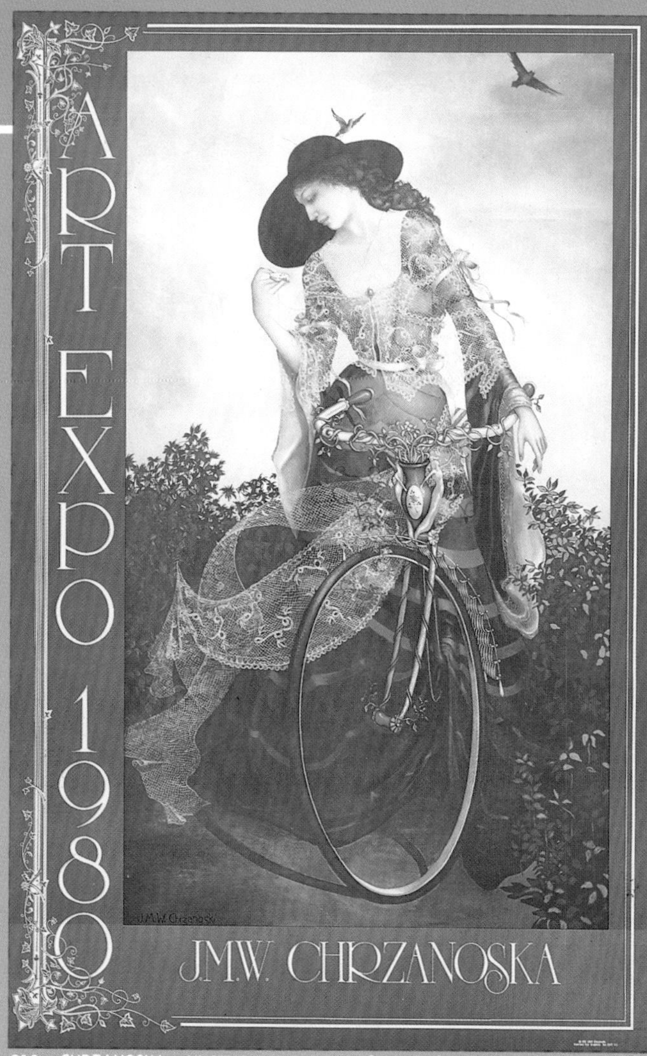
ART EXPO 1980
J.M.W. CHRZANOSKA

C19 CHRZANOSKA UNSTUCK IN TIME $39^{5}/_{8} \times 25^{3}/_{4}$

J.M.W CHRZANOSKA

C49 CHRZANOSKA PEARL 40×26

C76 CHRZANOSKA UNICORN $25^{5}/_{8} \times 39^{3}/_{4}$

swansbrook
galleries
J.M.W. CHRZANOSKA
wiltshire
england

B80 BARNET THE THREE MUSES $38^{3}/_{4} \times 30^{7}/_{8}$

THE DALLAS OPERA
SILVER ANNIVERSARY SEASON '81

J.M.W. CHRZANOSKA

C122 CHRZANOSKA SOLITAIRE $39^{1}/_{2} \times 25$

CHRISTA OGLAN
A BIRD FLEW BY

O15 OGLAN REFLECTION $36^{1}/_{4} \times 27^{3}/_{8}$

D I M S O N

D23 WINTER 28 × 20

WINTER
DIMSON

D24 SPRING 28 × 20

SPRING
DIMSON

SUMMER
DIMSON

D25 SUMMER 28 × 20

D26 AUTUMN 28 × 20

R9 LITTLE SPOONERS 36 × 24

Norman Rockwell

Art Collector's Gallery 1980

R31 SAYING GRACE 36 × 24

Saying Grace
Norman Rockwell

R6 UMPIRES 29 × 23*

SPECIAL TODAY
Norman Rockwell

R7 RUNAWAY 29 × 23*

Norman Rockwell

Art Collector's Gallery 1980

R8 TRIPLE SELF PORTRAIT 36 × 24

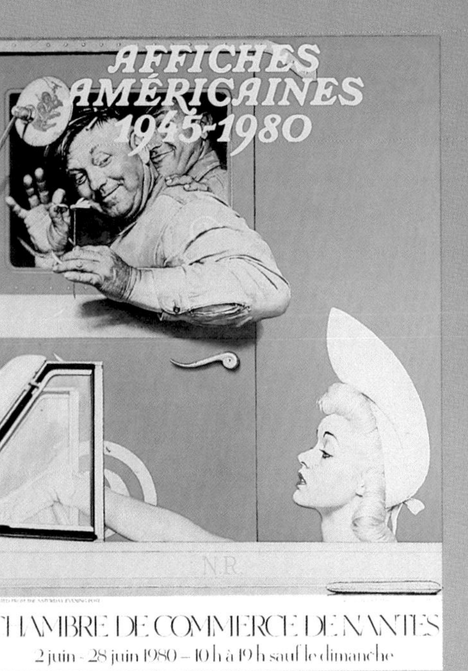
AFFICHES AMÉRICAINES 1945-1980
N.R.
CHAMBRE DE COMMERCE DE NANTES
2 juin - 28 juin 1980 – 10 h à 19 h sauf le dimanche

R22 AFFICHES AMERICAINES $31\frac{1}{2} \times 23\frac{1}{2}$

*Plus Margins

H O P P E R

H94 NEW ART FAIR 37 × 25

Pegge Hopper

H79 INCURABLE COLLECTOR 24 × 37

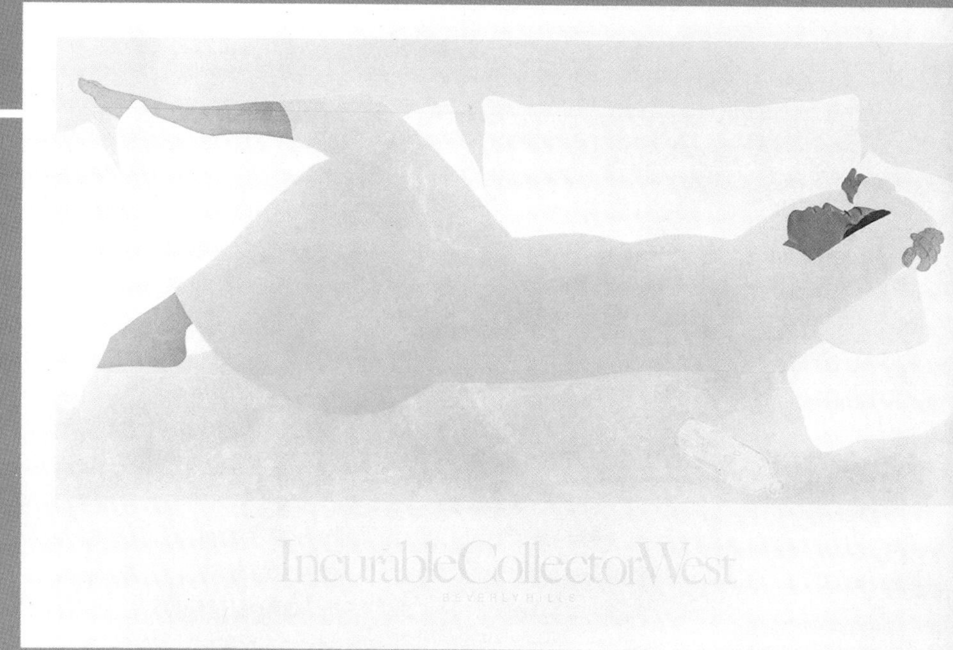
IncurableCollectorWest
BEVERLY HILLS

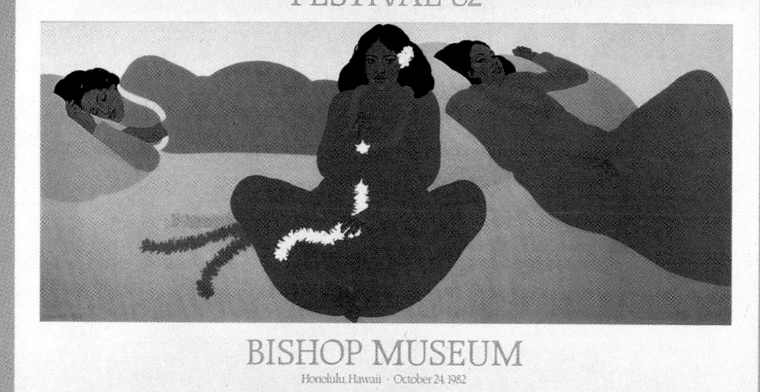
FESTIVAL '82
BISHOP MUSEUM
Honolulu, Hawaii · October 24, 1982

H71 BISHOP MUSEUM 26 × 39 7/8

WinnGalleries

H78 APRICOT SUMMER 36 1/2 × 24 1/2

L33 VIOLETTI *SERIGRAPH* 36 × 24

b.b. la femme

L39 MRS. JONES *SERIGRAPH* 24 × 36

SAN FRANCISCO
b.b. la femme

b.b. la femme

Hot Stuff

L24 HOT STUFF *SERIGRAPH* 30 × 20

b.b. la femme
Player
Greenwich Village Gallery, NYC., NY

L27 PLAYER *SERIGRAPH* 29 7/8 × 20

STEVEN KENNY

K100 KENNY THE THREE VIRTUES ☆ 34 × 25

A L S

lowers are the universal language—when I translate their beauty, I communicate with all." Artist Sandra Stevens is speaking of her own work, but could well be commenting on floral art in general.

ter shops are literally abloom with floral posters. And why not? Flowers are picturesque.

e demand for floral art is as strong as ever as artists continue to produce fresh new images to add to the ter of these best selling posters. Unlimited in its design applications, floral art is as appropriate in a el suite as in a private living room.

live in a society where we are constantly bombarded with unpleasant images. What a welcome respite aze at the loveliness of the lasting blooms of a floral poster.

wers symbolize love, the excitement of spring, and warm weather. A poster like Yuriko Takata's Spring 1 be a poignant reminder of a gentle warm day in the middle of a harsh winter.

cata, whose posters include the award winning Bamboo, says of her work: "I use flowers as building cks to 'construct' a balanced and harmonious feeling in my watercolors. My mother has studied ikebana e art of Japanese floral arrangement) for years and I think I've been influenced by its selective principles. y to use a minimum of simple elements to make my statement."

ok at the images of artist Steven Kenny and you will see some very cosmopolitan flowers. These are not dflowers sitting in jelly jars. These are sophisticated Gladiolas and Black Tulips in stylish vases. amatic flowers and dramatic images for today's dramatic interiors.

ve judge art on its relevance to the future, then we are saying that this moment is an illusion and the ure is reality," says Kenny who pioneered the high style, airbrushed floral poster. "I don't look at my work floral subjects; I look at them in terms of shapes and colors." Notice, then, the masterly juxtaposition of ral forms with interesting background elements.

lliam Todd Haile exemplifies another approach to floral art. Taking a simply spray of Baby's Breath, Haile eates an elegant, quiet image. Haile's work is noteworthy for his flawless use of the airbrush and flair for derstated design.

owers reveal the eclectic range of Mother Nature's palette from the intensity of Michael Hardesty's Allium the softness of a pastel image such as Lilac Time by Babette. Their infinite variety leads to a multitude of sign options that range from Art Deco to traditional realism.

ore floral images can be found in the photography and still life sections of this book. Of particular note are ng Lee's photograph of Baby's Breath on a striking blue background and Deborah Denker's Calla Lilly ductively wrapped around a clarinet.

ere is no need to have a green thumb or a good florist to avail oneself of perennial blooms. Whether a rson lives in the country or the city, their walls can be their garden. Floral posters provide an abundance dogwood, poppies, tulips and roses throughout the four seasons.

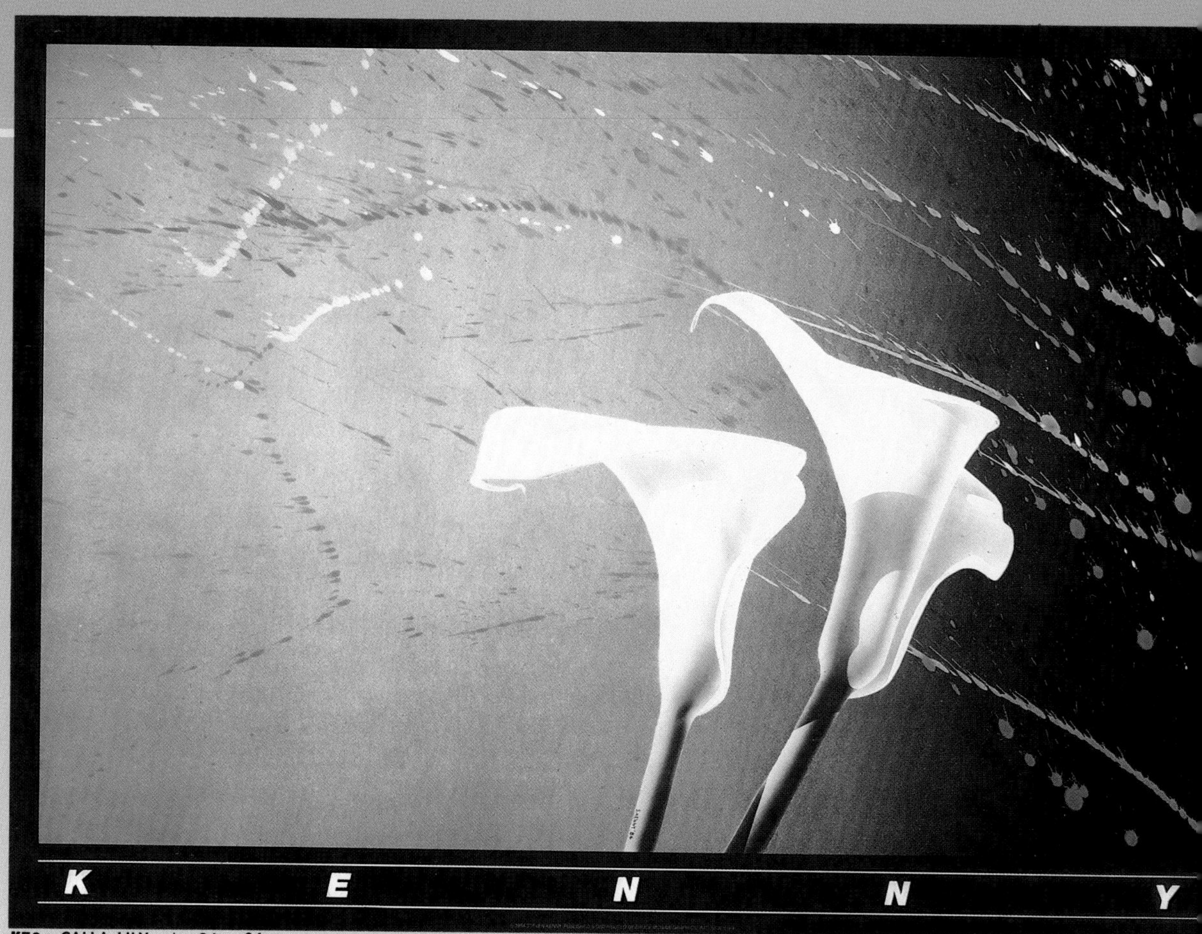
K E N N Y

K72 CALLA LILY ☆ 26 × 36

K E N N Y

K73 BIRD OF PARADISE II ☆ 26 × 36

K52 GLADIOLAS ☆ 38 × 24

K65 BLACK TULIPS ☆ 25 × 35

T E V E N K E N N Y

STEVEN KENNY

K33 BABY'S BREATH '82 ☆ $23^{7}/_{8} \times 33^{3}/_{8}$

S T E V E N

K29 BIRD OF PARADISE 25 × 35$^{3}/_{4}$

STEVEN KENNY
artworks fall '81

STEVEN KENNY
showplace square
SAN FRANCISCO 1981

K30 CATS 25 × 33$^{1}/_{2}$

K E N N Y

STEVEN·KENNY

K53 CYCLAMEN FAMILY ☆ 26 × 32

C56 PINK IRIS $34^1/_4 \times 12^5/_8$

C55 BLUE IRIS $34^1/_4 \times 12^5/_8$

ED COTA
DISCOVERY EDITIONS

C74 WHITE IRISES $34^7/_8 \times 24^7/_8$

ED COTA
DISCOVERY GALLERIES
Art Expo · San Francisco · 1981

ED COTA
DISCOVERY GALLERIES
Art Expo · San Francisco · 1981

ED COTA/DISCOVERY GALLERIES

C128 IRIS GARDEN 17×32

C92 WHITE ORCHID $34^7/_8$ × 25

ED COTA
DISCOVERY GALLERIES
SANTA MONICA · CALIFORNIA

ED COTA
DISCOVERY GALLERIES
SANTA MONICA · CALIFORNIA

C58 CACTUS FLOWER 36 × 26

C104 FRESH CUT 32 × 25

R65 REZNY FLOWERS IN GLASS VASE 22 × 28

Aaron Rezny
FLOWERS IN GLASS VASE

S153 SHICK SPRING NIGHT 18 × 24

S152 SCHEWE FLOWERS 34 × 25

GREGOIRE
CRYSTAL VISIONS

G99 GREGOIRE ORCHIDS 33 × 25

M132 MARIE ORCHIDS $35^{1}/_{2} \times 23^{1}/_{2}$

suzanne
marie
Art Expo West 81

M130 MARIE STILL LIFE 24 × 38

SUZANNE MARIE/VIVA GRAPHICS

SUZANNE MARIE / VIVA GRAPHICS

M131 MARIE DECO MOTIF 38 × 24

ROSLYN ROSE

R12 ROSE ☆ GENUS IRIS *OFFSET WITH EMBOSSING* 28 × 22

LONGWOOD GARDENS
KENNETT SQUARE PENNSYLVANIA
Takata

T46 LONGWOOD GARDENS ☆ 40 × 21

WATERCOLORS YORIKO TAKATA
C l a r k a n d W a d e G a l l e r y

T37 HELICONIA ☆ 34 × 24

T34 SPRING ☆ 23 × 38

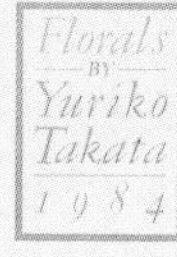
Florals
BY
Yuriko
Takata
1984

Yuriko Takata
WATERCOLORS

T28 BROMELIAD ☆ 21 × 39 3/4

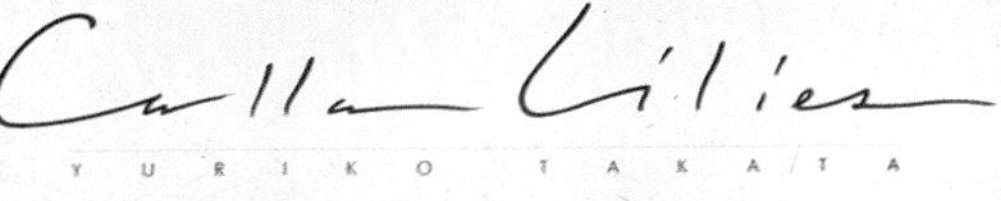
Calla Lilies
YURIKO TAKATA

T19 CALLA LILIES ☆ 39 × 17

TAKATA
SAN FRANCISCO

T18 AMARYLLIS ☆ 39 × 17

SEVENTH ANNUAL IBD ART AUCTION
GALLERIA · SAN FRANCISCO · 6 MARCH 1981 · 6 PM

T5 SAFEWAY ORCHID $33^{7}/_{8} \times 24^{3}/_{4}$

YURIKO TAKATA · IRIS
DASHER · SAN FRANCISCO

T11 IRIS $38 \times 12^{1}/_{2}$

YURIKO TAKATA · LILY
DASHER · SAN FRANCISCO

T10 LILY $38 \times 12^{1}/_{2}$

T24 CYCLAMEN ☆ 25 × 39

The Conservatory of Flowers / Golden Gate Park / Yuriko Takata

PHOENIX SYMPHONY ORCHESTRA
Yuriko Takata / Bruce McGaw Graphics / 1984

T33 CACTUS ☆ 24 × 36

T21 JAPANESE IRIS ☆ 26 × 40

YURIKO TAKATA - MCGAW EDITIONS

YURIKO TAKATA / WATERCOLORS · DASHER EDITIONS / SAN FRANCISCO

T4 WATERCOLORS $17^{1}/_{2} \times 39^{1}/_{4}$

T27 BAMBOO ☆ 19 × 40

Japanese Tea Garden · San Francisco
Takata

Water Lilies · Takata

T25 WATER LILIES ☆ 26 × 31

M83 MARTIN AMARYLLIS *LITHOGRAPH* 30 × 22

ANTHONY MARTIN • AMARYLLIS
STESSAN GALLERIES/FINE ART PUBLISHERS

M88 MARTIN RED POPPY *LITHOGRAPH* 30 × 24

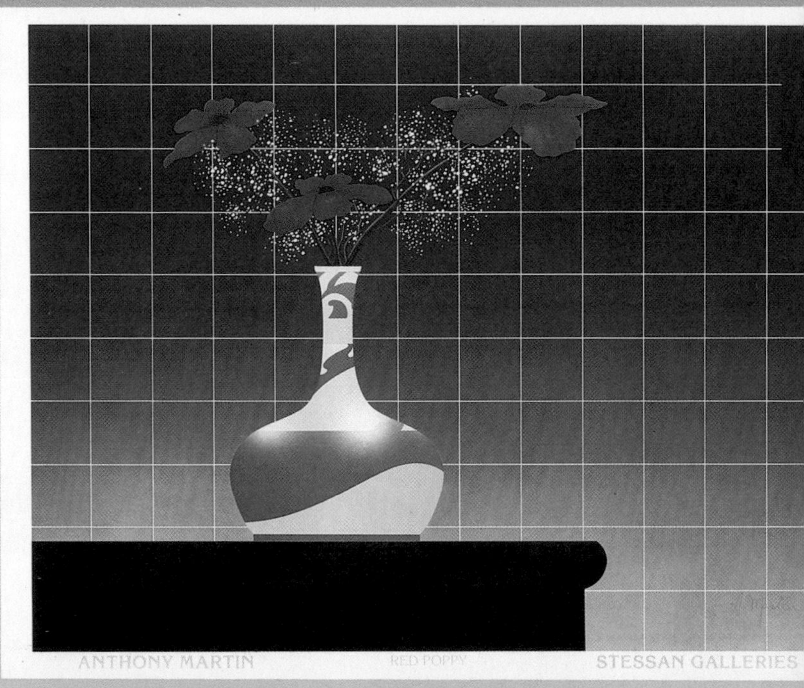
ANTHONY MARTIN
RED POPPY
STESSAN GALLERIES

GREGOIRE
CRYSTAL VISIONS

G120 GREGOIRE FREESIA 33 × 25

ALFRED M. WHITE

W42 WHITE BABY'S BREATH 36 × 24

CHARLES SCHNEIDER
NATURAL TOUCH

S115 SCHNEIDER NATURAL TOUCH 36 × 24

G55 GROSJEAN BABY'S BREATH 25 × 30

GROSJEAN

G78 GROSJEAN CASPIA 32 × 24

Grosjean

G74 GROSJEAN EVENING LIGHT 24 × 32

H93A SETTING "A" 32 × 24

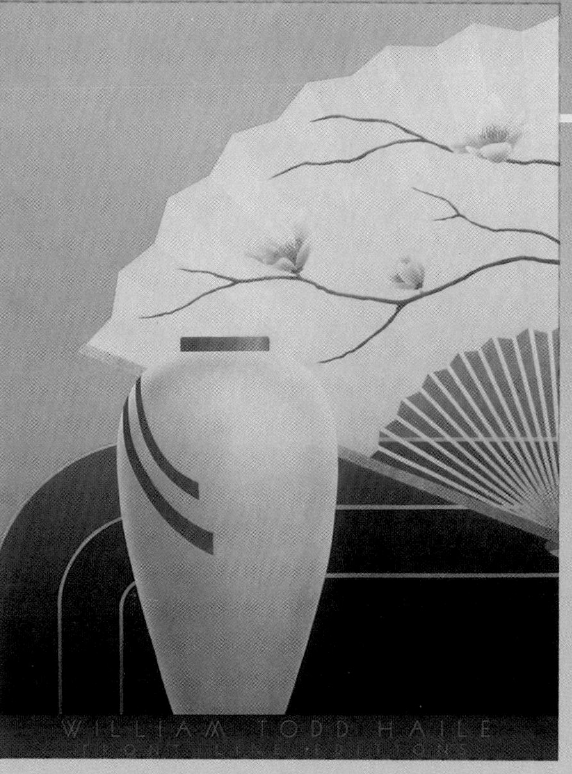
WILLIAM TODD HAILE
FRONT LINE EDITIONS

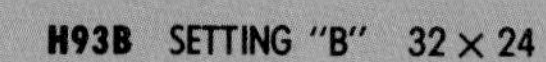
H93B SETTING "B" 32 × 24

MAY 3-31 1984
POSTERS INTERNATIONAL TORONTO

H87 GREEN VASE 24 × 32

H92 QUIET AFTERNOON $35^{3}/_{4}$ × 24

WILLIAM TODD HAILE
ART EXPO NEW YORK / APRIL
1982

H47 APPLE BLOSSOMS $24 \times 31^{3}/_{4}$

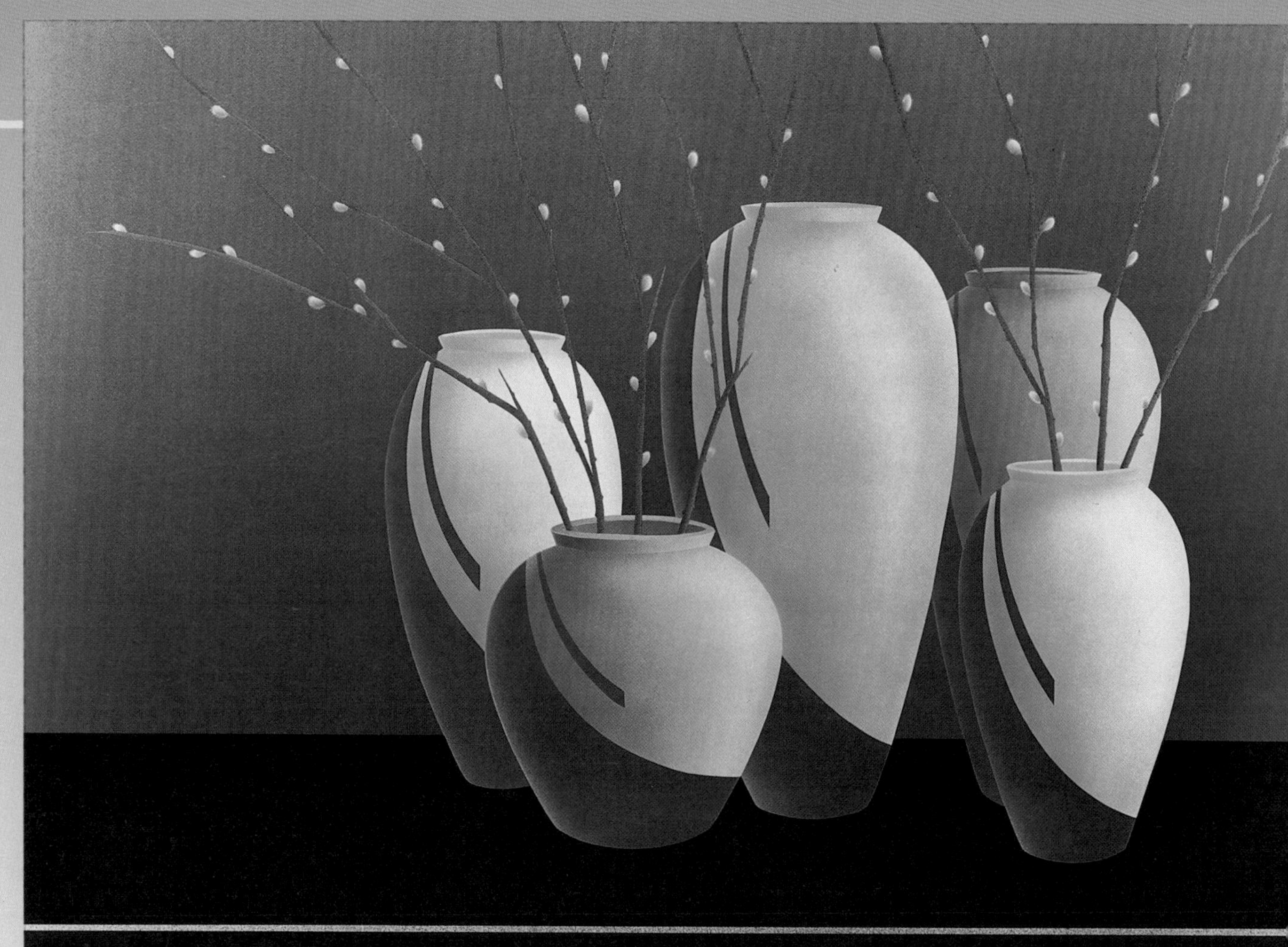
WILLIAM TODD HAILE
FRONT LINE EDITIONS / FEBRUARY 1983

H76 JARS $24^{1}/_{8} \times 32$

H77 EVENING STILL LIFE 36 × 24

WILLIAM TODD HAILE
ART EXPO NEW YORK/APRIL 7-11, 1983

H37 PUSSY WILLOWS 36 × 20

WILLIAM TODD HAILE
UP FRONT GALLERY/NOV-DEC. 1981

NSAI EXHIBITION · MIKI-SAN/OUR PLACE, SAN DIEGO · SEPT 1982 · WILLIAM TODD HAILE

H61 BONSAI 21 × 36

H24 BIRD OF PARADISE 36 × 24

WILLIAM TODD HAILE
TOPANGA GALLERY · JAN-FEB 198

WILLIAM TODD HAILE
TOPANGA GALLERY · JAN-FEB 1981

H25 CALLA LILIES 36 × 24

William Todd Haile · Talmadge Gallery 198

H34 TULIPS 24 × 36

WILLIAM TODD HAILE / GALLERY 415

H60 STATUS 36 × 20

WILLIAM TODD HAILE
ART EXPO NY · APRIL 22-26, 1982

H49 ANTHURIUM 36 × 20

Z8 ZUNGOLI IRIS 24 × 18

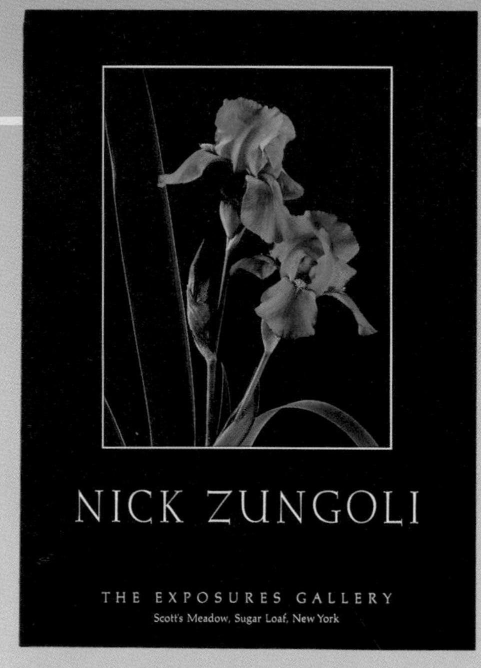
NICK ZUNGOLI
THE EXPOSURES GALLERY
Scott's Meadow, Sugar Loaf, New York

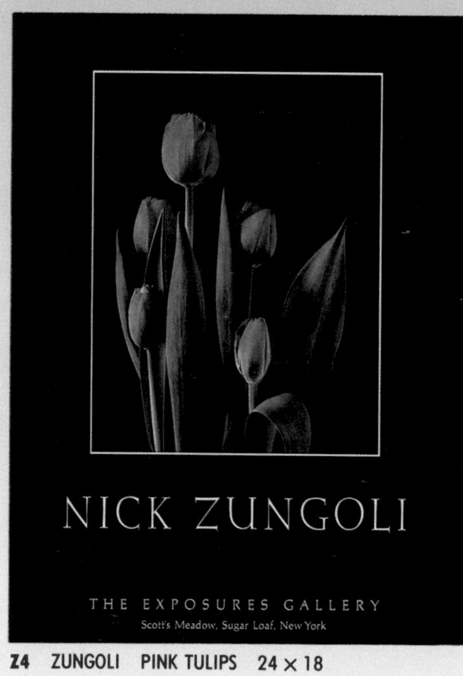
NICK ZUNGOLI
THE EXPOSURES GALLERY
Scott's Meadow, Sugar Loaf, New York

Z4 ZUNGOLI PINK TULIPS 24 × 18

A L L I U M

H88 HARDESTY ALLIUM ☆ 37 × 24

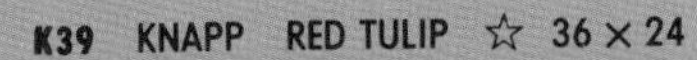

K39 KNAPP RED TULIP ☆ 36×24

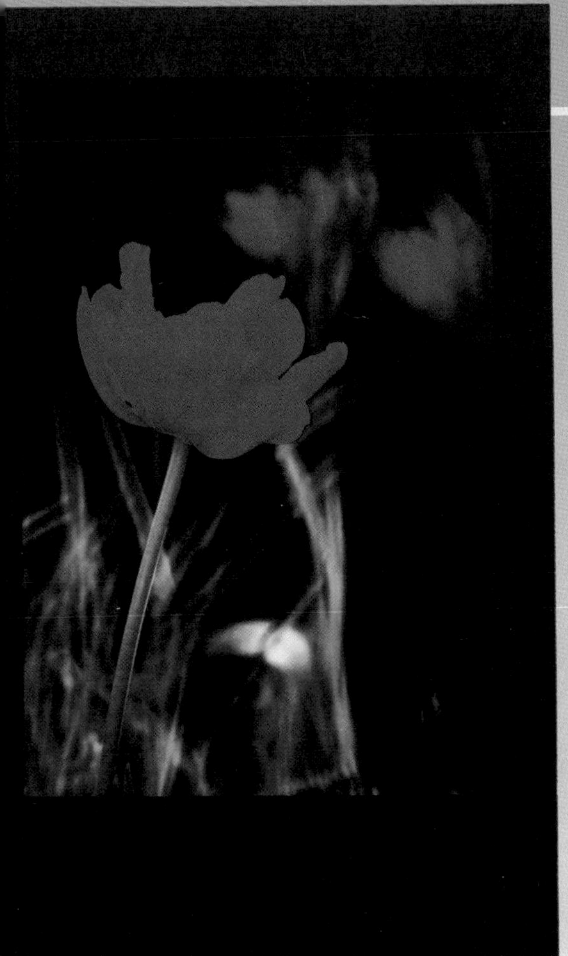

P33 PEMA IRISES $35^{3}/_{4} \times 23^{3}/_{4}$

PEMA
ART OF THE 80's
NEW YORK EXHIBITION

P34 PEMA ORCHIDS $35^{3}/_{4} \times 23^{3}/_{4}$

PEMA
ART OF THE 80's
NEW YORK EXHIBITION

WALTER HAMILTON
DISCOVERY GALLERIES

H90 HAMILTON ANTHURIUM STILL LIFE 33×24

BRIDGES FLORALIA $24 \times 29^{7}/_{8}$

F93 FRIEDMAN SPRING TULIPS ☆ 24 × 31

JERRY FRIEDMAN

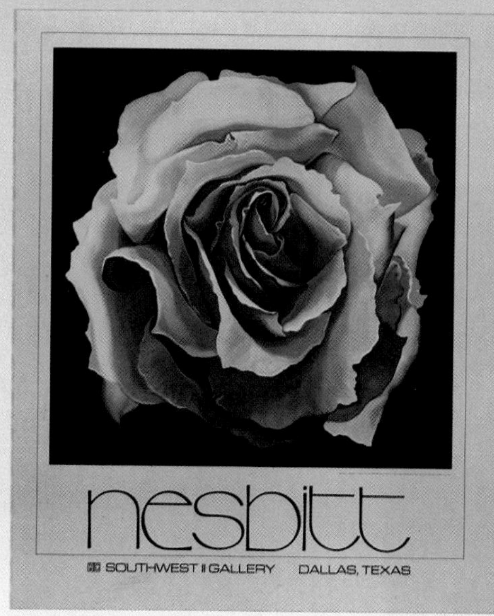
nesbitt
SOUTHWEST GALLERY DALLAS, TEXAS

N36 NESBITT THE ROSE ☆ 30 × 25

gregoire

G117 GREGOIRE BIRDS OF PARADISE 33 ×

M107A MENDELSOHN FAN DIPTYCH "A" *SERIGRAPH* 18 × 25

M107B MENDELSOHN FAN DIPTYCH "B" *SERIGRAPH* 18 × 25

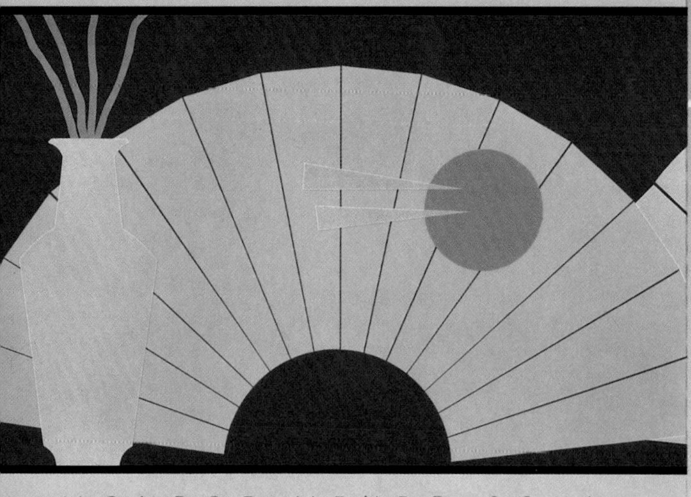

MONROE MENDELSOHN

DISCOVERY GALLERIES

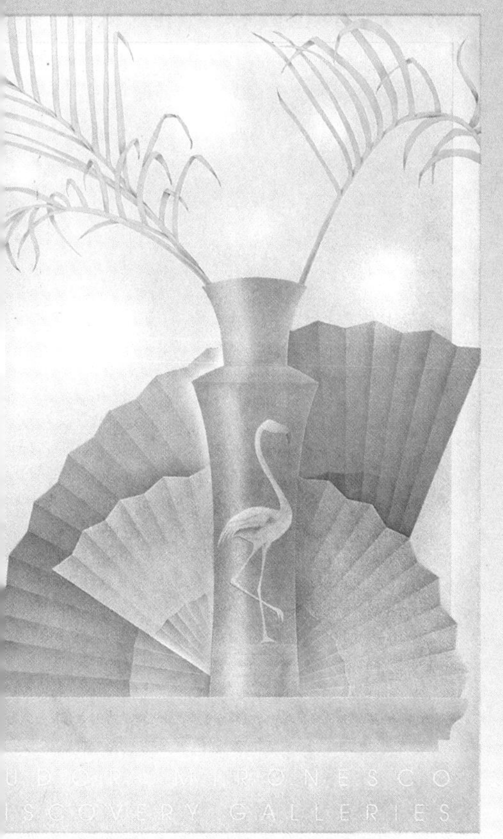
DISCOVERY GALLERIES

M90 MIRONESCO VASE WITH FAN 34 × 23

DISCOVERY GALLERIES

M89 MIRONESCO TULIPS STILL LIFE $31^3/_8 \times 22^3/_8$

B32 BABETTE LILAC TIME ☆ $32^3/4 \times 26$

BABETTE E. / WATERCOLORS

P72 POWELL STILL LIFE ON VERANDA 34 × 24

JOHN POWELL

FLORÉAL
MAIN ST. GRAPHICS · SANTA MONICA

F13 FLOREAL CYCLAMEN 25 × 19

FLORÉAL
MAIN ST. GRAPHICS · SANTA MONIC

F14 FLOREAL ORCHID 25 × 19

A42 ADAMS GARDEN ROSE $21^1/_2 \times 23$

"Garden Rose," 1982
Watercolor, 20½ x 18"
Poster published by
Allport Editions, Inc.
San Francisco

CHOICE EDITIONS

I8 IGER TIGER LILY 30×22

HOICE EDITIONS

I3 IGER LOTUS $31^3/_4 \times 22$

CHOICE EDITIONS

I2 IGER POPPIES 30×22

Y3 YOSHIKO COLLAGE FLORAL ☆ 34 × 24

yoshiko
mcgaw edition

E83 ELLESCAS PINK VASE 36 × 24

DICK ELLESCAS · DISCOVERY GALLERIES

MICHAEL CARSON

C157A CARSON ORCHIDS "A" 24 × 18

PACIFIC GALLERY

C157B CARSON ORCHIDS "B" 24 × 18

Y4 YOSHIKO IRISES ☆ 34 × 24

yoshiko
migaw editions

E82 ELLESCAS BLACK VASE 36 × 24

DICK ELLESCAS · DISCOVERY GALLERIES

CATHLEEN DALY
カサリン ディリー
Monotypes, Prints & Drawings Gallery Amelia Tokyo

D48 DALY RHODODENDRON 30 × 30

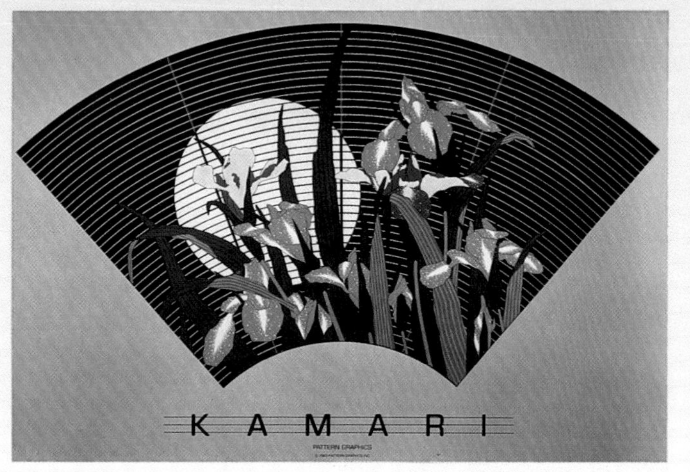
KAMARI
PATTERN GRAPHICS

K95 KAMARI IRIS I 24 × 36

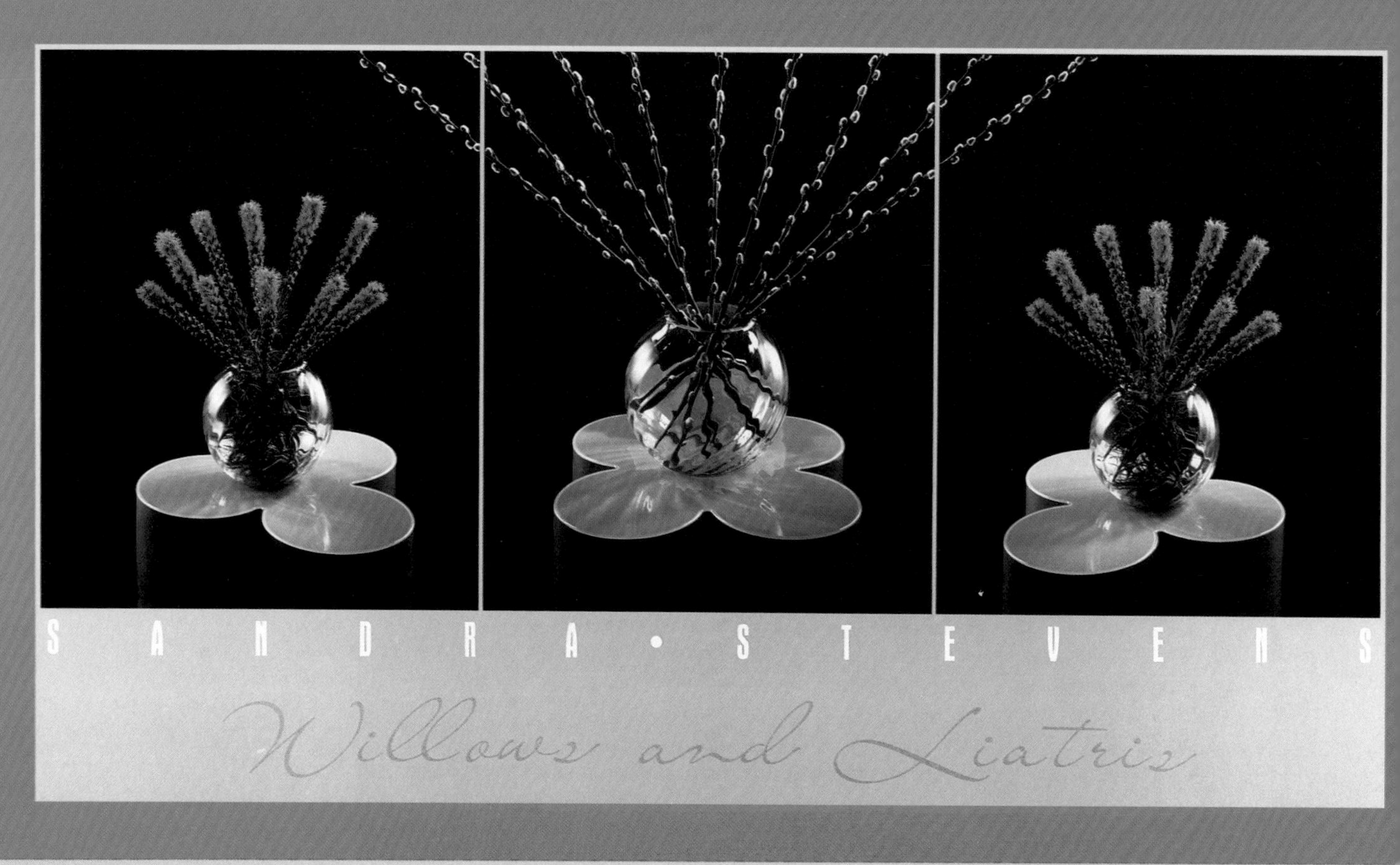
S A N D R A • S T E V E N S
Willows and Liatris

S161 WILLOWS & LIATRIS ☆ 22 × 38

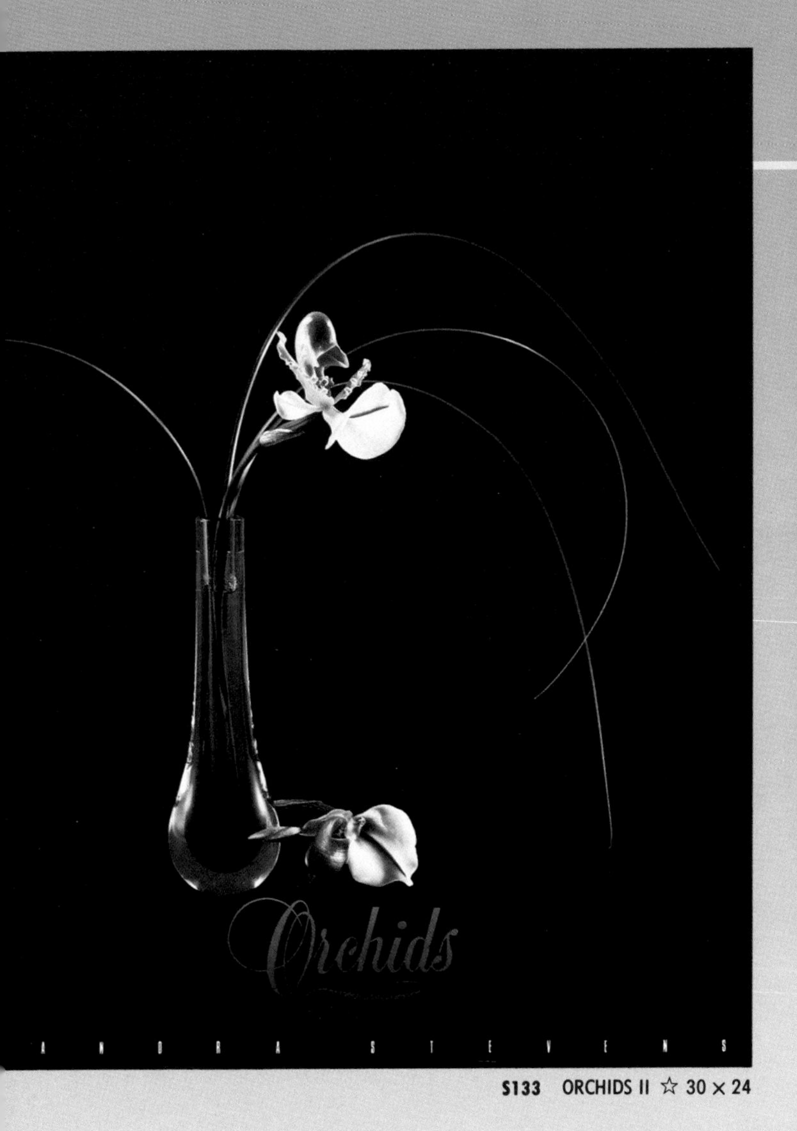
Orchids
A N D R A S T E V E N S

S133 ORCHIDS II ☆ 30 × 24

O R C H I D S

S130 ORCHIDS ☆ 30 × 24

P68 POWELL AVEC AMOUR-TULIPS 24 × 36

AVEC AMOUR

S46 SHIER ROSE 24 5/8 × 19

MARK SHIER

C154 CROWLEY PEACH VASE 20 × 16

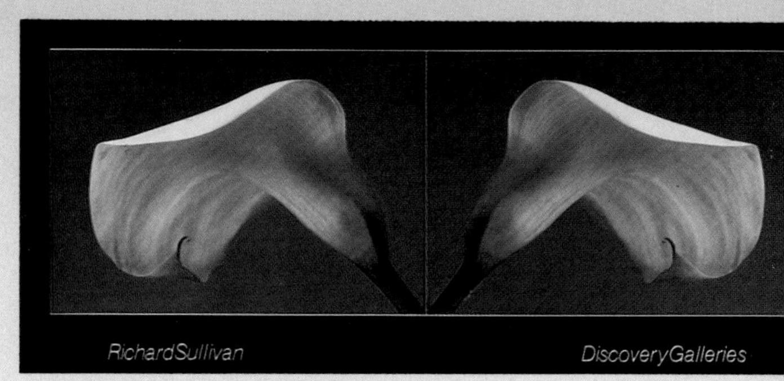
RichardSullivan
DiscoveryGalleries

S119 SULLIVAN CALLA LILY 18 × 39

T32 TRACK ROYAL BOTANICAL GARDENS 22 × 32 3/4

ROYAL BOTANICAL GARDENS
Hamilton
Ontario
Canada

K43 KIRKLAND YELLOW ROSE 38 × 24

B E T H · G A L T O N

G44 GALTON FLOWER ON LINEN 22 × 26

B31 CALIFORNIA POPPIES $20^{1}/_{4} \times 43$

GARY BUKOVNIK
Dryden Gallery, New York, New York

B41 GLOXINIA 38×25

V N I K

B27 WATERCOLORS 18 × 39 1/2

ARY BUKOVNIK/WATERCOLORS · ADI GALLERY/SAN FRANCISCO · JANUARY 17, 1980

B40 BEGONIA 38 × 25

D102 CALLA LILIES 36 × 24

BRIAN DAVIS
BRIAN DAVIS 83
THE HUNTINGTON
LIBRARY · ART GALLERY · BOTANICAL GARDENS
SAN MARINO · CALIFORNIA

BRIAN DAVI
LONG BEACH MUSEUM OF AR
BOOKSTORE/GALLERY SEPT. 7-OCT. 12, 198

D108 CAMELLIAS 36 × 24

BRIAN DAVIS / THE HUNTINGTO
LIBRARY · ART COLLECTIONS · BOTANICAL GARDENS · SAN MARINO · CALIFO

D143A WATER LILIES "A" 24 × 36

D137 ROSE 36 × 24

BRIAN DAVIS
THE HUNTINGTON
LIBRARY · ART GALLERY · BOTANICAL GARDENS

BRIAN DAVIS
THE HUNTINGTON
LIBRARY · ART GALLERY · BOTANICAL GARDENS
SAN MARINO · CALIFORNIA

D100 CACTUS ORCHID 36 × 24

IAN DAVIS / THE HUNTINGTON

D143B WATER LILIES "B" 24 × 36

D104 CYMBIDIUM V 36 × 24

BRIAN DAVIS
LAGUNA BEACH MUSEUM OF ART
POCHOIR PAINTINGS · APRIL 12 - MAY 24, 1981

D103 IRIS V 36 × 24

BRIAN DAVIS
NEW YORK BOTANICAL GARDEN
PRINT GALLERY/APRIL 10 - MAY 9, 19

BRIAN DAVIS / DAVIS·BLUE ARTWO

D140 TWO CYMBIDIUMS 18 × 24

D A V I S

D99 BIRD OF PARADISE 36 × 24

W17 ORCHID 25 × 32 7/8

JOHN WESA / ORCHID / WOODROSE FINE ARTS / FINE ART PUBLISHERS

W29 TWO ORCHIDS 25 × 33

JOHN WESA/TWO ORCHIDS/WOODROSE FINE ARTS/ART FOR THE 80'S

JOHN WESA / BIRD OF PARADISE
WOODROSE FINE ARTS / ARCATA, CALIFORNIA

W59 BIRD OF PARADISE 26 × 18

W37 ORCHIDS AT DAWN 36 × 24

JOHN WESA
WOODROSE FINE ARTS

W32 IRISES TWO 26 × 18

C R A N E

C143 GOLDEN LILIES 24 × 30

JEAN CRANE
ART EXPO

C164 YELLOW PEONIES 24 × 30

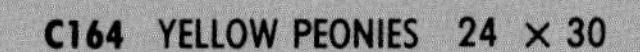

JEAN CRANE
ART EXPO

JEAN CRANE · ART EXPO

C105 BOUQUET 30 × 22

JEAN CRANE
ART EXPO

C106 MAGNOLIAS 24 × 30

JEAN CRANE
ART EXPO

C60 POSNER 24 × 30

C O O P E

C142A ORCHID ELEGANCE "A" $28^1/_2 \times 22$*

C142B ORCHID ELEGANCE "B" $28^1/_2 \times 22$*

C141 SUMMER ORCHID $31^1/_2 \times 25$*

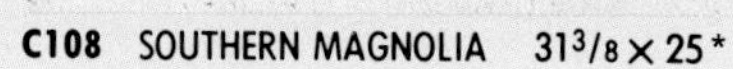

C108 SOUTHERN MAGNOLIA $31^3/_8 \times 25$*

C109 DECO IRIS $31^3/_8 \times 25$*

ALL SIZES ON THIS PAGE INDICATE IMAGES WITHOUT MARGINS

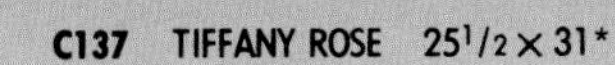

C137 TIFFANY ROSE $25^{1}/_{2} \times 31$*

C111 JAPANESE ORCHID $25^{1}/_{2} \times 31$*

C140 LAVENDER LADY $31^{1}/_{2} \times 25$*

C139 IMPERIAL LILY $25^{1}/_{2} \times 31$*

*ALL SIZES ON THIS PAGE INDICATE IMAGES WITHOUT MARGINS

C138 MOON VISTA $28^1/_4 \times 22^1/_4$

JUSTIN COOPERSMITH
New York Art Exposition

C110 EUROPEAN LILY $25^1/_2 \times 31$

Coopersmith

JUSTIN COOPERSMITH
IMPRESS GRAPHICS EDITIONS

C72 NIGHT LILY $28 \times 22^1/_4$

JUSTIN COOPERSMITH
IMPRESS GRAPHICS EDITIONS

C71 NIGHT FUCHSIA $28 \times 22^1/_4$

NEW YORK BOTANICAL GARDEN
PRINT GALLERY/JUSTIN COOPERSMITH

C69 NIGHT ORCHID $28 \times 22^1/_4$

C112 MAGNOLIA NOUVEAU 36¼ × 24¼

COOPERSMITH
NEW YORK BOTANICAL GARDEN
Print Gallery

COOPERSMITH
NEW YORK BOTANICAL GARDEN
Print Gallery

C113 CAMELLIA NOUVEAU 36¼ × 24¼

NEW YORK BOTANICAL GARDEN
PRINT GALLERY/JUSTIN COOPERSMITH

C68 NIGHT IRIS 28 × 22¼

M119 MANTELPIECE 24 × 36

KEITH MALLETT/NEW YORK ART EXPO

KEITH MALLETT
FRONT LINE EDITIONS · 1984

M101 TILE LILY 24 × 32

KEITH MALLETT GALLERY 415

M118 HENNESSEY III 24 × 32

E T T

GOLDEN
KEITH MALLETT
ART EXPO NEW YORK / APRIL 7-11 1983
REFLECTIONS

M97 GOLDEN 36 × 12

M75 GOLDEN REFLECTIONS 36 × 24

M98 REFLECTIONS 36 × 12

KEITH MALLETT/NEW YORK ART EXPO

M117 GOLDEN HORIZONS 24 × 36

jerry fruchtman
B R O O K E S • B O U Q U E T
photographer

F46 BROOKES BOUQUET $35^{3}/_{4} \times 25^{1}/_{8}$

F73 CHERRY BLOSSOMS, BLACK 24 × 36

F R U C H T M A N
PUBLISHED BY MIRAGE EDITIONS, INC & FRONTLINE EDITIONS

F R U C H T M A N

F78 CHERRY BLOSSOMS, WHITE 24 × 36

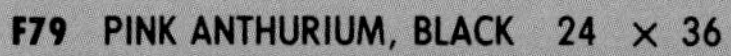

F79 PINK ANTHURIUM, BLACK 24 × 36

F27 FLORAL $33^{7}/_{8} \times 22^{3}/_{4}$

FRUCHTMAN

F80 PINK ANTHURIUM, WHITE 24 × 36

JERRY FRUCHTMAN
PORTFOLIO ONE ANTHURIUM
PUBLISHED BY MIRAGE EDITIONS INC SANTA MONICA CALIFORNIA

F64 ANTHURIUM 34 × 24

FRUCHTMAN
NIGHT MOODS
PUBLISHED BY MIRAGE EDITIONS, SANTA MONICA, CA

F81 NIGHT MOODS 36 × 24

M121 MONTEAUX VASE ON MANTEL 24 × 18

MICHEL MONTEAUX
PARIS • PHOTOGRAPHY • LOS ANGELES

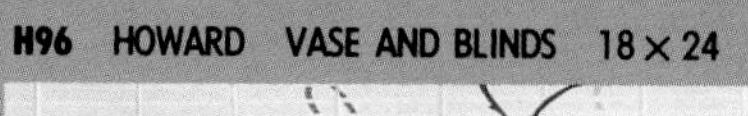

H96 HOWARD VASE AND BLINDS 18 × 24

LES FLEURS

D119 DENNISON LES FLEURS 34 × 25

FRIEDBERT RENBAUM, HELICO GRAPHICS, ART EXPO, N.Y. APRIL 22-26

R21 RENBAUM LILIES $20^{1}/_{8} \times 39^{3}/_{4}$

R40 RENBAUM BIRDS OF PARADISE 20 × 39 1/2

FRIEDBERT RENBAUM HELICO GRAPHICS ART EXPO N.Y. 83

R51 RENBAUM L'IMAGE DESIGN 36 × 24

FRIEDBERT RENBAUM, L'IMAGE DESIGN, TORONTO

FRIEDBERT RENBAUM HELICO GRAPHICS ART EXPO N.Y. 83

R41 RENBAUM IRIS 20 × 39 1/2

b.b. la femme
GEARY'S
Spring 1983
Beverly Hills, Ca.

L52 LA FEMME GEARY'S *SERIGRAPH* 30 × 22

M128 McCRUM CALLA 34 × 24

GUY McCRUM

S121 SCHAIR SILVER DOLLARS ☆ 24 × 18

MAL WATSON

W44 WATSON SPANISH IRIS 35 × 24

M109 MENDELSOHN GINGER STILL LIFE 26 × 20

MONROE MENDELSOHN
DISCOVERY GALLERIES

M95 MENDELSOHN GLORIOSA LILY 33 × 25

MONROE MENDELSOHN
DISCOVERY GALLERIES

M80 MENDELSOHN MOTH ORCHIDS - I

32 × 24

TROPICAL ORCHIDS
DISCOVERY GALLERIES

M87 MENDELSOHN TROPICAL ORCHIDS 25 × 32

MONROE MENDELSOHN
DISCOVERY GALLERIES

M96 MENDELSOHN HAWAIIAN ILLI 33 × 25

L11 FUCHSIA ORCHIDS $39\frac{3}{8} \times 24\frac{3}{4}$

Lander
galerie El-baz

L28 WATERMELON FLORAL $39\frac{1}{2} \times 27$

Lander
galerie El-baz

L25 SILVER VASE $39\frac{1}{2} \times 27$

Lander

5th Anniversary Marci Lipman Graphics J. Lander
TORONTO MAY 1979

L13 MAY BOUQUET $34 \times 23\frac{1}{8}$

Lander

L12 IRISES WITH CRANE $39\frac{3}{8} \times 24\frac{3}{4}$

D E R

L17 YELLOW VASE 39 1/2 × 27 1/2

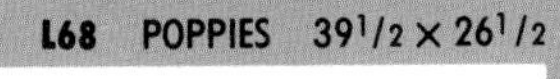

L68 POPPIES 39 1/2 × 26 1/2

L14 RIBBONED VASE 39 3/8 × 24 3/4

Lander
galerie Elbaz

John Lander
Toronto
Marci Lipman Graphics
Nov/80

L7 ANTHURIUM 39 × 27

JOHN LANDER EL·BAZ GALLERY SOHO NEW YORK

L69 CARNATIONS 39 3/8 × 26 3/4

I 10 IRWIN MISSISSIPPI MAGNOLIA $18^{3}/_{4} \times 39$

MISSISSIPPI/MAGNOLIA · DON IRWIN · DASHER EDITIONS/SAN FRANCISCO

I 12 IRWIN STEPHEN'S POPPIES $20^{7}/_{8} \times 39^{1}/_{2}$

STEPHEN'S POPPIES · DON IRWIN · DASHER EDITIONS/SAN FRANCISCO

Shiley's Petunias · Lucija Jovanovic · First Impressions · Carmel

J12 JOVANOVIC SHILEY'S PETUNIAS $22 \times 39^{3}/_{8}$

CALIFORNIA/GOLDEN POPPY · DON IRWIN · DASHER EDITIONS/SAN FRANCISCO

I 4 IRWIN GOLDEN POPPY $16^{1}/_{4} \times 39$

J13 JOVANOVIC MR. T'S BEGONIA 22 × 33 3/8

Mr. T's Begonia · Lucija Jovanovic · Dasher Editions · San Francisco

Mr. T's Nasturtiums · Lucija Jovanovic · Dasher Editions · San Francisco

J24 JOVANOVIC MR. T'S NASTURTIUMS 22 × 40

SQUASH BLOSSOMS · LUCIJA JOVANOVIC · DASHER EDITIONS/SAN FRANCISCO

J23 JOVANOVIC SQUASH BLOSSOMS 21 × 40

Lucija Jovanovic · Eucalyptus · Dasher · San Francisco

J11 JOVANOVIC EUCALYPTUS 24 × 39 1/2

D118 DER HACOPIAN CRYSTAL BLOSSOM $35^{3}/_{8} \times 24$

DER HACOPIAN
LOS ANGELES/PHOTOGRAPHY

P91 PETER ANTHURIUM 36×24

DOUGLAS PETER
PHOTOGRAPHY/LOS ANGELE
PHOTO/GRAPHICS A POSTER SERIES OF INTERNATION
PHOTOGRAPHIC ART PUBLISHED AND DISTRIBUTED
DAVIS · BLUE ARTWOR

$35^{3}/_{8} \times 24$

DER HACOPIAN
LOS ANGELES/PHOTOGRAPHY

D116 DER HACOPIAN BLACK BAMBOO

D112 DER HACOPIAN BLUE MORNING $23^{1}/_{4} \times 30$

L60 LACROIX CYCLAMEN $35^{3}/_{4} \times 24^{1}/_{2}$

AT LACROIX

L59 LECLAIRE FROST VASE 24 × 20

Leclaire
White

N49 NEWMAN ABSTRACT FLORAL $28^{1}/_{2} \times 22^{1}/_{2}$

S143 SHICK WILLOWS 24× 18

JIM SHICK PHOTOGRAPHY

S144 SHICK FEATHERS 24 × 18

K11 WHITE FLOWERS 24¼ × 32

BRIAN KELLEY
ART TORONTO 80 POSTERS INTERNATIONAL INC

BRIAN KELLEY
at the Elmwood club
18 elm st. toronto, canada - november 8 - december 5 1983

K71 ELMWOOD CLUB 24 × 32

L E Y

K57 CHAIR 27 × 34

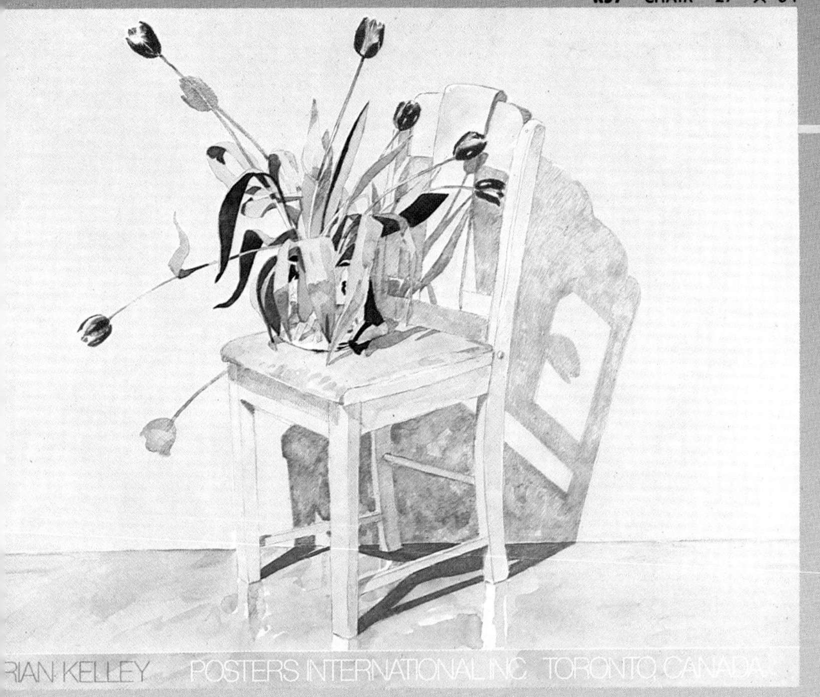
RIAN KELLEY
POSTERS INTERNATIONAL INC TORONTO CANADA

K3 STILL LIFE 24 × 36

BRIAN KELLEY

BRIAN KELLEY
POSTERS INTERNATIONAL 508 EGLINTON

K27 ORCHID $24^1/_2$ × 36

B19 BOTANICAL LAVENDER 36 x 24

Mattioli, Venice, 1565
The New York Botanical Garden Print Series

B88 BOTANICAL IRISES 36 x 24

Iris Calcedonica latifolia
Hortus Eystettensis, Eichstatt, 1613
The New York Botanical Garden Print Series

B89 BOTANICAL THISTLE 36 x 24

Cinera cum flore.
Hortus Eystettensis, Eichstatt, 161
The New York Botanical Garden Print Series

DOUG
HOOK
ART EXPO-
SAN
FRANCISCO,
CALIFORNIA
OCTOBER
22-26, 1981

H46 HOOK DAY LILIES 24¹/₄ × 36

SARA EYESTONE
AMERICAN BATT

E72 EYESTONE SPRING FLORAL ☆ 36 x 20

B21 BOTANICAL SUNFLOWER 36 x 24

Flos Solis maior.
Hortus Eystettensis, Eichstatt, 1613

B17 BOTANICAL AMARYLLIS 36 x 24

Wallich, London, 1830

B20 BOTANICAL ORCHID 36 x 24

Cattleya skinneri

SARA EYESTONE · AMERICAN BATIK

E30 EYESTONE AMERICAN BATIK ☆ 30 x 40

F105 ROLAND GARROS $29\frac{1}{2} \times 22\frac{1}{4}$

ROLAND GARROS
1982

F37 LA TOSCANA $37 \times 26\frac{7}{8}$

La Toscana nel '500
MOSTRE AD AREZZO GROSSETO IMPRUNETA LIVORNO LUCCA PISA PISTOIA PRATO SIENA
REGIONE TOSCANA PRIMAVERA-AUTUNNO 1980
CON IL PATROCINIO DEL COMITATO NAZIONALE DELLA 16ª ESPOSIZIONE EUROPEA D'ARTE SCIENZA E CULTURA

F97 BLUE ROSE $32\frac{1}{4} \times 22\frac{3}{8}$

THE BLUE
ROSE

ZARAGOZA
COPA DEL MUNDO DE FUTBOL ESPAÑA 82

F104 ZARAGOZA $37\frac{1}{4} \times 23\frac{1}{8}$

FOLON
Transworld Art

F6 UN MATIN $36\frac{1}{2} \times 24\frac{1}{4}$

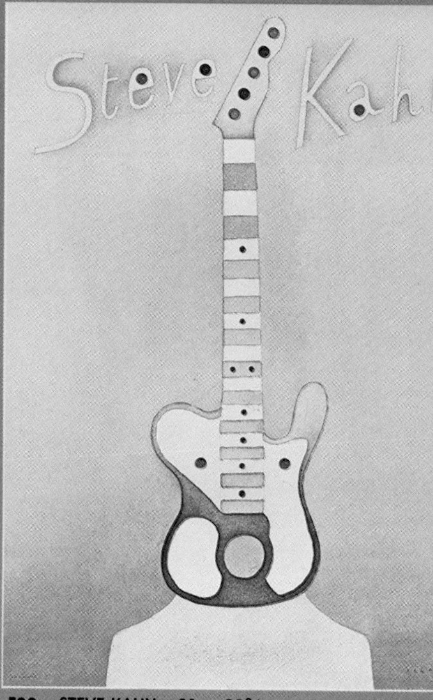
Steve

F98 STEVE KAHN $31 \times 22\frac{3}{8}$

F99 L'AMOUR NU $31^{3}/_{8} \times 22$

MARLENE JOBERT
JEAN-MICHEL FOLON
L'amour nu
UN FILM DE YANNICK BELLON

F100 L'ECOLOGIE $24^{3}/_{4} \times 17^{1}/_{2}$

AUJOURD'HUI
L'ECOLOGIE

F7 BASTILLE DAY $30^{3}/_{8} \times 23$

FOLON, THE GRAPHIC ART
HORN GALLERY 503 6TH AVENUE N.Y.C.
14

FOLON
images pour des mots

F101 IMAGES POUR DES MOTS $26^{1}/_{2} \times 17^{1}/_{2}$

IT'S LIKE A ROLLER COASTER RIDE FOR THE MIND.
THE NEW SCIENCE MUSEUM OF MINNESOTA
WILLIAM L. McKNIGHT-3M OMNITHEATER

F2 ROLLER COASTER 29×23

G54 MONK SEAL 32 × 22

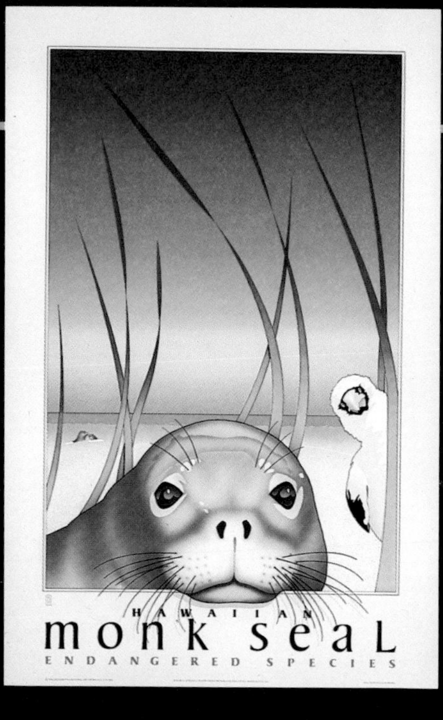
HAWAIIAN
monk seal
ENDANGERED SPECIES

G73 TIGER 28 × 20

DANIEL GILBERT
LITHOGRAPHY BY DESIGN, PETALUMA, CALIFORNIA

G53 RUNNER $33^{7}/_{8} \times 23^{7}/_{8}$

RUNNER

MILLER•GILBERT
MARRIED MARCH 10, NINETEEN-EIGHTY-TWO

G38 WEDDING POSTER 18 × 25

G115 TOUCANS 26 × 20

We Don't Want You To Smoke.

G32 TALK 36 × 22

T - A - L - K
KGO NEWSTALK RADIO 81 SAN FRANCISCO

G111 RADIO 32 × 20

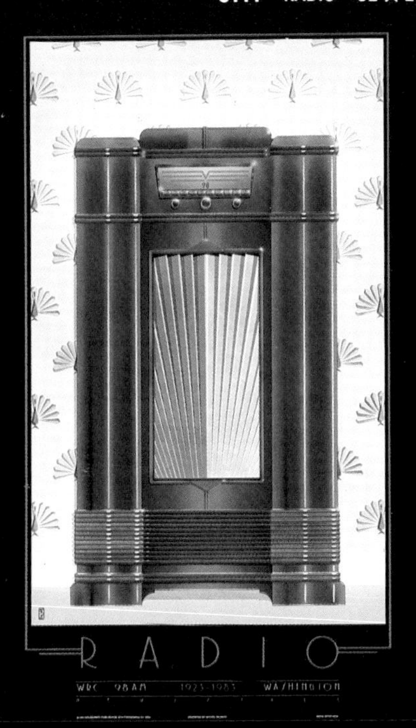
R A D I O

ART POSTERS OF DANIEL GILBERT
WALLER PRESS
SAN FRANCISCO, CALIFORNIA

G109 ZEBRA 32 × 25

YEAR OF THE OCEAN

G108 YEAR OF THE OCEAN 21 × 32

G52 MONET'S PALETTE 36 × 24

MONET
1840-1926
GIVERNY

G34 MOZART SNEEZES 36 × 24

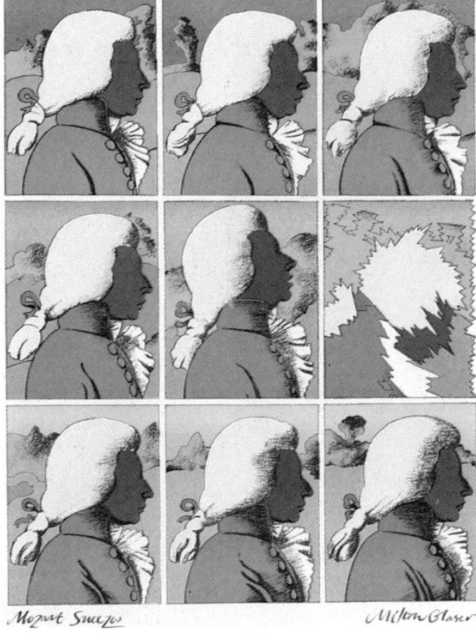
Mostly Mozart Festival
Lincoln Center
Mozart Sneezes
Milton Glaser

G69 SAN DIEGO JAZZ FEST. 36 × 24

Floating pear

G51 FLOATING PEAR 37 × 24

ELVIS
ELVIS BY ALBERT GOLDMAN
WITH THE RECOLLECTIONS OF LAMAR FIKE AND THE AMERICAN PEOPLE
PUBLISHED BY McGRAW-HILL BOOK COMPANY

G50 ELVIS 36 × 24

Sony Tape. Full Color Sound.

G36 SONY-LANDSCAPE 36 × 24

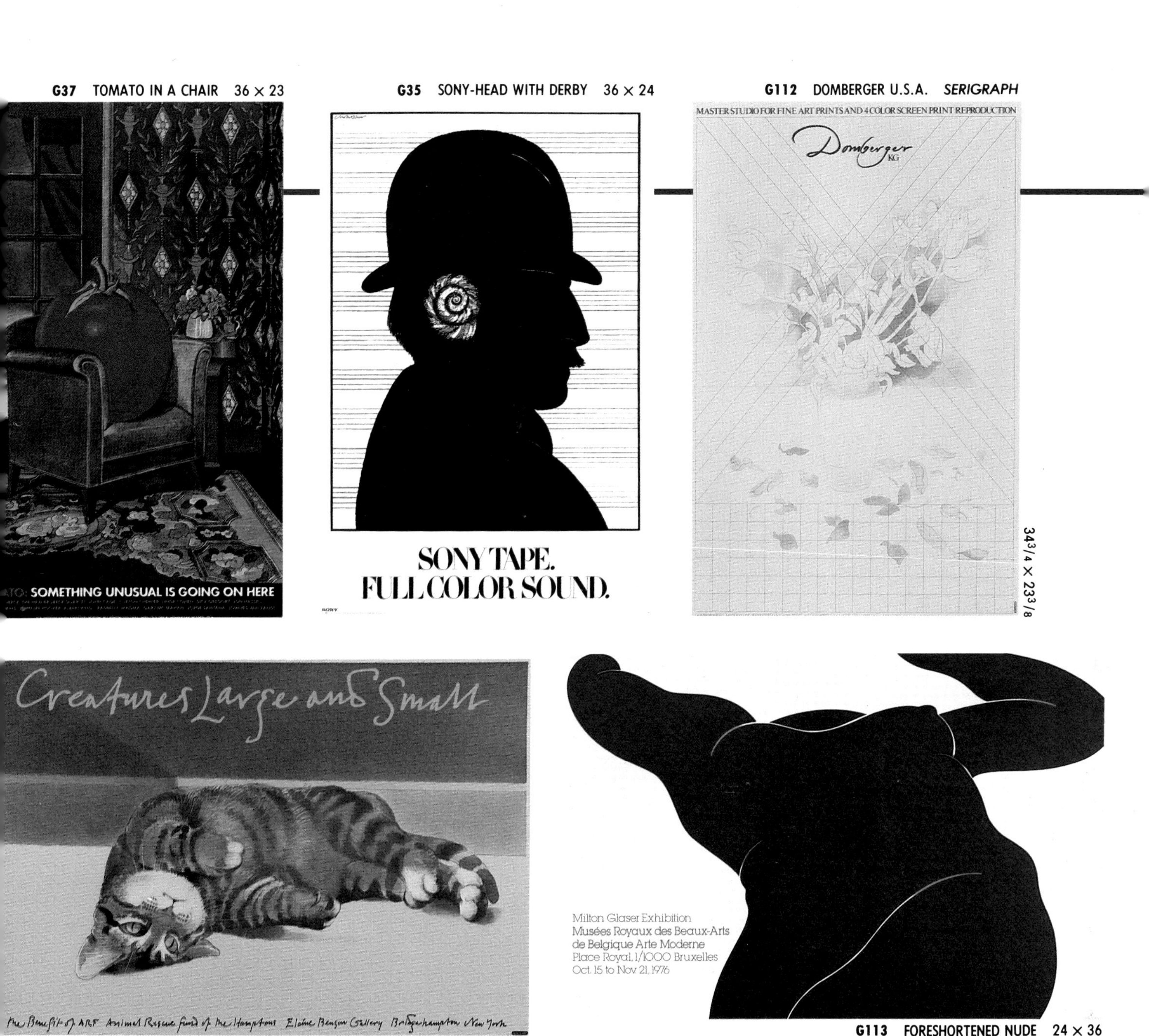

SOMETHING UNUSUAL IS GOING ON HERE
SONY TAPE.
FULL COLOR SOUND.
MASTER STUDIO FOR FINE ART PRINTS AND 4 COLOR SCREEN PRINT REPRODUCTION
Domberger KG
Creatures Large and Small
the Benefit of ARF Animal Rescue Fund of the Hamptons Elaine Benson Gallery Bridgehampton New York
Milton Glaser Exhibition
Musées Royaux des Beaux-Arts
de Belgique Arte Moderne
Place Royal, 1/1000 Bruxelles
Oct. 15 to Nov 21, 1976

G37 TOMATO IN A CHAIR 36 × 23

G35 SONY-HEAD WITH DERBY 36 × 24

G112 DOMBERGER U.S.A. *SERIGRAPH* 34 3/4 × 23 3/8

G114 CREATURES LARGE & SMALL 24 × 36

G113 FORESHORTENED NUDE 24 × 36

"The most successful posters balance familiar and understandable imagery with the unexpected or exotic to produce a surprise or visual joke.

is a well observed design paradox that the informed communication of ideas can often best be conveyed insights arrived at by the unconscious—where the imaginative and the functional fuse and become ally indistinguishable."

lton Glaser

C132 COLEN SUMMER DELIGHT ☆ 27 × 32

SUMMER
Delight

S93 SPAFFORD VEGETABLES $24^7/_8$ × 33

M E T

rtist Paul Gaugin once cryptically remarked: "Many cooks are spoiled by going into the arts." Today's artistic gastronomes satisfy their culinary and aesthetic appetites by indulging in gourmet posters.

criminating palates have discovered the fun of dining with these savory works. Food related images providing a feast for the eyes and a boon for the poster industry.

erest in these posters is a natural extension of the growing interest in food in our society. As tastes lve from hot dogs to haute cuisine, people spend more time in the kitchen and discover the bare walls re needing some attention. Food and other paraphernalia of cooking provide the logical imagery.

ple have also begun to appreciate food for aesthetic values rather than just as something to quell nger. Pink peppercorns, miniature vegetables, red lettuce and endless other foods we now dine on are d as much for how they look as for how they taste. So it seems only natural that people would respond husiastically to such delicious images as Bruce Curtis' Strawberries *or John Neubauer's* Le Champignon. *s is not just food, this is fine dining.*

ists like Rick Davis add another dimension to our appreciation of the food we consume. Davis uses very ple imagery to create very sophisticated posters. Look at his Oranges, *or his* Bananas *or his* Kiwis. *Then, t time you go to eat one of these fruits, take a second look and enjoy not only the taste, but the beauty of fruit as well.*

hat a shoot ... fruit! The pressure of new subtle images drove me crazy for weeks, but the greengrocer ed me at last," says Rick Davis. "Shapes that are easy on the eye and haven't changed in eons are the st difficult challenge and also produce the most rewarding images."

nere have been famous photographs done by fine art photographers that have used a screen as a textural ct against a nude," says photographer Corinne Colen speaking of her poster Summer Delight. *"I took the a and used it in the same way with food which is also sensual, but in a different way. I like the muted nding of textures and tones that was achieved in the image and the water adds a sense of freshness."*

er gourmet posters can be found in the photography and still life sections of this catalogue.

R I C K

D87 BANANAS ☆ 18 × 24

R I C K D A V I S

R I C K D A V I S

D88 LIMES ☆ 18 × 24

R I C K D A V I

D85 KIWIS ☆ 18 × 24

D A V I S

D90 STRAWBERRIES ☆ 18 × 24

R I C K D A V I S

I C K D A V I S

D86 ORANGES ☆ 18 × 24

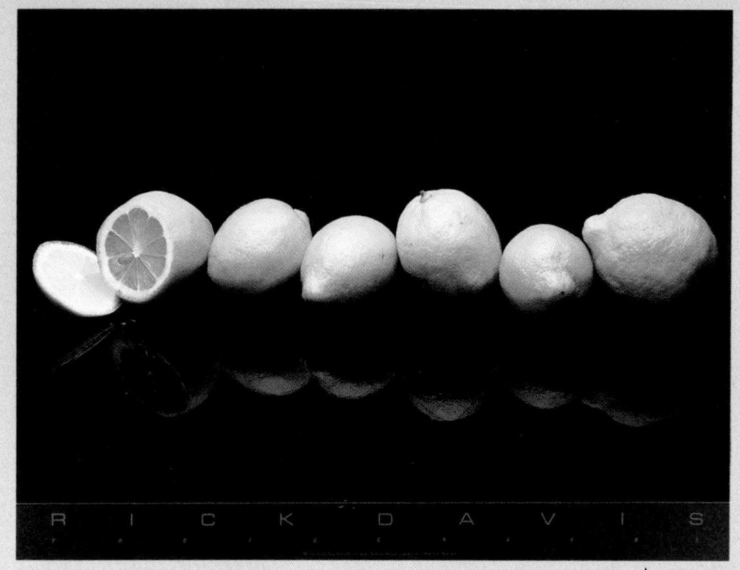
R I C K D A V I S

D89 LEMONS ☆ 18 × 24

H124 HALL STERLING VINEYARDS $31^{3}/_{8} \times 21^{3}/_{4}$

STERLING VINEYARDS
Napa Valley California

C120 CAUDLE ICE CREAM $16^{1}/_{8} \times 22$

ROD CAUDLE STUDIO

F103 FINMARK BLANC $24^{1}/_{2} \times 29^{1}/_{4}$

GRANDS VINS DE FRANCE
ROUGE

F102 FINMARK ROUGE $24^{1}/_{2} \times 29^{1}/_{4}$

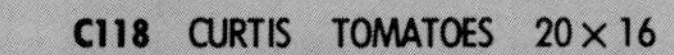

S128 SANTIAGO KU RASPBERRIES 34 × 24

PRINGLE & BOOTH

C118 CURTIS TOMATOES 20 × 16

C119 CURTIS ONIONS 20 × 16

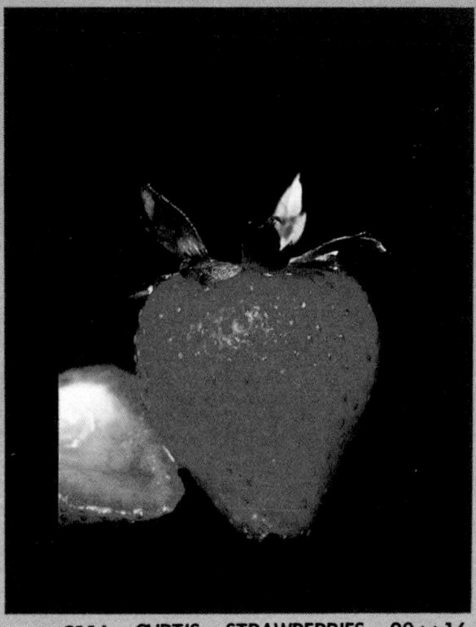

C116 CURTIS STRAWBERRIES 20 × 16

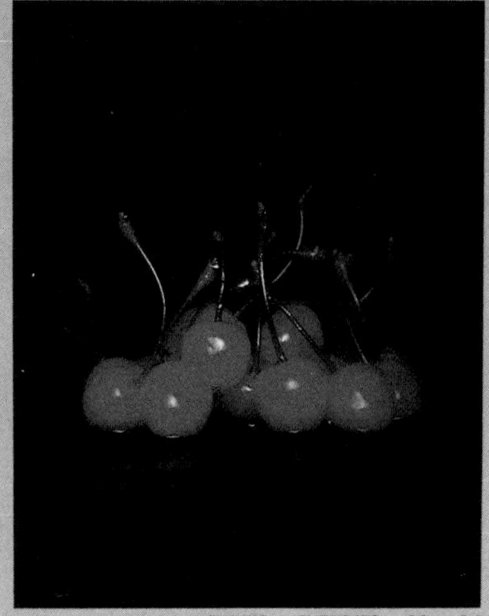

C117 CURTIS CHERRIES 20 × 16

S100 ST. JIVAGO EGG IN NEST 36 × 24

F63 FRENCH WINE 19 × 21 1/2

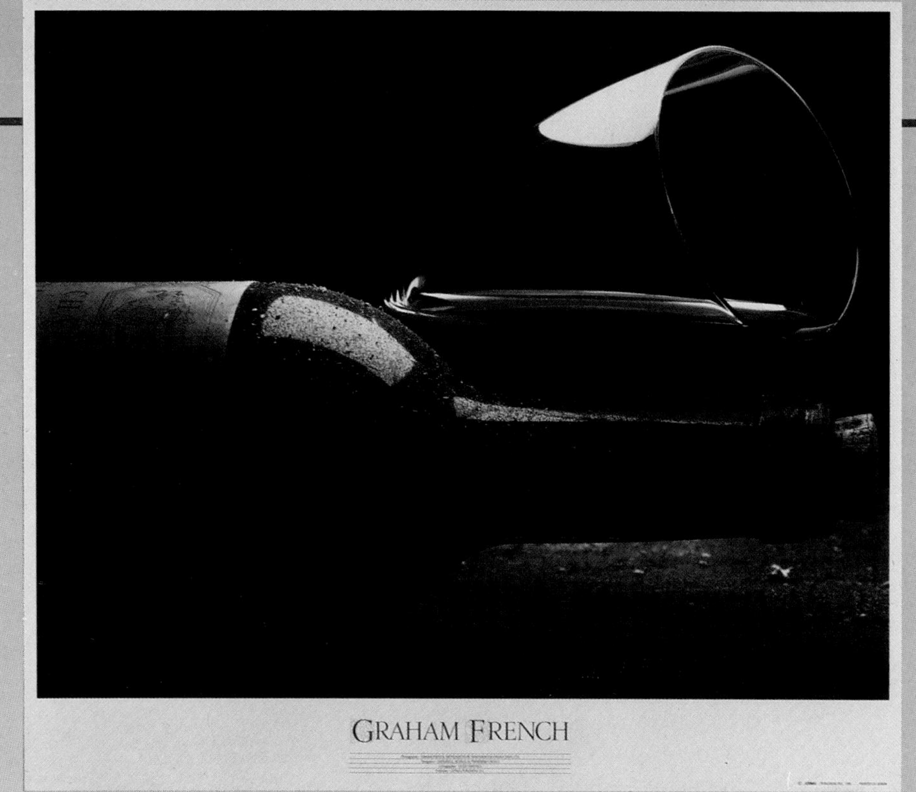
GRAHAM FRENCH

M108 MANNO HAPPY HOUR 32 × 23

MANNO
art spectrum · new york

Saint Emilion

F72 FRENCH SAINT EMILION 30 × 24

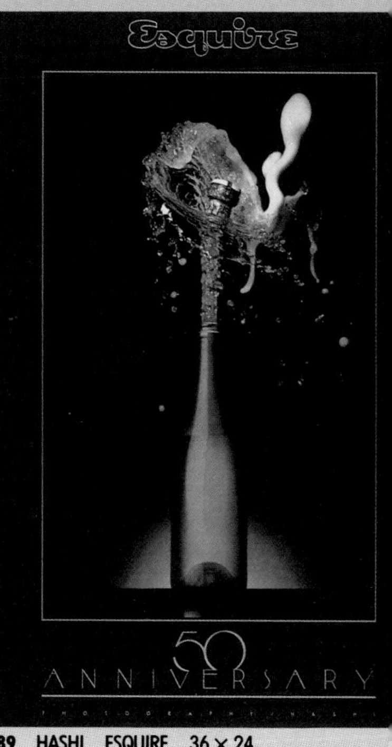
Esquire
50
ANNIVERSARY

H89 HASHI ESQUIRE 36 × 24

P88 PERWEILER TEA CUP 36 × 23 1/2

PERWEILER

P25 PERWEILER CROISSANTS 24 5/8 × 18 3/4

PERWEILER

P26 PERWEILER EGGS & FORK 24 1/8 × 18 1/8

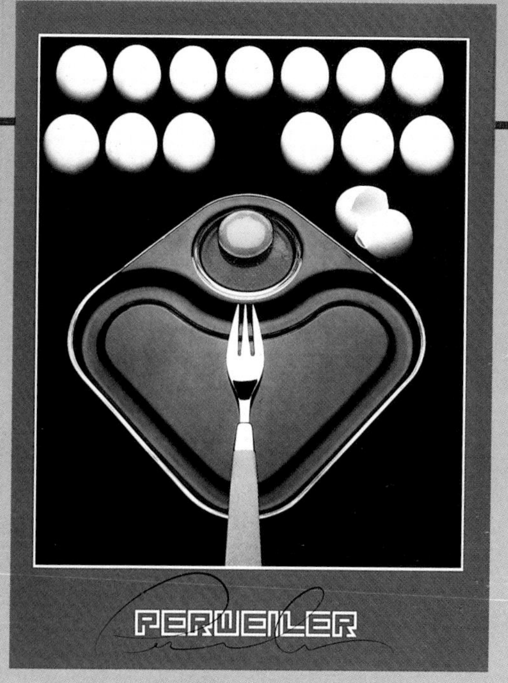
PERWEILER

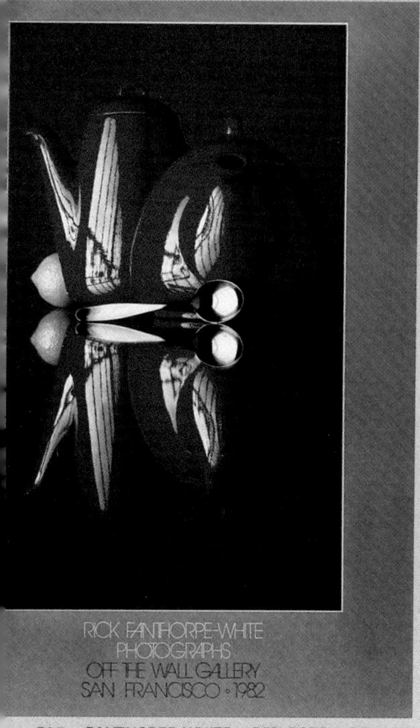
RICK FANTHORPE-WHITE
PHOTOGRAPHS
OFF THE WALL GALLERY
SAN FRANCISCO • 1982

F35 FANTHORPE-WHITE RED POTS 28 × 19

Colin Barker

B145 BARKER RED TEAPOT 19 × 25 1/2

D126 DUBIEL APPLES 32 × 25

Market Gallery

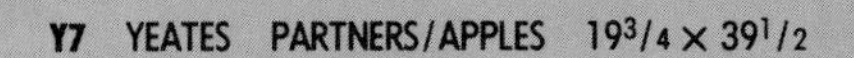
Y7 YEATES PARTNERS/APPLES 19 3/4 × 39 1/2

PARTNERS

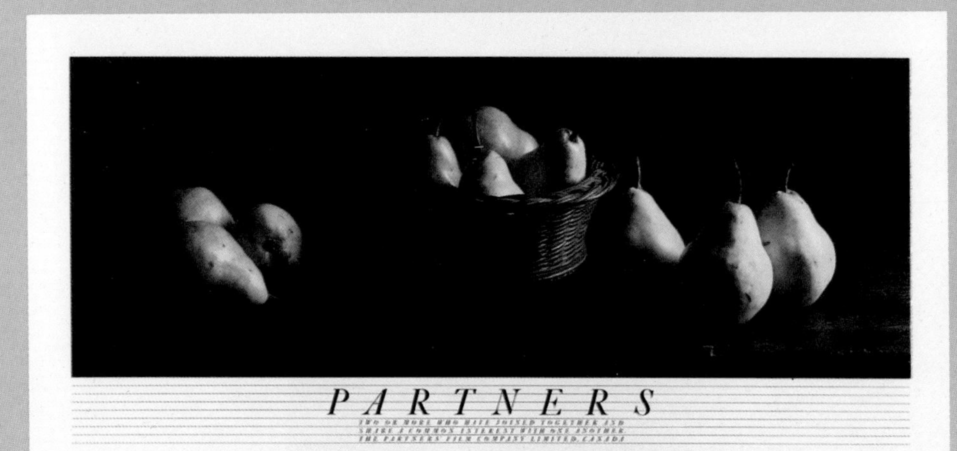
PARTNERS

Y6 YEATES PARTNERS/PEARS 19 3/4 × 39 1/2

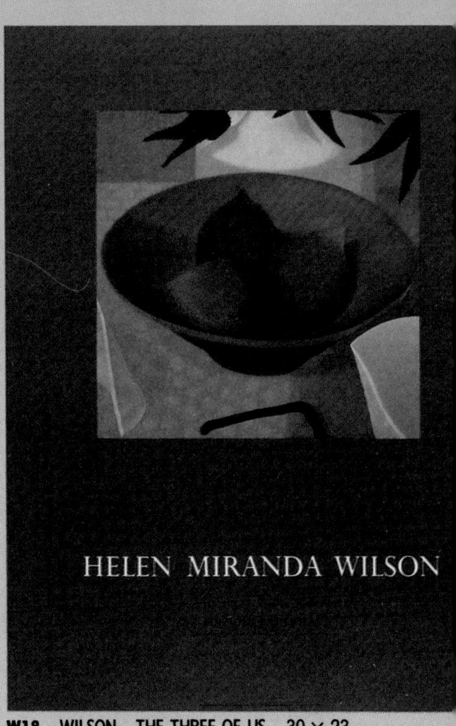
HELEN MIRANDA WILSON

W18 WILSON THE THREE OF US 30 × 23

M39 MILLER CALCAIRE 30 × 20¾

CALCAIRE

M40 MILLER MARLSTONE 30 × 20¾

MARLSTONE

B153 BATISTA—MOON PAUL MASSON '84 26 × 20

Paul Masson
Summer Series 84
JUNE 16-SEPTEMBER 16
PAUL MASSON MOUNTAIN WINERY SARATOGA CALIFORNIA

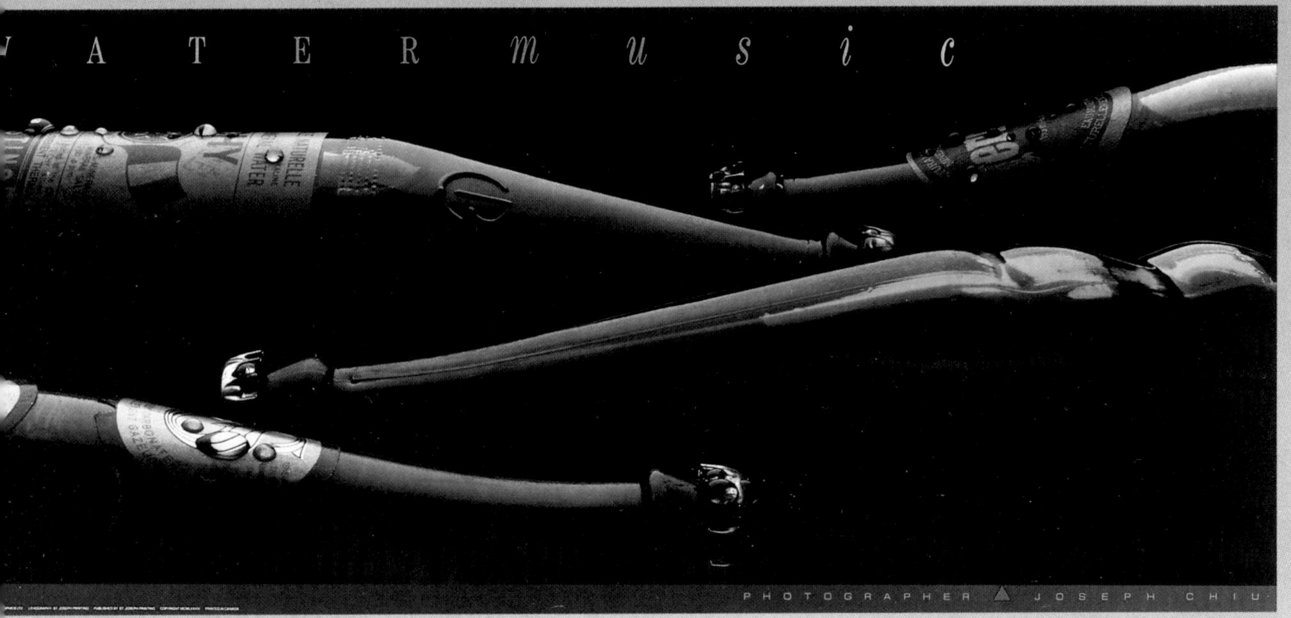
WATER music
PHOTOGRAPHER JOSEPH CHIU

C162 CHIU WATER MUSIC 15¾ × 35¼

N46 NEUBAUER LE PIMENT VERT 32 × 20

·LE·PIMENT·VERT·
Photography John Neubauer·Gourmet Grafiks·May 26,19

N52 NEUBAUER LA FRAISE 22 × 28

·LA·FRAISE·
·Photography John Neubauer·Gallery Prints·May 26,1982·

·LE·CHAMPIGNON·

N47 NEUBAUER LE CHAMPIGNON 22 × 28

LA BOTTE DE RADIS

N56 NEUBAUER LA BOTTE DE RADIS 24 × 34

LA GOUSSE D'AIL
JOHN NEUBAUER · GOURMET GRAFIKS · MARCH 1, 1983

N54 NEUBAUER LA GOUSSE D'AIL 34 × 2

C102 CHOU THE LAZY GOURMET 20 × 16

F66 FUKUDA COCOLAT $27^{3}/_{4} \times 19^{1}/_{8}$

D69 DAVIES WHITE EGGS PLUS 30 × 22

KEN DAVIES
"WHITE EGGS PLUS"
TRITON PRESS·NYC

DENNIS DUBIEL

D128 DUBIEL THE GARLIC BRAID $31^{1}/_{2} \times 18^{1}/_{2}$

H59 HILL JARS 18 × 24

T7 TARGAN LEMONS *OFFSET WITH EMBOSSING* 26 × 32

L'AFFICHE GALERIE - MAY 1978
145 SPRING ST. N.Y. N.Y.
145 SPRING ST. N.Y. N.Y.
JUDY TARGAN - GRAPHICS

T9 TARGAN PEAS *OFFSET WITH EMBOSSING* 26 × 2

JUDY TARGAN
PHILADELPHIA
L'AFFICHE GALERIE LTD.
NEW YORK

L'AFFICHE GALERIE - MAY 1979
THIRD ANNIVERSARY
145 SPRING ST. N.Y. N.Y.
JUDY TARGAN - GRAPHICS

T8 TARGAN GRAPES *OFFSET WITH EMBOSSING* 26 × 32

NEW YORK BOTANICAL GARDEN
· JUDY TARGAN · · 1982
NEW YORK BOTANICAL GARDEN

T13 TARGAN APPLES *OFFSET WITH EMBOSSING* 26 × 32

C70 CAMPBELL WATERMELONS $21 \times 33^1/_2$

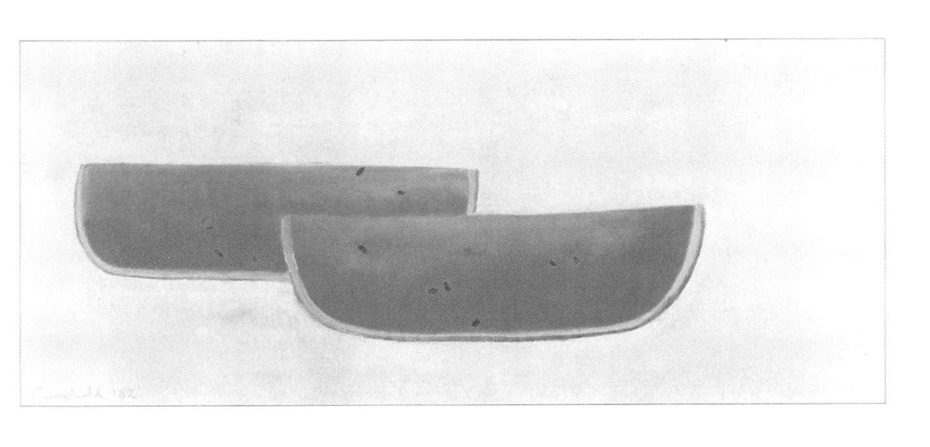
SHIRLEY
CAMPBELL
MARCI LIPMAN GRAPHICS
TORONTO·CANADA

W30 WIGINGTON PASTA 30×22

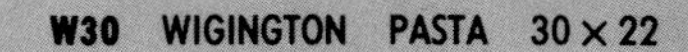

pasta

K74 KANFER CORN SILK 20×24

JUSTINE HILL PHOTOGRAPHY

H58 HILL CORN 18×24

F48 FRENCH CLASSROOM LE VIN $33^{3}/_{8} \times 26$

LE VIN
134

F50 FRENCH CLASSROOM LA SOUPE $32^{3}/_{4} \times 25$

LA SOUPE
542

F52 FRENCH CLASSROOM LES CONFITURES $33^{3}/_{8}$

LES CONFITURES

ANNE SILBER/SERIGRAPHS
ARTISTWORKS · BOSTON

S76 SILBER WEDGEWOOD TEAPOT $18^{5}/_{8} \times 34^{1}/_{8}$

$27^{1}/_{2} \times 12^{1}/_{2}$

ITALIAN
CAVIAR

J18 JOVANOVIC ITALIAN CAVIAR

$27^{1}/_{2} \times 12^{1}/_{2}$

MEXICAN
AMBROSIA

J19 JOVANOVIC MEXICAN AMBRO

LE PAIN
141

F49 FRENCH CLASSROOM LE PAIN $33^3/_8 \times 25^5/_8$

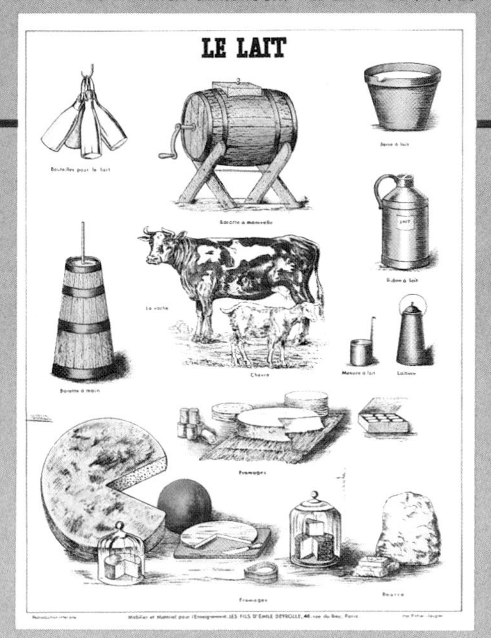
LE LAIT

F53 FRENCH CLASSROOM LE LAIT $33^3/_8 \times 26$

LE CAFÉ
144

F51 FRENCH CLASSROOM LE CAFE $33^3/_8 \times 26$

JOSEPH CRAIG ENGLISH

KRASKIN GARNER

E29 ENGLISH MARKET MORNING 36×24

JOSEPH
CRAIG
ENGLISH
KRASKIN
GALLERY

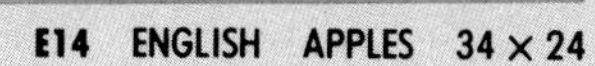

E14 ENGLISH APPLES 34×24

"My Cup of tea"

S94 STOCK MY CUP OF TEA $29^3/_4 \times 21^1/_4$

B51 BARRIS MALIBU, 1962 35 × 23

George Barris
Marilyn Monroe
Weston Editions Ltd.
PARIS·LOS ANGELES·LONDON·NEW YORK·MILAN

B73 BARRIS ALWAYS YOURS 35 1/8 × 23

George Barris
Marilyn Monroe
Weston Editions Ltd.
Paris·Los Angeles·London·New York·Milan

S36 STERN MONTAGE 28 1/2 × 22 1/2

ART EXPO WEST
LOS ANGELES CONVENTION CENTER
MARILYN MONROE
as photographed by
BERT STERN
"the Last Sitting"
EDWARD WESTON GRAPHICS

CERAVOLO
NEW YORK PALM BEACH LOS ANGELES

C156 CERAVOLO MARILYN 32 7/8 × 25

George Barris
Marilyn Monroe
Weston Editions Ltd.
Paris·Los Angeles·London·New York·Milan

B75 BARRIS ALL OF ME 34 7/8 × 22 7/8

MARILYN
MONROE
"the
Last
Sitting"
photographed by
BERT
STERN

S33 STERN RHYTHM 28 1/2 × 22

George Barris
Marilyn Monroe
Weston Editions Ltd.
Paris-Los Angeles-London-New York-Milan

B48 BARRIS WARM UP 29 × 23

he magic of Hollywood has a hold on the world. As long as movies have their fans, these Hollywood posters are sure to be a box office hit.

ny of these images are recently "rediscovered" photographs of stars who have become legends in the vie industry. Photography was an important part of studio promotion in the earlier years of Hollywood. dio photographers such as Clarence Sinclair Bull and Laszlo Willinger are today attracting renewed erest for the artistic merits of their dramatic work.

e Marilyn Monroe posters are a lasting look at this woman who continues to fascinate. These playful, vocative images capture the essence of the woman whom many people idolize.

lywood posters deliver a look at the mystery and romance of silver screen celebrities.

W7 WILLINGER GABLE & CRAWFORD

LASZLO WILLINGER
ART EXPO WEST
EDWARD WESTON GRAPHICS
PARIS·LOS ANGELES·NEW YORK·MILAN

$34\frac{1}{2} \times 22\frac{1}{4}$

H28 HURRELL YOUNG & POWER 40 × 26

HURRELL
ART EXPO
EDWARD WESTON GRAPHICS
PARIS·LOS ANGELES·NEW YORK·MILAN

H14 HURRELL HARLOW 40 × 26

HURRELL
Edward Weston Graphics
PARIS·LOS ANGELES·LONDON·NEW YORK·MILAN

SERIGRAPH 38 × 17

CHARLIE CHAPLIN
MIDNIGHT FILM FESTIVAL
CINEMA ARTS CENTRE

F96 FRANCIS CHARLIE CHAPLIN

CLARENCE SINCLAIR BULL
Edward Weston Graphics

B42 BULL GARBO 37 × 24

CLARENCE SINCLAIR BULL
Edward Weston Graphics

B49 BULL GRETA GARBO, INSPIRATION 30 × 24

J29 JUDY GARLAND 30 × 24

J U D Y

Tribute

G A R L A N D

J31 JAMES DEAN 30 × 24

J A M E S
Tribute
D E A N

W34 WILLINGER VIVIEN LEIGH 38 × 24

LASZLO WILLINGER
ART EXPO WEST
EDWARD WESTON GRAPHICS
PARIS·LOS ANGELES·NEW YORK·MILAN

Eugene R. Richee
LOUISE BROOKS 1928
Edward Weston Graphics
PARIS·LOS ANGELES·LONDON·NEW YORK·MILAN

JAMES DEAN

S176 SCHATT JAMES DEAN $28^{3}/_{4}$ × 20

H15 HAIG DIETRICH 30 × 23

LADIES OF THE SILVER SCREEN

H70 HAIG JEAN HARLOW 30 × 23

LADIES OF THE SILVER SCREEN

H16 HAIG MARILYN 28 × 23 1/4

LADIES OF THE SILVER SCREEN

LADIES OF THE SILVER SCREEN

H32 HAIG JOAN CRAWFORD 25 × 27 3/4

LADIES OF THE SILVER SCREEN

H122 HAIG VIVIAN LEIGH 30 × 23

LADIES OF THE SILVER SCREEN

H29 HAIG KATHERINE HEPBURN 29 × 23

D53 DOLACK CRYSTAL THEATRE $25^1/_2 \times 18^1/_2$

CRYSTAL THEATRE
515 SOUTH HIGGINS MISSOULA, MONTANA USA

G27 GABLE $22^1/_4 \times 29$

GABLE
1940
Edward Weston Graphics
PARIS·LOS ANGELES·LONDON·NEW YORK·MILAN

SKREBNESKI
OCTOBER 1982
PHOTOGALERIE THE COMPAGNIE
HAMBURG WEST GERMANY

LASZLO WILLINGER
ART EXPO WEST
EDWARD WESTON GRAPHICS
PARIS·LOS ANGELES·NEW YORK·MILAN

W36 WILLINGER CLARK GABLE $29 \times 22^1/_4$

STRAWBERRY SHAKE
KING
HEATHER'S DOLL
KING

K101 KING STRAWBERRY SHAKE ☆ 24 × 18

K102 KING HEATHER'S DOLL ☆ 24 × 18

big, burly man we know was recently spotted buying several of these posters. Although he professed to be buying them for his children, they were later spotted hanging in his den!

ight be kid's stuff, but kids of all ages seem to be interested in posters such as those by Mickey Myers. ces like The One With The Ruler or Rainbow Pencils *employ images we associate with childhood. The* ors are bright and happy; the shapes are simple and recognizable.

ough her images seem light, Myers is serious about her work and there is more to them than may first be parent as she explains: "In my work, objects we use every day are shown to have character in their form, mor in their detail and grandeur in relation to other things."

ers studied with Corita Kent whose poster work also spans the age gap. The two artists have much common—bold colors, cheerful imagery—but Corita's work uses more abstract forms and always orporates a written literal message.

ong colors and a humorous viewpoint characterize the posters of Anne Laddon. Her work may have even re adult appeal, but her use of primary colors and her direct style lend themselves equally well to kids.

night be said that today's poster industry is bullish on bears—teddy bears, that is. First created in honor Theodore, "Teddy," Roosevelt, this soft cuddly creature has become synonymous with the concept of ldhood. These posters, such as Theodore Bear *by Nicolas Sidjakov, are as friendly and lovable as the* ggable version of the bear. When a person is too adult to any longer have their stuffed animals, a teddy ır on their wall can remind them of the comforts of youth.

s believed a child's environment plays an important role in defining what kind of person that child will w up to be. Visual stimulation, such as these colorful posters, sparks a child's mental curiosity starting m on a path of intellectual development that will benefit them throughout their life.

the very nature of their simple, direct graphics, posters are suitable for children. As a present for a vborn or older child, posters provide years of pleasure. What could be a better way to send your best shes than by giving Mickey Myers's Happy Birthday *to any child, no matter what their age.*

erybody has a favorite child. A god daughter, a grandchild, or a best friend's baby are all "the most autiful child you've ever seen." For many people, hanging one of these posters in their home can be vely reminder of that special child.

y of these posters can brighten a room with their cheerful, refreshingly simple images. Whether young years or young at heart, these posters will bring a smile to a person's face while decorating their walls.

C25 CORITA BE OF LOVE . . . 29 × 23

Be of love
(a little)
more careful
than of
anything
CORITA
CORITA PRINTS - NORTH HOLLYWOOD, CALIFORNIA

C63 CORITA SPRING FROM WINTER ☆ *LITHOGRAPH* 26 × 30

spring
from
winter

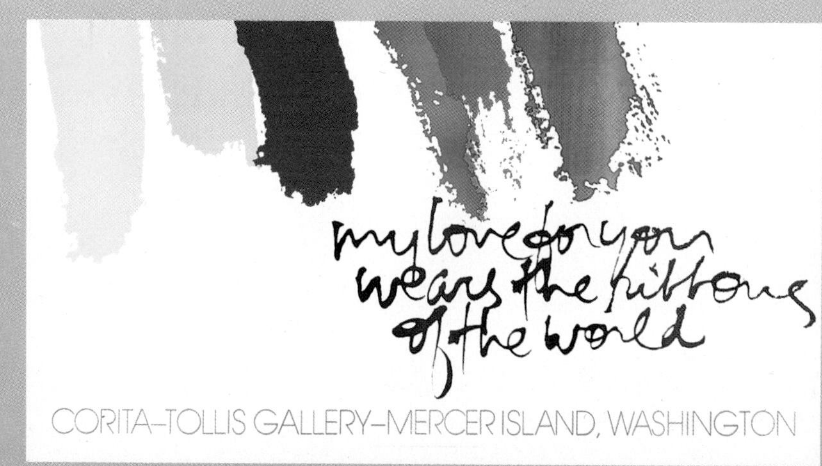
my love for you
wears the ribbons
of the world
CORITA–TOLLIS GALLERY–MERCER ISLAND, WASHINGTON

C45 CORITA RIBBONS ☆ *LITHOGRAPH* 21 × 39

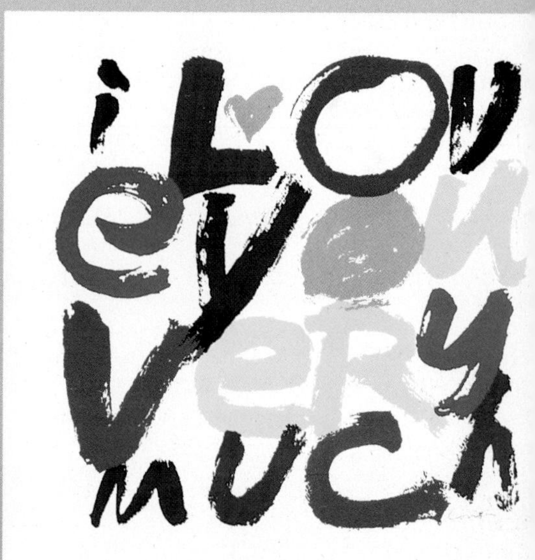
i Love you very much
Corita
December 1978
Muirhead Galleries - Costa Mesa, CA

C13 CORITA I LOVE YOU 29 × 33

D27 DAHL 5:01 ☆ 34 × 25

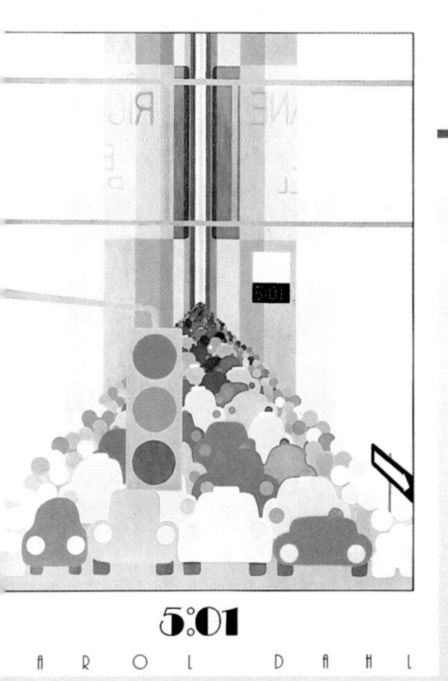
5:01
AROL DAHL

D41 DAHL CELEBRATE ☆ 34 × 25

CAROL DAHL · CELEBRATE

D83 DAHL LIVE ON STAGE 36 × 24

LIVE ON STAGE

Alan McCord
ICGAW EDITIONS

M17 McCORD FLYING HOUSE ☆ 32 × 22

PREMIERE
PREMIERE
OPENING NIGHT
Carol dahl

D138 DAHL OPENING NIGHT $24^1/_4 \times 30^1/_4$

B147 BURKE OUT FOR A WADDLE $25^1/_2 \times 19$

JANE MASON BURKE
FIRST IMPRESSIONS CARMEL CA

B149 BURKE THE FOREBEARS 21×26

The Forebears
Jane Mason Burke • First Impressions • Carmel

H98 HILL BEAR 18×24

Over the Hills and Far Away...

B152 BINZEN OVER THE HILLS & FAR AWAY . . . $19^1/_2 \times 25^1/_8$

B143 BURKE BEARLY BALLET $17^1/_4 \times 32$

S89 SIDJAKOV THEODORE BEAR *SERIGRAPH*

THEODORE BEAR

$30^1/_4 \times 22^1/_8$

TEDDY

W45 WHITING TEDDY & HIS TOYS 28 × 22

BEARU
B
E
A
R

M133 MIRONESCO THE TEDDY BEAR CHEERLEADERS 32 × 16

M10 EVEN MORE 39 x 25

MICKEY MYERS
CHOICE EDITIONS

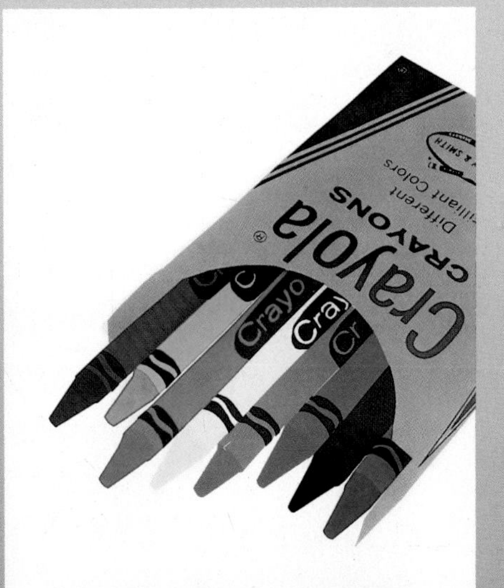
Crayola
CRAYONS
MICKEY MYERS
CHOICE EDITIONS

M9 BOX OF . . . 39 x 25

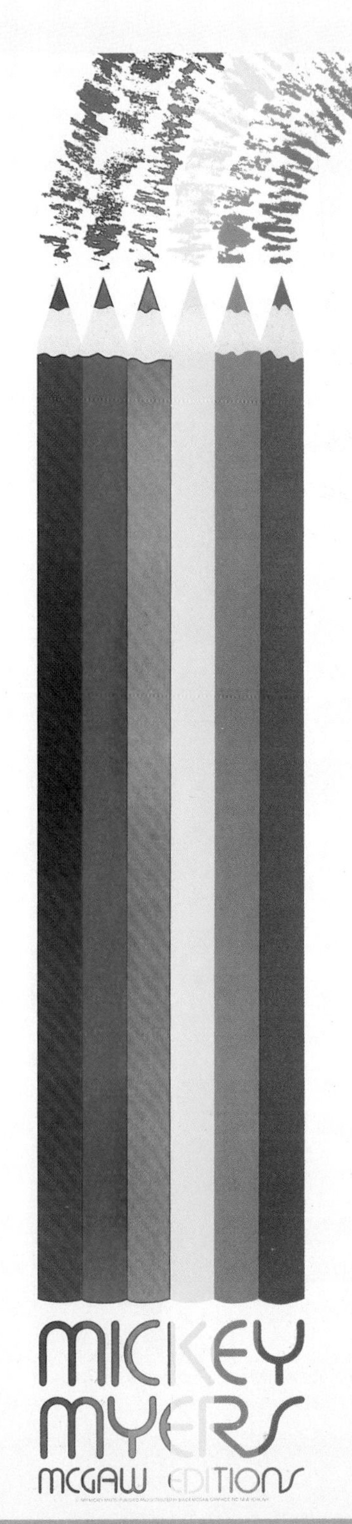
MICKEY
MYERS
MCGAW EDITIONS

M33 RAINBOW PENCILS ☆ *LITHOGRAPH* $38^{7}/_{8}$ x 20

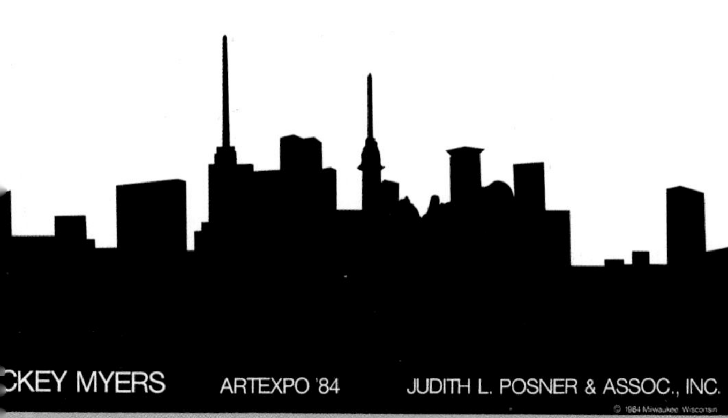
CKEY MYERS ARTEXPO '84 JUDITH L. POSNER & ASSOC., INC.

M115 ARTIST'S BALLOON *SERIGRAPH* 34 × 18

MICKEY MYERS ARTEXPO '83 JUDITH L. POSNER & ASSOC., INC.

M77 RED FLIGHT *SERIGRAPH* 35 x $17^7/_8$

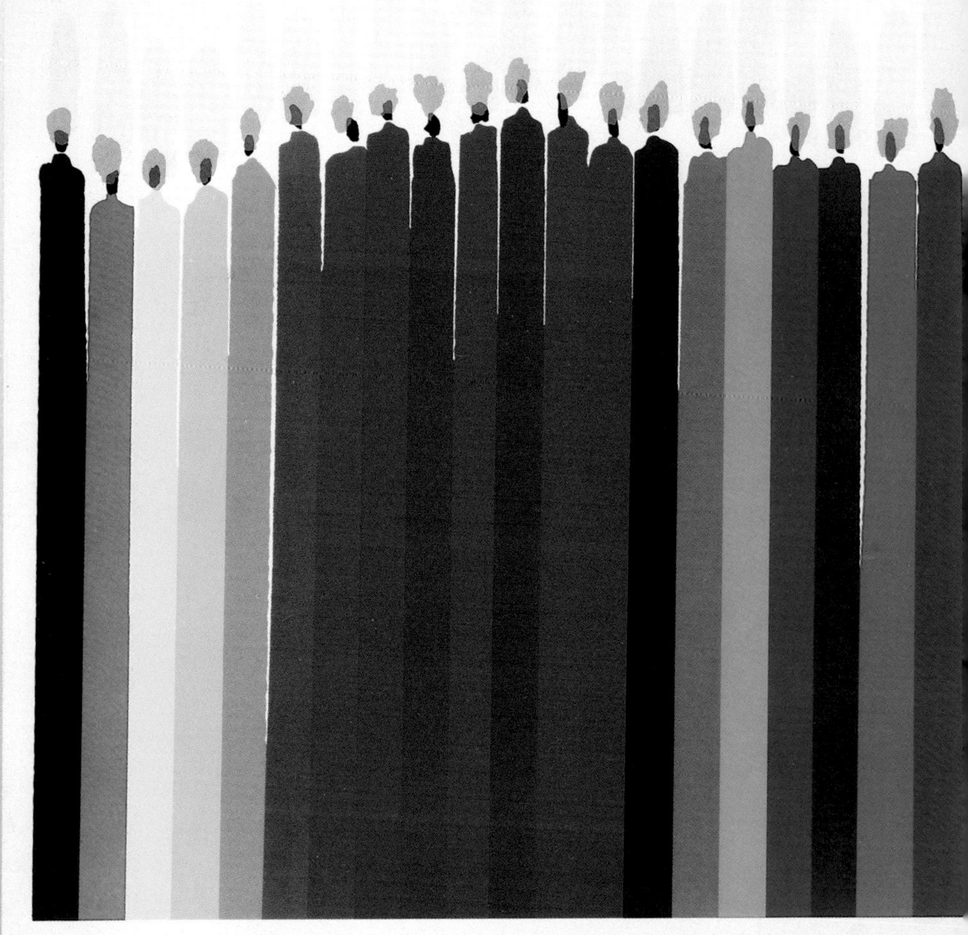
HAPPY BIRTHDAY
MICKEY MYERS
MCGAW EDITIONS · ART EXPO NY '83

M73 HAPPY BIRTHDAY ☆ 32 × 24

M32 THE ONE WITH THE RULER ☆ *LITHOGRAPH* 24 × 36

Crayola
Crayola
Crayola
Crayola
Crayola

KEY MYERS-MCGAW EDITIONS ART EXPO CAL-OCT

Thank You Note

CKEY MYERS GARNER GALLERIES

M114 THANK YOU NOTE 20 × 16

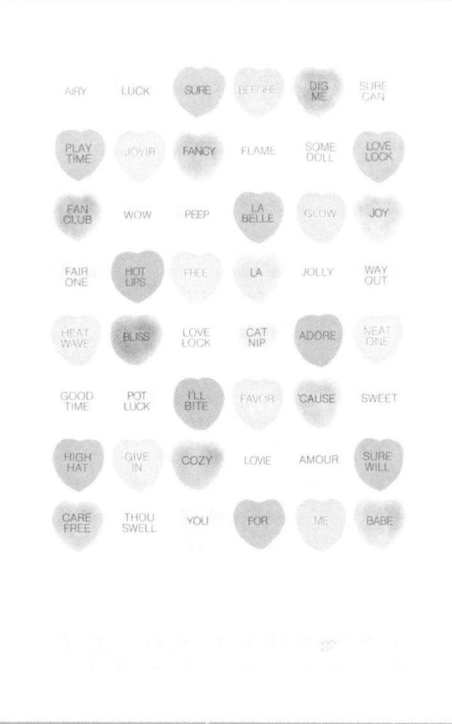
AIRY
LUCK
SURE
DIG ME
SURE CAN
PLAY TIME
FANCY
FLAME
SOME DOLL
LOVE LOCK
FAN CLUB
WOW
PEEP
LA BELLE
GLOW
JOY
FAIR ONE
HOT LIPS
FREE
LA
JOLLY
WAY OUT
HEAT WAVE
BLISS
LOVE LOCK
CAT NIP
ADORE
NEAT ONE
GOOD TIME
POT LUCK
I'LL BITE
FAVOR
'CAUSE
SWEET
HIGH HAT
GIVE IN
COZY
LOVIE
AMOUR
SURE WILL
CARE FREE
THOU SWELL
YOU
FOR
ME
BABE

M48 SWEETHEARTS 36 × 24

L9 MY CYCLE 30 × 22

ANNE LADDON
MY CYCLE

L47 POOR CINDERELLA 36 × 24

betty boop
ANNE LADDON
POOR CINDERELLA

L64 MIDNIGHT CAROUSEL 36 × 23 3/4

ANNE LADDON
MIDNIGHT CAROUSEL

ANNE LADDON LA COMIDA MEXICANA

L65 LA COMIDA MEXICANA 24 3/4 × 28 7/8

HYNAP
ANNE LADDON
AT THE COUNTER

L63 AT THE COUNTER 25 × 18

L22 SURE SHOT 34 × 25

ANNE LADDON
SURE SHOT
Nikon
F

L23 EXPOSED 36 × 25

PROCESS K-14
Kodachrome
ANNE LADDON
EXPOSED!

L38 PFFT! 35 × 24

ANNE LADDON
PFFT!
CHAMPIONSHIP
Wilson
3

ANNE LADDON
RETURN
SHIFT

L46 W.P. - V.D.T. 35 × 23

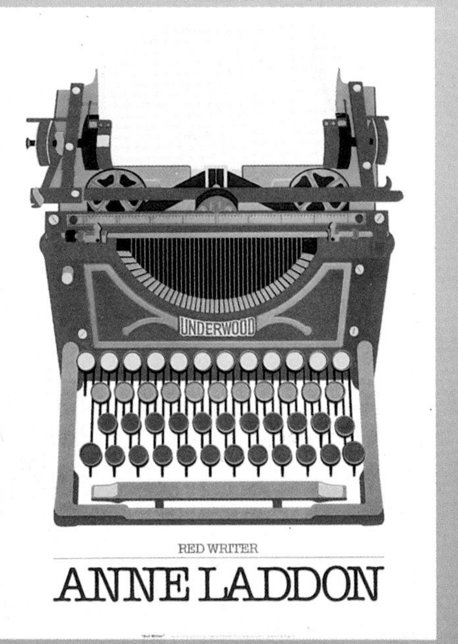
UNDERWOOD
RED WRITER
ANNE LADDON

L20 RED WRITER 36 × 25

S87 SUMICHRAST RUSSIAN ALPHABET 25 × 38

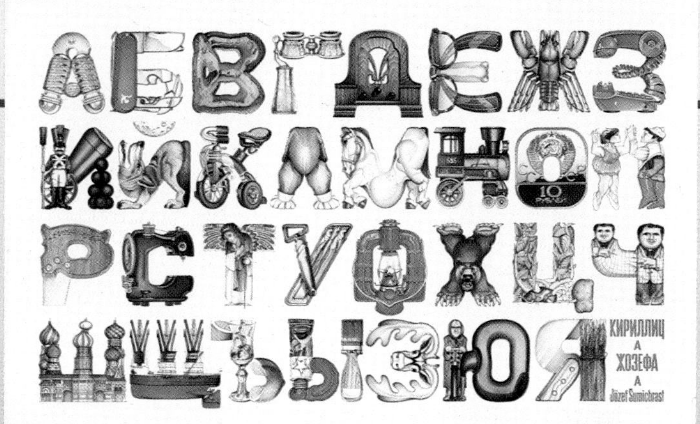
КИРИЛЛИЦ
А
ХОЗЕФА
А
Józef Sumichrast

S88 SUMICHRAST HEBREW ALPHABET 25 × 38

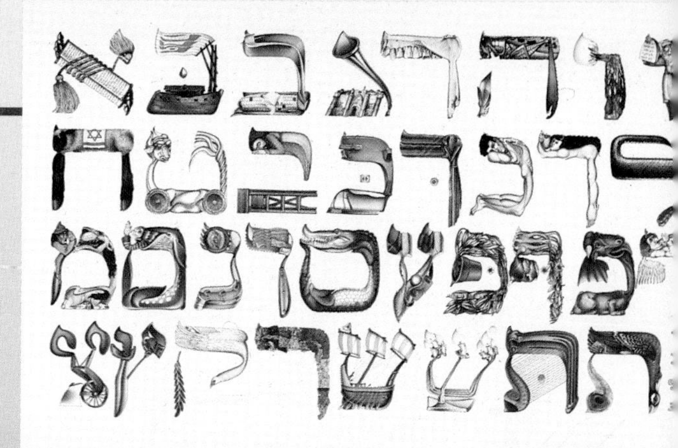

WOOLLY LAMB
IN HONOR OF THE TENTH ANNIVERSARY OF CHILDREN'S COUNCIL OF SAN FRANCISCO

S154 SIDJAKOV WOOLLY LAMB *SERIGRAPH* $30^{1}/_{2} \times 22$

RUBBER DUCKY

S108 SIDJAKOV RUBBER DUCKY *SERIGRAPH* 30 × 22

S86 SUMICHRAST ENGLISH ALPHABET 25 × 38

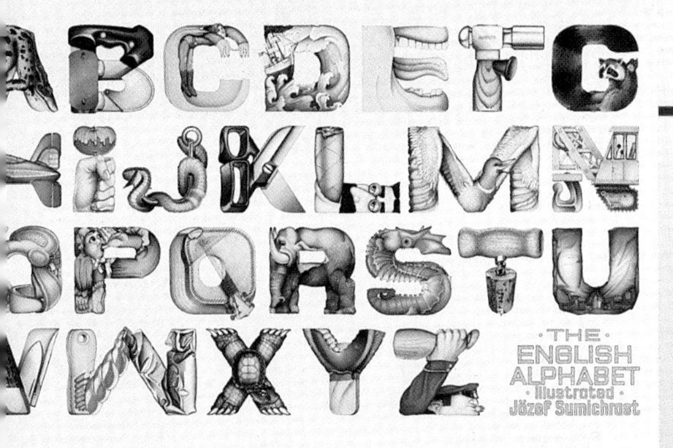
THE
ENGLISH
ALPHABET
Illustrated
Józef Sumichrast

K8 KOHL ONE HEART *LITHOGRAPH*

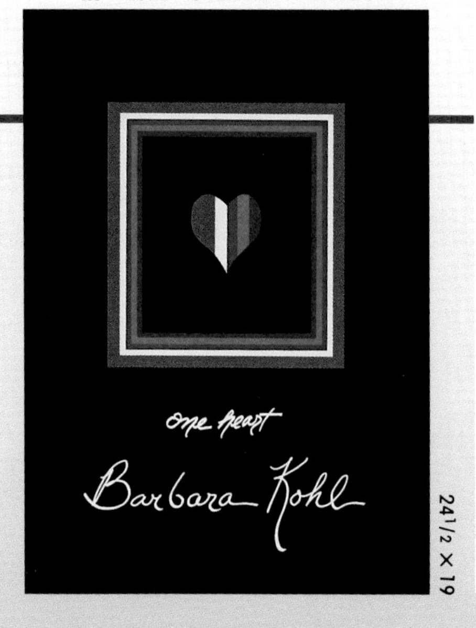
one heart
Barbara Kohl

$24^1/_2 \times 19$

T29 THORNYCROFT FOR LOVE AND MONEY

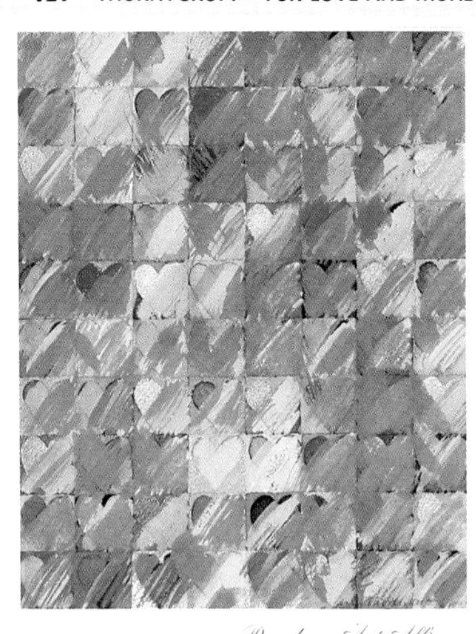
Pasadena Art Alliance

32 × 24

school of GRANT WOOD
TREASURES FROM
THE KERMITAGE COLLECTION

A64 AMERICAN GOTHIQUE 34 × 24

Mary Vickers
CHILDREN OF THE WORLD
for the UNITED NATIONS
INTERNATIONAL SCHOOL

V3 VICKERS CHILDREN OF THE WORLD 36 × 24

L40 LACROIX BALLOONS $34^1/_4 \times 25^1/_2$

B119 BROWND BUNNY LOVE 24 × 18

B128 BROWND APPLE BEAR 24 × 18

M156 MACKEY BUTTERFLY PUP 24 × 18

B129 BROWND CHINA CAT 24 × 18

B118 BROWND COUNTRY GOOSE 24 × 18

M157 MACKEY OLIVER OWL 24 × 18

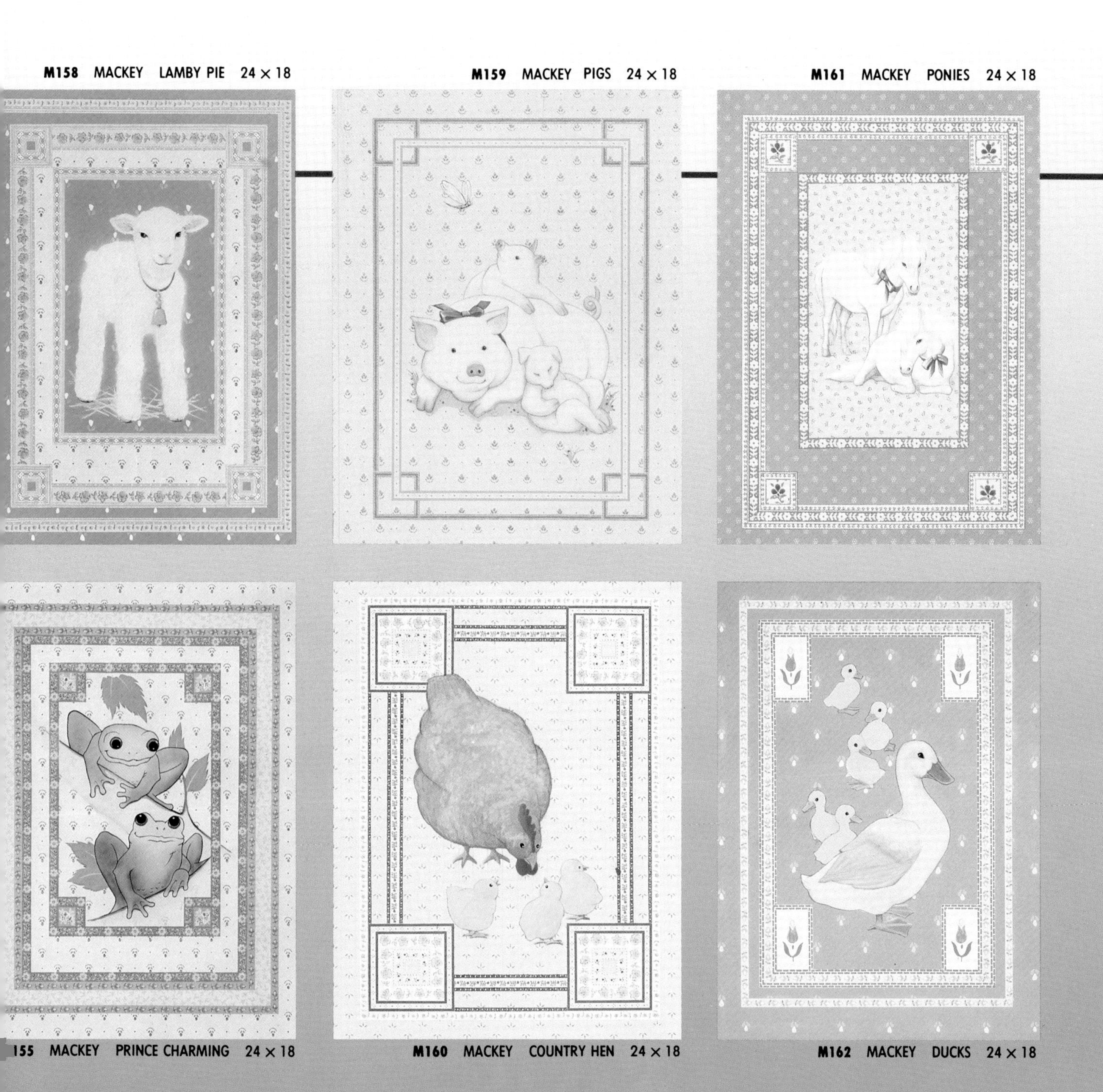

M158 MACKEY LAMBY PIE 24 × 18

M159 MACKEY PIGS 24 × 18

M161 MACKEY PONIES 24 × 18

155 MACKEY PRINCE CHARMING 24 × 18

M160 MACKEY COUNTRY HEN 24 × 18

M162 MACKEY DUCKS 24 × 18

M16 MEISEL WASHINGTON MONUMENT $32^{1}/_{2} \times 23$

M34 MEISEL TIMES SQUARE 37 × 24

Steven Klein
Middleton Gallery - Annapolis, MD

K63 KLEIN AMERICAN HERITAGE 36 × 24

SUSAN PEAR MEISEL
EDWARD WESTON GRAPHICS
NEW YORK, PARIS, LOS ANGELES

Susan Pear Meisel
SONY
Coca-Cola

ANNE LADDON
RAMA LAMA DING DONG

L34 LADDON RAMA LAMA DING DONG 36 × 25

THE AMERICAN
CAROUSELS
GENE SIEGRIST
JUMPERS · CARVED BY CHARLES LOOFF CIRCA 1906

S179 SIEGRIST THE AMERICAN CAROUSELS 30 × 22

8 MEISEL LINCOLN MEMORIAL $29^{7}/_{8} \times 24^{1}/_{8}$

Susan Pear Meisel
The Lincoln Memorial
Washington D.C.

M29 MEISEL JEFFERSON MEMORIAL $29^{3}/_{4} \times 24$

Susan Pear Meisel
The Jefferson Memorial
Washington D.C.

M168 MEISEL STATUE OF LIBERTY 24×20

Susan Pear Meisel
Statue of Liberty

B161 BAROV ZODIAC 38×25

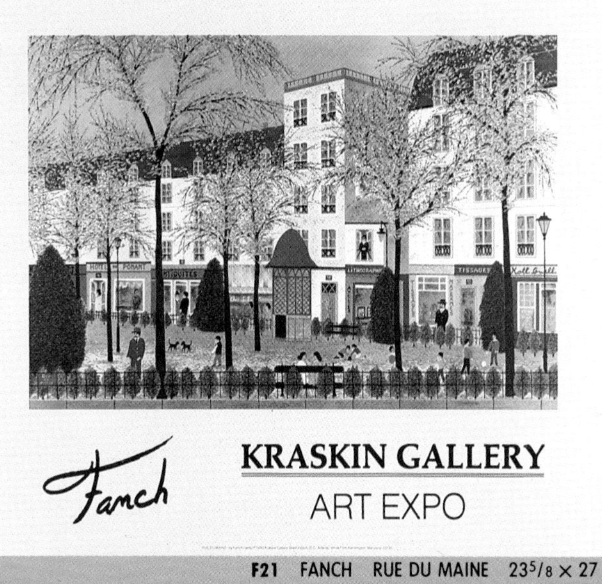
Fanch
KRASKIN GALLERY
ART EXPO

F21 FANCH RUE DU MAINE $23^{5}/_{8} \times 27$

DICK DURRANCE II

D146 DURRANCE WHITE CHAIRS ☆ 24 × 32

S180 STYCZYNSKI REFLECTIONS 25 × 30

C A P E S

"o say to the painter that nature is to be taken as she is, is to say to the player that he may sit on the
piano," said the great American artist Whistler. Today, as over the centuries, artists are applying their
distinctive vision to the portrayal of the landscape.

sider the work of Jerry Schurr, one of the most popular contemporary landscape artists. Schurr has
eloped a complex method of creating original images that is analogous to the multi-leveled imagery of
complicated vistas. The images are "built" layer upon layer recreating the spatial planes that exist in
actual landscape. The resulting serene landscapes seem to move forward in space visually and
positionally.

avelling through Europe, landscapes suddenly came into focus as a succinct way of expressing the
ic themes I was feeling," says Schurr. "The deep mountain canyons of the Alps spoke on a grand scale.
gan to see the landscape as an endless panorama of exciting encounters.

e technical problems seemed the most formidable when I first started. How was the structure of
ndscape best expressed, especially on a two dimensional surface? Silkscreen printing provided the
wer which I later adapted to painting.

se one screen to do all my colors, overprinting one color on top of another, changing stencils on the
een. It occurred to me that this technique was analogous to the landscape as I was conceiving it. I began
nderstand the organization of the landscape in very simple linear terms. I had inadvertently developed
analogue of the landscape through reduction stencil technique."

rcus Uzilevsky turned to the visual arts from a successful career in the performing arts. Still inspired
nusic, Uzilevsky now turns his muse to the creation of "linear landscapes" highly in demand.

the early '70s I initiated this linearesque technique. I was experimenting with mechanical drawing
s when I discovered I could create an impressionistic landscape by juxtaposing thin lines of color across
eet of paper," says Uzilevsky. "My art is inspired by the feeling for landscape and the challenge of
nipulating horizontal lines to define the images. I enjoy incorporating this technical approach to
ntaneous creativity." Using subtle earth tones or a rich impressionistic palette, Uzilevsky creates poster
ks that provide rich harmony in the contemporary environment.

ndscape artists have also taken a look at the urban landscapes that man has created. The high style Art
o metro in Paris and the glorious glass structure that is the Conservatory of Flowers in San Francisco
e inspired artists such as Quentin King and Jeffrey Nicholas.

ndscape posters are as wonderfully varied as the world in which we live offering an endless variety
esign options. Artists have applied every possible medium to the recording of their interpretations
he marvels of the world around us from majestic clouds to quiet beaches to the jeweled light of
ll day. The resulting art provides some of the industry's most popular images that know no bounds
contemporary design.

JERRY SCHURR

SUMMA GALLERY
152 Montague Street
Brooklyn Heights, NY 11201 • 212-875-1647

$140 CAPE FOUL WEATHER $36^3/_4 \times 27$

ERRY SCHURR SUMMA GALLERY BROOKLYN HEIGHTS, NEW YORK

S32 POINT LOBOS ☆ 24 × 40

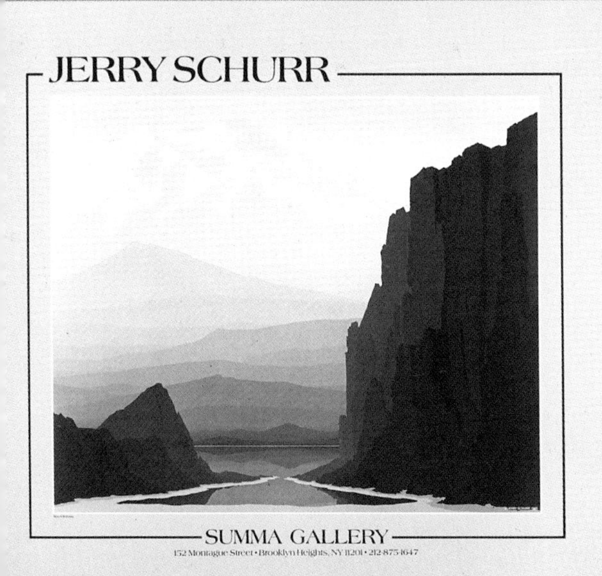
JERRY SCHURR
SUMMA GALLERY
152 Montague Street • Brooklyn Heights, NY 11201 • 212-875-1647

S129 MT. McKINLEY 26 x 30

JERRY SCHURR
CASTLE ROCK
Triangle Galleries
Galleria, White Plains, NY
Roosevelt Field, Long Island, NY
Published and Distributed by: John Szoke Graphics, Inc., 144 East 57th Street, NY, NY • 212-759-9405

S106 CASTLE ROCK 36 × 24

JERRY SCHURR
SUMMA
GALLERY
152 MONTAGUE STREET
BROOKLYN HEIGHTS, NEW YORK

S78 BAFFIN FJORD ☆ 38 × 26

JERRY SCHURR
SUMMA GALLERY • BROOKLYN HEIGHTS, NY

S35 MUIR WOODS ☆ $38^{3}/_{4} \times 21^{5}/_{8}$

Jerry Schurr
Estampe Gallery
Colorado Springs, Colorado

S44 SHADOW LAKE $39^{1}/_{2} \times 29^{1}/_{2}$

S27 PADRES BAY ☆ 25 x 38

JERRY SCHURR
SUMMA GALLERY

JERRY SCHURR
SUMMA GALLERY, INC.
152 Montague Street, Brooklyn Heights, New York

S53 SAN ANDRAES LAKE 26 × 29 1/8

JERRY SCHURR
SUMMA GALLERY

S20 OLYMPIA ☆ 38 x 26

K82 BRASSERIE $35^1/_4 \times 25^1/_4$

CAFE
BRASSERIE

Rick's
Café Americain
CASABLANCA

K41 CASABLANCA $35^3/_8 \times 24^1/_4$

K61 L'ASCENSEUR $35^1/_2 \times 25^1/_4$

ALL POSTERS ON THIS PAGE ARE SERIGRAPHS.

K81 ESPLANADE $25^1/_4 \times 35^1/_4$

ESPLANADE

MAXIM'S
PARIS

K40 MAXIM'S $35^3/_8 \times 25^1/_4$

MONTMARTRE

K76 MONTMARTRE $35^1/_4 \times 25^1/_4$

NEW YORK

K59 NEW YORK $35^1/_2 \times 25^1/_4$

ALL POSTERS ON THIS PAGE ARE SERIGRAPHS.

K77 RAFFLES $35^1/_4 \times 25^1/_4$

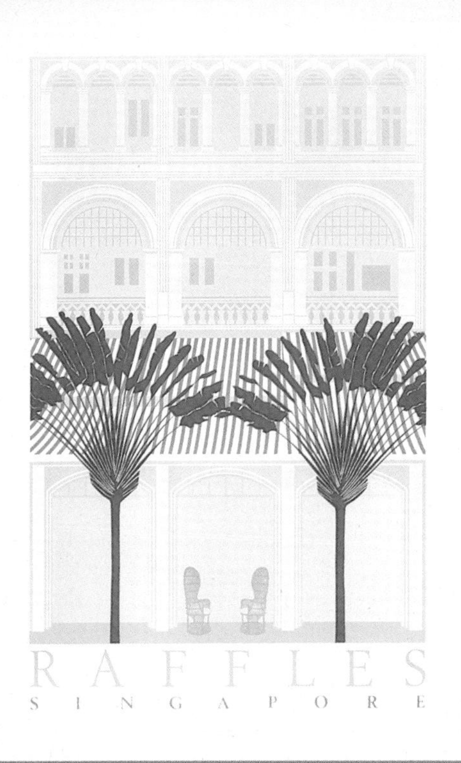
RAFFLES
SINGAPORE

K79 CANNES $35^1/_4 \times 25^1/_4$

HOTEL
CARLTON
CANNES

PEREGRINE KING

K78 PEREGRINE KING $35^1/_4 \times 25^1/_4$

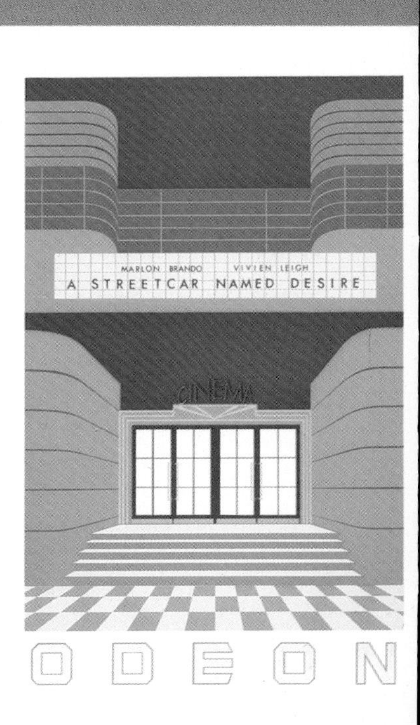
MARLON BRANDO VIVIEN LEIGH
A STREETCAR NAMED DESIRE
CINEMA
ODEON

K69 ODEON $35^1/_2 \times 25^1/_4$

ALL POSTERS ON THIS PAGE ARE SERIGRAPHS.

K80 DINER $35^1/_4 \times 25^1/_4$

DINER

K48 TAXI TO THE RITZ $35^1/_2 \times 25^1/_4$

RITZ
RESTAURANT
TAXI
LONDON

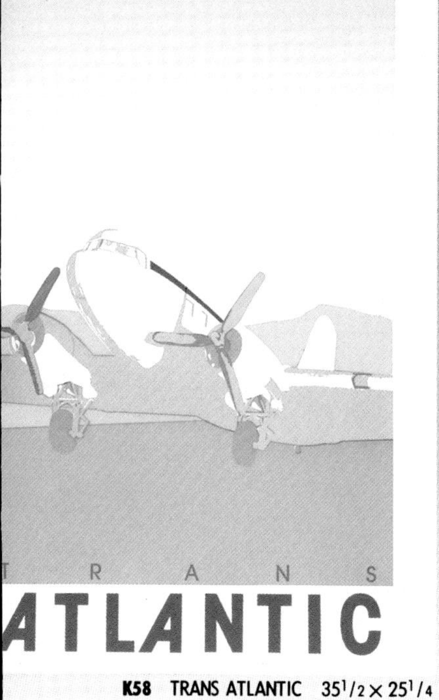
TRANS
ATLANTIC

K58 TRANS ATLANTIC $35^1/_2 \times 25^1/_4$

METROPOLITAIN
METRO

K70 METRO $35^1/_4 \times 25^1/_4$

ALL POSTERS ON THIS PAGE ARE SERIGRAPHS.

M43 MARKGRAF SUMMER MORNING 30 × 20 3/4

may 8 - june 3, 1981
markgraf
children of the raven gallery
vancouver british columbia

M51 MUTCHNIK THEME AND VARIATION ☆ 27 × 40

MARK MUTCHNIK • JOHN SZOKE GRAPHIC

CAMPBELL/RANGES
HIMALAYAS/MIRAG

C144A CAMPBELL RANGE SERIES "A" 26 × 26

C144B CAMPBELL RANGE SERIES "B" 26 × 26

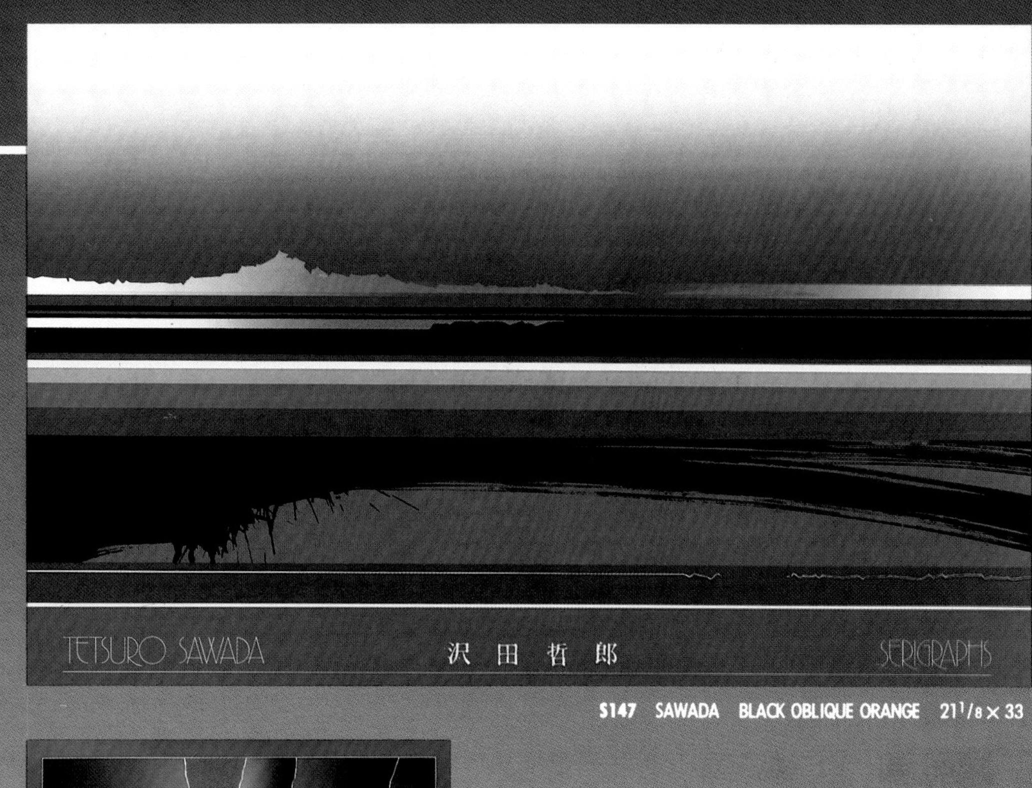
TETSURO SAWADA
沢 田 哲 郎
SERIGRAPHS

S147 SAWADA BLACK OBLIQUE ORANGE $21^{1}/_{8} \times 33$

THE NATURE COMPANY
Daniel Goldstein
TENTH ANNIVERSARY

G82 GOLDSTEIN 10th ANNIVERSARY 36 × 23

MUTCHNIK CLOUD CUCKOO LAND ☆ 40 × 12

U9 LILY OF THE VALLEY 25 × 39

Lily of the Valley–Marcus Uzilevsky 1983– Oaksprings Impressions–Fairfax, California

MARCUS UZILEVSKY

U4 CORNERSTONE $24^{3}/_{4} \times 38^{7}/_{8}$

U3 LANDSCAPE (GATEWAY) $24^1/_8 \times 38^1/_8$

MARCUS UZILEVSKY

MARCUS UZILEVSKY
EDITIONS LIMITED
GALLERIES
INDIANAPOLIS
&
SAN FRANCISCO

U24 MT. ZION 37×25

U Z

I L

Uzilevsky

U20 HOSANNA 39 × 25

U7 WINGS OF THE MORNING 27 × 39

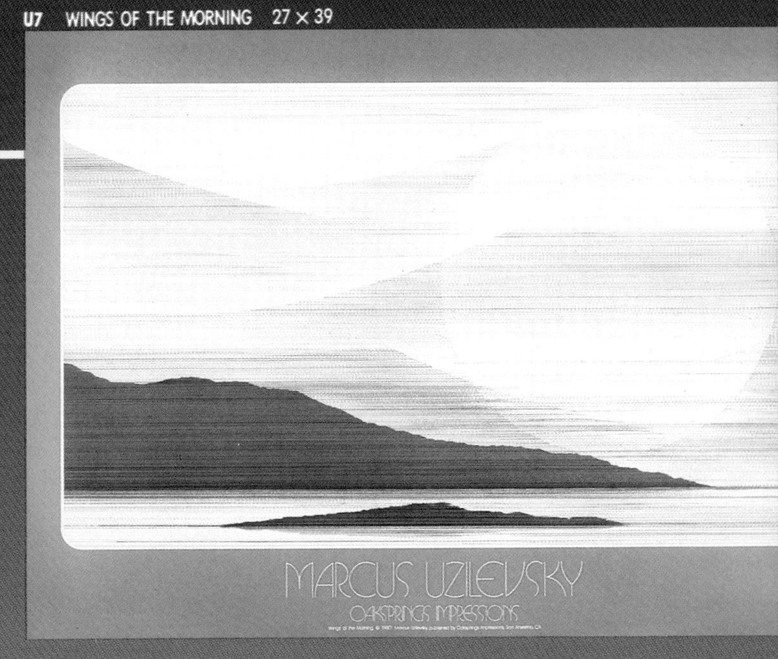
MARCUS UZILEVSKY
OAKSPRINGS IMPRESSIONS

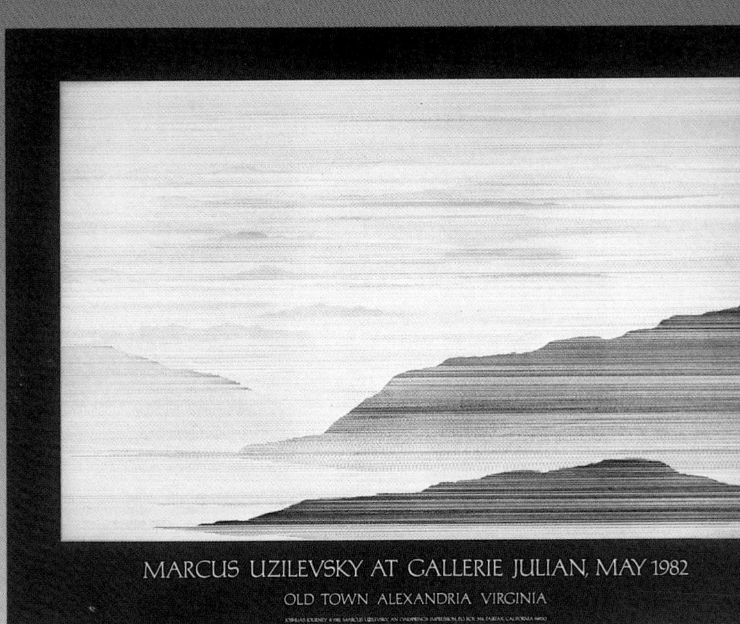
MARCUS UZILEVSKY AT GALLERIE JULIAN, MAY 1982
OLD TOWN ALEXANDRIA VIRGINIA

U14 JOSHUA'S JOURNEY 24 1/4 × 35

U21A DAMASCUS "A" 38 × 25

U21B DAMASCUS "B" 38 × 25

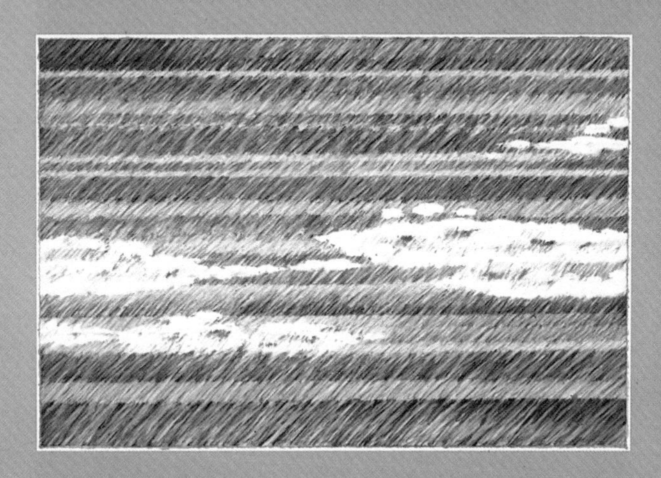
MARCUS UZILEVSKY · PORTLAND ART MUSEUM
U18 WATER LILIES 21 × 27

Tribute to Seurat
MARCUS UZILEVSKY AT RYAN/JOHNSON GALLERY
U26 TRIBUTE TO SEURAT 39 × 25

V S K Y

U19 GIVERNY $24^1/_2 \times 28$

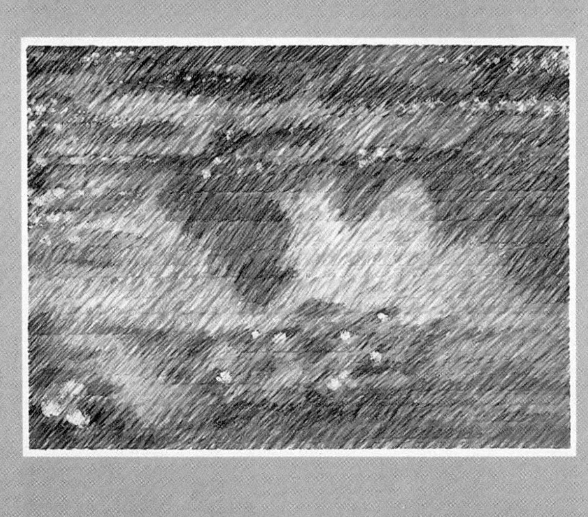
REFLECTIONS OF MONET - MARCUS UZILEVSKY - ART EXPO - 1981

U12 REFLECTIONS OF MONET $22 \times 27^1/_8$

L A N D S

M126A MELL THREE MESAS "A" 24 × 36

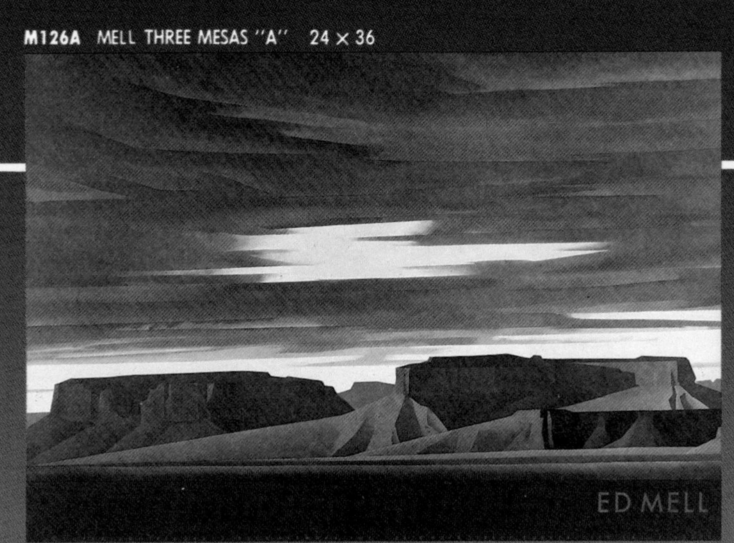
ED MELL

M126B MELL THREE MESAS "B" 24 × 36

HARRIS GALLERY, HOUSTON, TEXAS JUNE 1,

36 × 12

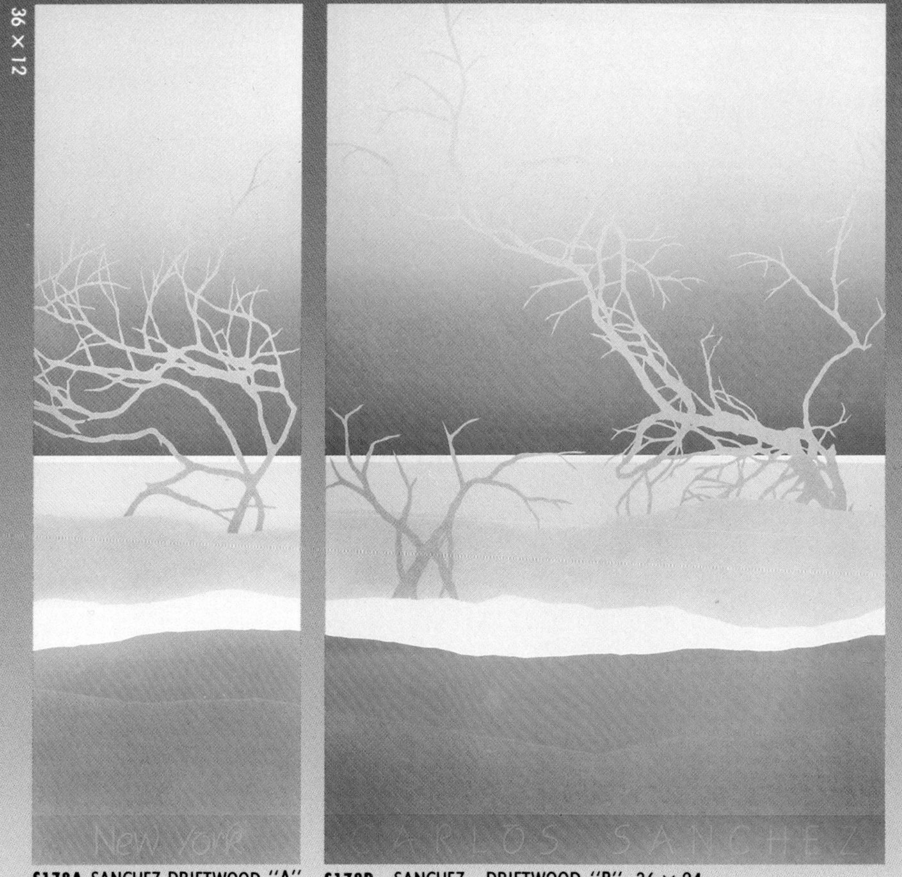
New York
CARLOS SANCHEZ

S178A SANCHEZ DRIFTWOOD "A" **S178B** SANCHEZ DRIFTWOOD "B" 36 × 24 **S178C** SANCHEZ DRIFTWOOD

MELL GRAND CANYON AFTERNOON 36 × 24

M127 MELL CANYON STORM 18 × 24

MELL
WEY/KOFRON GALLERY
NTA FE, NEW MEXICO
Y 30, 1983

D MELL HARRIS GALLERY, HOUSTON, TEXAS JAN.29-FEB.25,1982

M105 MELL SPACIOUS SKIES 25 × 37

R10 RODMAN REFLECTIONS ☆ 25 × 38

RODMAN SUMMA GALLERY BROOKLYN HEIGHTS, NEW YORK

E60 EISEMANN UNTITLED 36 × 24

MICHAEL EISEMANN
MUSEUM EDITIONS, LTD.
LOS ANGELES/NEW YORK

HAROLD E. HANSEN • ART EXPO
POSNER GALLERY • MILWAUKEE

H113 HANSEN CUMBERLAND FALLS 22 × 28

HAROLD E. HANSEN • ART EXPO
POSNER GALLERY • MILWAUKEE

H114 HANSEN BUFFALO VALLEY 22 × 28

K93 KEATING SAWMILL BARNS 23 × 31

THE PHILADELPHIA ART SHOW
ST. CHRISTOPHER'S HOSPITAL FOR CHILDREN
C.B.C. the Adam's Mark Hotel – November 17 to 20 1983

K36 KEATING GRANDADDY'S $21^{5}/_{8}$ × 28

PETER KEATING
GRANDADDY'S
PRIMROSE PRESS NEW HOPE, PA.

HAROLD E. HANSEN • ART EXPO
POSNER GALLERY • MILWAUKEE

H112 HANSEN FOX RIVER 22 × 28

A59 PATHWAY $19^{5}/_{8} \times 25^{1}/_{2}$

HAROLD ALTMAN
EL·BAZ GALLERY
SOHO
NEW YORK

A32 GALERIE EL BAZ $26^{1}/_{4} \times 19^{1}/_{8}$

HAROLD ALTMAN
GALERIE EL·BAZ

HAROLD ALTMAN
EL·BAZ GALLERY
SOHO
NEW YORK

A58 RUNNER $19^{5}/_{8} \times 25^{1}/_{2}$

A36 CHILDREN, PARC MONCEAU 24 × 30 3/8

harold altman at editions limited

A25 MARKET STAND 25 × 33 7/8

HAROLD ALTMAN / EDITIONS LIMITED

HAROLD ALTMAN GALERIE ELBAZ TORONTO SEPTEMBER 1982

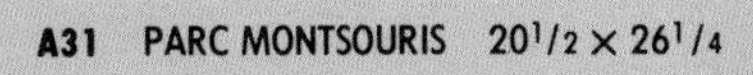

A31 PARC MONTSOURIS 20 1/2 × 26 1/4

harold altman at editions limited

A11 EDITIONS LTD. 24 × 30 1/2

15A IRWIN CALIF. FOOTHILLS "A" $21^1/_8 \times 35^3/_4$

15B IRWIN CALIF. FOOTHILLS "B" $21^1/_8 \times 35^3/_4$

CALIFORNIA HILLS · DON IRWIN · DASHER EDITIONS/SAN FRANCISCO

I11 IRWIN CALIFORNIA HILLS $22 \times 39^3/_8$

NORTHWEST / NEW YORK 1980
BAYARD GALLERY
may 13 - june 15

N15 NORDIN OCTOBER MARSH ☆ 22×34

C A P E S

T31 TALBOT SEASCAPE 24 × 32

T A L B O T
PHOTOGRAPH

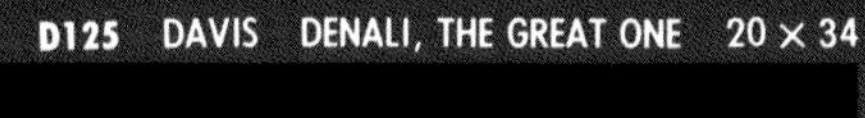

D125 DAVIS DENALI, THE GREAT ONE 20 × 34

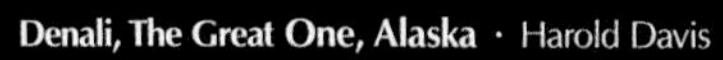
Denali, The Great One, Alaska · Harold Davis

KANFER
art spectrum · new york

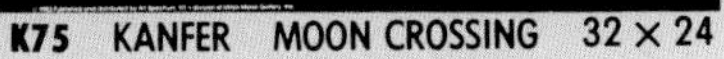

K75 KANFER MOON CROSSING 32 × 24

THE CONSERVATORY OF FLOWERS SAN FRANCISCO

N50 NICHOLAS CONSERVATORY OF FLOWERS 16 × 28

H45 HOLSTEIN SINGAPORE $24^{1}/_{8} \times 32^{1}/_{2}$

BENT HOLSTEIN AT FUTURA · ART EXPO WEST · SAN FRANCISCO · 1981

P18 PRATT EXIT $38^{7}/_{8} \times 22$

EXIT
CHRISTOPHER PRAT
Mira Godard Gallery
TORONTO·CALGARY·DECEMBER 1980

DOORS OF SOHO

M112 MANNING DOORS OF SOHO 28×19

Doorways of Chester County

M66 MANNING DOORWAYS $28 \times 18^{7}/_{8}$

M21 MURRAY GREAT AMERICAN DOOR PAINTINGS ☆ 22 × 39 1/4

JOHN MURRAY · GREAT AMERICAN DOOR PAINTINGS BAYARD GALLERY FEB. 3-MAR. 3, 1981

HRISTOPHER PRATT MIRA GODARD GALLERY CALGARY TORONTO

P17 PRATT COTTAGE 24 × 34 1/4

SEASIDE

B135 BROOKE SEASIDE 35 × 23

H39 HARRILL ADOBE $30^3/_4 \times 21^3/_4$

JAMES HARRILL
LESLIE LEVY GALLERY
SCOTTSDALE, ARIZONA
1981

H74 HARRILL STEPS $38^3/_4 \times 19$

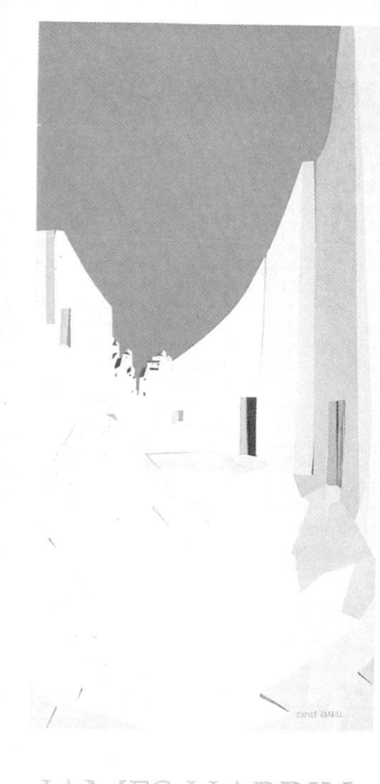
JAMES HARRILL
Museum Editions, Ltd.
Los Angeles · New York

H75 HARRILL AEGEAN MONASTERY

LESLIE LEVY GALLERY
SCOTTSDALE, ARIZONA

35 × 15

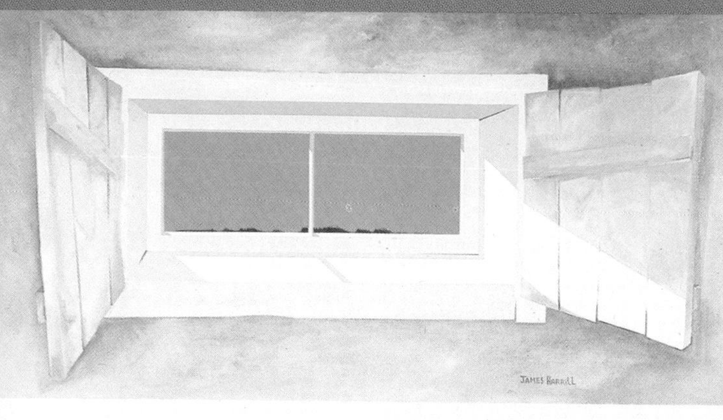
JAMES HARRILL
Museum Editions, Ltd. Los Angeles · New York

H73 HARRILL WINDOW $25^1/_8 \times 38^7/_8$

JAMES HARRILL
Leslie Levy Gallery
Scottsdale, Arizona

H108 HARRILL CRETE STEPS $25 \times 32^1/_2$

S171 SIMPSON WASHINGTON SQUARE $27\frac{1}{2} \times 22\frac{3}{4}$

WASHINGTON SQUARE, NEW YORK CITY 1979
GRETCHEN DOW SIMPSON

S173 SIMPSON SALEM, NEW YORK $31\frac{5}{8} \times 24\frac{3}{4}$

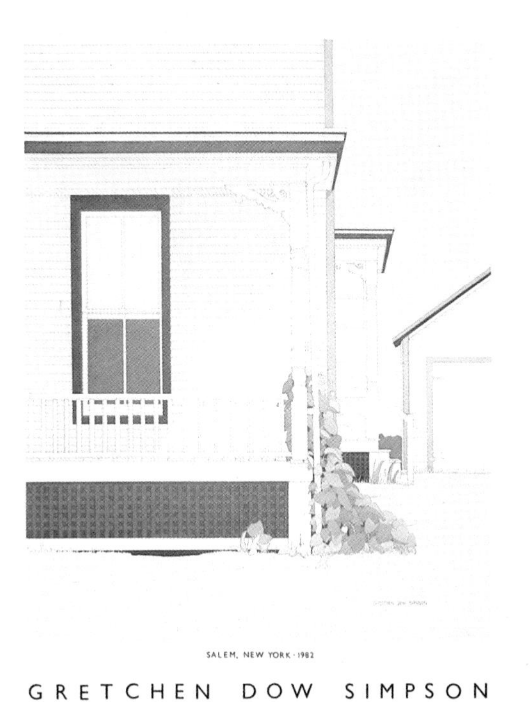
SALEM, NEW YORK · 1982
GRETCHEN DOW SIMPSON

DOUG WEST Aspen Mountain Gallery

W56 WEST BORN ON THE WING 38×25

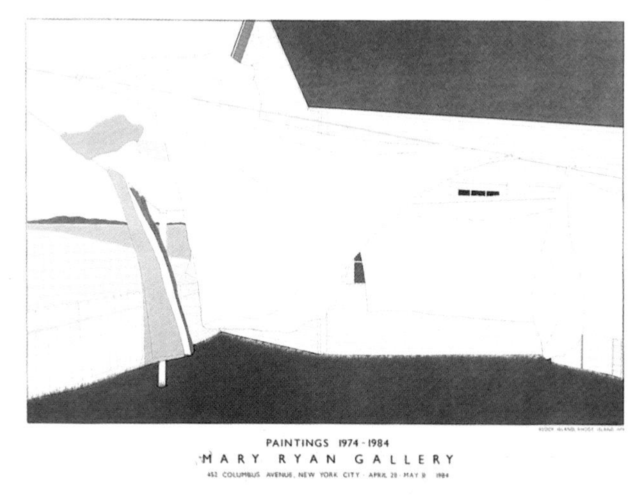
GRETCHEN DOW SIMPSON
PAINTINGS 1974 · 1984
MARY RYAN GALLERY

S172 SIMPSON BLOCK ISLAND $24 \times 29\frac{1}{2}$

H100 HEDLEY TABLE FOR TWO 20 × 30

RALPH HEDLEY

H101 HEDLEY YELLOW CHAIR 20 × 30

RALPH HEDLEY

WHITE SANDS

F92 FONTANA WHITE SANDS $19^{3}/_{8} \times 24^{7}/_{8}$

Schoolhouse Gallery

S82 SQUIRES COTTAGE VIEW $36^{1}/_{2} \times 24^{1}/_{2}$

Schoolhouse Gallery

S83 SQUIRES AFTERNOON REST 37 × 25

28 JACKSON TORONTO SUMMER 35 × 18

TORONTO
SUMMER 1984

PANORAMA
MICHEL TRONEL

T44 TRONEL PANORAMA $21^1/_2 \times 35^3/_4$

KATE HEPBURN

H103 HEPBURN SAILING 24 × 16

KATE HEPBURN

H102 HEPBURN LIGHTHOUSE 24 × 16

L30 LUONGO BEACH UMBRELLAS 39 × 30 1/2

ALDO LUONGO
MARTIN LAWRENCE LIMITED EDITIONS
LOS ANGELES, CALIFORNIA
1982

P90 PEDRONO BEACH CHAIR 33 1/2 × 25 1/2

PEDRONO

GALERIE
DU CENTRE
5 rue Pierre-au-Lard

872 MASSACHUSETTS AVE. CAMBRIDGE MA 02139
IMPRESSIONS

S117 SALMONA FAUTEUIL SUR LA PLAGE 31 1/2 × 24 1/2

J8 JINKS SUMMER 39 × 24 3/4

SUMMER
REMIER EDITIONS

B115 BARTNICK LAKE PLACID PORCH 24 × 36

HARRY BARTNICK

Manhattan Beach

F16 FRANSEN MANHATTAN BEACH 32 × 24

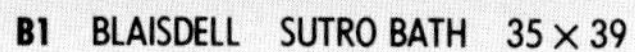
B1 BLAISDELL SUTRO BATH 35 × 39

A61 ANDREOLO LA VERANDA $22^1/_4 \times 28^1/_4$

ALDO ANDREOLO
L'AFFICHE ILLUSTREE Via Guelfa 14r · Via dei Servi 69r · Firenze

A24 ANDREOLO ESTATE $22^1/_8 \times 27^3/_8$

A N D R E O L O
KUNSTHANDEL P.D. VAN VOORST VAN BEEST

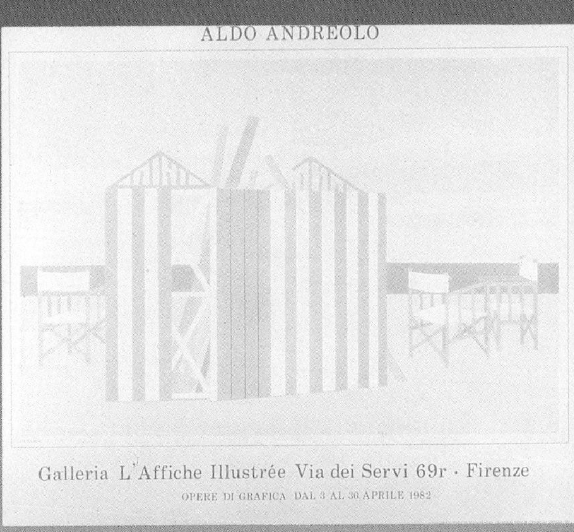
ALDO ANDREOLO
Galleria L'Affiche Illustrée Via dei Servi 69r · Firenze
OPERE DI GRAFICA DAL 3 AL 30 APRILE 1982

A37 ANDREOLO LA SPIAGGIA $22^1/_4 \times 27^1/_2$

ALDO ANDREOLO
ART 14'83 BASEL 15-20.6.83

A62 ANDREOLO EVA $29^1/_2 \times 18^3/_4$

ALDO ANDREOLO

A23 ANDREOLO LA VENEXIANA $31^1/_8 \times 20^1/_2$

G101 GOCKEL SEASIDE 28 × 22

G100 GOCKEL AFTER THE SUN 28 × 22

ART EXPO NEW YORK '84

CAROL CHAPMAN

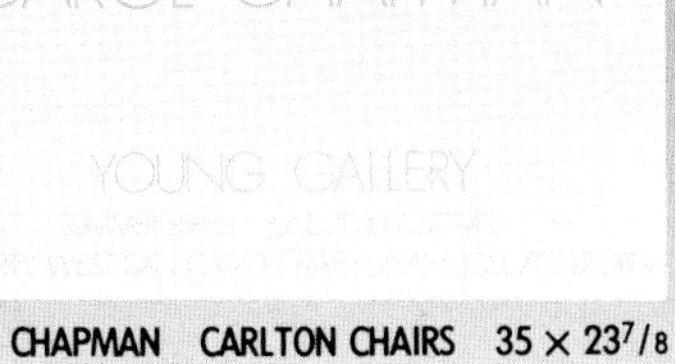
YOUNG GALLERY

CHAPMAN CARLTON CHAIRS 35 × 23 7/8

AVEC AMOUR

G102 GILBERT AVEC AMOUR 24 × 36

D40 DAVIS NEW YORK, NEW YORK ☆ 25 × 31 3/4

NEW YORK – NEW YORK
HAROLD DAVIS MUSEUM OF THE CITY OF NEW YORK

P121 PARKINSON HAT FASHIONS 21 1/4 × 26

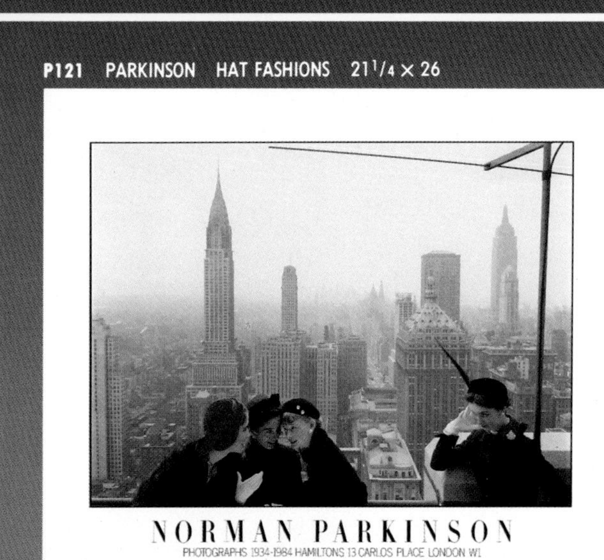
NORMAN PARKINSON
PHOTOGRAPHS 1934-1984 HAMILTONS 13 CARLOS PLACE LONDON W1

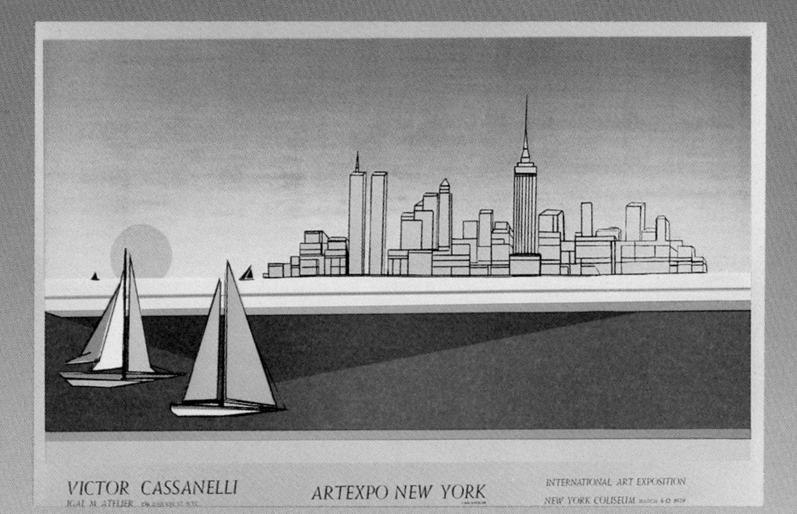
VICTOR CASSANELLI
ARTEXPO NEW YORK
INTERNATIONAL ART EXPOSITION
NEW YORK COLISEUM

C10 CASSANELLI NEW YORK SKYLINE 23 × 35

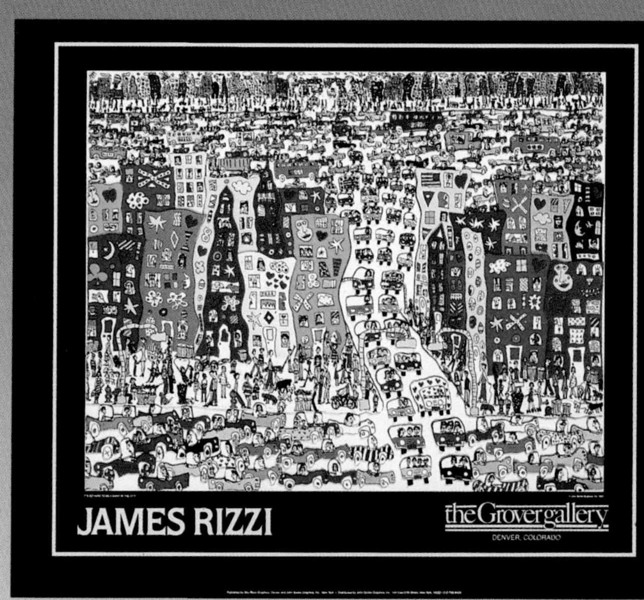
JAMES RIZZI
theGrovergallery
DENVER, COLORADO

R54 RIZZI SAINT IN THE CITY 24 × 28

N E W Y O R K

G65 GRAHAM MANHATTAN!! 32 × 25

Manhattan!!
tony Graham

G64 GRAHAM MINI MANHATTAN!! 20 × 16

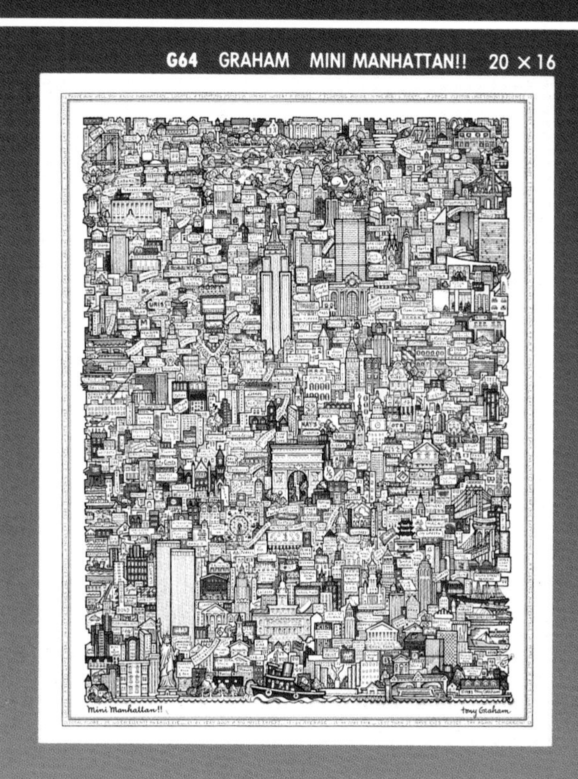

Mini Manhattan!!
tony Graham

G62 GRAHAM BROADWAY!!

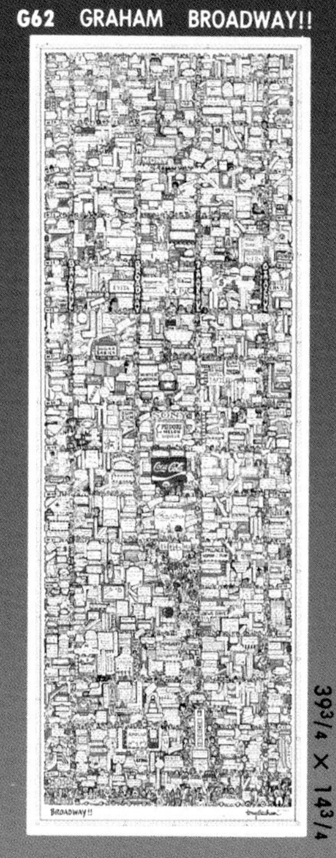

39 3/4 × 14 3/4

Manhattan Skyline
tony Graham

G63 GRAHAM MANHATTAN SKYLINE 13 × 48

H1 HILDENBRAND BROOKLYN BRIDGE $16^1/4 \times 59$

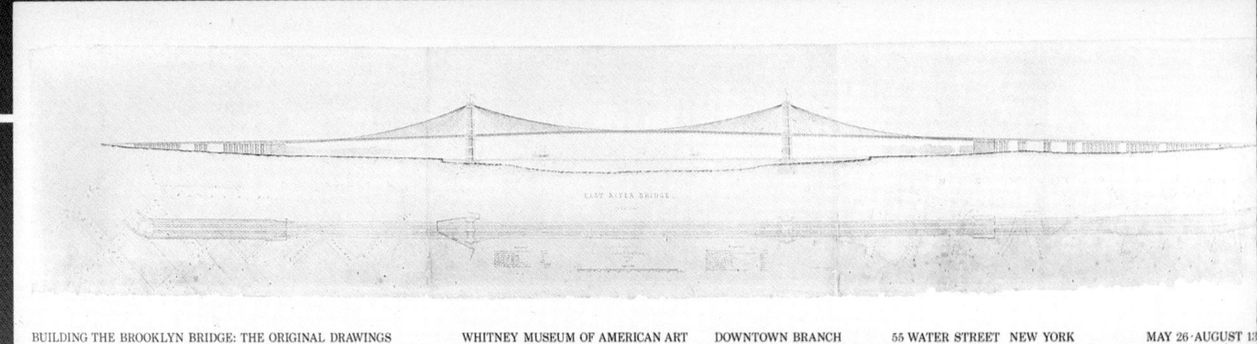
EAST RIVER BRIDGE
BUILDING THE BROOKLYN BRIDGE: THE ORIGINAL DRAWINGS
WHITNEY MUSEUM OF AMERICAN ART
DOWNTOWN BRANCH
55 WATER STREET NEW YORK
MAY 26-AUGUST 1

ONE HUNDRED YEARS IN CENTRAL PARK 1880-1980 THE METROPOLITAN MUSEUM OF ART
A DRAWING OF THE McKIM, MEAD & WHITE ADDITIONS TO THE FIFTH AVENUE FACADE

M30 METROPOLITAN MUSEUM OF ART 16×59

NEW YORK NEW YORK NEW YORK NEW YOR

P22 PITIGLIANI NEW YORK, NEW YORK 24×36

9 DAVIES THE CHRYSLER BUILDING 40 × 30

CHARD DAVIES
THE CHRYSLER BUILDING
USEUM OF THE CITY OF NEW YORK

D56 DAVIES EMPIRE STATE BLDG. $33^1/_2 \times 24^5/_8$

THE MANHATTAN SUITE
RICHARD DAVIES
Empire State Building
FUTURA Nov. 1981

ROOKLYN BRIDGE
NTENNIAL 1883-1983

S111 SHERMAN BROOKLYN BRIDGE $30 \times 21^3/_4$

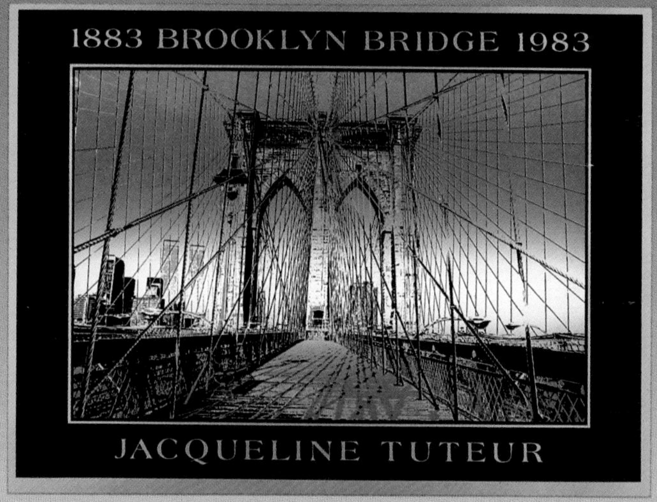

1883 BROOKLYN BRIDGE 1983
JACQUELINE TUTEUR

T26 TUTEUR BROOKLYN BRIDGE *SERIGRAPH* 23 × 31

M124 McKNIGHT COLD SPRING HARBOR $26^1/_2 \times 27^1/_2$

McKNIGHT CHALK & VERMILION ART EXPO 1984

M123 McKNIGHT BENNINGTON $26^1/_2 \times 27^1/_2$

McKNIGHT GEORGETOWN FINE ARTS WASHINGTON, D.C

THOMAS McKNIGHT ROLLY-MICHAUX GALLERIES 1982

M76 McKNIGHT FLOWERED COUCH $26^3/_4 \times 27^3/_4$

McKNIGHT CHRISTIES CONTEMPORARY ART LONDON

M122 McKNIGHT NEWPORT SAILING $26^1/_2 \times 27^1/_2$

P24 PRATT BED $35^{7}/_{8} \times 24$

CHRISTOPHER PRATT

MIRA GODARD GALLERY
CALGARY · TORONTO · 1981

S65 ST. CLAIR 3 CHAIRS $32^{1}/_{2} \times 22^{3}/_{4}$

Bruce St. Clair

S64 SOLOMBRE LANDSCAPE $24^{3}/_{4} \times 19^{3}/_{4}$

B146 BECK STEPS $22^{1}/_{4} \times 26^{1}/_{4}$

B144 BECK ARCHWAY $22^{1}/_{4} \times 26^{1}/_{4}$

E61 ENGLISH FROZEN DAIRY BAR $23^{1}/_{8} \times 26^{3}/_{8}$

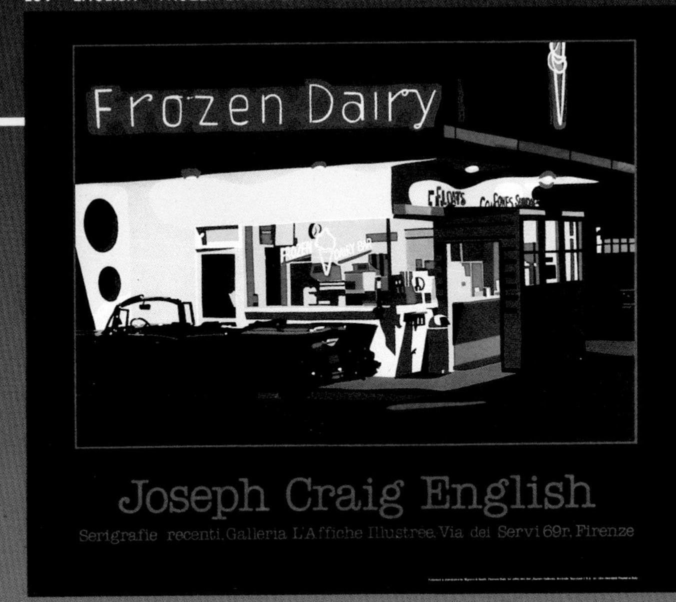
Frozen Dairy
Joseph Craig English
Serigrafie recenti, Galleria L'Affiche Illustree, Via dei Servi 69r, Firenze

032 ODGERS NEW YORK IN LOS ANGELES $24^{1}/_{2} \times 29^{1}/_{4}$

N E W Y O R K I N L O S A N G E L E S

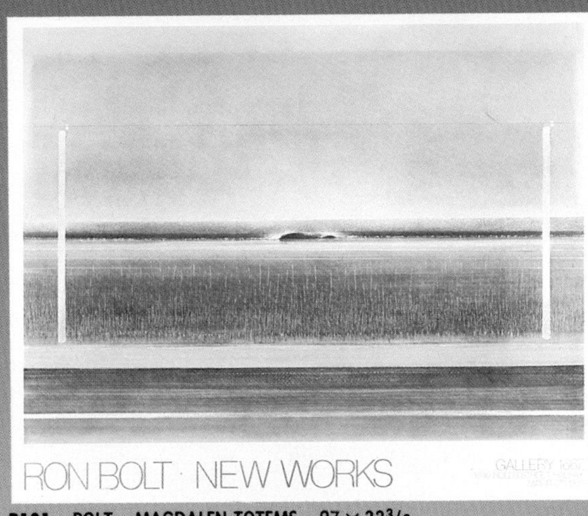
RON BOLT NEW WORKS

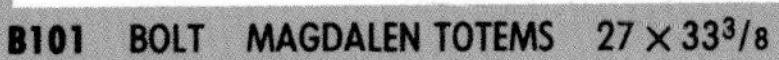

B101 BOLT MAGDALEN TOTEMS $27 \times 33^{3}/_{8}$

M I D D A Y

C163 COULON MIDDAY $23 \times 31^{5}/_{8}$

L54 LLOYD WINDOW 36 × 22 1/2

DAVID LLOYD

R49 ROSENTHAL FARMERS MARKET 23 1/2 × 31 1/2

Phone
Phone
Phone
FARMERS MARKET
PIERRE ROSENTHAL

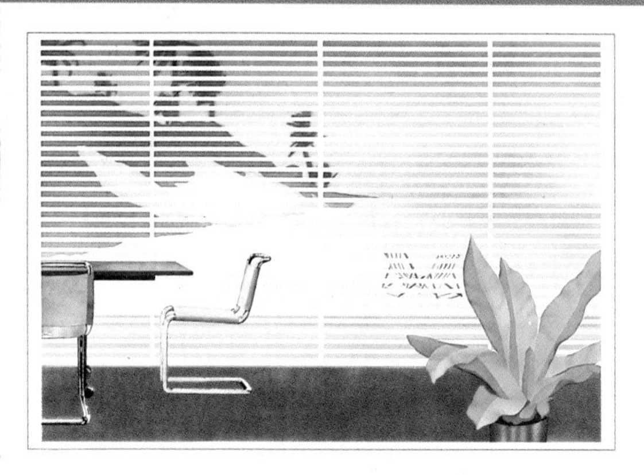
TIMOTHY-V BIRCH

B70 BIRCH OCEAN VIEW 25 × 35

TIMOTHY-V BIRCH

B60 BIRCH WINDOW 25 × 35

W57 WEST RETURN $21^3/_4 \times 34^7/_8$

DOUG WEST
1983

D120 De ARCE EL PRESIDIO GALLERY 24 × 35

R43 RUSH MORNING MIST 24 × 36

DIANE RUSH · DUSK

R50A RUSH ISLANDS/BLOSSOMS "A" 36 × 24

D107 De ARCE GALLERY VANDER WOUDE 24 × 35

D109 De ARCE WEAVER'S NEEDLE 24 × 36

MANUEL de ARCE GALLERY THREE PHOENIX

FRONT LINE EDITIONS

R50B RUSH ISLANDS/BLOSSOMS "B" 36 × 24

SEPIA SUNSET • DIANE RUSH

R60 RUSH SEPIA SUNSET 24 × $35^{7}/_{8}$

W35 WEIL WIMBLEDON '82 $29^{1}/_{2} \times 19$

ROBERT WEIL
WIMBLEDON 1982

W39 WEIL TENNIS $15 \times 22^{3}/_{4}$

ROBERT WEIL
TENNIS 1980

ROBERT WEIL

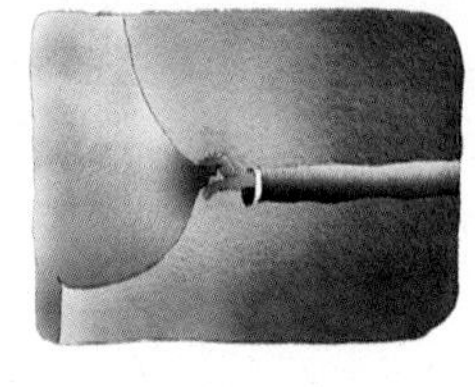

MULTIPLES

ROBERT STEIN FINE ARTS SAN FRANCISCO

W28 WEIL MULTIPLES 20×15

ROBERT WEIL
SUNSHINE GRAPHICS
Johannesburg, South Africa

W23 WEIL SUNSHINE GRAPHICS 25×18

ALPI WINTER
RUN 80
FEB 6 — 24
1980 ST. MORITZ

W49 WEIL ST. MORITZ 29×21

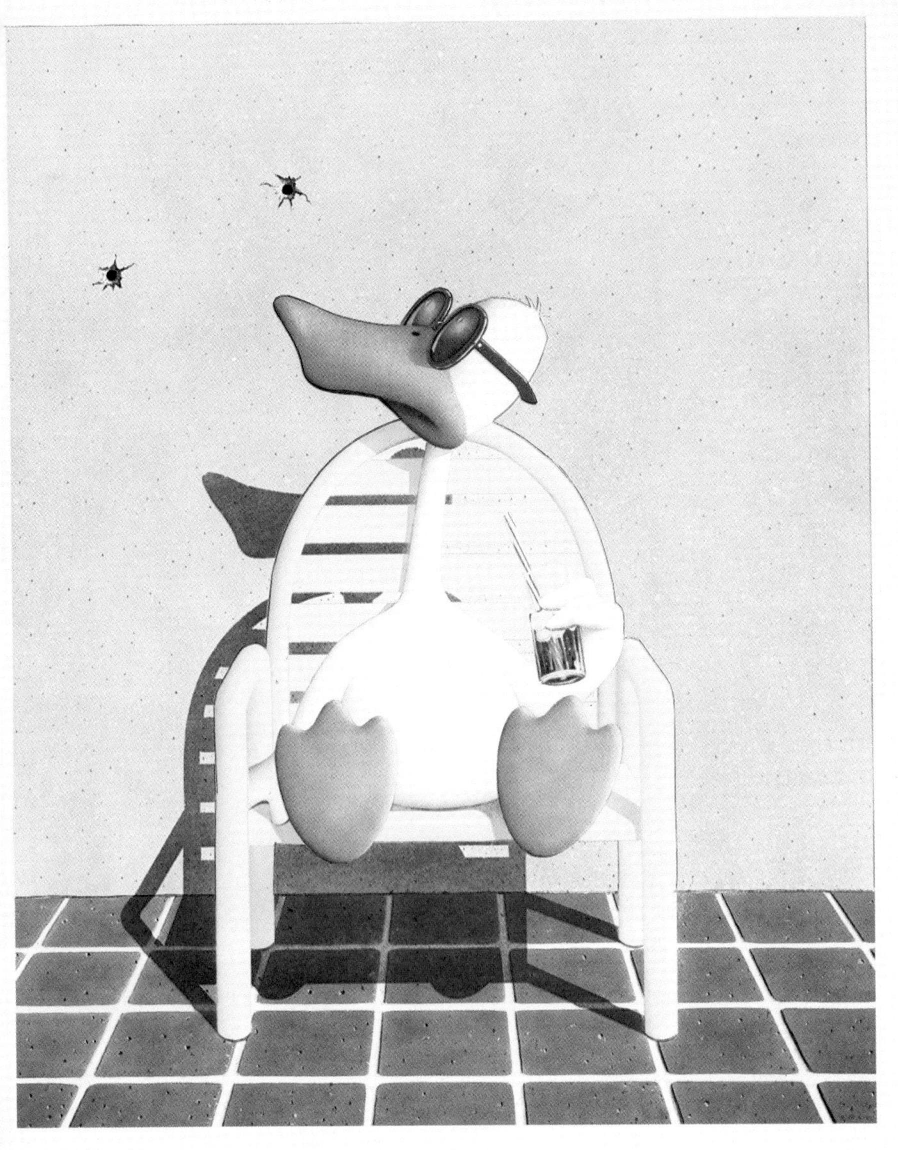
'Sitting Duck'
B E D A R D

B108 BEDARD SITTING DUCK 30 3/4 × 22 1/2

One of America's most famous comedians, Will Rogers, once declared, "We are all here for a spell, get all the good laughs you can." This group of artists are doing their best to make that so.

Humor provides a release from the growing complexity of our lives. Just when we begin to take ourselves too seriously, along comes an artist like Charles Bragg who says the artistic equivalent of, "Hey, wait a minute. Let's take a look at the other side of the matter." That other side, of course, being the levity of the whole thing.

Humorous posters take a very close look at life. They find the funny little things that we have overlooked, exaggerate them to bring them to our attention, and make us laugh. In a sense, all they do is tell us the truth about human nature.

Without doubt, the most fun stock in any inventory will be the laughing stock.

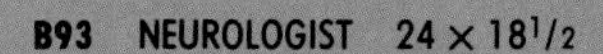

B93 NEUROLOGIST $24 \times 18^1/_2$

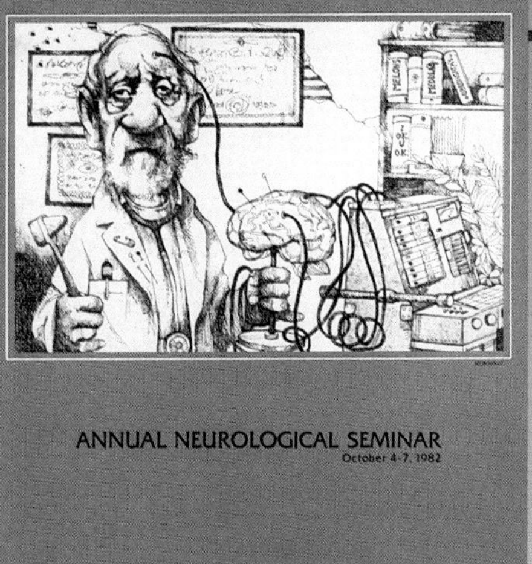
CHARLES BRAGG
ANNUAL NEUROLOGICAL SEMINAR
October 4-7, 1982
LINDEN FINE ARTS

B95 GYNECOLOGIST $24 \times 18^1/_2$

CHARLES BRAGG
NATIONAL CONVENTION OF GYNECOLOGISTS
The New York Coliseum
September 14-20th 1982
LINDEN FINE ARTS

B97 OBJECTION SUSTAINED 24×18

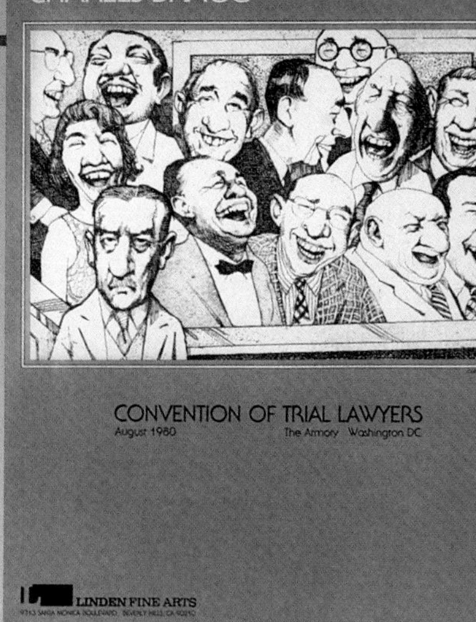
CHARLES BRAGG
CONVENTION OF TRIAL LAWYERS
August 1980
The Armory Washington DC
LINDEN FINE ARTS

CHARLES BRAGG
SOCIETY OF GENERAL PRACTITIONERS
Seminar on Family Medicine
Topeka, Kansas Nov. 1907
LINDEN FINE ARTS

B90 DR. SNEED 24×18

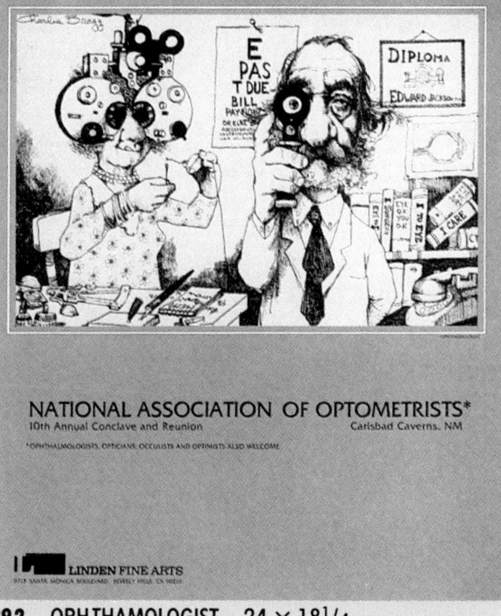
CHARLES BRAGG
DIPLOMA
NATIONAL ASSOCIATION OF OPTOMETRISTS*
10th Annual Conclave and Reunion
Carlsbad Caverns, NM
LINDEN FINE ARTS

B92 OPHTHAMOLOGIST $24 \times 18^1/_4$

CHARLES BRAGG
MARDI GRAS
Saints and Sinners Ball French Quarter
NEW ORLEANS LOUISIANA
February 1983
LINDEN FINE ARTS

B98 MARDI GRAS 24×18

B94 OUT OF COURT SETTLEMENT 24 × 18

HARLES BRAGG

CONVENTION OF TRIAL LAWYERS
August 1980 The Armory Washington DC
LINDEN FINE ARTS

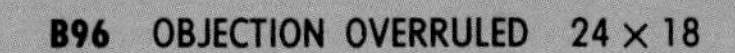

B96 OBJECTION OVERRULED 24 × 18

CHARLES BRAGG
ACLU AMERICAN CIVIL LIBERTIES UNION
Autumn Festival October 1982 Los Angeles Chapter CA
LINDEN FINE ARTS
9713 SANTA MONICA BOULEVARD BEVERLY HILLS CA 90210

B13 THE RIDDLE 24 × 18

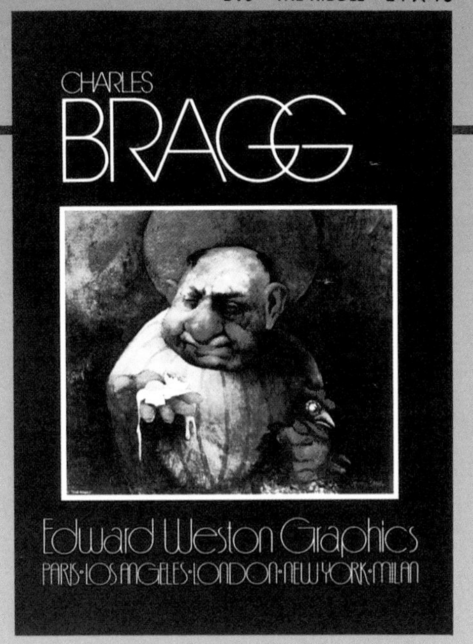
CHARLES
BRAGG
Edward Weston Graphics
PARIS·LOS ANGELES·LONDON·NEW YORK·MILAN

CHARLES BRAGG

MARDI GRAS
Saints and Sinners Ball French Quarter
NEW ORLEANS LOUISIANA
February 1983
LINDEN FINE ARTS

B99 SAINTS & SINNERS BALL 24 × 18

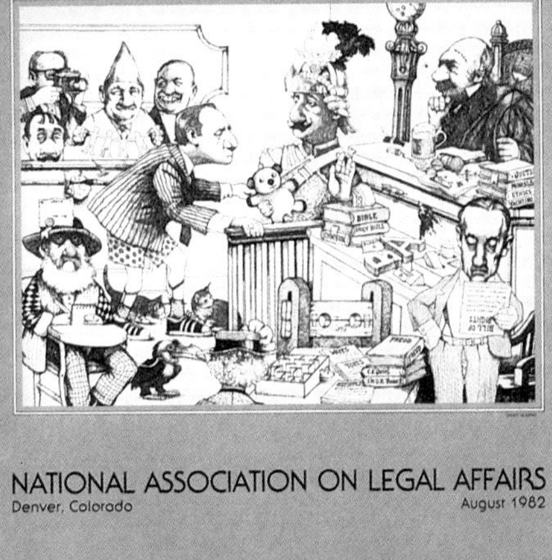
CHARLES BRAGG
NATIONAL ASSOCIATION ON LEGAL AFFAIRS
Denver, Colorado August 1982
LINDEN FINE ARTS
9713 SANTA MONICA BOULEVARD BEVERLY HILLS CA 90210

B91 SANITY HEARING 24 × 18

CHARLES BRAGG
ART EXPO 82 NEW YORK NY APRIL 22-26.1982
LINDEN FINE ARTS

B100 SHIP OF FOOLS 28 × 21

B59 IN THE BEGINNING 28 × 22

CHARLES
BRAGG

SUTTON GALLERIES
437 ROYAL ST. NEW ORLEANS, LOUISIANA 70130 (504) 581-1551

B77 SELF PORTRAIT 30 × 22

CHARLES
BRAGG
JULY 1976 BEVERLY HILLS
GEARY'S
NORTH

B58 KING OF ME'S 32 × 24

CHARLES
BRAGG

SUTTON GALLERIES
437 ROYAL ST. NEW ORLEANS, LOUISIANA 70130 (504) 581-155

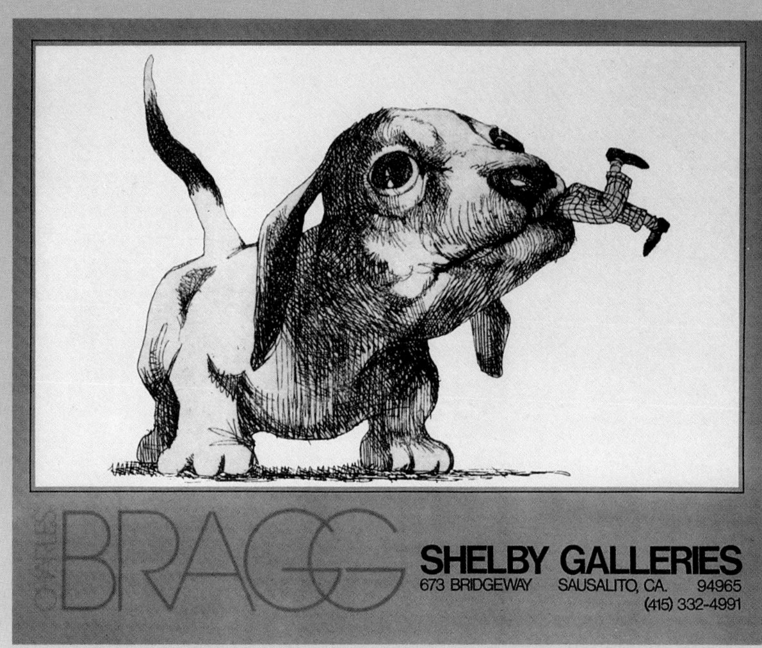
CHARLES
BRAGG
SHELBY GALLERIES
673 BRIDGEWAY SAUSALITO, CA. 94965
(415) 332-4991

B64 A DOG & HIS MASTER 19 × 24

CHARLES
BRAGG

THE ART COLLECTOR
San Diego, CA

B62 GARDEN OF EROS $30^{3}/_{4} \times 23^{1}/_{8}$

B68 ANIMAL DOCTOR 24 × 20

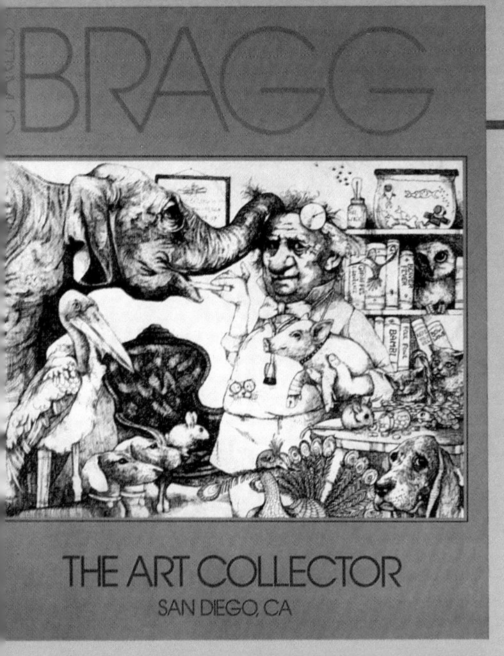
BRAGG
THE ART COLLECTOR
SAN DIEGO, CA

B65 JURISTS 20 × 26 1/2

CHARLES
BRAGG
NATIONAL CONVENTION
OF JURISTS
GEORGETOWN, VIRGINIA
SEPTEMBER 1979

CHARLES
BRAGG
SUTTON GALLERIES
316 ROYAL ST. NEW ORLEANS, LOUISIANA 70130 (504) 581-1551

B56 THE 6th DAY 30 × 20

charles bragg
Aaron Brothers 35th anniversary 1981
"the lovers"

B61 THE LOVERS 20 × 24

W61 WEIL STOCKBROKER 33 × 17

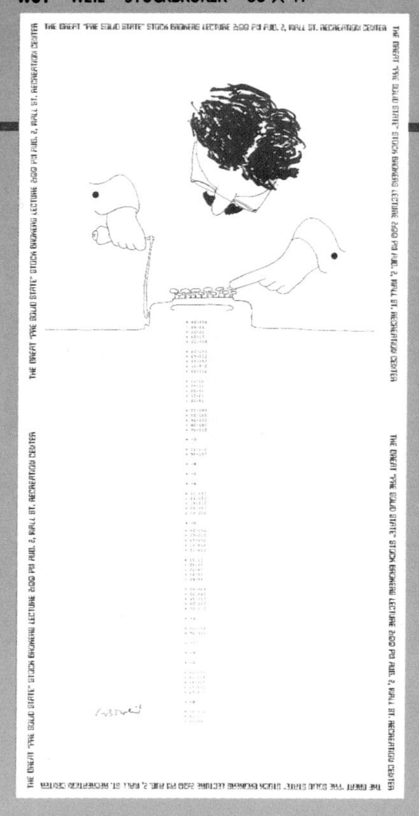

S55 SARIANO AMERICAN BIOGRAPHY ☆ *LITHOGRAPH WITH EMBOSSING* 25 × 28

jean sariano · mcgaw editions

R4 REINHARD REHEARSAL 19 1/2 × 27 1/2

LOS ANGELES 1984
Reinhard
FOR PEACE SAKE...
All Together Now!

R59 REINHARD ALL TOGETHER NOW 34 × 24

S34 SARIANO HANDEL WITH CARE ☆ *LITHOGRAPH* 36 × 24

JEAN SARIANO
HANDEL WITH CARE

expose yourself to art

R20 RYERSON EXPOSE YOURSELF TO ART 23 × 17

Reinhard
PAPER SCULPTURE GRAPHICS/81

R19 REINHARD HOLEY SMOKE 25 × 20

Jim Dine
monotypes et gravures
Galerie Maeght s.a.
du 12 avril au 20 mai 1983 - 14, rue de Téhéran, Paris 8e

D145 DINE MONOTYPES & GRAVURES $31^1/_4 \times 21^5/_8$

SANTA FE
CHAMBER MUSIC
FESTIVAL THE TWELFTH SEASON
July 8—August 17, 1984

038 O'KEEFFE SUMMER DAYS 36×24

E U M

To have beheld or heard the greatest works of any great painter or musician, is a possession added to
 the best things of life," said the English poet Swinburne. Museum art posters allow each of us access
ıese works which are at the pinnacle of mankind's artistic achievements.

poster industry, as we know it today, has, at its historical source, museum art posters. The
ouncement of museum and gallery exhibitions was a primary function of the poster when it first caught
oublic's eye.

e concept of today's commercially acceptable decorative posters must be historically linked with
seum art posters," says Bruce McGaw, a leading poster publisher/distributor. "When we first entered
industry, it was necessary for us to search galleries and museums worldwide to find the images we
ded to supply to poster shops.

day's poster industry has evolved into one where sophisticated marketing techniques bring the public
e very different kinds of images from those of museum art posters. We believe it is important to offer not
the decorative posters so much in style, but the truly fine art that museum art posters represent as
l."

ay's artistic trends are important avenues for aesthetic expression, but museum pieces remain among
most important art work the world has ever produced and is still producing. And while trends may come
go, fine art exhibition posters are here to stay.

believe the future of the industry hinges on a commitment to images with solid design and artistic
ility rather than fleeting trends," McGaw adds. "In dedicating ourselves to quality, it is good to take an
asional look at the posters in this section which, in fact, are the most aesthetically important pieces we
e to offer."

seum art posters provide an entree to the works of eminent artists, both past and present. Jim Dine's
ters, for example, reveal the fascination with certain imagery this contemporary artist is well known for
le visually enchanting the viewer with his interpretations of tools, hearts, and robes.

scope of David Hockney's talent is evident when looking at the collection of his posters. Reflected in
se images is the versatility and strength of drawing associated with this artistically active artist. These
kney poster images range from delicately rendered representational pieces to brightly colored, more
tract works.

rgia O'Keeffe was one of the first women artists to gain prominence in the 20th century. Her posters
vide an overview of her work, the subtle colorations and organic forms that have made her one of our
st artists.

ere once posters merely announced museum shows, the growing popularity of the medium has led
or cultural institutions to utilize posters to increase public interest in the artists, the exhibitions and the
seums themselves. Posters such as Monet's Water Lilies or Tiffany's Autumn Landscape bring museums
as The Metropolitan Museum of Art to the attention of a heretofore untapped audience.

eum art posters encompass every facet of art—they are realistic and they are abstract; they are brightly
red and they are subtly colored. Their subjects are as diverse as the sections in this Catalogue. But
ve all, they are fine art. These images transcend styles. They are the finest art the world has to offer,
ver synonymous with culture and aesthetic integrity.

D133 PACE GALLERY 1980 $29^{7}/_{8} \times 38$

JIM DINE PAINTINGS PACE GALLERY JANUARY 1980

Jim Dine: Five Themes
Walker Art Center, 15 February-15 April 1984

D134 FIVE THEMES $34 \times 23^{1}/_{2}$

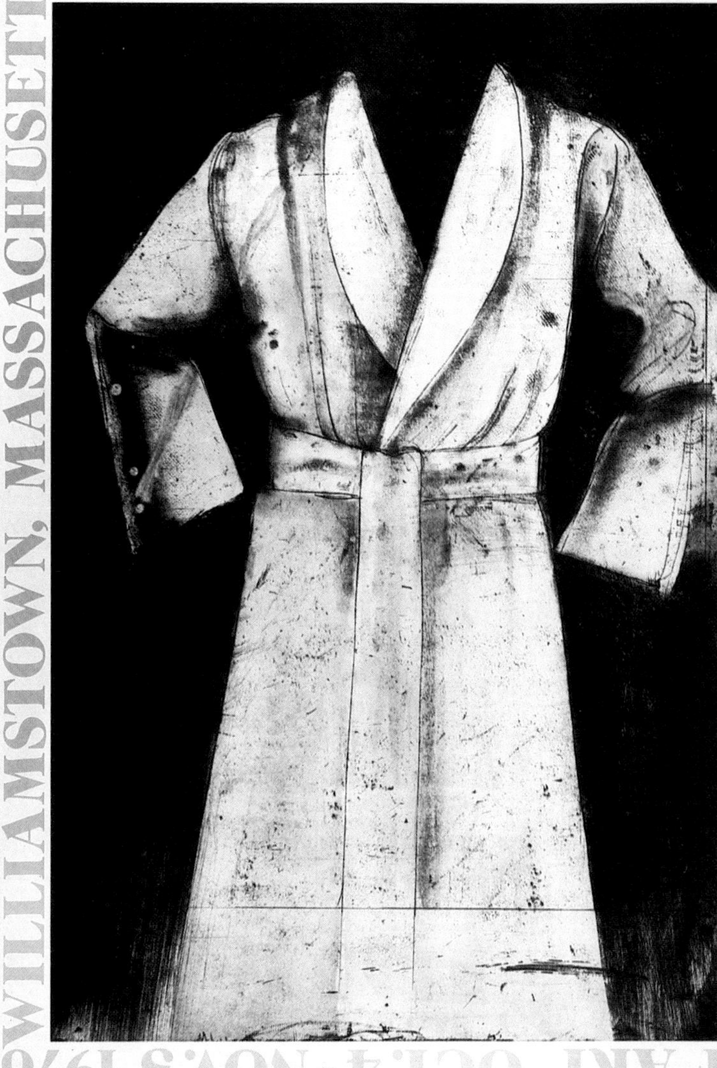
JIM DINE PRINTS: 1970
WILLIAMSTOWN, MASSACHUSETTS
OF ART OCT. 4 - NOV. 5 1976

D135 WILLIAMS COLLEGE MUSEUM *LITHOGRAPH* $35^{1}/_{4} \times 25$

D79 HEARTS 26 × 36

Red
Orange
Yellow
Green
Blue
Black
Silver
Look at
Dine

D77 COLORFUL TOOLS *LITHOGRAPH* $40^3/_4 \times 34^1/_4$

אמנות אמריקאית במאה העשרים
AMERICAN ART IN THE TWENTIETH CENTURY

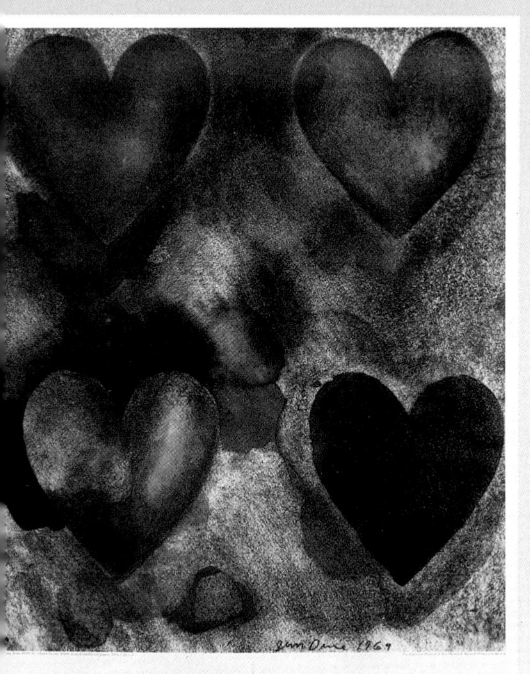
THE BALTIMORE MUSEUM OF ART

D94 HEARTS II 28 × 22

JIM DINE
Walker Art Center 15 February to 15 April 1984

D105 CARDINAL 40 × 24

Jim Dine
Pace Gallery 32 East 57th Street Nov 6-Dec 5,1981

D136 PACE GALLERY 1981 $35^3/_4 \times 25$

W50 WARHOL NUN $39^1/_2 \times 27^1/_2$

ANDY WARHOL
GALERIE BÖRJESON
HAMNGATAN 4, 211 22 MALMÖ SWEDEN
DECEMBER 3-23, 1983

W52 WARHOL WITH HAT $39^1/_2 \times 27^1/_2$

ANDY WARHOL
GALERIE BÖRJESON
HAMNGATAN 4, 211 22 MALMÖ SWEDEN
DECEMBER 3-23, 1983

W51 WARHOL HERSELF $39^1/_2 \times 27^1/_2$

ANDY WARHOL
GALERIE BÖRJESON
HAMNGATAN 4, 211 22 MALMÖ SWEDEN
DECEMBER 3-23, 1983

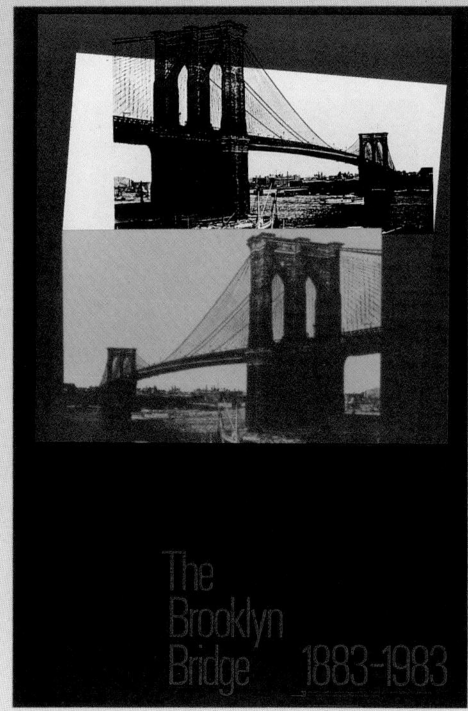
The Brooklyn Bridge
1883-1983

W38 WARHOL BROOKLYN BRIDGE $36^1/_2 \times 24^1/_2$

The Tate Gallery 17 FEBRUARY-28 MARCH 1971
Warhol

W60 WARHOL MARILYN 36×25

T38 TROVA PACE/COLUMBUS 35 × 25

TROVA
PACE/COLUMBUS

T39 TROVA PACE GALLERY EXHIBITION $26^{7}/_{8} \times 26$

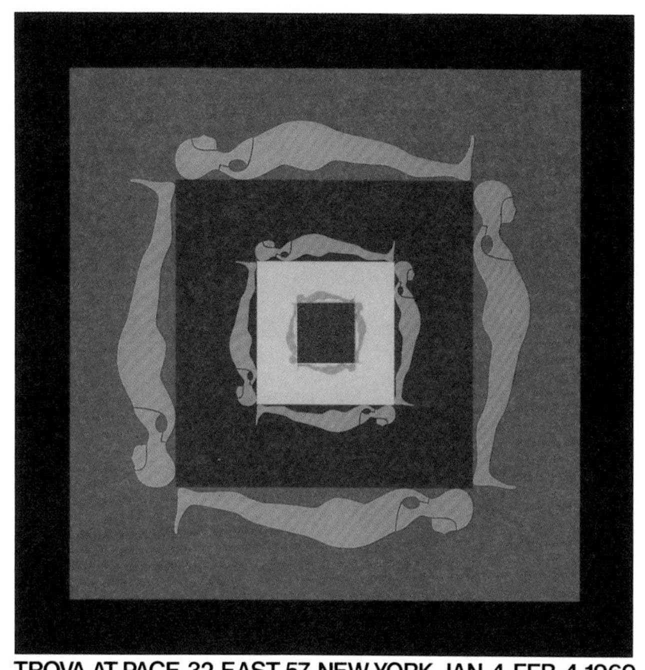
TROVA AT PACE 32 EAST 57 NEW YORK JAN. 4-FEB. 4, 1969

CAGE
WALL TO WALL JOHN CAGE + FRIENDS
MAR 13 82
FREE

R38 RAUSCHENBERG CAGE & FRIENDS 42 × 30

T40 TROVA M.I.T. RECENT SCULPTURE $25^{5}/_{8} \times 25^{7}/_{8}$

H50 MT. FUJI & FLOWERS 36 × 24

THE METROPOLITAN MUSEUM
OF ART DEPARTMENT OF
TWENTIETH CENTURY ART

H54 EDITIONS HERSCHER 37 1/2 × 34

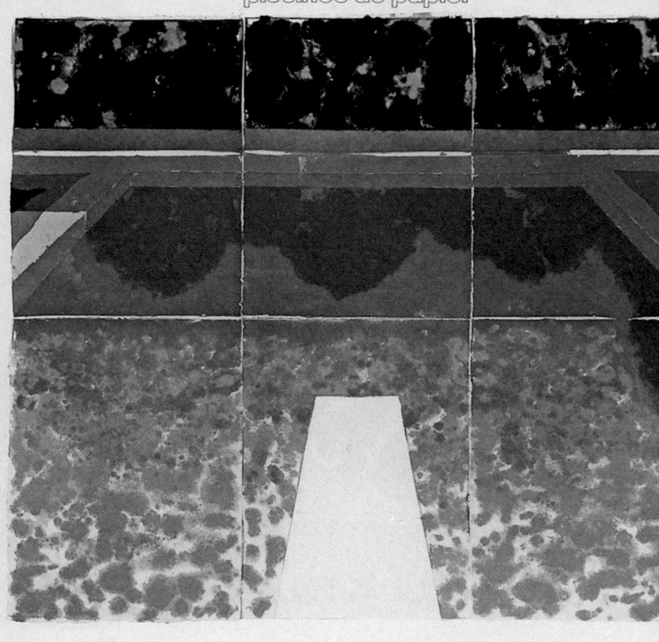
David Hockney
piscines de papier
Editions Herscher
Paris

RAVELS GARDEN
Hockney Paints the Stage
Walker Art Center 20 November 1983 to 22 January 1984

H120 RAVELS GARDEN 34 × 27

LOS ANGELES BICENTENNIAL 1781 1981

H22 SKATERS VENICE 30 1/2 × 25

H52 TATE GALLERY 30 × 20

David Hockney
The Tate Gallery
July 2 – August 3 1980

H69 ARUN ART CENTRE 32 × 20

David Hockney Modern Graphics 1969-1979
The Arun Art Centre Arundel West Sussex
23 August - 27 September 1980 9am - 5.30pm
Closed Sundays & Bank Holidays Free Adm.

H121 MR. CLARK & PERCY 37 × 25

The Tate Gallery
National Collection of Modern Painting
The Tate Gallery, Millbank, London SW1 Weekdays 10-6 Sundays 2-6

ckney Paints the Stage Walker Art Center 20 November 1983 to 22 January 1984

H119 HOCKNEY PAINTS THE STAGE 27 × 37

V15 VASARELY VASARELY CENTER 32 × 24

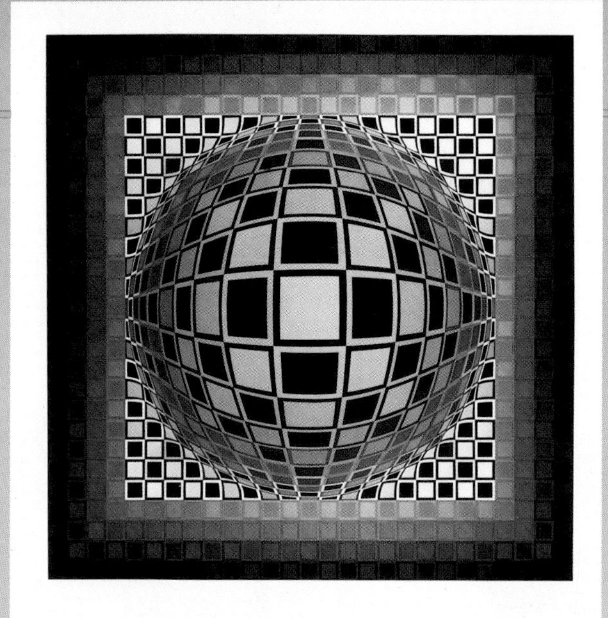

VASARELY CENTER
NEW YORK
Vasarely
CENTER

V17 VASARELY ART EXPO ☆ 33 1/2 × 24

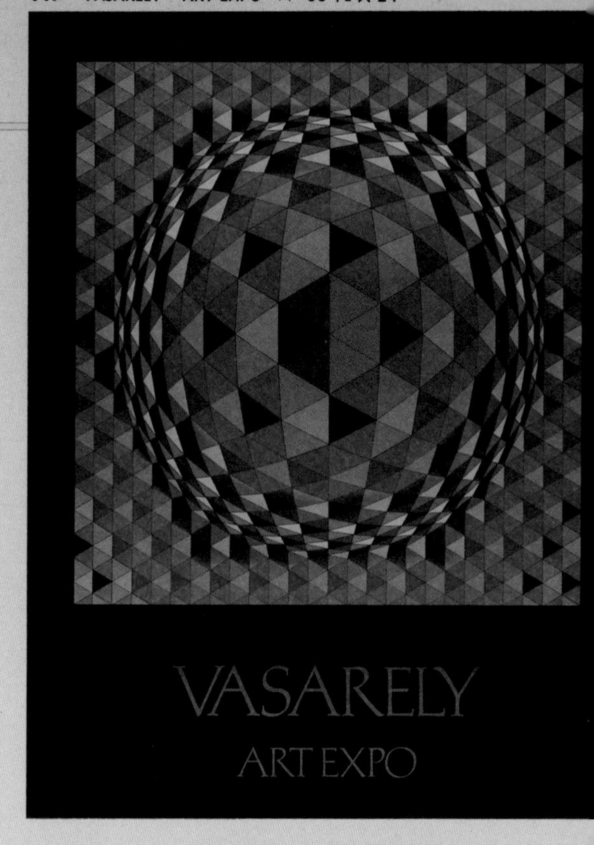
VASARELY
ART EXPO

VASARELY IN NEW YORK 4/84

New York University

GUGGENHEIM
MUSEUM

Vasarely
CENTER

New School for Social Research

PACE UNIVERSITY

V18 VASARELY VASARELY IN NY 24 1/8 × 32 3/4

33 × 24 1/4

V16 VASARELY PITTSBURGH INT'L *SERIGRAPH*

P117 POLLOCK NO.1 $23^1/_2 \times 33^1/_2$

SHOW PAINTING AND SCULPTURE FROM EIGHT COLLECTIONS 1940-1980 THE MUSEUM OF CONTEMPORARY ART, LOS ANGELES NOVEMBER 20, 1983 FEBRUARY 19, 1984

A65 AVERY RED ROCK FALLS 31×26

Milton Avery
Walker Art Center 18 September–30 October 1983

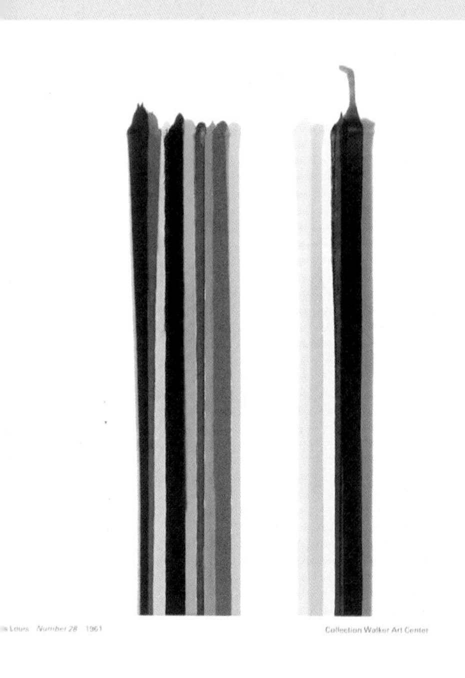
Collection Walker Art Center
Walker Art Center

L6 LOUIS #28 34×23

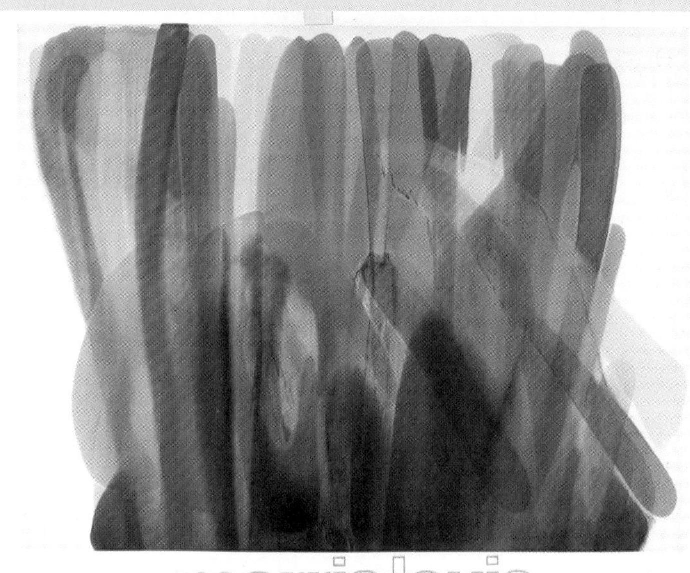
morris louis
the tel aviv museum february-march 1981

L29 LOUIS FLORAL II $27^1/_2 \times 36$

M24 MAGEE STONES $29^{1}/_{4} \times 29^{1}/_{2}$

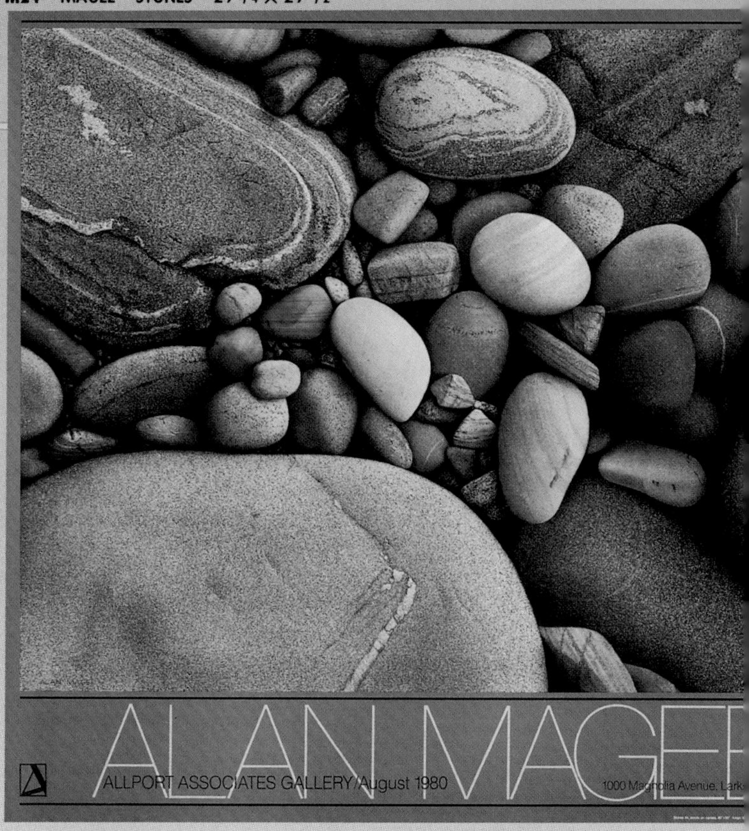
ALAN MAGE
ALLPORT ASSOCIATES GALLERY/August 1980

M70 MAGEE CONSTELLATION 25 × 25

A L A N

M A G E E

TELEPHONE
TELEPHONE
TELEPHONE
THE METROPOLITAN MUSEUM OF ART

E84 ESTES TELEPHONE BOOTHS 30 × 37

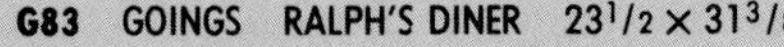

G83 GOINGS RALPH'S DINER $23^1/_2 \times 31^3/_8$

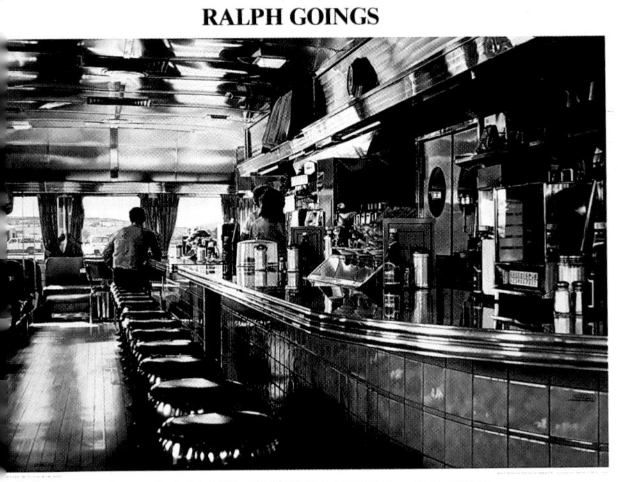
RALPH GOINGS
O.K.HARRIS FEBRUARY 5—26.1983
3 WEST BROADWAY NEW YORK N.Y. 10012 (212) 431-3600

G67 GOINGS DINER 27×36

Ralph Goings

G40 GUERRINI RED VOLKSWAGON $21^1/_4 \times 31$

FERNANDO GUERRINI · CALIFORNIA · L'AFFICHE ILLUSTREE · Via Guelfa 14r · Via dei Servi 69r · FIRENZE

G116 GUERRINI CALIFORNIA 21×31

03 GREY LINE WITH BLACK 35 × 23

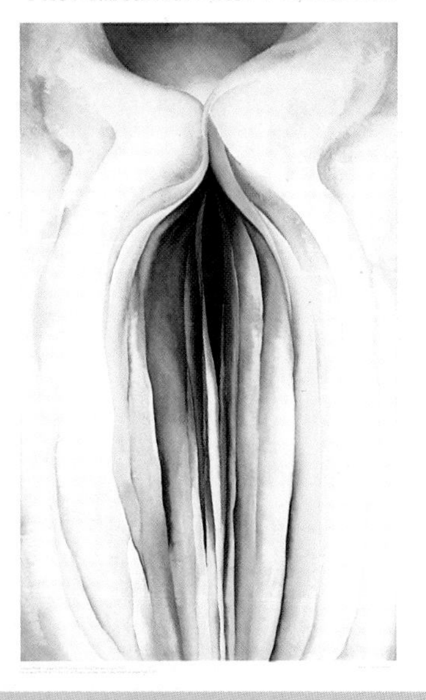
The Museum of Fine Arts, Houston

013 LAWRENCE TREE $34^7/_8 \times 28^1/_8$

SANTA FE
CHAMBER MUSIC
FESTIVAL THE NINTH SEASON
July 12 - August 17, 1981

08 WHITE SHELL $34^3/_4 \times 28$

SANTA FE
CHAMBER MUSIC
FESTIVAL THE FOURTH SEASON
June 27 - August 1, 1976

THE PHILLIPS COLLECTION

019 RANCHOS CHURCH 25 × 34

Walker Art Center

012 LAKE GEORGE BARNS 25 × 28

02 BLACK AND PURPLE PETUNIAS $34^1/4 \times 26^3/4$

ANTA FE
CHAMBER MUSIC
FESTIVAL *THE FIFTH SEASON*

ly 3 August 7, 1977

01 BLACK PLACE III 35 × 25

SANTA FE
CHAMBER MUSIC
FESTIVAL *THE SIXTH SEASON*

July 2 August 7, 1978

05 FARAWAY NEARBY 35 × 25

SANTA FE
CHAMBER MUSIC
FESTIVAL *THE THIRD SEASON*

June 29 August 3, 1975

027 WATERFALL 1 36 × 22

034 ANOTHER CHURCH 15 x 25

011 CLIFFS BEYOND ABIQUIU 39 × 24¹/4

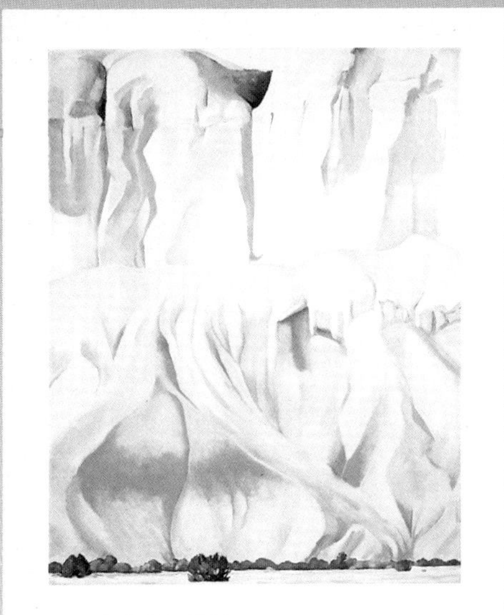
SANTA FE
CHAMBER MUSIC
FESTIVAL THE EIGHTH SEASON
July 6–August 11, 1980

04 LADDER TO THE MOON 36³/4 × 24

SANTA FE
CHAMBER MUSIC
FESTIVAL THE SECOND SEASON
June 30–August 4, 1974

09 CITY NIGHT 37 × 22¹/2

WILLIAM CARLOS WILLIAMS
and the American Scene, 1920-1940

SAVE OUR PLANET SAVE OUR AIR

037 SAVE OUR AIR 25 × 36

LOCH HAVEN ART CENTER
Orlando, Florida

010 LOCH HAVEN 33 × 28

07 TWO JIMSON WEEDS 39 × 25

SANTA FE
CHAMBER MUSIC
FESTIVAL THE SEVENTH SEASON
July 1–August 6, 1979

028 JACK - IN - THE - PULPIT II 39 1/4 × 24

SANTA FE
CHAMBER MUSIC
FESTIVAL THE ELEVENTH SEASON

021 SERIES 1 - NO. 1 39 × 24 1/4

SANTA FE
CHAMBER MUSIC
FESTIVAL THE TENTH SEASON

Whitney Museum of American Art
Fairfield County
ONE CHAMPION PLAZA · STAMFORD, CONNECTICUT
TUESDAY · SATURDAY 11–6
SUPPORTED BY CHAMPION INTERNATIONAL CORPORATION

014 WHITE CALICO FLOWER 37 1/4 × 32

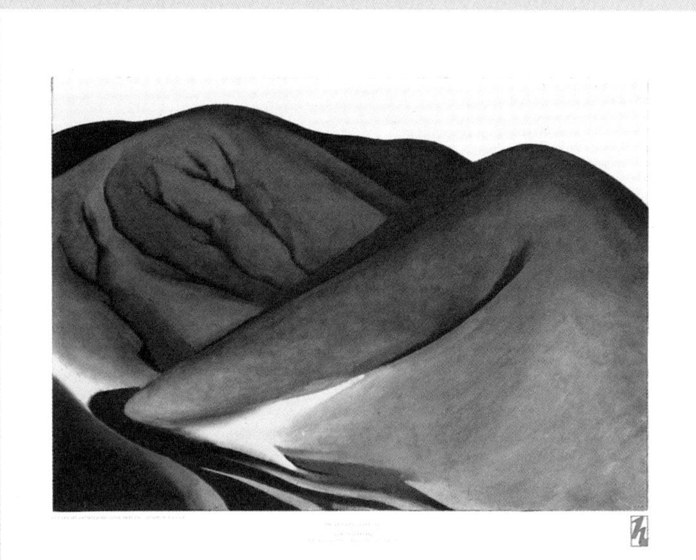

035 THE RED HILLS 19 × 24

M1 MAN RAY THREE PEACHES 32⅝ × 19¼

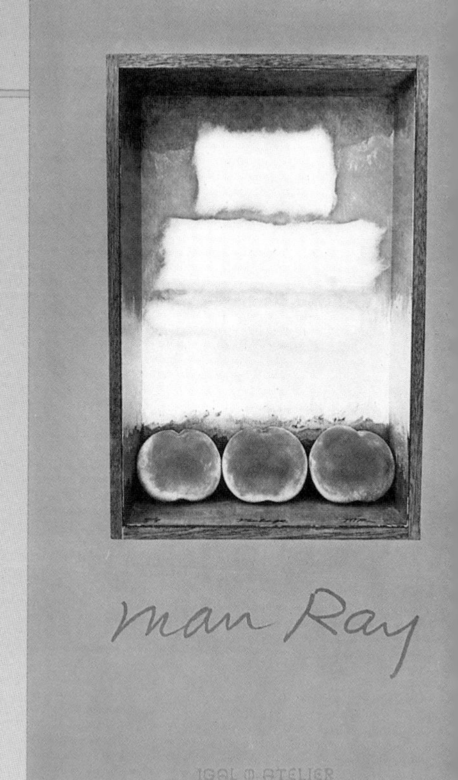
man Ray
IGAL ® ATELIER

M120 MONDRIAN BALTIMORE MUSEUM OF ART

MONDRIAN: DRAWINGS & WATERCOLORS

33⅞ × 21

F89 FRANK AMARYLLIS 39 × 24

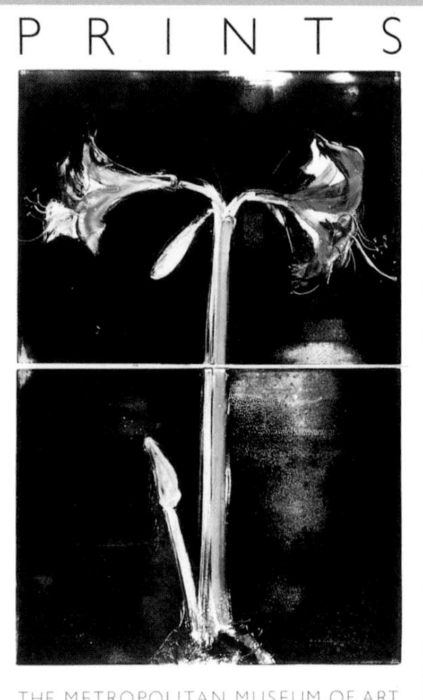
PRINTS
THE METROPOLITAN MUSEUM OF ART

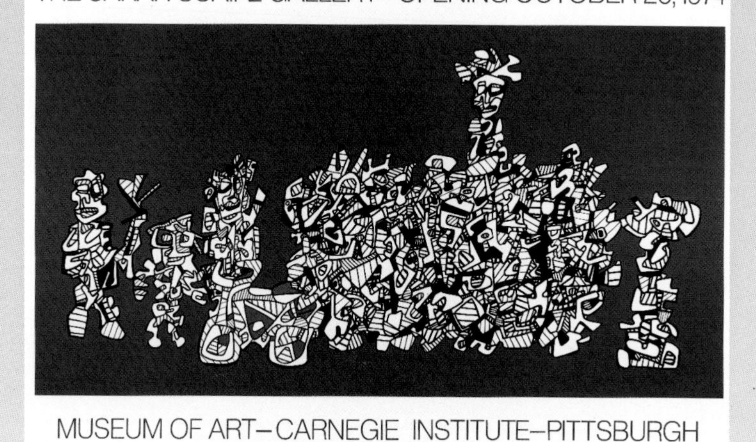
THE SARAH SCAIFE GALLERY–OPENING OCTOBER 26, 1974
MUSEUM OF ART–CARNEGIE INSTITUTE–PITTSBURGH

D113 DUBUFFET CARNEGIE INSTITUTE 35 × 51

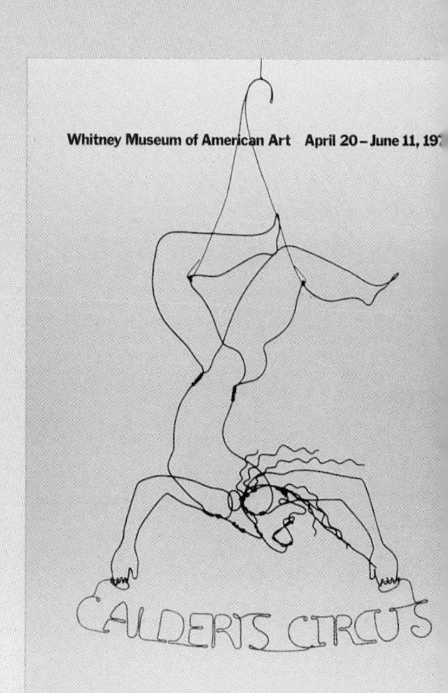
Whitney Museum of American Art April 20–June 11, 19
CALDER'S CIRCUS

C7 CALDER CIRCUS 36 × 26

P122 PICASSO DORA MAAR 38 × 20

Picasso
from the Musée Picasso, Paris
Walker Art Center
10 February through 30 March 1980

P15 PICASSO STILL LIFE ON PEDESTAL 38 × 20

Picasso
from the Musée Picasso, Paris
Walker Art Center
10 February through 30 March 1980

P16 PICASSO PORTRAIT OF OLGA 38 × 20

Picasso
from the Musée Picasso, Paris
Walker Art Center
10 February through 30 March 1980

Picasso
Norton Simon Museum

P3 PICASSO WOMAN WITH BOOK 34 × 33

Picasso
The Pace Gallery 32 East 57th Street Jan 30-Mar 14, 1981

P101 PICASSO PACE GALLERY 35 × 23 1/2

M164 MATISSE THE PINK NUDE $27^3/_4 \times 33^1/_2$

THE BALTIMORE MUSEUM OF ART

M151 MATISSE PARAKEET & MERMAID *SERIGRAPH* $22^1/_4 \times 39$

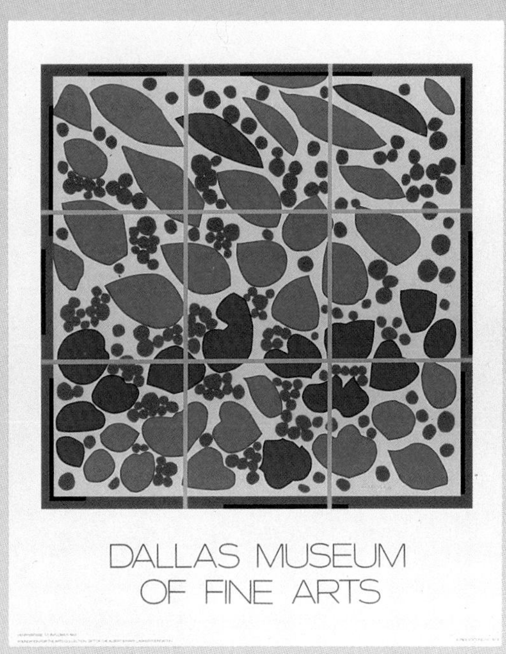
DALLAS MUSEUM
OF FINE ARTS

M145 MATISSE DALLAS MUSEUM $35^5/_8 \times 27^7/_8$

Les quatre Saisons
Le Printemps

S167 SAINT LAURENT LE PRINTEMPS 31 × 24

Les quatre Saisons
L'été

S168 SAINT LAURENT L'ETE 31 × 24

M144 MATISSE CARNEGIE INSTITUTE $28^{1}/_{2} \times 53^{1}/_{2}$

MUSEUM OF ART-CARNEGIE INSTITUTE-PITTSBURGH

Les quatre Saisons

L'Automne

S166 SAINT LAURENT L'AUTOMNE 31 × 24

Les quatre Saisons
L'Hiver

S169 SAINT LAURENT L'HIVER 31 × 24

THE BALTIMORE MUSEUM OF ART

M146 MATISSE BALTIMORE MUSEUM $34^{1}/_{4} \times 24^{3}/_{4}$

M4 GARDEN AT VETHEUIL 34 × 22

Claude Monet
NORTON SIMON MUSEUM

M5 WATER LILIES 30 × 20

Claude Monet

M56 POPLARS 31 × 24¼

MONET'S YEARS AT GIVERNY
THE METROPOLITAN MUSEUM OF ART · APRIL 22-JULY 9 1978

MONET'S YEARS AT GIVERNY
THE METROPOLITAN MUSEUM OF ART
APRIL 22-JULY 9 1978

M52 WATER LILIES (GIVERNY) 27½ × 49

THE ANDRÉ MEYER GALLERIES
The Metropolitan Museum of Art

M64 PARC MONCEAU 38 × 23⅞

E T

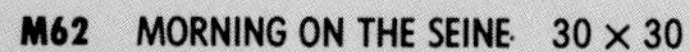

M53 WATER LILIES & BRIDGE $30 \times 24^1/_4$

ONET'S YEARS AT GIVERNY
THE METROPOLITAN MUSEUM OF ART · APRIL 22-JULY 9 1978

M62 MORNING ON THE SEINE 30×30

The André Meyer Galleries · The Metropolitan Museum of Art

HE ANDRÉ MEYER GALLERIES
HE METROPOLITAN MUSEUM OF ART

M60 PATH, VETHEUIL $36^7/_8 \times 24$

Impressionist and Post-Impressionist Paintings
in The Metropolitan Museum of Art · A New Book

M61 TERRACE AT STE. ADRESSE $29^7/_8 \times 33$

P118 PRENDERGAST SWINGS 37 × 24

The Metropolitan Museum of Art
The Robert Lehman Collection

Z1 ZURBARAN STILL LIFE 25 × 38

ZURBARAN
Norton Simon Museum

38 × 20

MODIGLIANI
NORTON SIMON MUSEUM

M154 MODIGLIANI FEMME DE L'ARTISTE

DIEGO RIVERA
NORTON SIMON MUSEUM

R26 RIVERA GIRL WITH LILIES $37^{7}/_{8} \times 32^{7}/_{8}$

C159 CURRIER & IVES THE YACHT MOHAWK 28 × 37

DEPARTMENT OF PRINTS AND PHOTOGRAPHS
THE METROPOLITAN MUSEUM OF ART

C160 CHASE CENTRAL PARK 30 × 37

WILLIAM MERRITT CHASE
AT THE METROPOLITAN MUSEUM OF ART

THE NEW AMERICAN WING
THE METROPOLITAN MUSEUM OF ART

K96 KENSETT LAKE GEORGE 30 × 38

42 × 24

Prendergast: Large Boston Public Garden Sketchbook

P119 PRENDERGAST PERAMBULATOR

C12 CHAGALL DAPHNE & CHLOE 25 × 33 3/8

CHAGALL AT PACE / COLUMBUS
EXHIBITION JUNE 25th Through JULY 23rd, 1977
1460 EAST BROAD STREET COLUMBUS, OHIO 43205

C52 CHAGALL THE LOVERS 37 3/4 × 24

marc chagall
from the tel aviv museum collection

kandinsky
NORTON SIMON MUSEUM

K91 KANDINSKY STREET IN MURNAU 33 × 34

36 × 24

THE ANDRÉ MEYER GALLERIES
THE METROPOLITAN MUSEUM OF ART

R67 RENOIR TWO YOUNG GIRLS AT THE PIANO

C20 CEZANNE TULIPS IN VASE 36 × 24

Cezanne
ORTON SIMON MUSEUM

V13 VAN GOGH PORTRAIT OF A PEASANT 32 × 24

NORTON SIMON MUSEUM

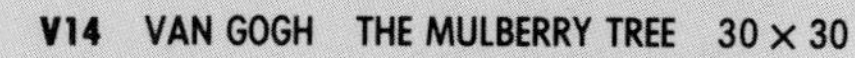
V14 VAN GOGH THE MULBERRY TREE 30 × 30

Vincent Van Gogh
Norton Simon Museum

IE METROPOLITAN MUSEUM OF ART GUIDE

36 × 24

RENOIR MADAME CHARPENTIER & HER CHILDREN

THE ANDRÉ MEYER GALLERIES
The Metropolitan Museum of Art

R37 RENOIR IN THE MEADOW 35 × 24

D131 DEGAS DANCERS PRACTICING AT THE BAR 30 × 34

Degas
THE METROPOLITAN MUSEUM OF ART GUIDE

D130 DEGAS DANCERS IN THE WINGS 34 ×

NORTON SIMON MUSEUM

THE CLOISTERS · FORT TRYON PARK
THE METROPOLITAN MUSEUM OF ART

U22 THE UNICORN IN CAPITIVITY 39 × 22

THE NEW AMERICAN WING
THE METROPOLITAN MUSEUM OF ART

T22 TIFFANY AUTUMN LANDSCAPE 40 × 24

43 × 18

THE NEW AMERICAN WING
THE METROPOLITAN MUSEUM OF ART

T42 TIFFANY GRAPEVINE PANEL

D67 DEGAS REHEARSAL ON THE STAGE 30 × 36

THE METROPOLITAN MUSEUM OF ART • The André Meyer Galleries

T43 TIFFANY FOUR SEASONS 36 × 24

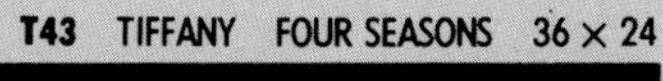

CHICAGO TRIBUNE PRESENTS
THE TREASURES OF
T·I·F·F·A·N·Y
Museum of Science and Industry · June 10 · November 14, 1982

THE NEW AMERICAN WING
THE METROPOLITAN MUSEUM OF ART

T14 TIFFANY MAGNOLIAS & IRISES 39 × 24

THE NEW AMERICAN WING
THE METROPOLITAN MUSEUM OF ART

T15 TIFFANY VIEW OF OYSTER BAY 32 × 24

W58 WARD THE HOME MY DADDY BUILT 35 × 24

America: the third century

H63 HOPPER THE LIGHTHOUSE 28 7/8 × 37

DEPARTMENT OF TWENTIETH CENTURY ART
The Metropolitan Museum of Art

The Metropolitan Museum of Art · American Paintings and Sculpture

H80 HOMER FLOWER GARDEN & BUNGALOW 24 × 33

The Metropolitan Museum of Art · American Paintings and Sculpture

H111 HOMER PALM TREE, NASSAU 34 × 24

H27 HOPPER EARLY SUNDAY MORNING 32 × 39 3/4

EDWARD HOPPER THE ART AND THE ARTIST
WHITNEY MUSEUM OF AMERICAN ART · SEPTEMBER 23, 1980–JANUARY 18, 1981

B155 BAILEY STILL LIFE WITH EGGS 35 × 24

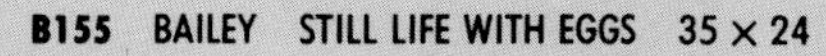

America: the third century

THE METROPOLITAN MUSEUM
OF ART DEPARTMENT OF
TWENTIETH CENTURY ART

W55 WELLIVER THE BIRCHES 37 × 30

The Metropolitan Museum of Art · American Paintings and Sculpture

H81 HOMER A WALL, NASSAU 24 × 33

P37 PORTER ROSEBUD TREES 34 × 22

Eliot Porter: Intimate Landscapes
THE METROPOLITAN MUSEUM OF ART, NEW YORK

P36 PORTER MAPLE & BIRCH 34 × 22

Eliot Porter: Intimate Landscapes
THE METROPOLITAN MUSEUM OF ART, NEW YORK

P69 PORTER DESERT ROSES 34 × 22

Eliot Porter: Intimate Landscapes
THE METROPOLITAN MUSEUM OF ART, NEW YORK

ANSEL ADAMS: AMERICAN ARTIST

A53 ADAMS AMERICAN ARTIST $17^{3}/_{4} \times 22$

Eliot Porter: Intimate Landscapes

P70 PORTER COLUMBINE LEAVES 34 × 22

P38 PORTER COLORFUL TREES 34 × 22

R39 ROTHKO VIOLET, BLACK, ORANGE 33 × 22

A RETROSPECTIVE
THE SOLOMON R. GUGGENHEIM MUSEUM, NEW YORK OCTOBER 27, 1978 - JANUARY 14, 1979

R64 ROTHKO GREEN-RED ON ORANGE $37^{7}/_{8} \times 22^{7}/_{8}$

MARK ROTHKO
SOLOMON R. GUGGENHEIM MUSEUM

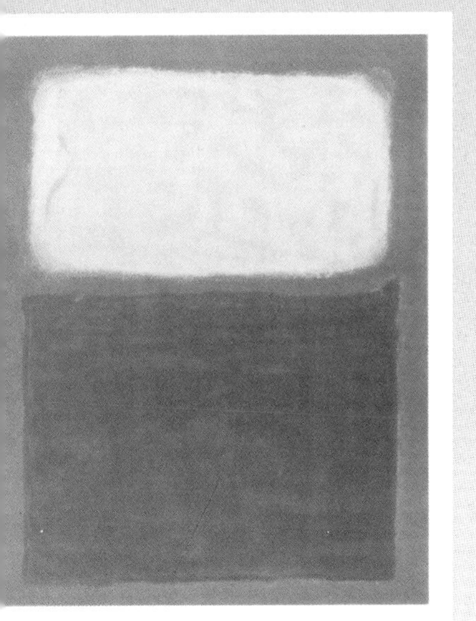

R63 ROTHKO ORANGE, YELLOW $37^{1}/_{2} \times 27^{7}/_{8}$

ROTHKO

R62 ROTHKO GREYED OLIVE GREEN 32 × 25

E80 ENDRESS PIANO & BRASS ☆ 23 × 38

J O H N P A U L E N D R E S S · P I A N O & B R A S S

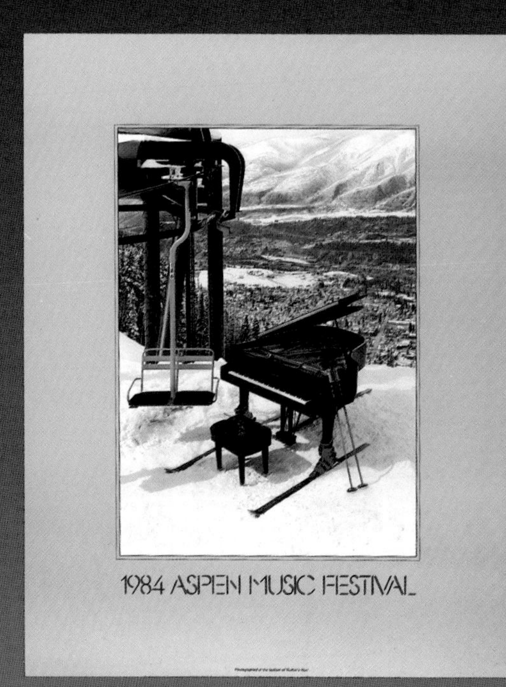
1984 ASPEN MUSIC FESTIVAL

D147 DIESS 1984 ASPEN MUSIC FESTIVAL 28 × 22

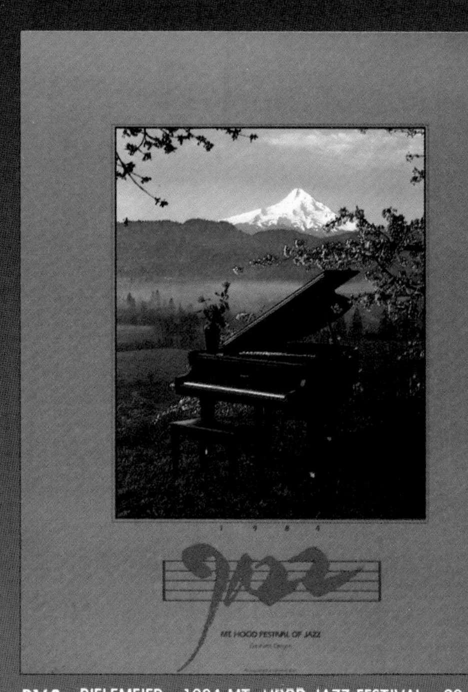
1 9 8 4
jazz
MT. HOOD FESTIVAL OF JAZZ

B162 BIELEMEIER 1984 MT. HOOD JAZZ FESTIVAL 28 × 2

onsider the craze for the Sony Walkman and you will begin to understand why so many people tune in to musical posters. People love music. Whether their passion is Handel or jazz, Broadway musical or ng sonata, there is bound to be a poster in concert with their taste.

cal posters combine the best of the audio and graphic arts. The harmony achieved by these two art s produces decorative images in tune with contemporary lifestyles.

e a good look at one of today's most successful images, Piano & Red Roses *by Jim DeVault. Why are those roses on the piano and who do they belong to? Were they put there in anticipation of someone's arrival ft there in a hasty retreat? The evocativeness of this poster and its simple, strong graphic design make piece with terrific impact.*

is poster DeVault says: "There was a story to be told in a strong graphic sense. The cleanness of the gn is the perfect juxtaposition to the air of mystery the roses present. The roses are much more lyrical than the piano whose clean, hard edge provides just the right visual balance."

with Piano & Red Roses, *musical imagery often provides a foundation for artists to build upon.* Lady and *for example, may allude to music, but it is certainly a "sexy" image as well.*

ical images in outdoor settings are a winning combination employed by many of the Batista-Moon ers. For example, Monterey Jazz '80 *sets a trumpet in the sunset-reflecting tide's edge. So, let your gination run wild. You are walking along the water's edge with the surf lapping at your feet, listening to favorite music...*

y of these posters immortalize important musical events. Been to the Bach Festival? What better inder of that transitory experience than a commemorative poster on the wall.

is hot and some of these posters are screaming that message. High contrast, hot colors, sharp edges clean lines broadcast this message while complimenting contemporary decor.

ic is a part of our daily life. Our musical tastes are translated into the visual through the medium of ers. No matter how one plays it, these posters are a hit.

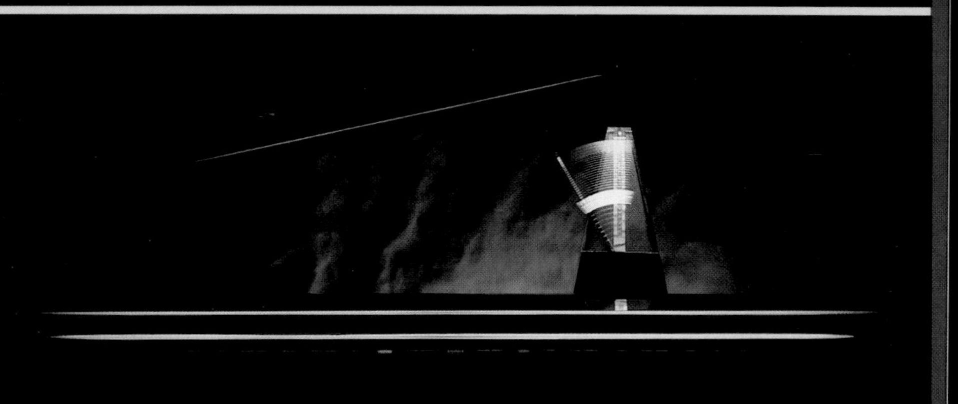

G79 GROSJEAN COLOR KEYS 24 × 30

Joseph Chiu Helico Graphics Art Expo N.Y. '83
Rhapsody in Blue

SUZANNE NYERGES & DANA JONES STUDIOS
1983 SANTA BARBARA JAZZ FESTIVAL
NOVEMBER 18 · 19 · 20

J30 JONES / NYGERES TWO CYMBALS 18 × 24

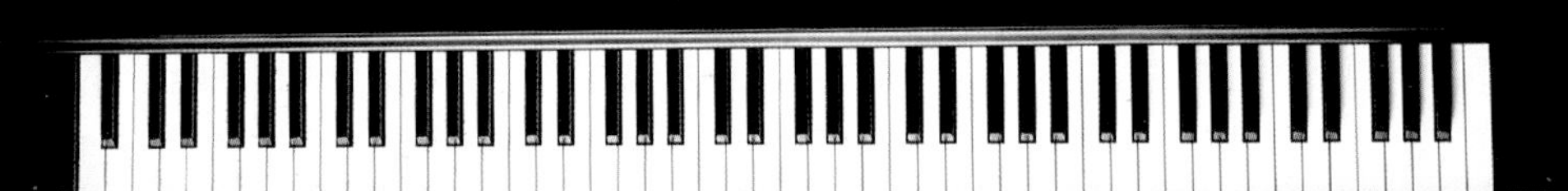

D65 DeVAULT PIANO & RED ROSES ☆ $23^{3}/_{4} \times 39$

R71 RESNIC GALA NO. 1 *LITHOGRAPH* 20 × 38 3/8

H110 HESSEL COMPOSER'S DREAM 23 7/8 × 33

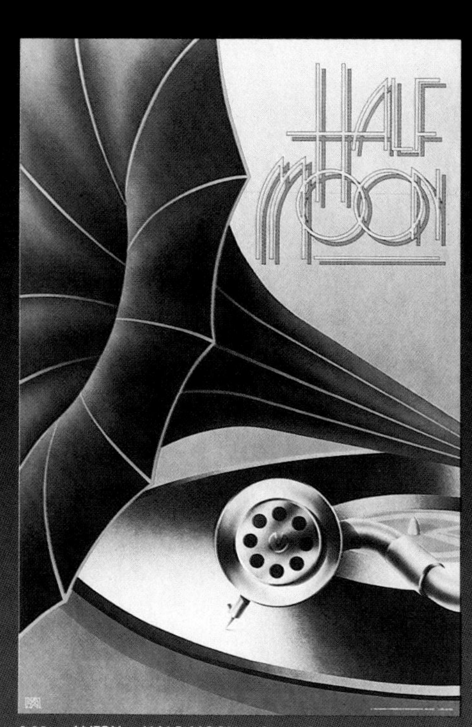
HALF
MOON

A41 AVERY HALF MOON 36 × 24

Classical Art

36 × 12

S164 SHICK CLASSICAL ART

Z5 ZASLOW INSPIRATION ON IVORY 23 × 29

Francine Zaslow / INSPIRATION ON IVORY

T41 TURNER BRASS 38 × 24

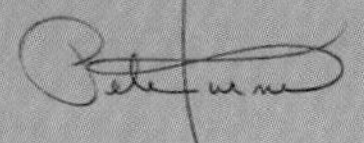

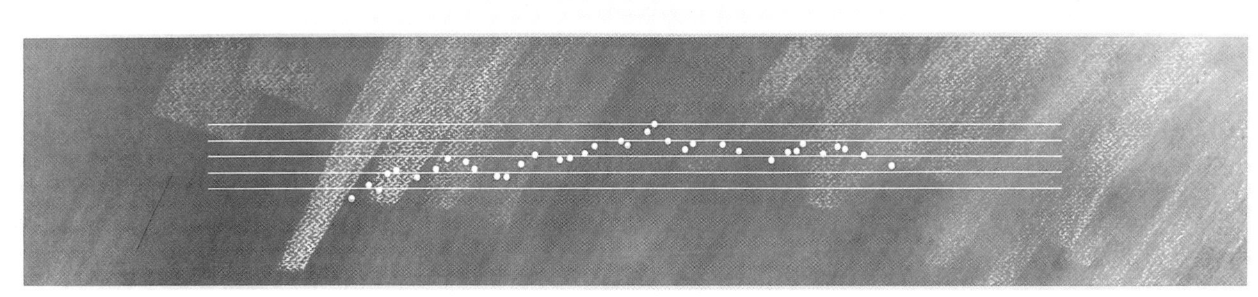
Palo Alto Chamber Orchestra / 17 Seasons
Whitson, Conductor

S97 SMIDT PALO ALTO CHAMBER MUSIC 12 × 38

M100 MYER FRENCH HORN 33 × 24

E R I C M Y E R
MUSIC CENTER OF LOS ANGELES COUNTY

ROSE, WOOD
&
SILK

Interlude

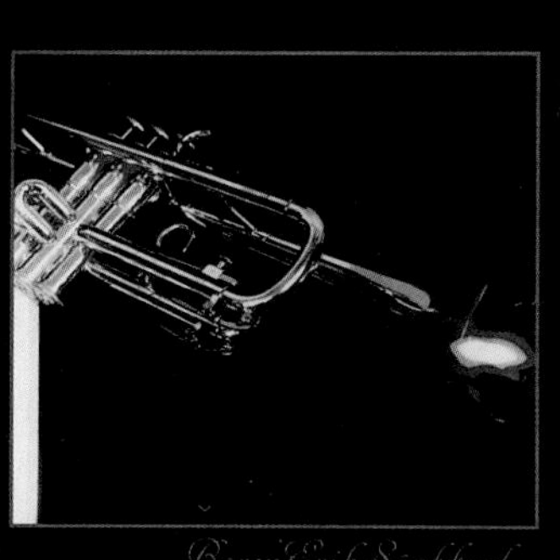
Baron Erik Spafford

S151 SPAFFORD INTERLUDE 12 × 36

L58 LEEDS SONATA $28^1/_4 \times 22^3/_8$

L55 LEEDS SERENADE $23^3/_8 \times 28^1/_2$

Sonata/KAREN LEEDS

Serenade/KAREN LEEDS

ROSNICK

R52 ROSNICK ROSNICK'S MUSIC 21 × 36

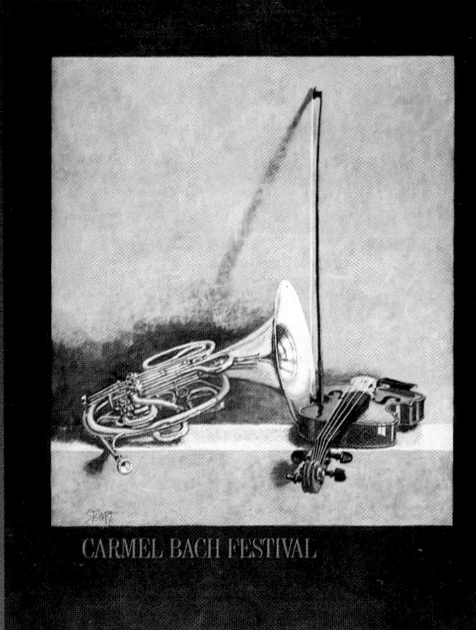
CARMEL BACH FESTIVAL

S72 STEWART BACH FESTIVAL 27 × 22

E32 VIOLIN $25^1/_2 \times 37^1/_2$

HARVEY EDWARDS
LIMITED EDITIONS
GOLDMAN ART
LOS ANGELES, CA.

HARVEY EDWARDS
NEW YORK PHILHARMONIC
AVERY FISHER HALL, LINCOLN CENTER

E64 LE STRAD 35 × 27

HARVEY EDWARDS
PRINT COLLECTORS GALLERY

E42 CELLO $39^3/_8 \times 25^3/_8$

HARVEY EDWARDS
JOEL MEISNER GALLERY
APR. 3 - APR. 30, 1982

E31 FRENCH HORN $25^{5}/_{8} \times 37^{1}/_{4}$

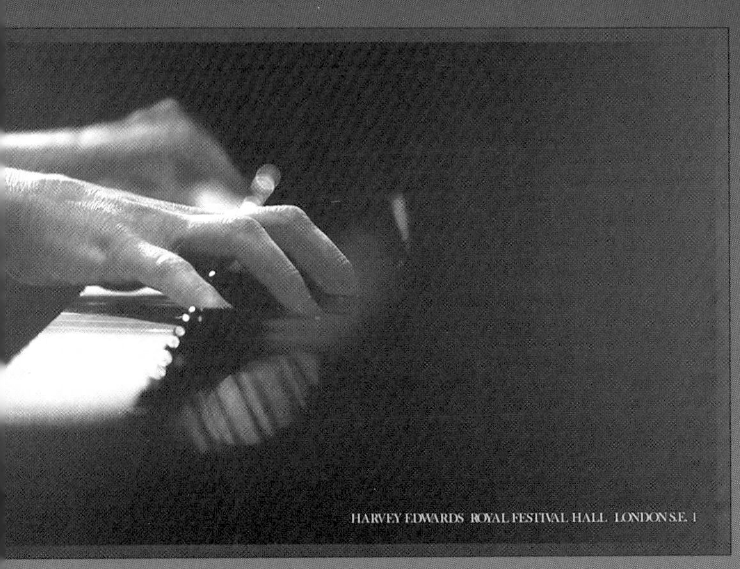
HARVEY EDWARDS ROYAL FESTIVAL HALL LONDON S.E. 1

E33 PIANO $25^{1}/_{2} \times 38^{1}/_{4}$

J A

S136 SHICK JAZZ QUARTET 36 × 24

S137 SHICK HOT SESSIONS 24 × 36

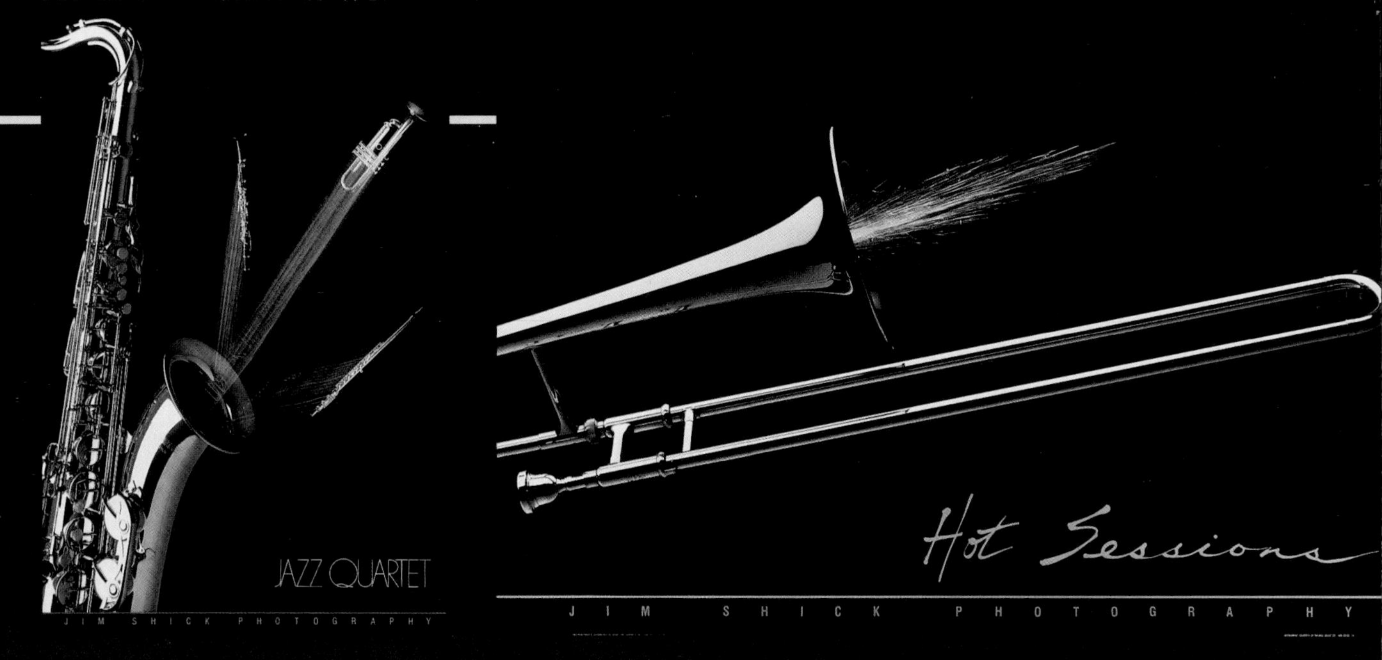

JAZZ QUARTET
JIM SHICK PHOTOGRAPHY
Hot Sessions
JIM SHICK PHOTOGRAPHY

JAZZ FUSION

R48 ROTH JAZZ FUSION $25\frac{5}{8} \times 19\frac{1}{2}$

S110 SPAFFORD JAZZ 34 × 25

D96 DAHLSTROM MT. HOOD JAZZ 28 × 32

1983 MT. HOOD FESTIVAL OF
JAZZ

C66 COIT JAZZ IN THE 80'S 24 × 20

JAZZ
IN THE 80'S

MT HOOD FESTIVAL OF
JAZZ 82

Duke Ellington/The Music Lives On/1899-1974

S175 SHERMAN DUKE ELLINGTON *SERIGRAPH* 20³/₄ × 28

F43 FORSTER MT. HOOD FESTIVAL OF JAZZ 27⁷/₈ × 22

S156 SHICK HOT JAZZ TRUMPET 16 × 33

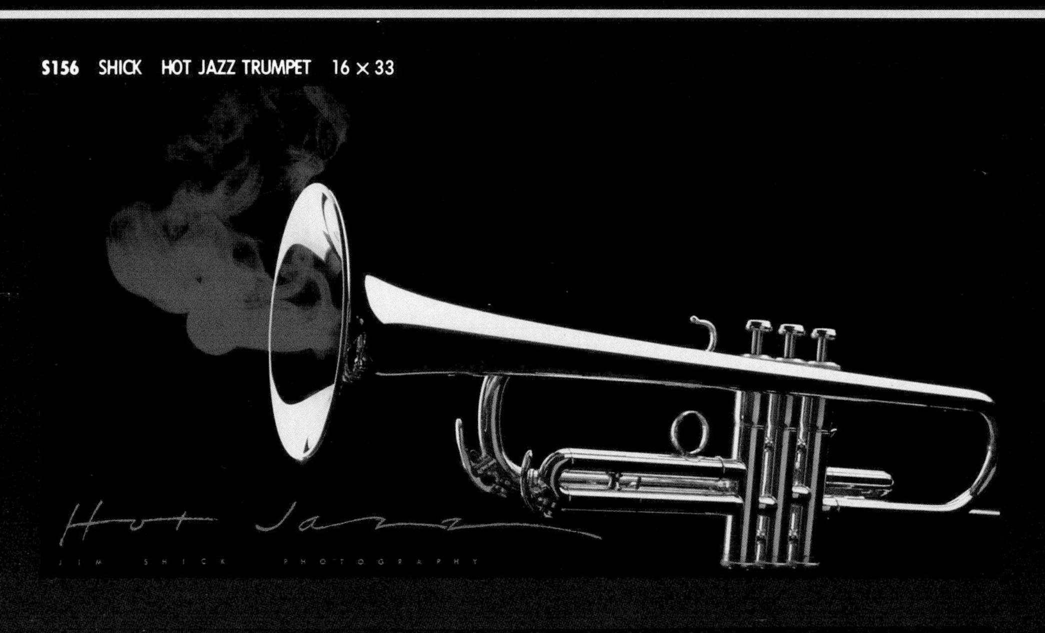
Hot Jazz
JIM SHICK PHOTOGRAPHY

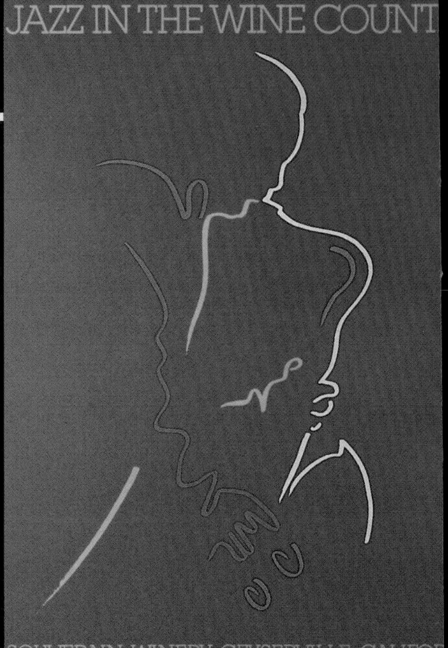
JAZZ IN THE WINE COUNT
SOUVERAIN WINERY, GEYSERVILLE, CALIFOR
AUGUST 14, 1982, 4-8 P.M. IN ASSOCIATION WITH

Hot Jazz
ED MASTERSON · PHOTOGRAPHY

M81 MASTERSON HOT JAZZ 16 × 33

HEART AND SOUL

P112 PATERSON MY HEART BELONGS TO ESTHER 32 ×

S157 SHICK NIGHT OUT 24 × 20

S158 SHICK SUITE SCENT 24 × 20

SUITE
SCENT

S159 SHICK ASHLEY 28 × 22

IRA
the words
GEORGE
the music
GERSHWIN
A SPECIAL EXHIBITION MAY 6 THROUGH SEPTEMBER 2, 1968
MUSEUM OF THE CITY OF NEW YORK
FIFTH AVENUE, 103RD TO 104TH STREET

R68 RIVERS GERSHWIN 37 × 26

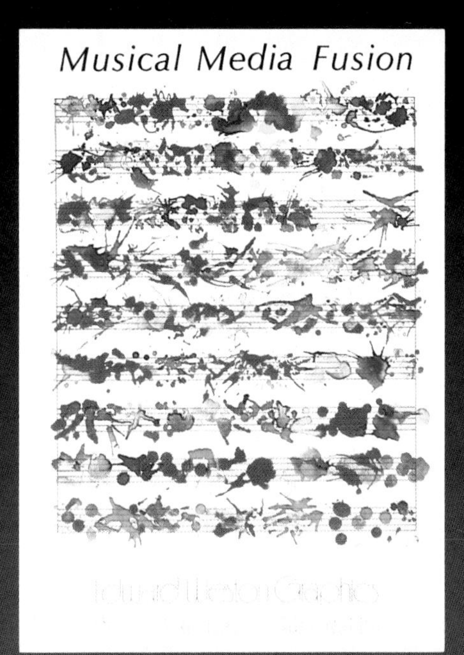
Musical Media Fusion

S8 SPRINGER JAZZ $34^1/_2 \times 22^1/_2$

B159 MONTEREY WINE & FOOD FEST. '84 28 × 20

FESTIVAL OF
MONTEREY COUNTY
Wine & Food
MONTEREY COUNTY FAIRGROUNDS
JUNE 9 & 10, 1984

B125 MONTEREY JAZZ 82 28 x 20

MONTEREY
FESTIVAL · 1982
SEPTEMBER 17·18·19 · 25TH ANNIVERSARY

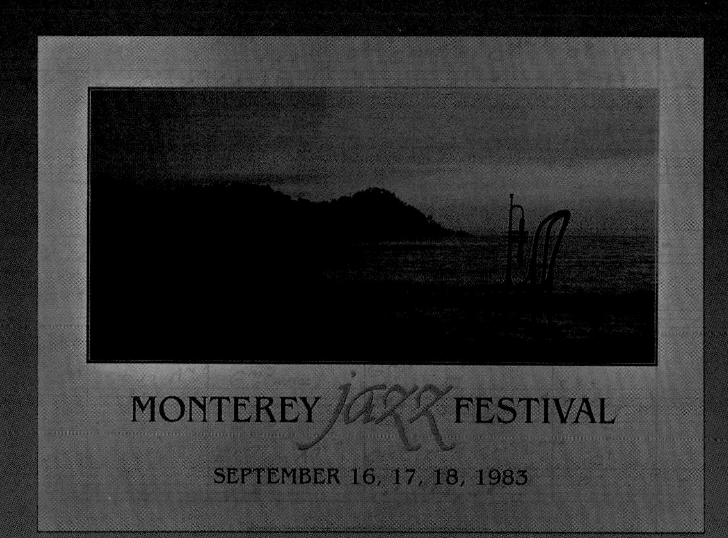
MONTEREY jazz FESTIVAL
SEPTEMBER 16, 17, 18, 1983

B131 MONTEREY JAZZ 83 23 x 32

MONTEREY
FESTIVAL 1981
SEPTEMBER 18, 19, 20

B126 MONTEREY JAZZ 81 29 3/4 x 19 3/4

POSTERS BY
BATISTA-MOON STUDIO
MONTEREY, CALIFORNIA

MONTEREY JAZZ FESTIVAL
SEPTEMBER 19-20-21
1 9 8 0

B123 MONTEREY JAZZ 80 $24^3/_8$ x 19

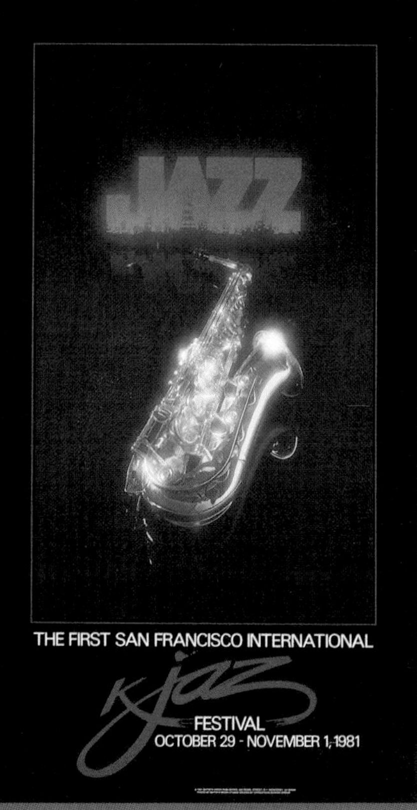
JAZZ
THE FIRST SAN FRANCISCO INTERNATIONAL
KJAZ
FESTIVAL
OCTOBER 29 - NOVEMBER 1, 1981

B124 S.F. JAZZ FESTIVAL $24^1/_2$ x 19

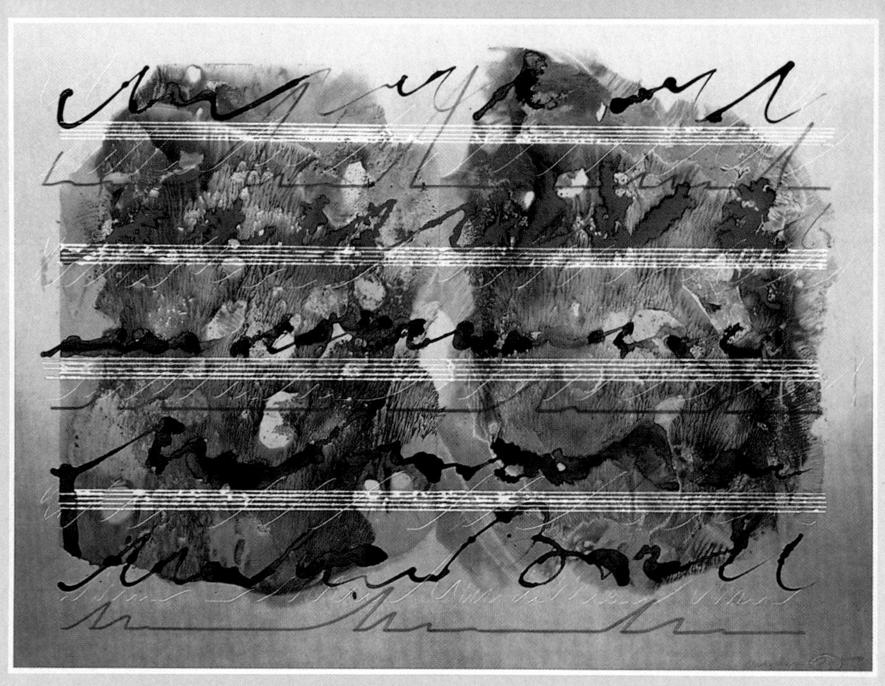
The Musical Series
U Z I L E V S K Y

U15 LINEAR MODE $24^{1}/_{2} \times 28^{1}/_{4}$

V S K Y

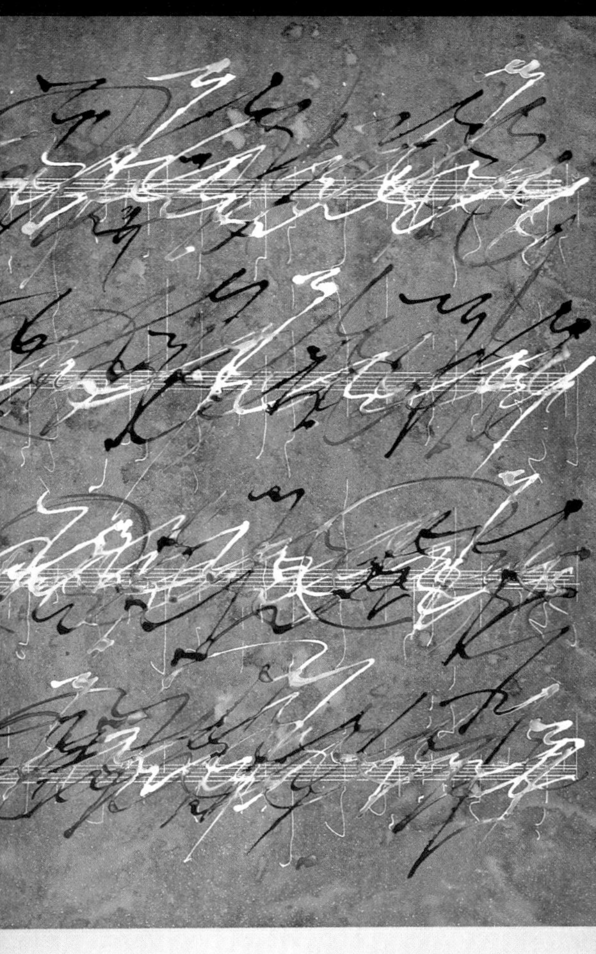
Mill Valley Chamber Music Society

U25 MILL VALLEY CHAMBER MUSIC SOCIETY 39 × 25

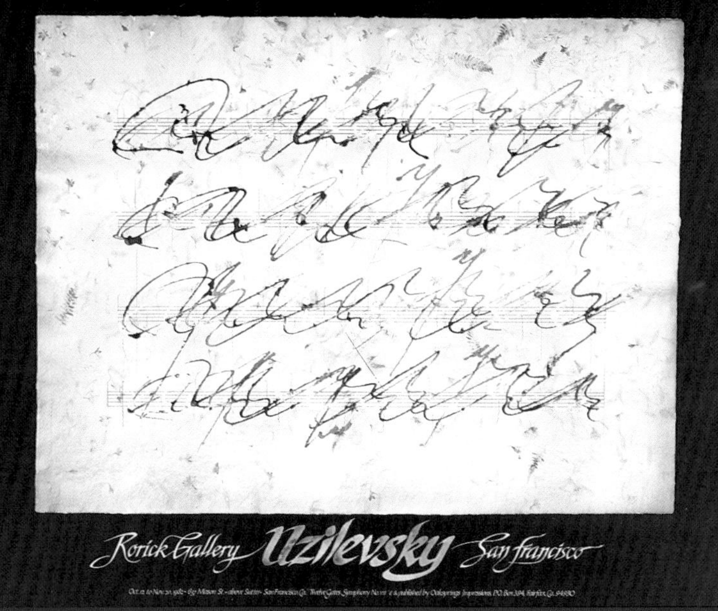
Rorick Gallery Uzilevsky San Francisco

U16 TWELVE GATES 27 × 33 3/8

Rolling Stones
1981 WORLD TOUR

STEVE STEIGMA
THE WEAVER GALLE

THE DOORS · FRIDAY AUGUST 8, 1969 · ELECTRIC CIRCUS · NEW YORK, N.Y.

F61 FRANCIS JIM MORRISON *SERIGRAPH* 17 × 41

A34 ANTEAU 50's MODERNE $24^1/_2 \times 35^7/_8$

W43 WAHLBERG HOT SAX 30×23

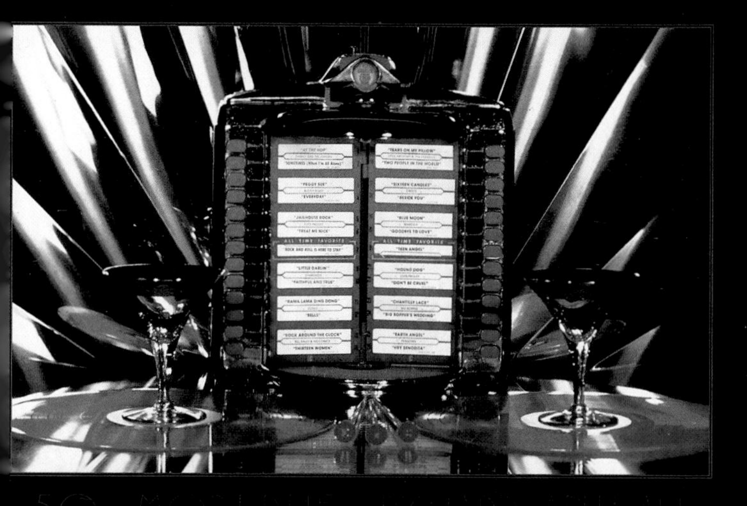

CHRIS WAHLBERG

THE MYTHOLOGICAL MUSIC MACHINE
Erickson

E71 ERICKSON MUSIC MACHINE $30^1/_2 \times 20^3/_4$

S160 SHICK HOT SENSATIONS 28×22

H2 HIROSHIGE BRIDGE 35 × 23

カシオピア画廊
日本木版画広重（一七九六－一八五八）
JAPANESE WOODBLOCK PRINTS HIROSHIGE (1797-1858)
CASSIOPEIA FINE ARTS
219 THOMPSON ST NEW YORK

H3 HIROSHIGE CHERRY BLOSSOMS

35 × 23

カシオピア画廊
日本木版画広重（一七九六－一八五八）
JAPANESE WOODBLOCK PRINTS HIROSHIGE (1797-1858)
CASSIOPEIA FINE ARTS
219 THOMPSON ST NEW YORK

K28 KUNISADA DIPTYCH ☆ 25 × 30

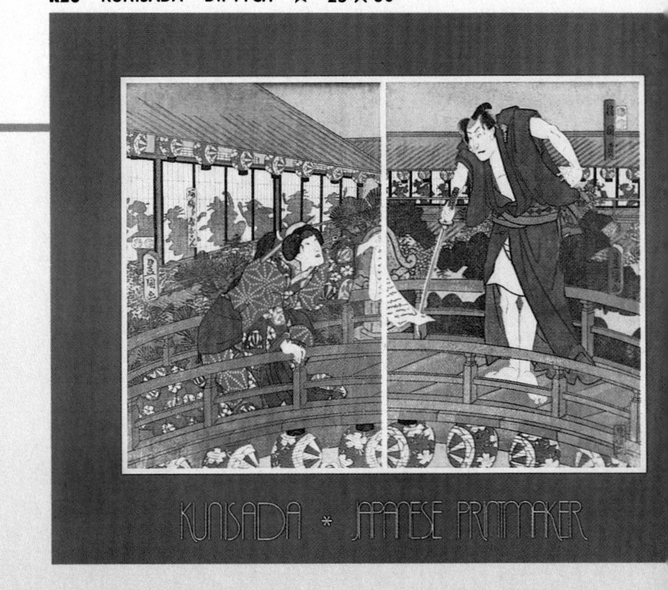
KUNISADA * JAPANESE PRINTMAKER

35 × 23

カシオピア画廊
日本木版画広重（一七九六－一八五八）
JAPANESE WOODBLOCK PRINTS HIROSHIGE (1797-1858)
CASSIOPEIA FINE ARTS
219 THOMPSON ST NEW YORK

H11 HIROSHIGE RAINBOW BRIDGE

カシオピア画廊
日本木版画祥邨（一八七七－一九四五）
JAPANESE WOODBLOCK PRINTS O. KOSON (1877-1945)
CASSIOPEIA FINE ARTS
219 THOMPSON ST NEW YORK

K21 KOSON IRIS 35 × 23

EISEN
PRINTMAKER

E27 EISEN PRINTMAKER ☆ 33 × 22

N T A L

ɔer since Marco Polo made his way to the Orient, western civilization has been intrigued by the ɱysteries of the culture he discovered there. Today, this fascination with eastern civilization continues is manifested as much in the popularity of oriental posters as in the proliferation of sushi bars.

imagery of these posters derives from an ancient art form that has much to say about oriental culture. se are artists whose innate sense of style and love of beauty was, and still is, encouraged by the society hich they worked.

Japanese clothing designers who are taking today's fashion world by storm have the cultural heritage ese artists behind them. Their understanding of the use of color and form is their legacy from the artists created the images on these posters.

EIZAN
COURTISAN HANAOGI, FROM THE HOUSE OF OGIYA, AND HER TWO ATTENDANTS c.1830

E13 EIZAN COURTESAN HANAOGI ☆ 33 × 24

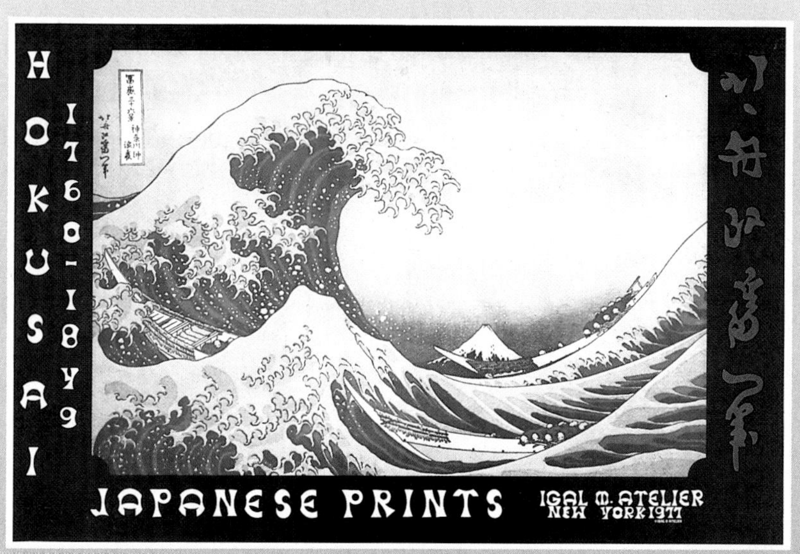
HOKUSAI
1760-1849
JAPANESE PRINTS
IGAL M. ATELIER
NEW YORK 1977

H5 HOKUSAI GREAT WAVE $23^1/_8 \times 35^1/_4$

K37 KIYOCHINKA JAPANESE PRINTS $24^1/_8 \times 38^1/_2$

Japanese Prints Greengrass Gallery in Macy's Cellar

$38^1/_2 \times 25^7/_8$

the tikotin museum of japanese art 89 hanassi ave. haifa israel open: sunday–thursday 10–13, 16–19 saturday 10–14

K2 KAIGETSUDO A COURTESAN

$27^1/_2 \times 18$

The Pins Collection, Jerusalem.
Chinese and Japanese Paintings and Prints.

U11 UTAGAWA BEAUTY OF YOSHIWARA

THE TIKOTIN MUSEUM OF JAPANESE ART
89 HANASSI AVE. HAIFA open: Sun.-Thu. 10-13, 16-19 Sat. 1

U10 UTAMARO TWO WOMEN $28^1/_4 \times 18^1/_2$

K9 KUNITERU TRIPTYCH ☆ 24 × 38

KUNITERU * JAPANESE PRINTMAKER * cica 1848

Galerie El-baz 222 avenue rd toronto 137 thompson st new york

G25 GEISHA WOMAN 37 × 24 1/4

the tikotin museum of japanese art 89 hanassi ave. haifa israel beautiful women · ukiyoe · bijin ga spring 1982

מוזיאון טיקוטין לאמנות יפנית שדרות הנשיא 89, חיפה דיוקן האשה באמנות היפנית אביב 1982

U13 UTAMARO BEAUTIFUL WOMAN 37 1/4 × 26 3/4

מוזיאון טיקוטין לאמנות יפנית
שדרות הנשיא 89, חיפה
פתוח: ימים ראשון-חמישי
14-10 שבת 19-16,13-10
THE TIKOTIN MUSEUM
OF JAPANESE ART
89 HANASSI AVE. HAIFA
SUN.–THU. 10-13,16-19
SAT. 10-14

32 1/8 × 21 7/8

U2 UTAMARO GEISHA & ATTENDANT

T3 TERAOKA FRENCH VANILLA 18 × 56 1/4

MASAMI TERAOKA
Whitney Museum of American Art, New York
October 24, 1979-January 6, 1980

PEASANT PAINTINGS FROM HUHSIEN COUNTY
ART EXPO NEW YORK COLISEUM

D21 DONG ZHEN GYI GOLD LILY 21 7/8 × 34 1/2

KUNISADA · CHERRY BLOSSOMS

40 1/4 × 26 1/4

K23 KUNISADA CHERRY BLOSSM SAMURAI ☆

KUNISADA · CHERRY BLOSSC

K24 KUNISADA CHERRY BLOSSOM GEISHA ☆

K12 KNIGIN REFLECTION ☆ 26 × 18

K13 KNIGIN PROFOUND LOVE ☆ 26 × 18

MICHAEL KNIGIN
UTAMARO SUITE

SHUBERT
THEATRE
MICHAEL KNIGIN
UTAMARO SUITE

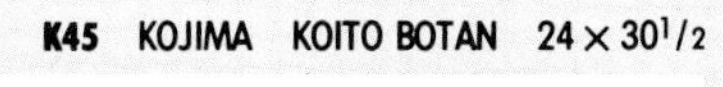

K45 KOJIMA KOITO BOTAN $24 \times 30^{1}/_{2}$

KIMIKO KOJIMA

OTSUKA
NEW YORK ART EXPO

039 OTSUKA THE KISS $36 \times 24^{1}/_{4}$

OTSUKA

017 OTSUKA DANCE OF THE 12 KIMONOS 22 × 28

P4 PANG LANDSCAPE FLORAL $31^{1}/_{2} \times 23$

Pang
Guild Gallery
New York
April, 1980

P29 PANG ART EXPO CAL. 24×36

PANG

Artexpo CAL

PRINTS
'80
LOS
ANGELES
CALIFORNIA
FEBRUARY
7 - 10
1980
pang

P5 PANG VERTICAL $37^{3}/_{4} \times 22^{1}/_{4}$

Pang WASH ART '79
MAY 2-7, 1979-12 TO 9P
DC NATIONAL ARMO

P1 PANG WASH. ART '79 25×29

G57 GATEWOOD BLACK KIMONO ☆ *OFFSET WITH FOIL STAMPING* 36 1/4 × 24 3/4

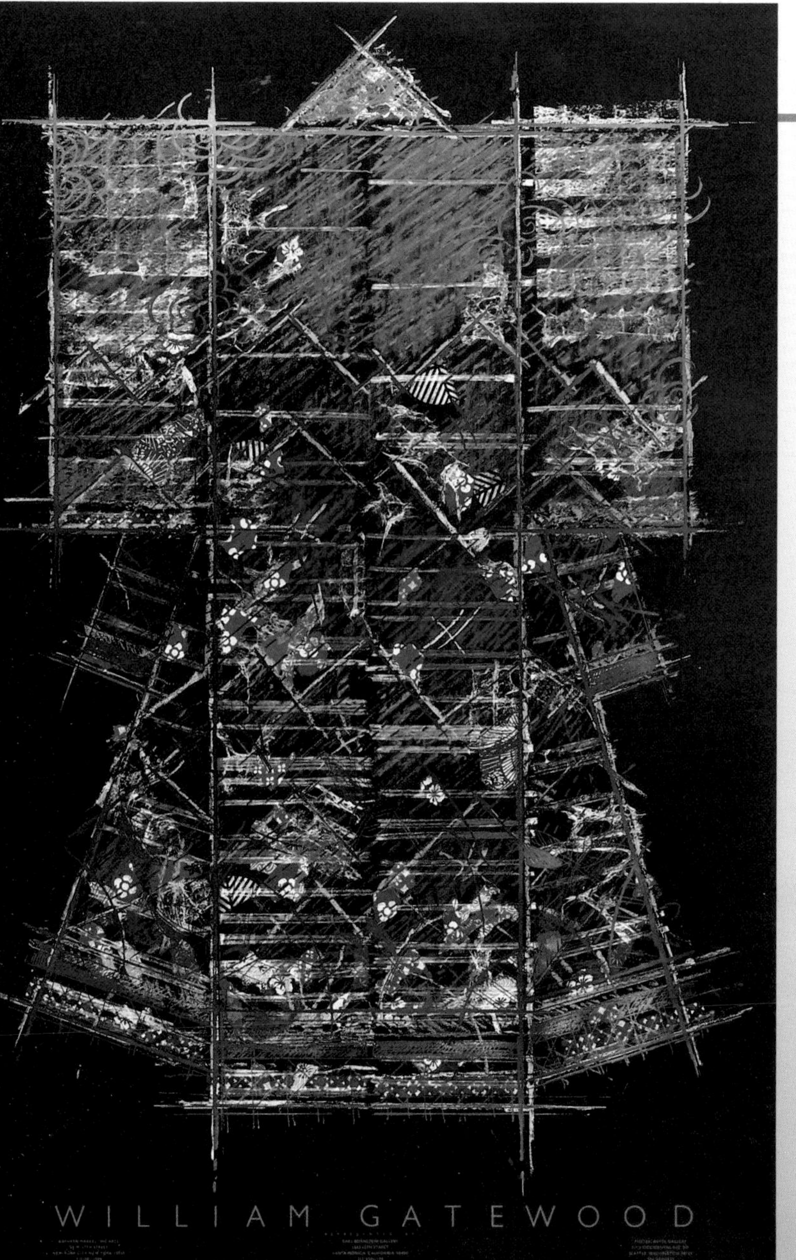
WILLIAM GATEWOOD

G106 GOODE JAPANESE SUITE 24 × 24

JAPANESE SUITE / FREDERICK GOODE / OCTOBER 28 THRU NOVEMBER 18 1981 / SUBRA GALLERY, LTD. / SEATTLE

A N T O N I O
Antonio Peticov / Published and Distributed by Bruce McGaw Graphics, Inc., New York,

P75A THE TABLE "A" ☆ 24 × 38

Antonio Pericov / Published and Distributed by Bruce McGaw Graphics, Inc., New York, New York

P75B **THE TABLE "B"** ☆ **24 × 38**

Intuition plays an essential role in my art. It is very important to have some technique, good information and the best tools available to help an artist. I often portray my brushes, paint pots, hammer, easel, as my personal helpers, trying to unveil their inner life. But intuition alone tells me where to go."

P113 NATURA II ☆ 26 × 29

ANTÔNIO PETICOV
NATURA II
©1984 ANTÔNIO PETICOV · PUBLISHED & DISTRIBUTED BY BRUCE MCGAW GRAPHICS INC., NEW YORK & JUDITH L. POSNER & ASSOCIATES, MILWAUKEE

GALERIA GB ARTE · RIO DE JANEIRO · ABRIL 1984 · DESENH

LABYRINTH

ANTONIO PETICOV

P126 LABYRINTH $23^1/_2 \times 29^1/_2$

N I G H T   F A L L

P E T I C O V

P124 LIGHT RINGS ☆ 35 × 25

P E T

ANTÔNIO PETICOV
THE WINDOW
© 1982 ANTONIO PETICOV PUBLISHED & DISTRIBUTED BY BRUCE MCGAW GRAPHICS, INC. & JUDITH POSNER & ASSOCIATES

P42 THE WINDOW ☆ 32 × 25

ANTÔNIO PETICOV
THE WINDOW II

P74 THE WINDOW II ☆ $31^{3}/_{4} \times 25$

PETICOV

P64 INTUITION ☆ $30\frac{1}{2} \times 24$

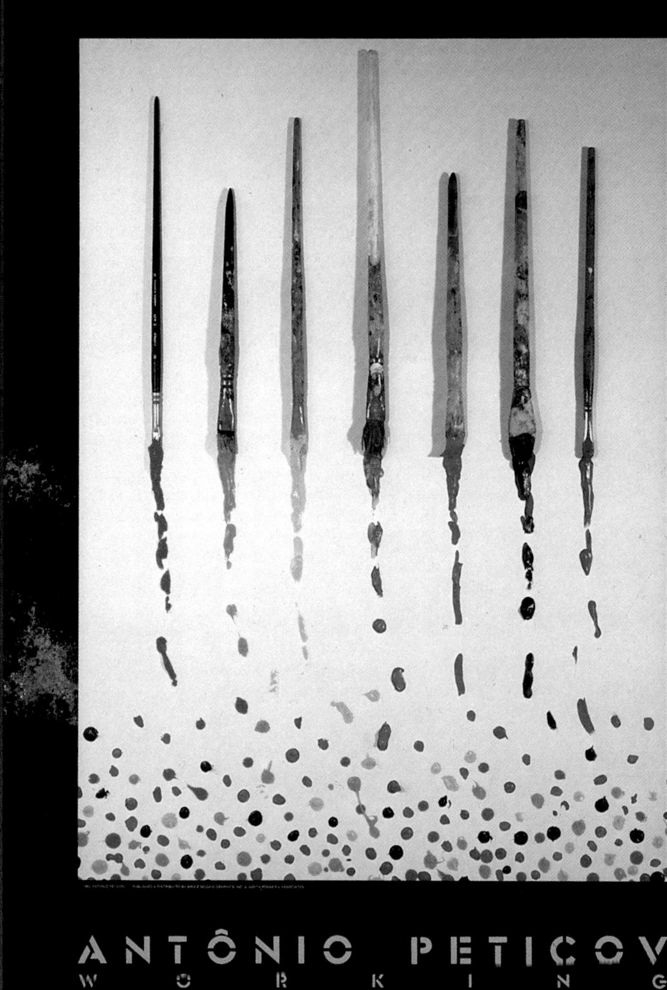
ANTÔNIO PETICOV
WORKING

A N T Ô N I O P E T I C O V
NATURA · WOOD, CERAMIC & NEON SCULPTURE · FRED DORFMAN, INC., NEW YORK

THE LADDER
ANTONIO PETICOV
ANTONIO PETICOV / PUBLISHED & DISTRIBUTED BY BRUCE MCGAW GRAPHICS, INC. AND JUDITH L. POSNER ASSOCIATES

P100 THE LADDER ∴ 39 × 24

P · E · T · I · C · O · V
S · P · R · I · N · G   L · I · G · H · T

S O U L F O O D

H91 HUIBREGTSE SOUL FOOD ☆ 24×18

JAY BRENNER
JAY BRENNER STUDIO • 18 EAST 17TH STREET, NEW YORK, NEW YORK 10003 • 212-741-2244 • REPRESENTED BY DAVID GOLDMAN •

B103 BRENNER CORPORATE SNACK ☆ 24 3/8 × 18 3/8

Before photography became such a popular avocation, people dismissed fine photographs believing it was a matter of luck that they too could have achieved had they been in the right spot," says ntographer Paul Hoffman. "Now that everyone takes pictures they realize how hard it is to get a really ıd photograph. The hand of the maker is so much on it when it's been done right."

fman is among a group of photographers whose work is becoming an increasingly important factor in poster industry. "This is an image from my youth," Hoffman adds speaking of his piece Morning Still *:. "It reminds me of my first cross country ramble. Going through Nebraska in 1964 I stopped at a diner. ɔas a fine good morning, and I must have subconsciously recreated that here."*

fman's photograph exemplifies one aspect of the medium's appeal. "It may not really be the truth, but it ms to be what it is," notes Hoffman. "It says to people this can exist—with the right point of view, the rld can be beautiful because here is a picture of it."

ch good photographer brings their own viewpoint to these images. "I try to capture something that ople see all the time, but transform it in such a way that I can express myself," Robert Farber comments. lets people share what my vision is; they are seeing through my eyes.

rber's moody images share a certain evocativeness with Hoffman's work. Both take photography and sh it beyond mere reportage, stretching the medium till it crosses the boundaries of other mediums.

ese artists are working with the same aesthetic criteria as any other visual artist. As Farber notes, "To press yourself with a camera is like expressing yourself with a paint brush, only the technique is ferent."

ented in 1839, photography has become a common medium producing the thousands of images that pear daily in magazines and on television. It is because people are so used to these images that they are le to respond to them so easily and so heartily when they become poster art. Advertising-type otography provides the poster market with some of its strongest images and the people who are sponsible for it are often successful commercial photographers. Farber's photographs, for example, have en used in ads for Revlon and movie posters for Paramount.

classic of the poster industry, Fresh Paint, *was produced by a man who says: "To be successful, a poster ould be memorable and have clarity of idea. Then it will remain in the landscape long after its initial tent." Julius Friedman's fresh, witty images have certainly succeeded in this respect.*

otography is an exciting medium and one which is only now beginning to be fully explored. Using their meras, photographers can create impelling visual images. They can record the tiniest dew drop with ystal clarity or skillfully manipulate their tools to create an altered reality. Applied to posters, these ages are one of the most dynamic aspects of today's fine art poster industry.

nce photography is a medium rather than a subject, photographic posters can be found in nearly every her section of this book. Artists included in the photography section are those who consistently use their meras to capture diversified subject matter.

LAURIE
RUBIN

R72 FLYING FISH ☆ 36 × 24

S H O T W E L L

S181 THE WINDOW ☆ 30 × 24

WHIPPED WHITE/KAREN LEEDS

L53 LEEDS WHIPPED WHITE $24^{1}/_{4} \times 18^{1}/_{4}$

MORNING STILL-LIFE

PHOTOGRAPH / PAUL HOFFMAN

H57 HOFFMAN MORNING STILL LIFE ☆ 30 × 23

J21 JONES TOOTHPICKS $23^{1}/_{8} \times 19^{3}/_{8}$

OOTHPICKS

S149 SHARABURA SUSHI 27×21

sushi!
PHOTOGRAPH BY SHARABURA

HARLES GREER
LPORT EDITIONS · 126 POST STREET · SAN FRANCISCO CALIFORNIA

G24 GREER OREO COOKIE $24 \times 17^{3}/_{8}$

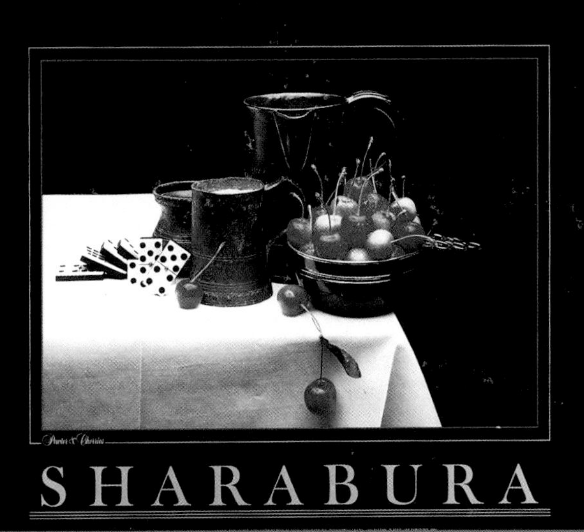
Pewter & Cherries
SHARABURA

S148 SHARABURA PEWTER & CHERRIES $21 \times 25^{1}/_{2}$

C L E

C82 DUSENBERG ☆ 26 × 30

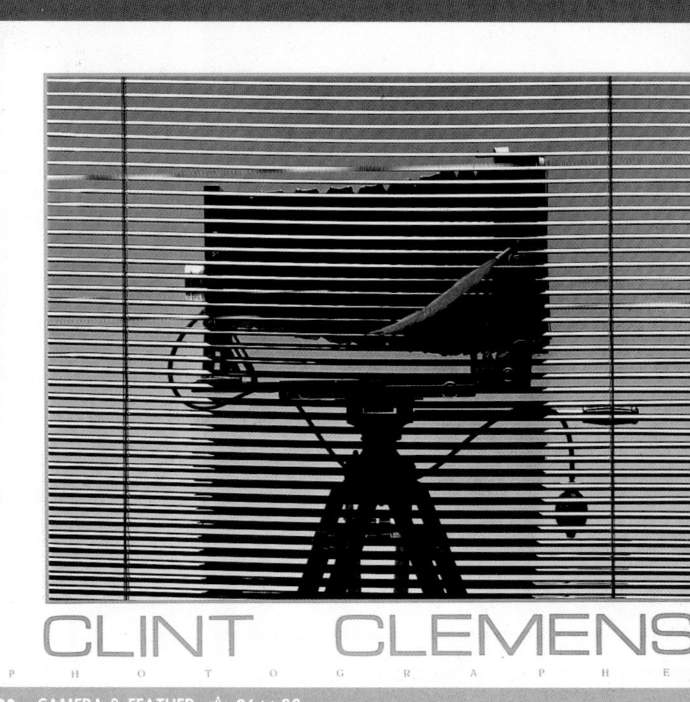
CLINT CLEMENS
PHOTOGRAPHE

C83 CAMERA & FEATHER ☆ 26 × 30

A BARREL OF LAUGHS
LINT CLEMENS

C81 A BARREL OF LAUGHS ☆ 29 × 24

CORINNE COLEN ■ SUMMER DREAMS

C148 COLEN SUMMER DREAMS ☆ 31 × 24

Spaventa

S131 SPAVENTA TULIPS ☆ 34 × 24

C99 CHOU APPLE 18 × 14

C101 CHOU LEMON 18 × 14

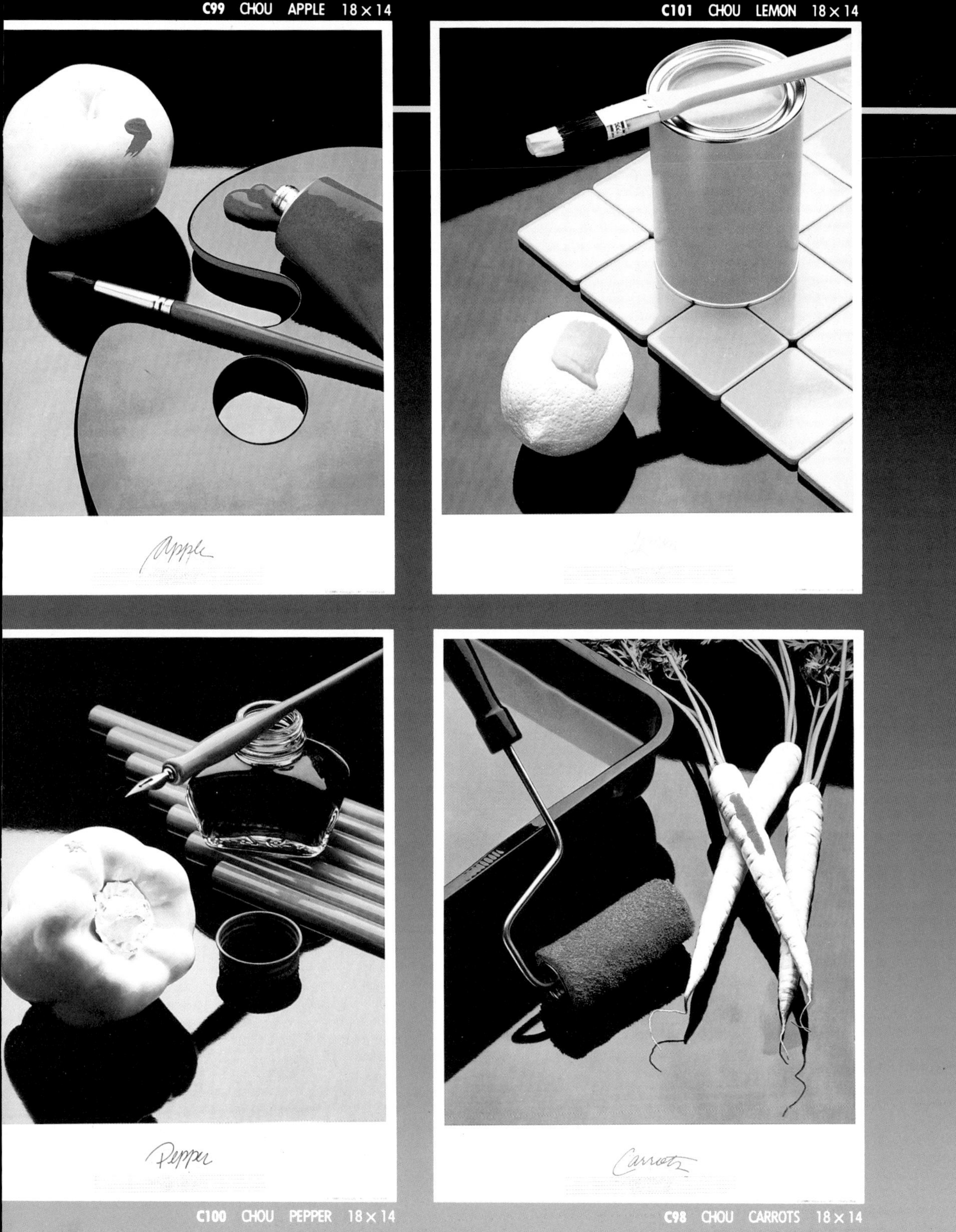
Apple
Pepper
Carrots

C100 CHOU PEPPER 18 × 14

C98 CHOU CARROTS 18 × 14

A35 AMMANN EIGHTBALL 24 1/8 × 27 1/8

EIGHT BALL BY MICHAEL AMMANN FOR ANDERSON LITHOGRAPH COMPANY, LOS ANGELES • SAN FRANCISCO

G93 GILMORE ZIPOLA 24 1/4 × 18 1/4

Zipola

SPRING SONATA BY MICHAEL AMMANN / W.C. PALMS GALLERY, PALM SPRINGS, CALIFORNIA

A44 AMMANN SPRING SONATA 30 × 24

ROSEY

C77 COATES ROSEY 25 × 20 3/4

B160 BRENNER LEMON/RED VISE 27 × 19

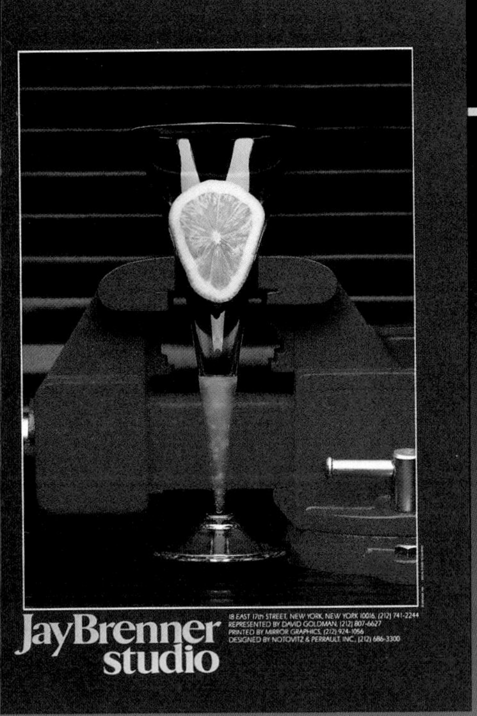
JayBrenner studio
18 EAST 17th STREET, NEW YORK, NEW YORK 10016, (212) 741-2244
REPRESENTED BY DAVID GOLDMAN, (212) 807-6627
PRINTED BY MIRROR GRAPHICS, (212) 924-1056
DESIGNED BY NOTOVITZ & PERRAULT, INC., (212) 686-3300

W40 WATSON ART OF ITALIAN COOKING

THE ART OF ITALIAN COOKING

24 × 18

H72 HOPTMAN WET PAINT 33 × 27 7/8

DAVID HOPTMAN
MUSEUM EDITIONS WEST
LOS ANGELES CALIFORNIA

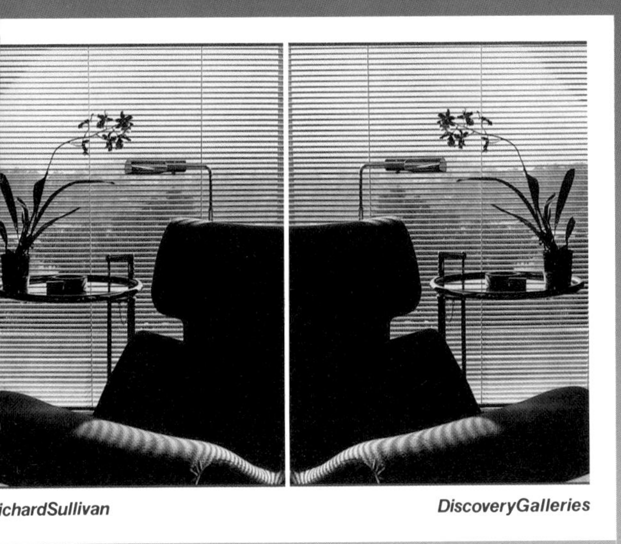
ichardSullivan
DiscoveryGalleries

S92 SULLIVAN HARRY'S CHAIR 26 × 33

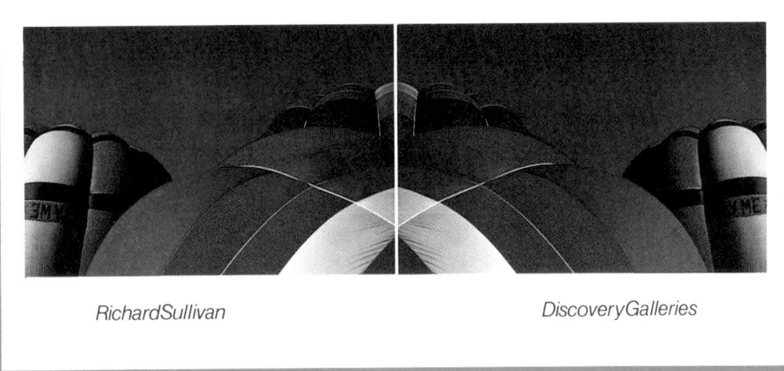
RichardSullivan
DiscoveryGalleries

S91 SULLIVAN FLY ME 18 × 37 7/8

D38 WOODEN SPOON & EGG $25 \times 19^1/_2$

YURI DOJC

D81 EGG II $30 \times 23^1/_2$

Yuri Dojc

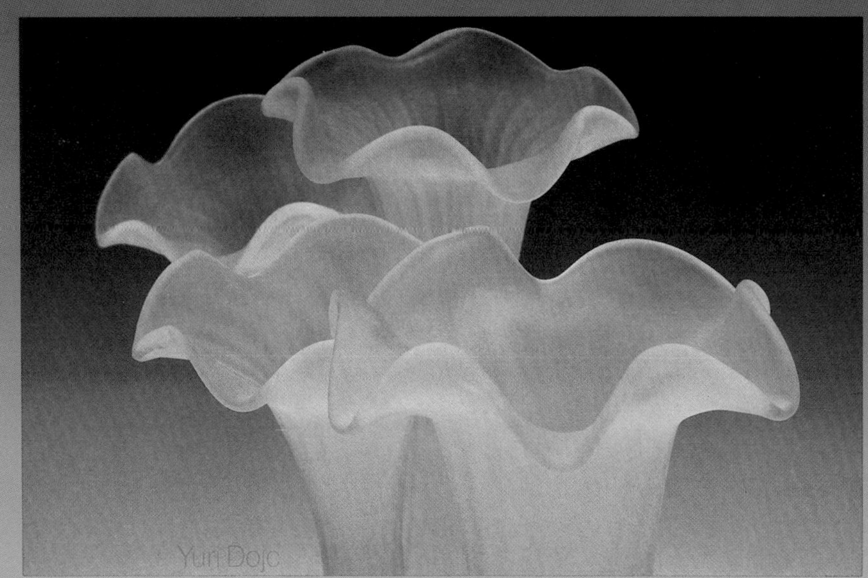
Yuri Dojc

D95 GLASS VASES $24^1/_4 \times 38^1/_2$

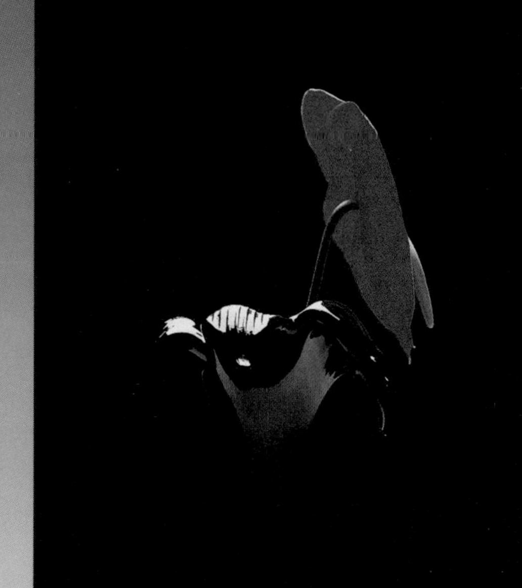

D97 RED & BLACK 30×23

D62 LEGS $26^{3}/_{4} \times 26^{3}/_{4}$

D58 FLORAL 30×22

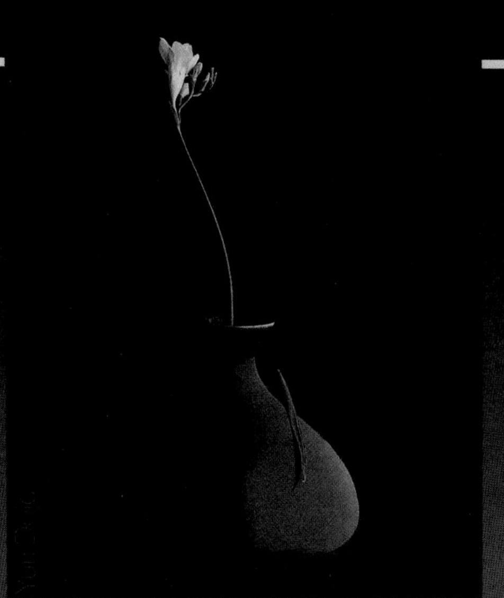

·Y·U·R·I· D·O·J·C·

D80 SILVER DOLLAR $18 \times 33^{1}/_{4}$

Yuri Dojc

D114 TULIP $30^{3}/_{8} \times 20^{5}/_{8}$

Marsh

F83 MARSH $27 \times 19^{1}/_{2}$

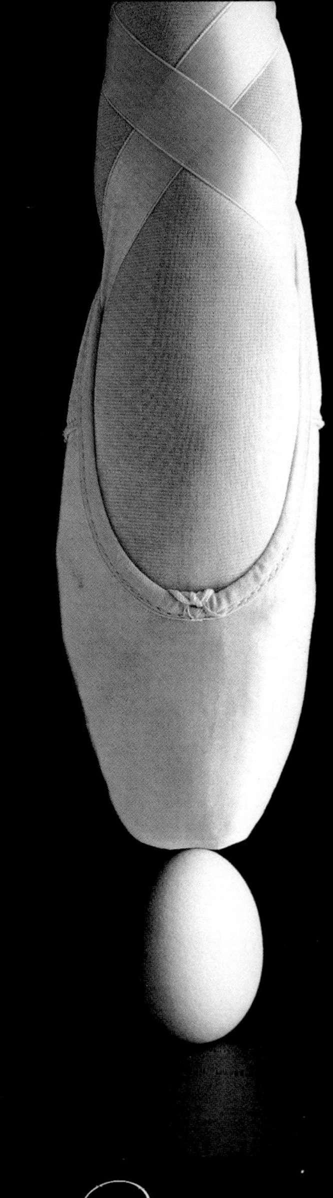

Louisville Ballet

F12 SHOE & EGG $35 \times 21^{3}/_{4}$

F R E S H P A I N T

FINE TUNING

F40 FINE TUNING $20 \times 27^7/8$

F9 FRESH PAINT 24×18

F87 RUN FOR THE ARTS 35 7/8 × 24

F84 COLORIFIC 27 × 19 1/2

Run for the arts.

COLO

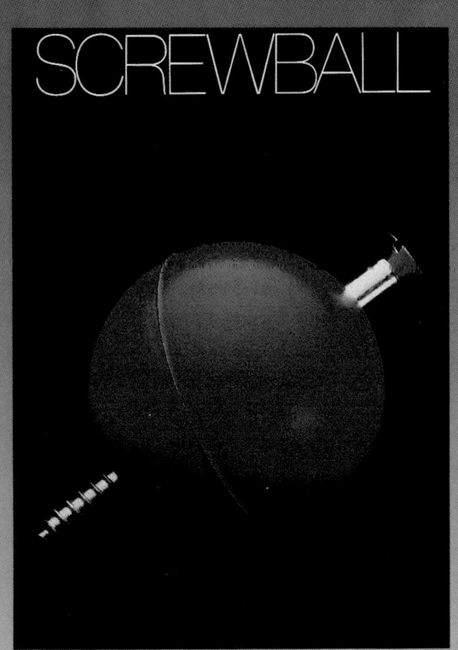
SCREWBALL

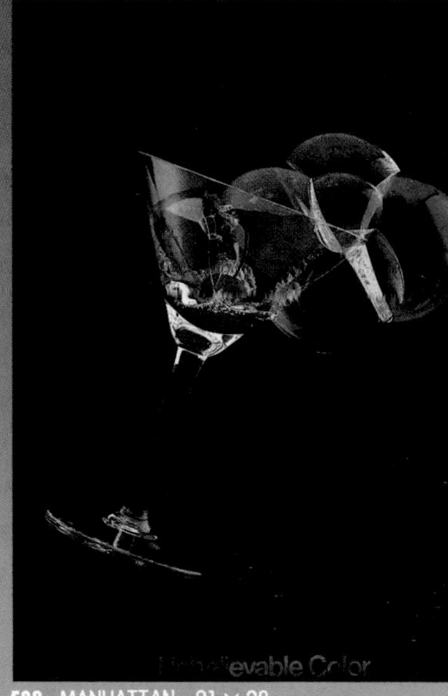

F88 MANHATTAN 21 × 28

F42 SCREWBALL 27 × 19 1/2

F39 UNBELIEVABLE APPLE 30 × 21

Unbelievable Color

Unbelievable Color

F24 UNBELIEVABLE COLOR $33^{1}/_{2} \times 22^{3}/_{4}$

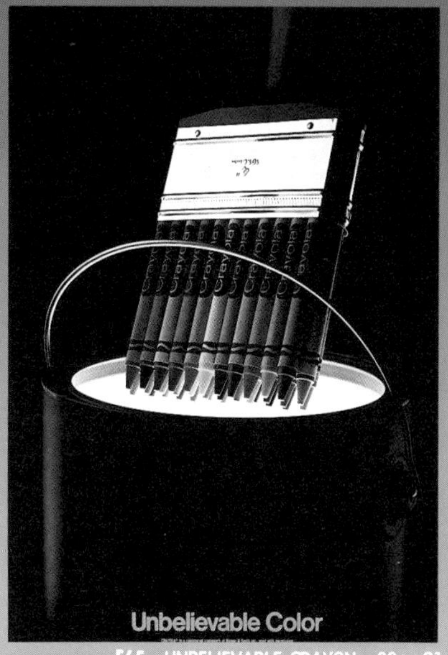
Unbelievable Color

F65 UNBELIEVABLE CRAYON 30 × 21

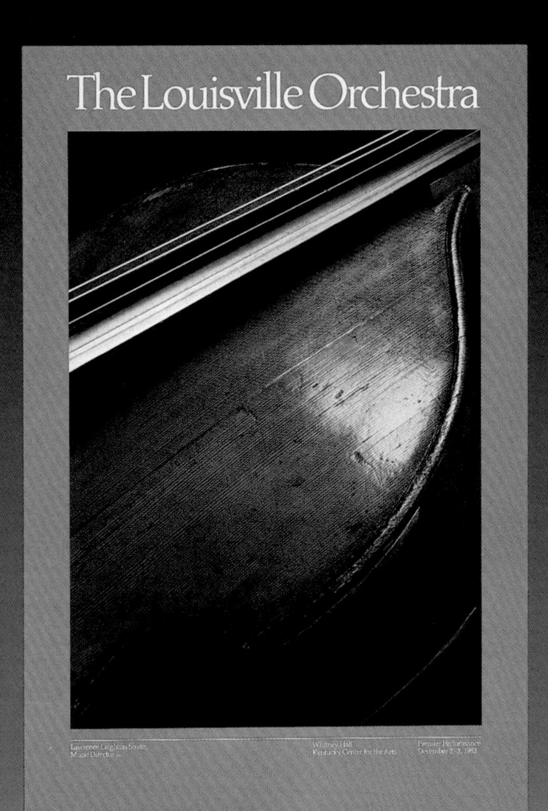
The Louisville Orchestra
Lawrence Leighton Smith,
Music Director
Whitney Hall
Kentucky Center for the Arts
Premier Performance
December 2-3, 1983

F75 THE LOUISVILLE ORCHESTRA 36 × 24

The Louisville Orchestra
Music Director

F68 MUSICAL TREAT 29 × 22 3/4

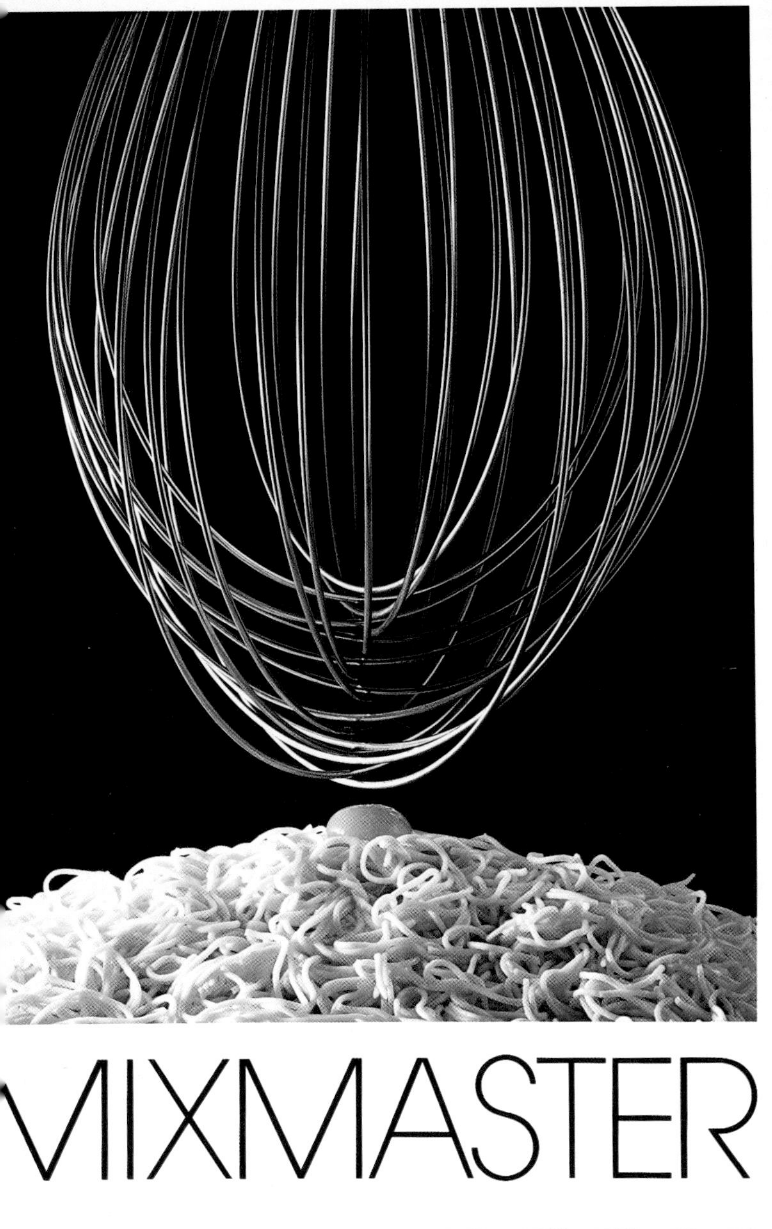
MIXMASTER

F82 MIXMASTER 36 × 24

Martha White Gallery The Real & The Unreal

F17 APPLES 30 × 23

F60 AMISH QUILTS 36 × 24

AmishQuilts

F38 PRESERVATION 36 × 24

Preservation: An eye for detail.

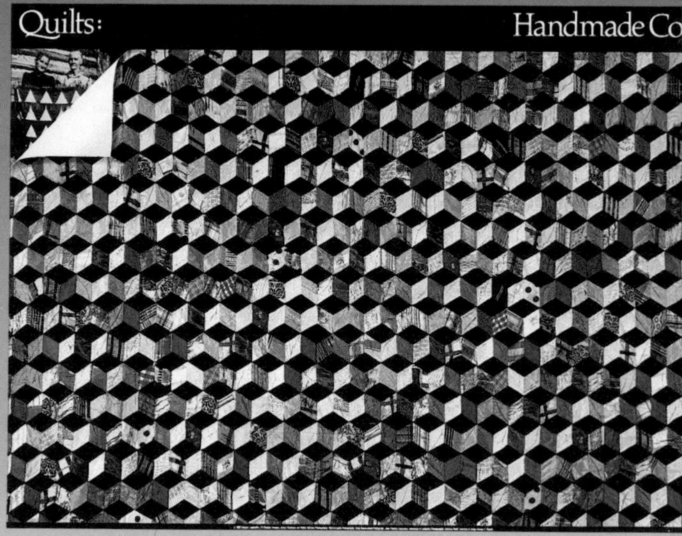
Quilts:
Handmade Co

F41 HANDMADE COLOR 23 × 32

F28 DERBY FESTIVAL $36 \times 23\frac{1}{2}$

Kentucky
Derby Festival
1982

F19 WATER I 36×24

WATER I
ART CENTER ASSOCIATION

he American Weigh

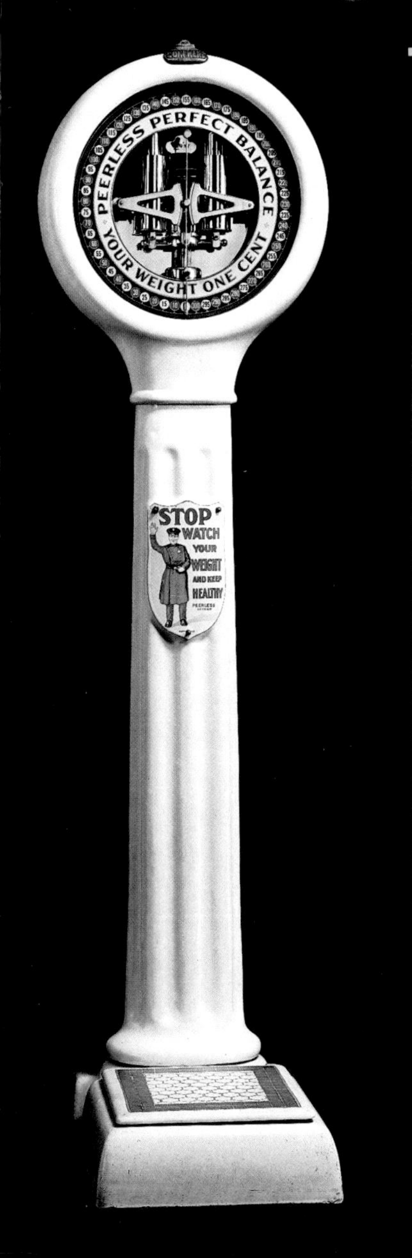
PEERLESS PERFECT BALANCE
YOUR WEIGHT ONE CENT
STOP
WATCH
YOUR
WEIGHT
AND KEEP
HEALTHY

F85 THE AMERICAN WEIGH $47\frac{7}{8} \times 16\frac{7}{8}$

sixth avenue

F74 SIXTH AVENUE $19\frac{1}{2} \times 27$

C L O U G H
©1983 Terry Clough Studio/Published and Distributed by Bruce McGaw Graphics, Inc., New York, New York

C124 VIOLETS & LACE ☆ 24 × 27

C T L E O R U R G Y H

C123 EGGCENTRIC ☆ 26 × 28 1/2

JAMES RANDKLEV
PUBLISHED BY MIRAGE EDITIONS / PRINTED BY GORE GRAPHICS

JAMES RANDKLEV
PUBLISHED BY MIRAGE EDITIONS / PRINTED BY GORE GRAPHICS

R28 RANDKLEV POOL OF LEAVES/GREY 27 × 34½

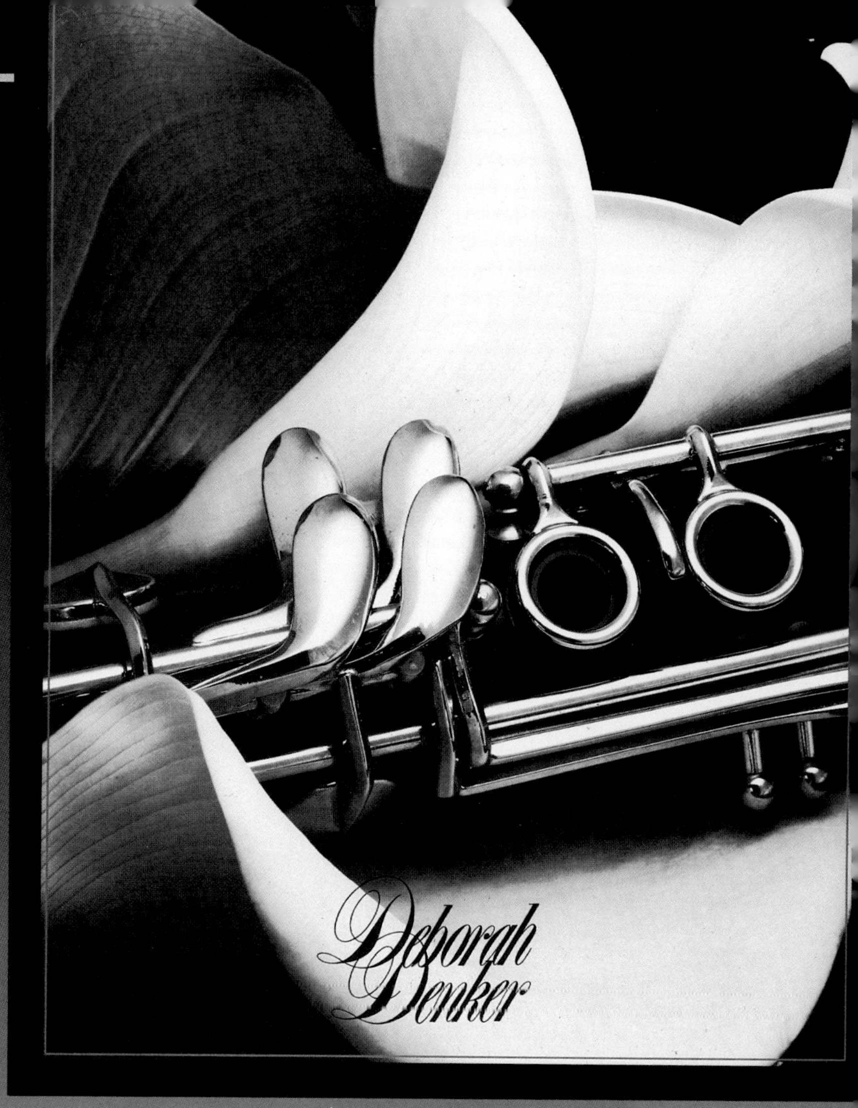
Deborah Denker

D98 DENKER CLARINET & CALLA LILY ☆ 30 × 24

P30 PATTERSON FOR THE JOY OF IT 24 × 30 1/8

FREEMAN PATTERSON / PHOTOGRAPHY FOR THE JOY OF IT

P31 PATTERSON THE ART OF SEEING 23 7/8 × 30 1/8

FREEMAN PATTERSON · PHOTOGRAPHY AND THE ART OF SEEING

32 1/2 × 23

THE
SANTA FE OPERA
1984

P114 PORTER MOON & EVENING CLOUDS

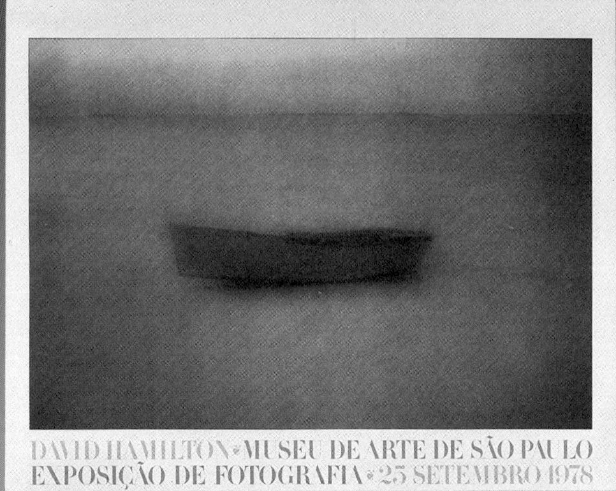
DAVID HAMILTON • MUSEU DE ARTE DE SÃO PAULO
EXPOSIÇÃO DE FOTOGRAFIA • 25 SETEMBRO 1978

H99 HAMILTON SAO PAULO 18 × 24

J U N G · L E E

L50 BABY'S BREATH ☆ 24× 19

UNG/LEE

PEARLS IN A POD
JUNG LEE

L51 PEARLS IN A POD ☆ 24 × 28

H43 RED CHAIR $29^1/_2 \times 19^1/_2$

H44 CAROUSEL $35 \times 23^1/_2$

H42 DEUX TIES $26^1/_8 \times 19^5/_8$

DEUX

LE CHAPITRE
36 RUE SAINT LOUIS EN L'ISLE 75004 PARIS FRANCE

LE CHAPITRE
36 RUE SAINT LOUIS EN L'ISLE 75004 PARIS FRANCE

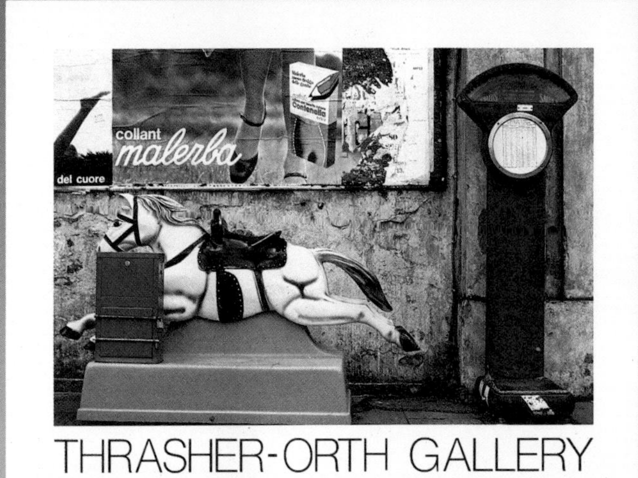
collant
malerba
del cuore
THRASHER-ORTH GALLERY

H20 HORSE $19 \times 25^1/_2$

THRASHER-ORTH GALLERY

H19 TREES $25^1/_2 \times 19$

H7 DEUX BIKES $25 \times 18^{3}/4$

DEUX

H36 GATE $25^{1}/4 \times 18$

THRASHER-ORTH GALLERY

H95 ST. JAMES $25 \times 18^{1}/2$

DEUX

H9 DEUX MEN $25 \times 18^{3}/4$

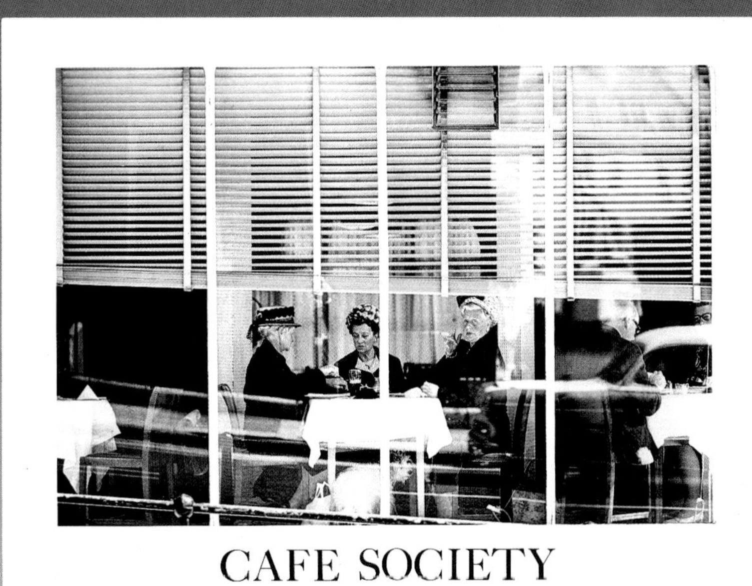

CAFE SOCIETY

H26 CAFE SOCIETY $19 \times 25^{1}/2$

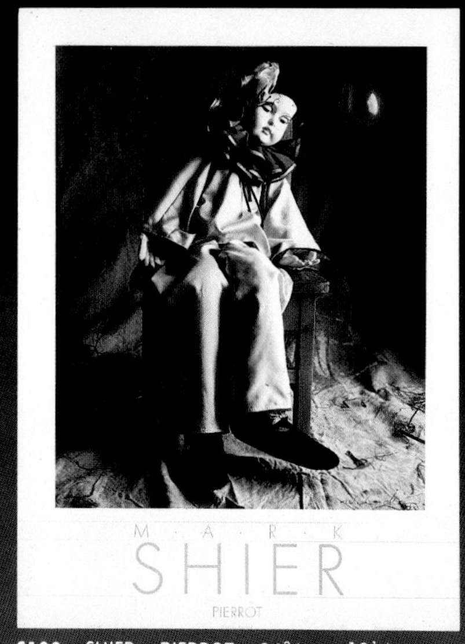
M A R K
SHIER
PIERROT

S102 SHIER PIERROT $24^{3}/_{4} \times 18^{1}/_{4}$

$30 \times 22^{1}/_{2}$

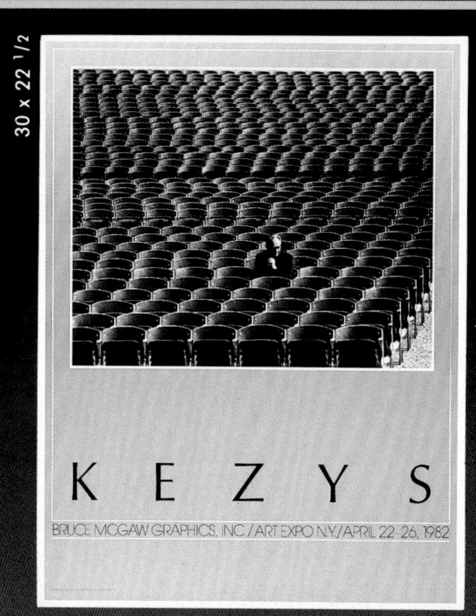
K E Z Y S
BRUCE MCGAW GRAPHICS, INC./ART EXPO N.Y./APRIL 22-26, 1982

K31 KEZYS AMONG PARK BENCHES ☆

K32 KEZYS WOMAN ON STAIRCASE ☆ $30 \times 22^{1}/_{2}$

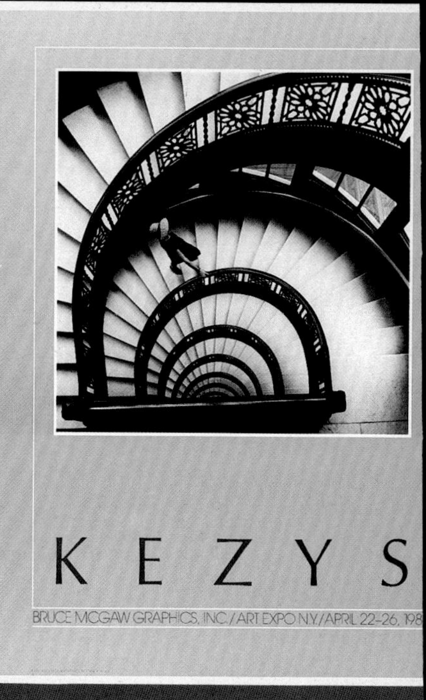
K E Z Y S
BRUCE MCGAW GRAPHICS, INC./ART EXPO N.Y./APRIL 22-26, 198

38×21

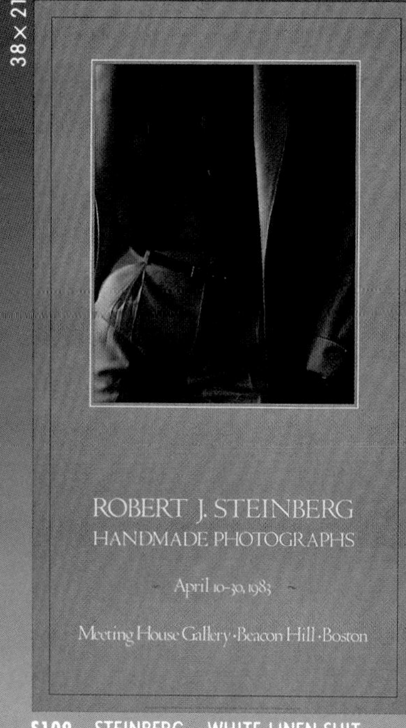
ROBERT J. STEINBERG
HANDMADE PHOTOGRAPHS
April 10-30, 1983
Meeting House Gallery · Beacon Hill · Boston

S109 STEINBERG WHITE LINEN SUIT

$37^{3}/_{4} \times 21$

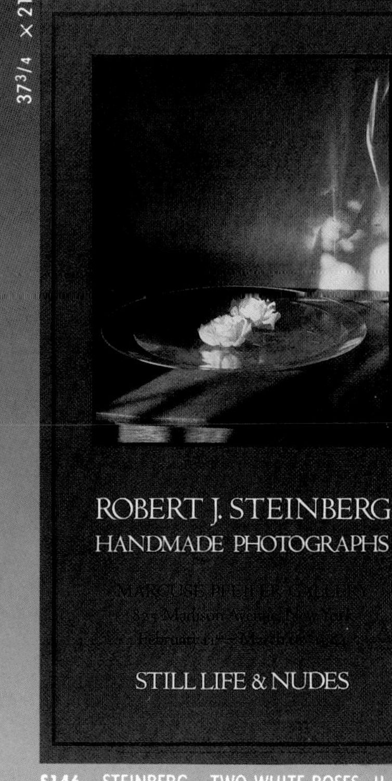
ROBERT J. STEINBERG
HANDMADE PHOTOGRAPHS
STILL LIFE & NUDES

S146 STEINBERG TWO WHITE ROSES, II

47 PENN WOODY ALLEN AS CHAPLIN

RVING PENN

36 × 25

M14 McDOWELL MOONRISE OVER ROLLS ROYCE $22^{1}/_{2} \times 22^{1}/_{2}$

ELLIOTT Mc DOWELL

M13 McDOWELL BOOTS & [illegible]LITZER $26^{1}/_{2} \times 22^{1}/_{2}$

RIDING HIGH

NTAGE PHOTOGRAPHS & ANTIQUE BICYCLES

IDING HIGH $39 \times 18^{3}/_{4}$

hand colored

P103 POLIER HAND COLORED $17^{7}/_{8} \times 24^{7}/_{8}$

F56 SEPARATE TABLES $25\frac{1}{4} \times 36\frac{1}{4}$

F A R B E R
S E P A R A T E T A B L E S

F55 FENETRE DES FLEURS $36\frac{1}{8} \times 24\frac{3}{8}$

FARBER
Fenetre des Fleurs

ROBERT FARBER
M O O D S

F33 VENICE/MOODS $36\frac{1}{4} \times 24\frac{1}{4}$

U M B R E L L A S

R O B E R T F A R B E R

F34 UMBRELLAS $24\frac{1}{2} \times 36\frac{1}{2}$

ROBERT FARBER

F18 CROSS'S FLOWERS ☆ 37 × 25

ROBERT FARBER

ROUSSEAU'S STUDIO

F29 ROUSSEAU'S STUDIO $36^{3}/_{8} \times 24^{1}/_{4}$

F32 MOONSCAPE $24^{3}/_{8}$ x $36^{3}/_{8}$

Robert Farber/Moods

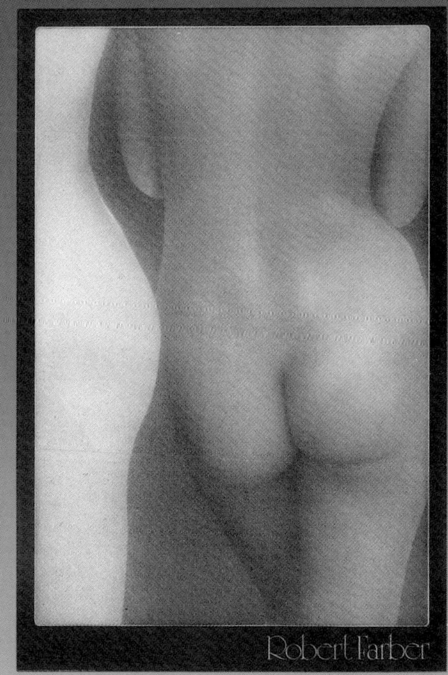
Robert Farber

F30 BEHINDS $36^{7}/_{8}$ x 25

F54 CARESS $36^{1}/_{8}$ x $24^{3}/_{8}$

F20 CURVES ☆ 30 x 40

ROBERT FARBER

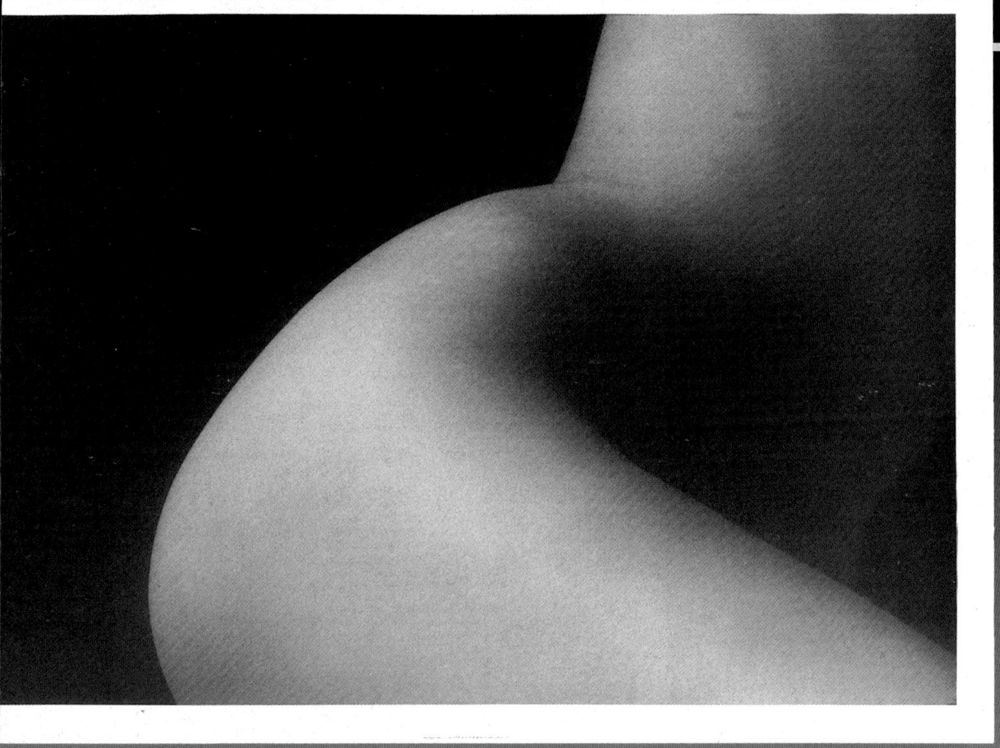

Robert Farber/Images of Woman

F31 JILL 37 x 25

R61 ROWELL LE CAPITANE $35^{7}/_{8} \times 23$

THE WRUBEL GALLERY INAUGURAL EXHIBITION GALEN ROWELL: CALIFORNIA VIEWS
THE NATURE COMPANY FOURTH STREET CENTER BERKELEY CALIFORNIA

D121 DEWITT LAKE ALBERT 25 × 36

DEBORAH DEWITT
DEWITT
EDITIONS LIMITED

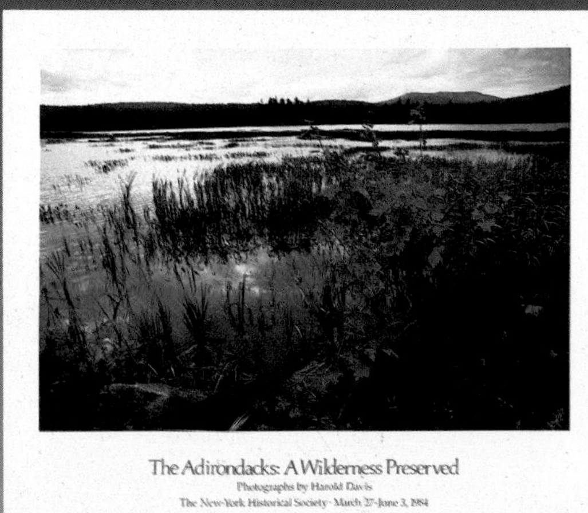
The Adirondacks: A Wilderness Preserved
Photographs by Harold Davis
The New-York Historical Society · March 27-June 3, 1984

D124 DAVIS THE ADIRONDACKS 25 × 30

THE ART OF PHOTOGRAPHER
TUPPER ANSEL BLAKE
WILDLANDS & WILDLIFE OF CALIFORNIA

B157 BLAKE WILDLANDS & WILDLIFE 24 × 32

D123 DAVIS DANCE OF SPRING 25 × 31 1/8

~ The Dance of Spring is the Dance of Life ~

R44 ROWELL MOUNTAIN WILDFLOWER 36 × 22 1/2

Sierra Club
WILDERNESS SERIES

ierra Club
LDERNESS SERIES

HOLMES CANYON WATERFALL 36 × 22 1/2

DEBORAH DEWIT
EDITIONS LIMITED

D122 DEWITT LUNA 25 × 36

H104 HAMILTON GALERIE MONA $26^3/_4 \times 18$

DAVID HAMILTON
Galerie
Mona
15 DÉCEMBRE 1983 · 18 AVENUE MATIGNON · PARIS 8e

F94 FOULKE NUDE $23^7/_8 \times 17^7/_8$

DOUGLAS · FOULKE
40 West 24th Street New York City 212·243·0822

David Hamilton

La Coupole
Exposition de Photographie
Boulevard du Montparnasse-Paris
Juillet Août 1982

H105 HAMILTON LA COUPLE 24×18

KIPTON KUMLER
HARCUS KRAKOW GALLERY · BOSTON

K87 KUMLER FRONDS, WELLESLEY $27^3/_4 \times 21$

G98 GREENE NELLIE NYAD IN BLACK HAT 29 × 24

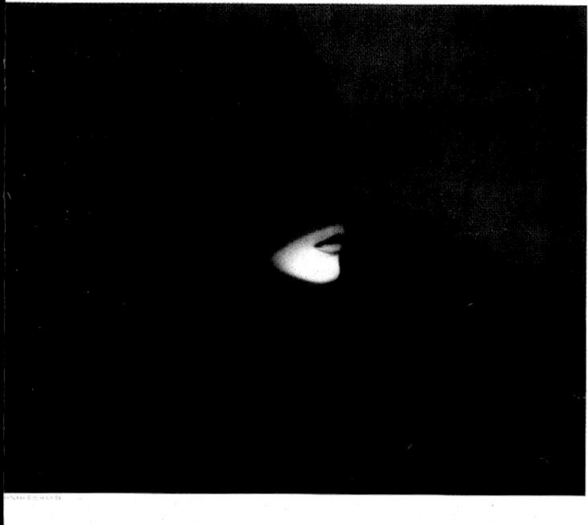

PHOTOGRAPHY WEST GALLERY

B151 BAER GARRAPATA 29 × 24

PHOTOGRAPHY WEST GALLERY

PHOTOGRAPHY WEST GALLERY

W48 WESTON CANAL-NETHERLANDS 29 × 24

PHOTOGRAPHY WEST GALLERY

W46 WESTON MENDENHALL GLACIER 29 × 24

C152 CARTER HOMECOMING 22 3/4 × 17

C149 CARTER SEA & AIR 23 × 17 1/4

M19 MOTI ROSES 20 × 26

M20 MOTI SUNRISE 16 × 28

M163 MOTI CHAMPS DE VIANDE 15 3/4 × 26 1/4

*ALL SIZES ON THIS PAGE INDICATE IMAGES WITHOUT MARGINS

N T S

CARTER FEATHERED MOBILE $23 \times 17^{1}/_{4}$

C151 CARTER CLOSE UP $22^{7}/_{8} \times 17$

M18 MOTI CHRYSANTHEMUMS 20×28

M12 MOTI LE GRAND ARBRE 22×28

**ALL SIZES ON THIS PAGE INDICATE IMAGES WITHOUT MARGINS*

B7 PROMENADE A TROIS 24 × 19 1/4*

B2 TOUR DE FRANCE 23 5/8 × 23 5/8*

B12 BALLOON PLAYERS 27 1/2 × 22 7/8*

B54 LE VIOLON DE JULIETTE 24 × 19 1/4*

B10 FILLE AU VIOLONCELLE 24 × 19 5/8

*ALL SIZES ON THIS PAGE INDICATE IMAGES WITHOUT MARGINS

B3 HOLIDAY ON WHEELS $23^5/_8 \times 23^5/_8$*

B4 JUMP ROPE $29^7/_8 \times 24^3/_8$*

B6 TROTINETTES $22^3/_8 \times 22^3/_8$*

B8 THE TEAM $22^7/_8 \times 28^1/_4$*

*ALL SIZES ON THIS PAGE INDICATE IMAGES WITHOUT MARGINS

B9 LA MATERNITE 31 × 19 1/4 *

B142 LE CHAT DE LA MARIEE 30 1/2 × 25 *

B141 L'ANNONCIATION 23 1/2 × 19 *

B11 BIRD VENDOR 23 3/4 × 23 5/8 *

B5 PRELUDE 19 5/8 × 24 *

ALL SIZES ON THIS PAGE INDICATE IMAGES WITHOUT MARGINS

B139 MADONE DU LAC 23 1/2 × 19 *

B137 OPUS I 25 1/2 × 29 1/4 *

B138 OPUS II 31 1/4 × 25 1/2 *

B140 MADONE AUX TROIS ANGES 23 1/2 × 19 *

**ALL SIZES ON THIS PAGE INDICATE IMAGES WITHOUT MARGINS*

D3 ICE CREAM VENDOR 28×22*
D3A ICE CREAM VENDOR 24×18*

HOTEL EXCELSIOR
A LA BOUTIQUE BLEUE
QUINCAILLERIE-BAZAR-JOUETS
ENTRÉE DE L'HOTEL
Comestibles des

D9 KIOSQUE $24\frac{1}{2} \times 30\frac{1}{4}$*

HOTEL
TABAC

D141 MOULIN DE LA GALETTE $21 \times 28\frac{5}{8}$*

D142 PLACE FURSTENBERG $19\frac{1}{2} \times 24\frac{1}{2}$*

*ALL SIZES ON THIS PAGE INDICATE IMAGES WITHOUT MARGINS

D11 AU BON MUSCADET 24 × 30*
D11A AU BON MUSCADET 14 1/2 × 18*

ALFRED
BROCANTEUR
ESTAMINET
COURS DES HALLES
HOTEL DE ST MALO
FRUITS & LEGUMES
GRANDE CONFISERIE MODERNE
RESTAURANT Cie DE VINS

D2 LES HALLES 27 3/4 × 21 7/8*
D2A LES HALLES 24 × 18*

LIEBIG
TRAITEUR
TABAC
COURS DES HALLES
CAFE-RESTAURANT
FRUITS AGRUMES LEGUMES PRIMEURS
Michel Delacroix

HOTEL
PENSION DE
RESTAURANT

D32 MONTMARTRE 29 3/4 × 21 3/4*

TABAC
EBENISTE
AU GANT D'OR
BOULANGERIE
BUVETTE
OCCASIONS
CAFE TABAC
CONFECTION POUR DAMES & ENFANTS
Michel Delacroix

D10 LA CIVETTE PARISIENNE 24 × 30*
D10A LA CIVETTE PARISIENNE 14 1/2 × 18*

**AII* ALL SIZES ON THIS PAGE INDICATE IMAGES WITHOUT MARGINS*

D E L A

D6 EIFFEL TOWER $31\frac{5}{8} \times 15\frac{7}{8}$*

CAFE RESTAURANT DU PROGRES
CHARCUTERIE MODERNE

D31 LA GARDE REPUBLICAINE $22 \times 29\frac{7}{8}$*

DENTIST
Michel Delacroix

*ALL SIZES ON THIS PAGE INDICATE IMAGES WITHOUT MARGINS

GOULET-TURPIN
RESTAURANT
CONFISEUR
COMESTIBLES

D7 LA COURSE $21\frac{1}{4} \times 25\frac{3}{4}$*
D7A LA COURSE $16 \times 19\frac{1}{2}$*

TEINTURERIE
CAFE-TABAC-BILLARD-VINS
CONFISERIE
HOTEL DU CENTRE

D5 PARADE $18\frac{1}{2} \times 22\frac{3}{8}$*

D34 NUIT DE DECEMBRE 20 × 28*

RESTAURANT
HOTEL
DEBIT DE BOISSONS

HOTEL

D35 PLACE DAUPHINE $23^{3}/_{4}$ × 30*

D33 MOUNT VERNON 22 × 28*

*ALL SIZES ON THIS PAGE INDICATE IMAGES WITHOUT MARGINS

G2 MUIRHEAD 25 × 28 7/8

R.C. GORMAN
March 11th. - April 7th., 1978
Muirhead Galleries Ltd.
South Coast Plaza - Costa Mesa, California

BAYARD GALLERY
R.C. GORMAN 1980

G4 MARIA ☆ 30 × 23

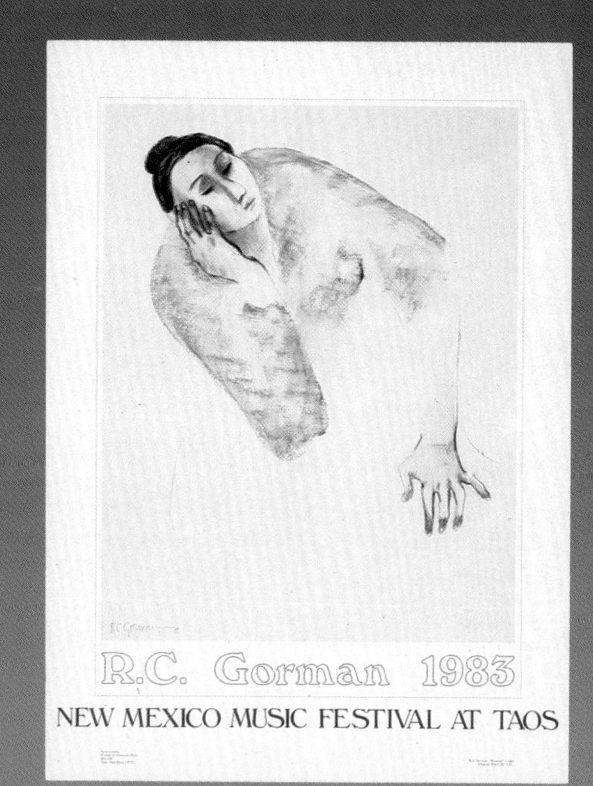
R.C. Gorman 1983
NEW MEXICO MUSIC FESTIVAL AT TAOS

G71 ROWENA 32 × 24

W E S T

*ne night he came striding through the door, resplendent in necklaces of turquoise and a bright red headband. He flung out his hands in greeting. Every fingernail was painted a deep turquoise, ectly matching his rings. We loved it." Lan and Elisabeth Farley are talking not about a rock star, but t R.C. Gorman, who The New York Times has referred to as the "Picasso of Indian artists."**

nan is one of the more prominent Southwestern artists working today providing a body of exciting work is being embraced by the entire population. While the popularity of these posters may once have been ional phenomenon, you can now find these works in museums and galleries, offices and homes, nd the country and around the world.

nan's work is particularly well suited to the poster medium. In his powerfully, understated renditions of jo women, he has depicted not only shapes, lines, and angles, but beauty, dignity, and tradition.

nan and Amado Peña use similar themes in their work, but with each it is the quality of images that es them exceptional. The warm, earth tones, the delicate lines, and the full voluptuous forms make e images as popular as they are. The use of color in conjunction with white spaces leads to visually resting patterns.

draws upon his south Texas background for his work. "I want my audience to know about a group of le—people from my past and from my present—Mexicans, Indians, my children, my friends, the people e southwest," says Peña.

late T.C. Cannon is yet another important artist who used Indian imagery to create very colorful works. in, we see contemporary images that at first appear somewhat amusing, but on closer inspection speak e plight of today's American Indian.

American cowboy is a romantic figure who fascinates people as much today as when he first rode onto plains of the wild west. But these poster images go beyond mere stereotypes showing, for example, the norous viewpoint of D.G. Smith.

striking patterns of Indian pottery make for powerful posters well suited to contemporary decor. Works as Hopi Pottery *are dramatic design statements that also remind people of the wonderful things man pable of creating with his hands.*

and open spaces, tradition and ancient culture, the sun baked colors of the desert and the brilliant s of the Arizona sky are all a part of the imagery of these posters. It is an imagery that has no raphical boundaries and reflects, in a sense, the modernization of America.

Nudes and Foods: Gorman Goes Gourmet *© 1981 by R.C. Gorman and published by Northland Press, Flagstaff, Arizona.*

G48 ROSE'S SHAWL 26 × 17

WESTWOOD GALLERIES
PORTLAND, OREGON
R.C. Gorman

G43 LILY 36 × 24

R.C. GORMAN
NEW MEXICO MUSIC FESTIVA
AT TA
FIFTH SEASON 19

R.C. GORMAN
HOBAR GALLERY SANTA BARBARA, CA DECEMBER 1982

G47 TRILOGY $22^{3}/_{8} \times 24^{7}/_{8}$

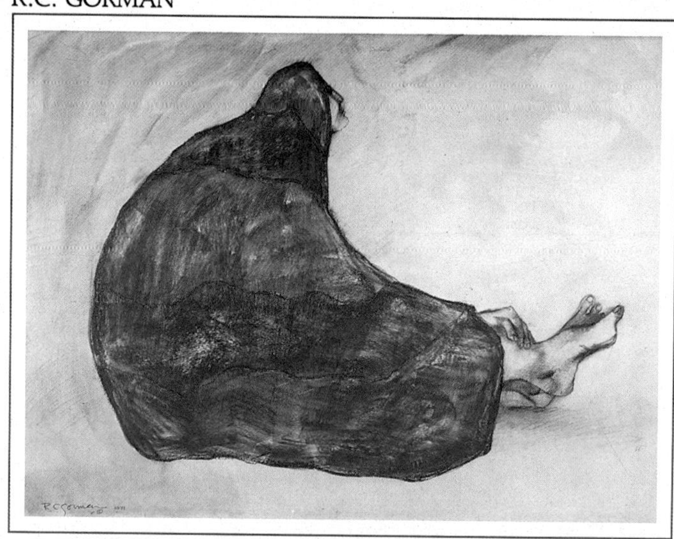
R.C. GORMAN
NEW MEXICO MUSIC FESTIVAL AT TAOS
SCHOLARSHIP PROGRAM 1981

G23 FRANCINE 24 × 30

G3 JEANETTE ☆ 26 × 31

BAYARD GALLERY
R.C. GORMAN 1980

RC Gorman 1981
SUZANNE BROWN GALLERY
SCOTTSDALE, ARIZONA

G61 TAZZIE'S BABY ☆ 22 × 24 1/4

RC GORMAN · 1983 · PB GRAPHICS

G80 LADY IN RED 24 × 30

G86 ANGELINA ☆ 25×18

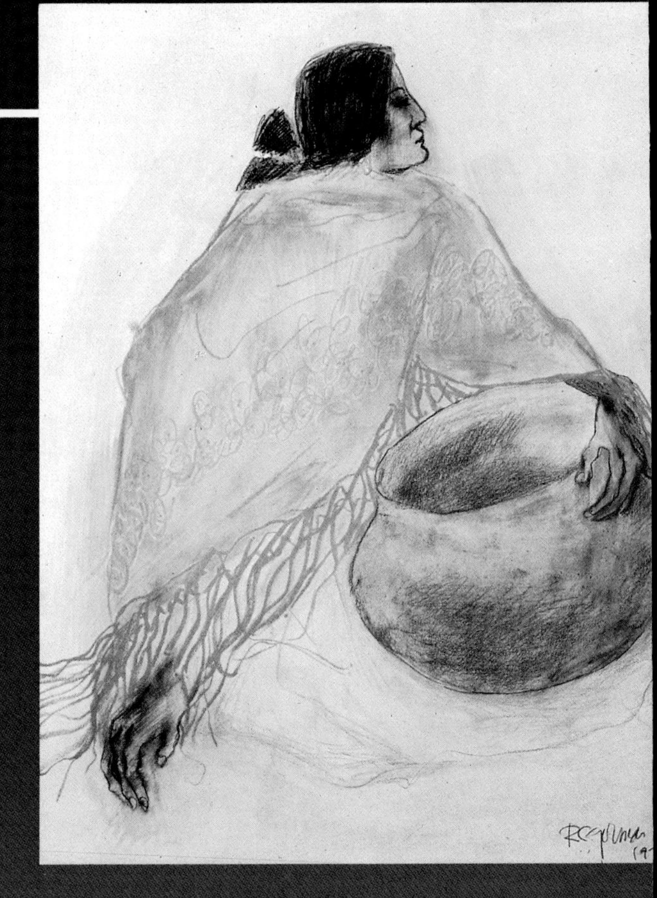

G85 SUE-BAH ☆ $20\frac{3}{4} \times 20\frac{1}{4}$

R. C. GORMAN / SUZANNE BROWN GALLERY / SCOTTSDALE, ARIZONA

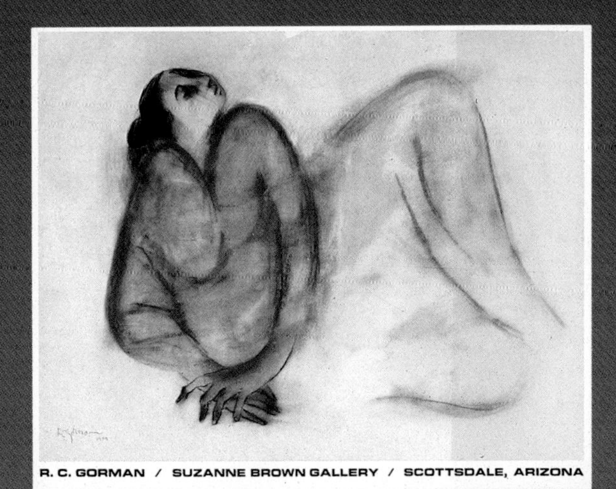
R. C. GORMAN / SUZANNE BROWN GALLERY / SCOTTSDALE, ARIZONA

G60 RECLINING WOMAN ☆ $23 \times 28\frac{1}{2}$

R. C. GORMAN / SUZANNE BROWN GALLERY / SCOTTSDALE, ARIZ

G91 PENSIVE WOMAN ☆ $22 \times 24\frac{3}{4}$

G81 OCT. '83 34 × 24

R.C. Gorman
OBER 1983
NOW & THEN GALLERY
EAST MEADOW, N.Y.

G90 LADY SNOOZING ☆ 28 × 22

ARIZONA THEATRE COMPANY
THE 1982 SEASON
THE PROFESSIONAL RESIDENT THEATRE OF ARIZONA

C. GORMAN / SUZANNE BROWN GALLERY / SCOTTSDALE, ARIZONA

G58 RED RIBBON ☆ $21^{3}/_{4} \times 25^{1}/_{2}$

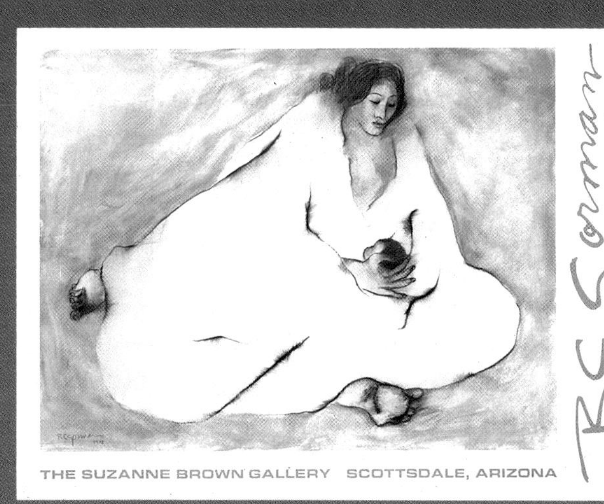
THE SUZANNE BROWN GALLERY SCOTTSDALE, ARIZONA
R.C. Gorman

G92 MOTHER AND CHILD ☆ 18 × 25

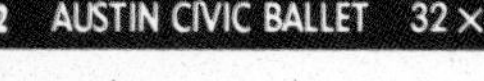
P82 AUSTIN CIVIC BALLET 32 × 22

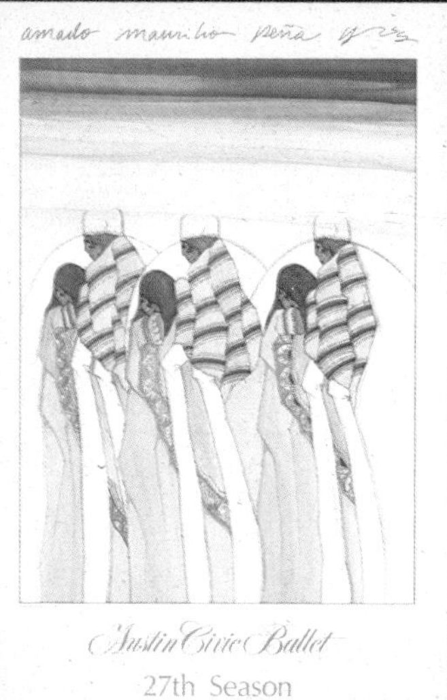
Austin Civic Ballet
27th Season

P77 INDIAN MARKET 25 × 29

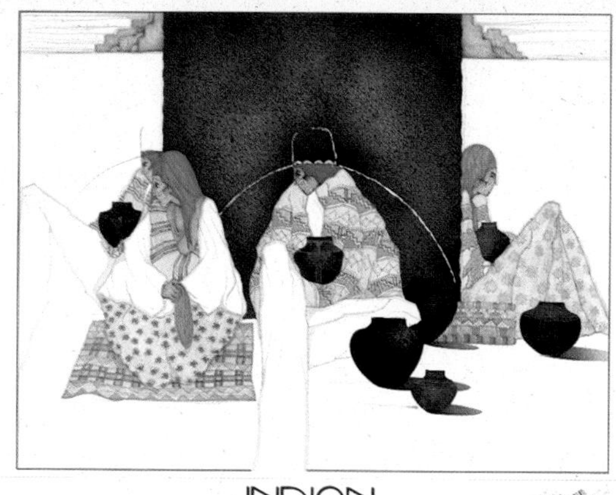
INDIAN
MARKET

P81 OLLA ELEGANTE 32 × 24

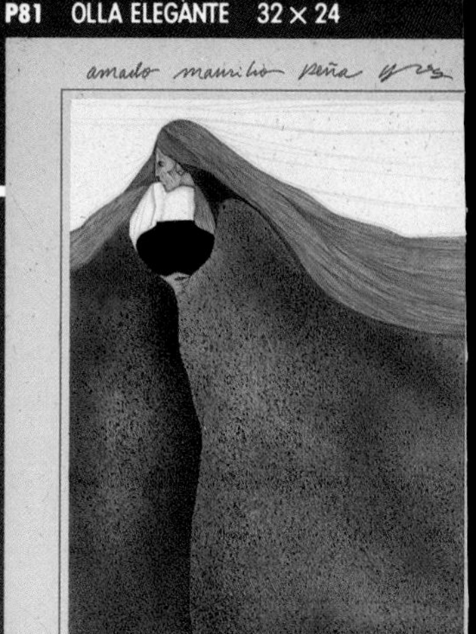
Kokopelli Galleries, Ltd.
Old Town, Albuquerque
1983

P45 CHULOS 32 × 26

E L P I N T O R
T A O S
P79 EL PINTOR 33 × 21

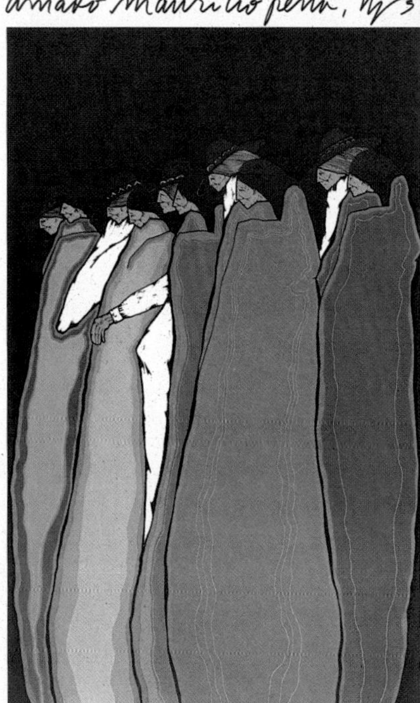
PEOPLESCAPE TWO – DANZANTES
DAGENBELA GALERIA – NOVEMBER 15, 1980 – SAN ANTONIO, TEXAS
P52 DANZANTES $34\frac{7}{8} \times 21\frac{7}{8}$

P80 ARTESANOS 24 × 31$^{7}/_{8}$

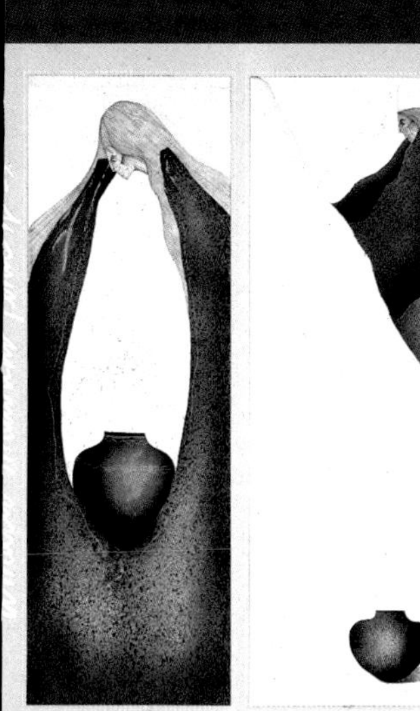

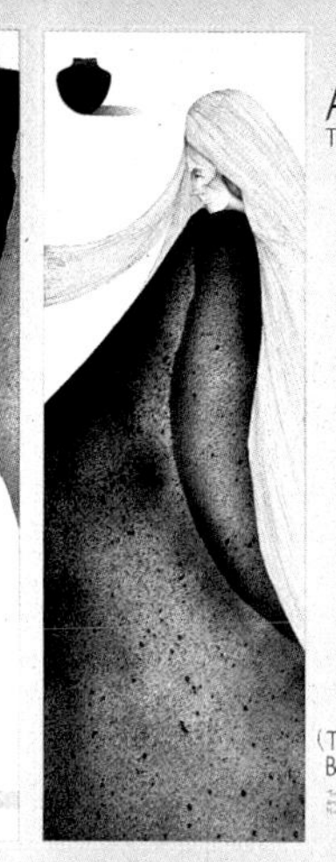
ARTESANOS
The artist and his craft
The Albatross Gallery
Boulder 1983

P76 MUSIC AT ANGEL FIRE 24 × 32

amado maurilio peña jr.
FIRST SEASON · MUSIC AT ANGEL FIRE · SUMMER 1984

amado maurilio peña, jr.
Dagen Bela Galeria San Antonio, Texas
November 14, 1981

P51 PAREJA DOS 35 × 24

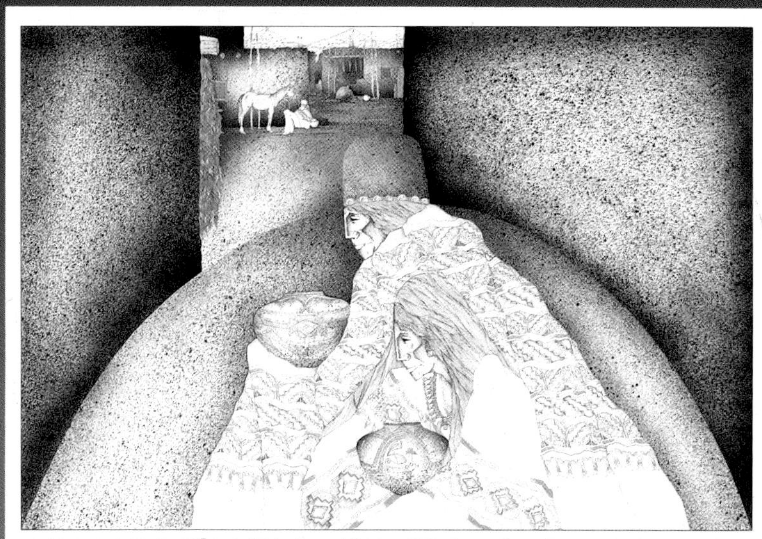
MAURILIO PEÑA, Jr. Fifth Annual Exhibit 1983 DagenBela Galeria San Antonio Texas

P94 DAGEN BELA '83 25 × 35

P40 LA PORTADORA DEL AGUA 28 × 22

amado maurilio peña, jr

P96 EL TALLER OCT. '83 24 × 28

el taller
october 1983

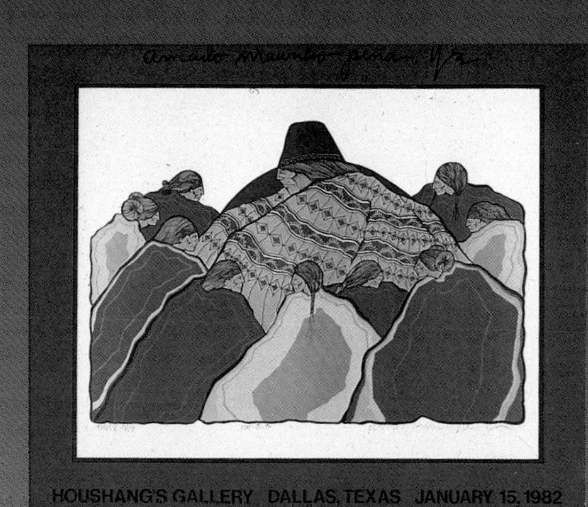
HOUSHANG'S GALLERY DALLAS, TEXAS JANUARY 15, 1982

P57 CUENTISTA $25^1/_2 \times 32$

Su Clinica Familiar
HARLINGEN, TEXAS

P86 MESTIZOS 24 × 30

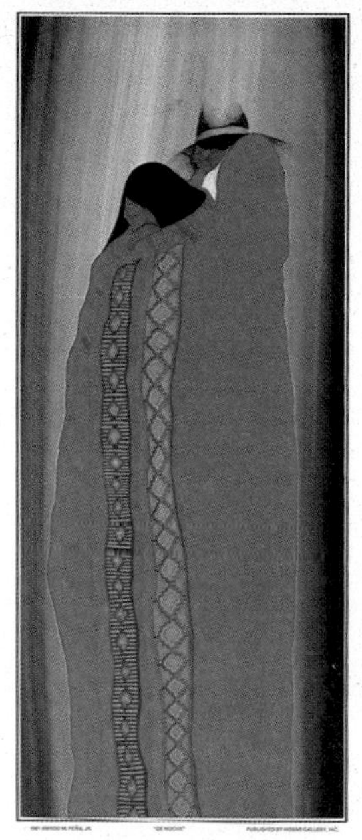
AMADO M. PEÑA, JR.
HOBAR GALLERY
SANTA BARBARA, CALIFORNIA
DECEMBER 5-23, 1981

P55 DE NOCHE $30^1/_2 \times 15^1/_2$

P53 JUNTOS 21 × 38 7/8

amado maurilio peña jr

P93 SOUTHWEST SPIRIT 30 × 24

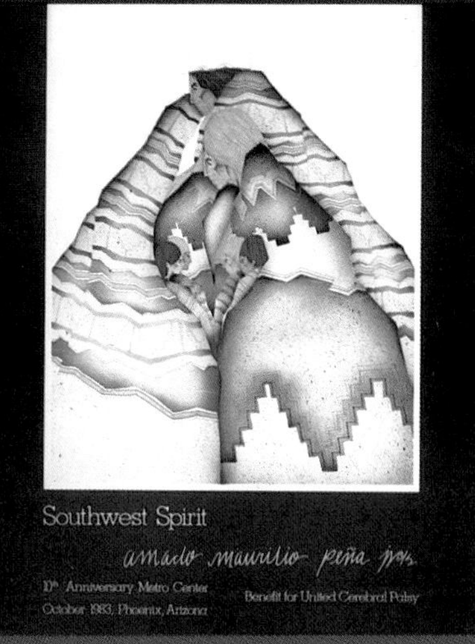
Southwest Spirit
amado maurilio peña jr
10th Anniversary Metro Center
October 1983, Phoenix, Arizona
Benefit for United Cerebral Palsy

amado maurilio peña jr
The Image of Southwest Indian Pottery
THE GRAPHIC IMAGE ☐ MILLBURN, NEW JERSEY ☐ NOVEMBER, 1982

P56 OLLAS VIEGAS 30 1/8 × 22

Kauffman Galleries
Amado Maurilio Peña, Jr.
November 1983
Houston

P95 KAUFFMAN GALLERY '83 21 × 34

P97 GRAPHIC IMAGE '83 30 × 22

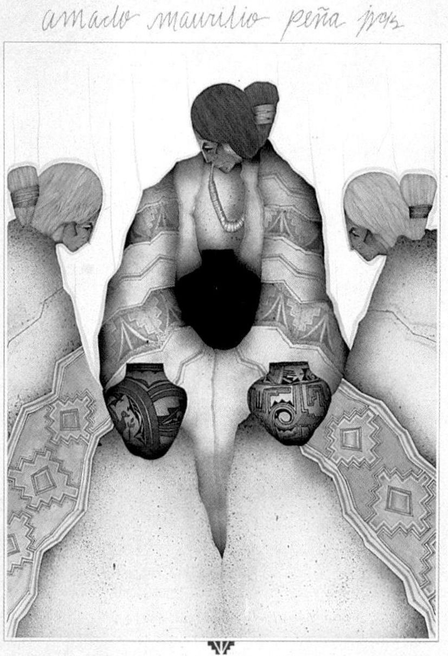
amado maurilio peña
The Image of Southwest Indian Pottery II
THE GRAPHIC IMAGE MILLBURN, NEW JERSEY 1983

P46 FIESTA 32 × 22

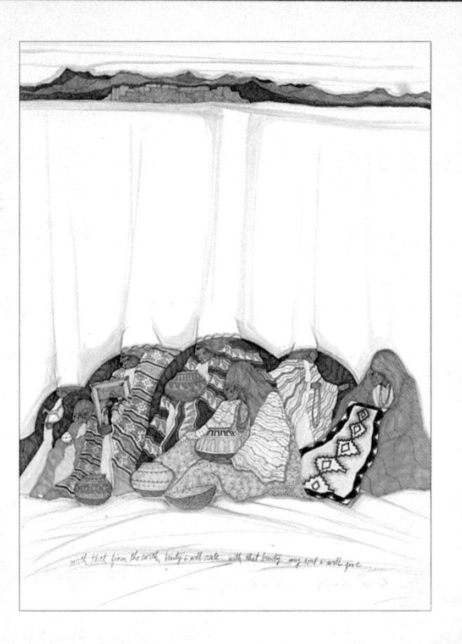
FIESTA 1982
LAGUNA GLORIA ART MUSEUM

P110 CUATRO Y EL VALLE 33 × 20

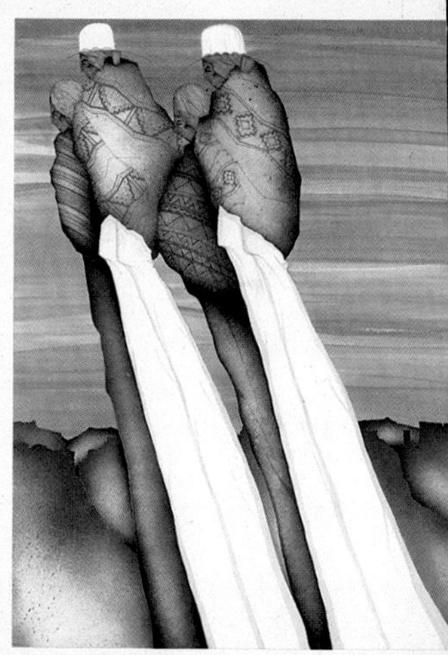
amado maurilio peña
Canyon Gallery
Ft. Lauderdale
January, 1984

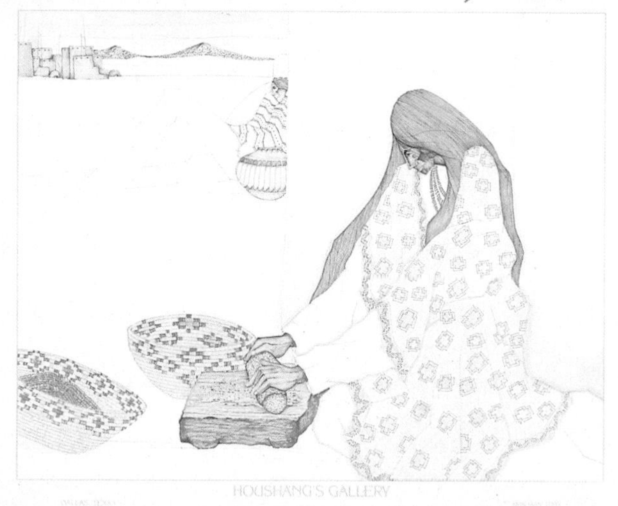
amado maurilio peña
HOUSHANG'S GALLERY

P85 EL METATE 24 × 30

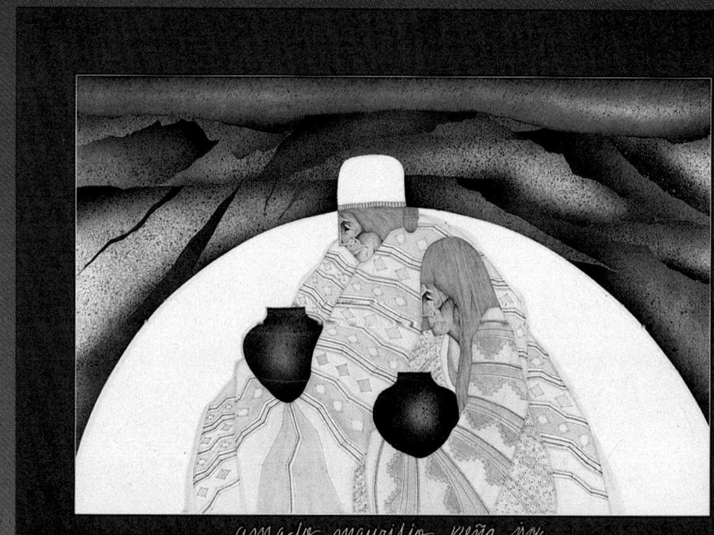
amado maurilio peña
Jubilee Of The Arts
Amarillo Art Center
The second weekend in August

P87 JUBILEE OF THE ARTS 26 × 34

P54 HERMANOS DEL VALLE 31 × 21 1/2

AMADO M. PEÑA, JR.
BAR GALLERY SANTA BARBARA, CA NOVEMBER 1982

P107 WINTER IN COLORADO 33 × 24

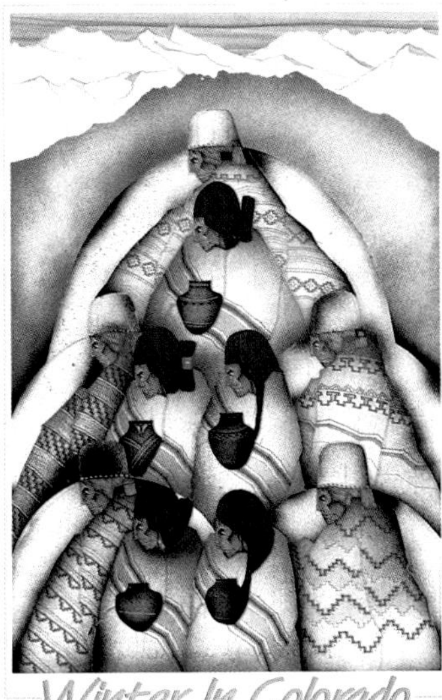
Winter In Colorado
the Squash Blossom
Aspen · Colorado Springs · Denver · Vail

P108 POR LA VENTANA 32 × 20

JOY TASH
GALLERY
March 1984
Scottsdale

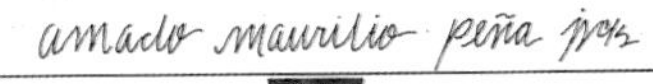
ADAGIO GALLERIES
PALM SPRINGS, CALIFORNIA

P106 OFERTA NUEVA 33 × 24

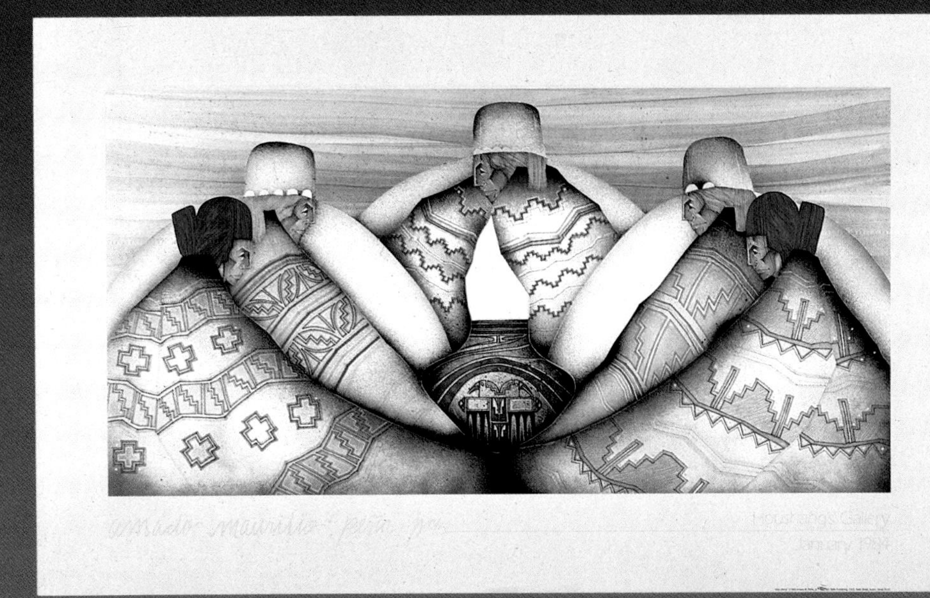

P109 UNA OFERTA 23 × 38

C16 CANNON TWO GUNS 33 × 23 3/8

T. C. CANNON
MEMORIAL EXHIBIT DECEMBER 1979
ABERBACH FINE ART 988 MADISON AVENUE NEW YORK

C17 CANNON WICKER CHAIR 34 1/4 × 23 3/8

TC Cannon
THE WHEELWRIGHT MUSEUM
SANTA FE, NEW MEXICO

T.C. CANNON MEMORIAL EXHIBITION
BUFFALO BILL HISTORICAL CENTER
Cody, Wyoming
MARCH 1981

C50 CANNON GRANDMOTHER 33 × 23 3/8

33 × 23 1/4

TURN OF THE CENTURY DAN
TC Cannon
ABERBACH FINE ART • NEW YORK

C26 CANNON TURN OF THE CENTURY DANDY

All Cannon Posters Offset with Foil Inserts

O20 OREN RODEO $34^{7}/_{8} \times 24$

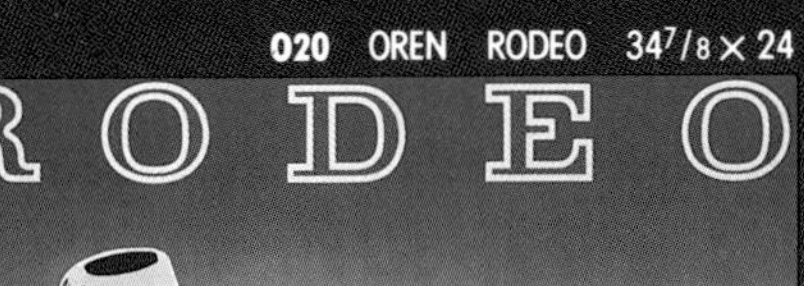
RODEO

F23 FREEMAN COWGIRL *LITHOGRAPH* 26×20

FREEMAN
Serigraphs
Sculptures
EXHIBITION

SMITH NEW WEST '82 *LITHOGRAPH* $34^{3}/_{4} \times 22^{1}/_{4}$

D.G. SMITH
SoHo Gallery
Santa Monica
August 1981

S61 SMITH SANTA MONICA BOOT *LITHOGRAPH* $34^{1}/_{2} \times 14^{5}/_{8}$

M15 MORRISSEAU SHAMAN ☆ 38 × 25

MORRISSEAU
SEPTEMBER 20–
OCTOBER 26, 1980
BAYARD
GALLERY

N35 NIETO POTTER 22 × $26\frac{1}{2}$

JOHN NIETO/ENTHIOS GALLERY/SANTA FE

The Southwest Museum
Los Angeles, California
Hopi Indian Pottery from the Museum's Gift Shop photographed by Monroe Mendelsohn, Discovery Galleries

H86 HOPI POTTERY 25 × 19

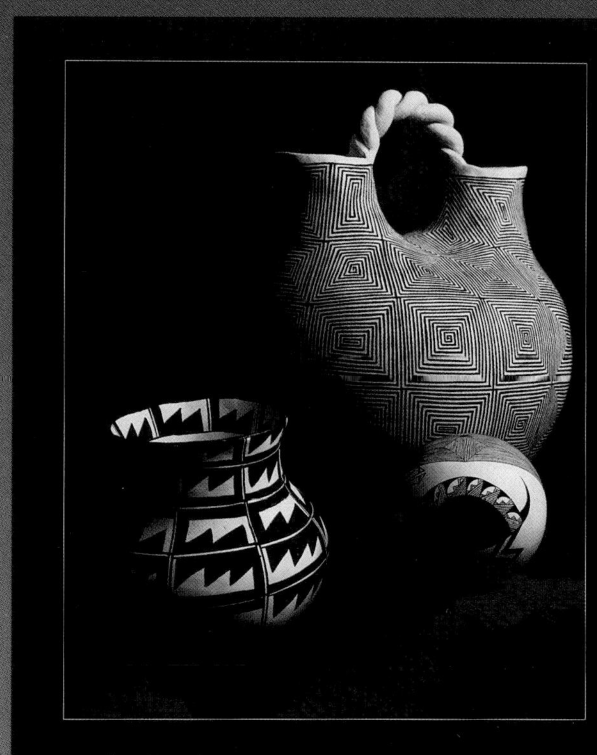
The Southwest Museum
Los Angeles, California
Acoma Indian Pottery from the Museum's Gift Shop photographed by Monroe Mendelsohn, Discovery Galleries

A45 ACOMA POTTERY 25 × 19

CAROL GRIGG/EDITIONS GALLERY/PORTLAND, OR.

AYNARD DIXON

D44 DIXON EARTH KNOWER $28^{3}/_{4} \times 19^{1}/_{2}$

JOHN NIETO / Impressions II, Ltd. / Tucson, Arizona

N34 NIETO DRUMMERS $27^{1}/_{8} \times 21^{7}/_{8}$

D73 De ARCE GUADALOUPE PEAK 25 × 34⁷/8

MANUEL de ARCE
MANY HORSES GALLERY
LOS ANGELES

Justin Coopersmith
BEVERLY HILLS GALLERIES

C67 COOPERSMITH DESERT BLOOM 29 × 23

Justin Coopersmith
BEVERLY HILLS GALLERIES

C54 COOPERSMITH CACTUS FLOWER 29 × 23

C41 CURTIS CACTUS $32^3/_8 \times 23$

RT CURTIS
DISCOVERY GALLERIES
CENTURY CITY • LOS ANGELES

C79 CURTIS CACTUS GARDEN II 33×23

ART CURTIS
DISCOVERY GALLERIES
SANTA MONICA • CALIFORNIA

ART CURTIS
LUNADA BAY GALLERY
PALOS VERDES ESTATES, CALIFORNIA, U.S.A.

C94 CURTIS WINDOW 25×18

ART CURTIS
LUNADA BAY GALLERY
PALOS VERDES ESTATES, CALIFORNIA, U.S.A.

C93 CURTIS TERRA COTTA 25×18

P111 PITIGLIANI 75 YEARS OF FLIGHT 39 × 25

N-X-211
75 Years of Powered Flight
National Air and Space Museum
Smithsonian Institution, Washington, D.C

W62 WILLEBRANT MIXED DOUBLES 26 1/2 × 32 1/2

JAMES WILLEBRANT
Philip Bacon Galleries. Brisbane, Australia. 18 November to 14 December 1983.

CANADY
ART EXPO NEW YORK 1982
BRUCE MAGAW GRAPHICS

C62 CANADY RUNNING '82 30 1/2 × 22

CANADY
ART EXPO NEW YORK 1982

C61 CANADY BASEBALL 30 1/2 × 22

R T S

ci enthusiasts spend the summer bemoaning snowless days. Boaters, on the other hand, suffer through vinter waiting to get their boats back into the water. Joggers sing the praises of their favorite shoes and ll know what Monday night means.

ple are crazy about sports and these posters have as many fans as the events themselves. As interest in ts continues to grow, so will our appreciation for sports art.

st LeRoy Neiman can be credited with bringing sports images to the attention of the public. His keen eye detail combined with vivid brush strokes and exciting colors make for powerful, action paintings. With es of posters already to his credit, the interest in these energetic, bright images remains strong.

nan captures the color, spectacle, and excitement of today's sporting scene. Neiman, who is described as o living, pro adventure, and pro excitement," believes it is the artist's responsibility to be where the ion is taking place. "You have to be there, you have to go to the event when it happens. Then you can nt it," he says.

air ballooning is certainly the most colorful sport to have captured the public's imagination. These ages naturally translate into cheerful, decorative posters.

lear day and a good wind are a sailor's delights. Posters such as the Challenge 12 or Australia II capture essence of the best days and the best boats. They transport one to Newport, the capital of the boating rld, and to the America's Cup, the ultimate boating event.

ce considered mainly a male domain, sports are now embraced by everyone. Whether one's passion is nis or cycling or baseball, there is no doubt that sports posters are very much a part of the picture.

N13 N.B.A. 34 1/4 × 21 3/8

LEROY NEIMA
HAMMER GRAPHICS
33 West 57th Street, New York, N.Y. 10019

N53 SUMMER OLYMPICS, '84 22 3/4 × 32 3/4

LEROY NEIMAN
OFFICIAL ARTIST U.S. OLYMPIC COMMITTEE
Games of the XXIII OLYMPIAD Los Angeles 1984

LEROY NEIMAN
HORSES
HAMMER GRAPHICS 33 West 57th Street, New York, N.Y. 10019

N2 HORSES 37 × 24 1/4

HARRODS LTD.
KNIGHTSBRIDGE LONDON SWIX 7XL
LEROY NEIMAN
OCTOBER 4–OCTOBER 18, 1982

N64 KEVIN KEEGAN 33 1/2 × 24

N7 THE RACE $37^7/_8 \times 23^1/_2$

EROY NEIMAN

BOSTON MARATHON
THE RACE

N12 MIXED DOUBLES $29^1/_2 \times 21^1/_2$

LEROY NEIMAN

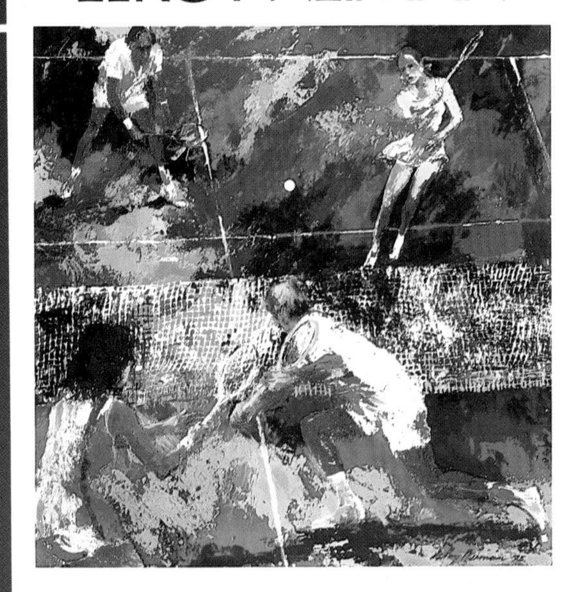

HAMMER GRAPHICS
33 West 57th Street, New York, N.Y. 10019

WESTCHESTER CLASSIC

N11 WESTCHESTER CLASSIC $28^5/_8 \times 22^5/_8$

LEROY NEIMAN

Hammer Graphics
33 WEST 57th STREET, NEW YORK, NY 10019

N8 ARNIE IN THE RAIN $23^3/_8 \times 29^1/_4$

N66 BARYSHNIKOV $35^{7}/_{8} \times 23^{7}/_{8}$

MIKHAIL BARYSHNIKOV
Presented by
The Des Moines Ballet
Des Moines Civic Center July 21, 1983

N65 ROGER STAUBACH $34^{1}/_{2} \times 22^{1}/_{4}$

LEROY NEIMAN
"AMERICA'S QUARTERBACK"
HAMMER GRAPHICS
33 West 57th Street, New York, N.Y. 10019

N67 JOE NAMATH $33^{1}/_{2} \times 25$

HAMMER GRAPHICS

F.X. McRORY'S WHISKEY BAR · SEATTLE

N33 F.X. McRORY'S WHISKEY BAR $22^{1}/_{8} \times 38^{1}/_{8}$

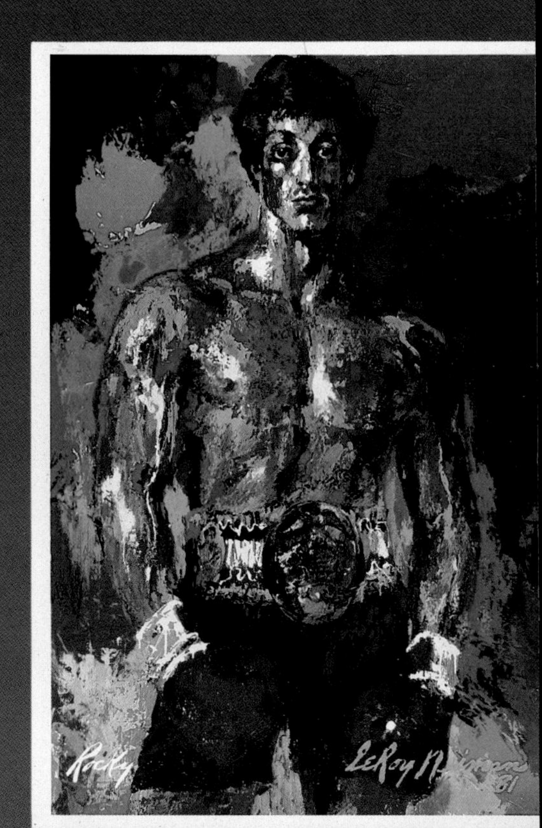
Rocky

N68 ROCKY III $32^{1}/_{4} \times 22^{1}/_{4}$

N10 SAILING $25^{5}/_{8} \times 29^{3}/_{4}$

LEROY NEIMAN
HAMMER GRAPHICS 33 WEST 57th STREET, NEW YORK

LEROY NEIMAN
MMER GRAPHICS 33 West 57th Street, New York, N.Y. 10019

N24 BASEBALL $33^{5}/_{8} \times 23$

N28 LITTLE HITTER 32 × 24

"THE STAGS HEAD"

N57 DUBLIN BAR *SERIGRAPH* $22^{3}/_{4} \times 33^{1}/_{2}$*

LeRoy Neiman '80

N58 OLYMPIC SLALOM *SERIGRAPH* $17^{1}/_{2} \times 24$*

*ALL SIZES ON THIS PAGE INDICATE IMAGES WITHOUT MARGINS

N59 AMERICA'S CUP *SERIGRAPH* 23 × 28 1/4*

LeRoy Neiman fans should take special note of his plate signed serigraphs. Printed in a manner similar to Neiman's original numbered serigraphs, these dynamic pieces provide a unique opportunity for the discriminating collector.

These exciting hand pulled serigraphs have been printed in as many as 16 colors to Neiman's exacting specifications. Although somewhat more costly than his poster images, these impelling pieces offer a viable alternative to Neiman's still more expensive originals.

N60 NEW YORK SCENE *SERIGRAPH* 16 1/4 × 28 1/2*

*ALL SIZES ON THIS PAGE INDICATE IMAGES WITHOUT MARGINS

C134 CHALLENGE 12 27 × 19³/₄

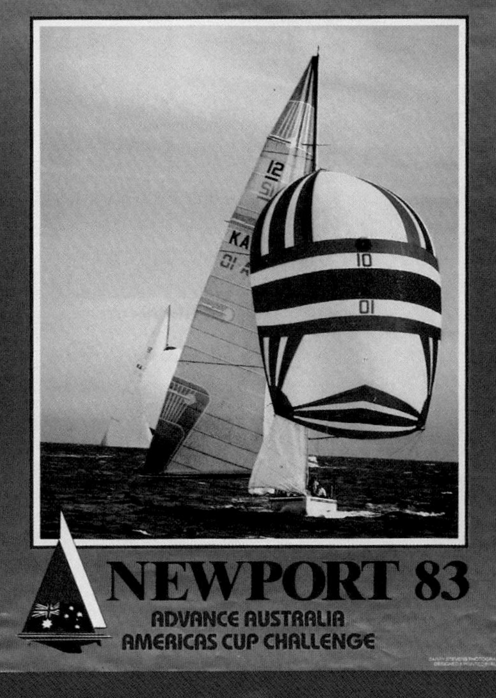
CHALLENGE 12
NEWPORT 83
ADVANCE AUSTRALIA
AMERICAS CUP CHALLENGE

D111 DANBY CANADA I 30 × 22

KEN DANBY
CANADA I
CHALLENGING CLIPPER
AMERICA'S CUP YACHT RACES, NEWPORT 1983

ALEX COLVILLE
MIRA GODARD GALLERY
CALGARY · TORONTO

C24 COLVILLE SAILING 24¹/₈ × 33

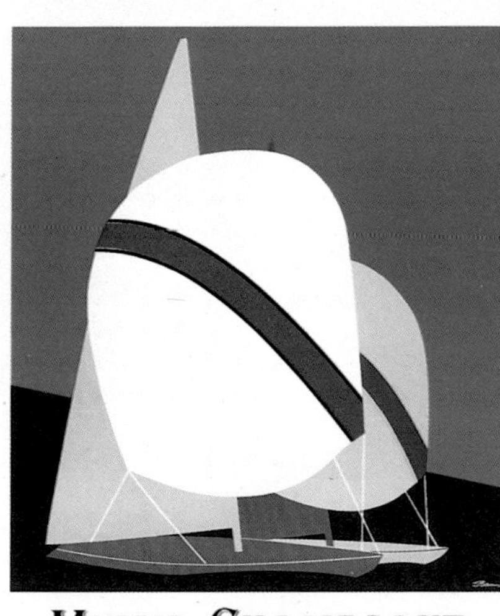

MUMM CHAMPAGNE
SPONSORING
25TH DEFENSE
AMERICA'S CUP
NEWPORT, R.I. 1983

B134 BARNS 25th AMERICA'S CUP 24 × 18

N51 NAGATA THE CHASE 36 × 24

NAGATA

L61 LA FEMME WORLD CUP '83 SERIGRAPH $30^1/_8 \times 22^1/_4$

WORLD CUP '83
Art 2Go
Manhattan Beach California

BILL BINZEN
LE CHAPITRE

B110 BINZEN LE CHAPITRE $28^3/_4 \times 22$

NANTUCKET
The Rainbow Fleet
c. 1920

G121 GARDINER RAINBOW FLEET 23 × 28

F91 FANCH LES BALLOONS 30 × 24

FANCH
Christie's Contemporary Art

D45 DAGGETT SHATTERED SILENCE 30 × 21 1/2

NOËL DAGGETT
art expo NY 81
Triton Press NYC

O22 OREN HOT AIR BALLOONS 36 × 24

THE BATTLE CREEK
JUNE 20 THRU JUNE 28, 1981
WORLD HOT AIR BALLOON CHAMPION
BATTLE CREEK, MICHIGAN

greg curnoe

C33 CURNOE MARIPOSA T.T. 25 × 32 7/8

Michael Potter
Christie's
Contemporary Art

P28 POTTER SKIER 28 × 22

N55 NAGATA TAKE OFF $35^{7}/_{8} \times 24$

NAGATA

B76 BERGEN HOT AIR BALLOONS $33^{7}/_{8} \times 25$

Hot Air Balloons
LORENZO BERGEN GALLERY · 730 ROYAL ST. · NEW ORLEANS

H97 HANSEN THE MAGIC OF FLIGHT 22×28

THE MAGIC OF FLIGHT
HAROLD E. HANSEN

S ANGELES 1984

C145 CZILLER L.A. '84 $36 \times 22^{1}/_{2}$

DEAUVILLE

R53 RAZZIA DEAUVILLE $34^{3}/_{8} \times 24^{7}/_{8}$

S H O T W E L L

S96 SHOTWELL BLINDS & WINE ☆ 24 × 18

L I F E S

ve always wanted to be a zebra breeder, but when I saw the graphics of this image my mania for tripes was satisfied," jokes photographer Chuck Shotwell about his award winning poster, Blinds & *. In the hands of artists such as Shotwell, common objects become the elements for striking and ual still life images.*

ife posters take the very ordinary and transform it into something quite extraordinary. Everyday ts that have been looked at countless times suddenly become an integral part of a larger picture of ımmate beauty.

etimes a simple task for the eye makes for a wonderful visual experience and I think that is what has ened here," Shotwell adds on a more serious note. "A pretty, simple, quiet photograph can give a very rful graphic image."

is a tranquility in the imagery of still life posters that offers a calming respite from the frenetic pace of rn day life. To look at a piece by an artist such as Jeff Kahn is a chance to visually catch your breath. e are quiet, lovely images that give one a chance to pause from the demands of life.

e are images that often confront us in a very nonthreatening manner. They are images that soothe. rs such as Brian Kelley's Orchid *are still lifes not only because they are an arrangement of still objects, ecause they visually offer one a stillness that is a moment of peace.*

s are objects of intricate beauty that fascinate people and still life posters such as those by Ed Cota an abundance of images that confirm this. Eclectic shapes and delicate hues make these posters l delights. After seeing these posters, take a walk on the beach. Stop to pick up some shells and notice your appreciation for their many nuances has increased.

ifes add a touch of humaness to our environment. They are images that one can easily relate to and, are conducive to use in any kind of design situation, be it in the home or in a more public space. gh often associated with traditional forms of artistic expression, still lifes, in fact, cover a broad rum of styles including the more new wave, high tech images of artists like Piero Vinci and Michael

ole played by the artist is that of a teacher, showing people a new way of looking at things. Still life es can provoke people to take a fresh look at the things they see all the time and discover the beauty might otherwise be too preoccupied to find.

J E F F

K67A STILL LIFE "A" 24 × 30

JEFF KAHN-GRAPHIKS-BOSTO

JEFF KAHN-GRAPHIKS-BOSTON-

MIAMI-FT. LAUDERDALE-DALLAS

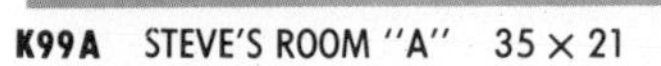

K99A STEVE'S ROOM "A" 35 × 21

K99B STEVE'S ROOM "B" 35 × 21

K A H N

K67B STILL LIFE "B" 24 × 30

AMI-FT. LAUDERDALE-DALLAS

JEFF KAHN-GRAPHKS-BOSTON-

K98A BLACK TABLE "A" 24 × 30

MIAMI-FT. LAUDERDALE-DALLAS

K98B BLACK TABLE "B" 24 × 30

S T I L L

M58 MELCHER RANCH VISIT 37 ×

Nell Melche

E66 EGGS AND EARTH $16\frac{1}{2} \times 36$

THE NATURE COMPANY 10 YEARS

BETH · GALTON

G56 GALTON SEWING BASKET $27\frac{1}{8} \times 22$

T Y L E R · D E A

PARASOL STILL LIFE / © 1984 MIRAGE EDITIONS INC SM C

D127 DEAN PARASOLS $21\frac{7}{8} \times 36$

E77 ELLESCAS JAPANESE LANTERN 36 × 24

DICK ELLESCAS
DISCOVERY GALLERIES

D129 DUNLAP TWO VASES 24 × 18

SCOTT DUNLAP/PHOTOGRAPHY/LOS ANGELES

CHARLES SCHNEIDER AT SEWELL & CO

S155 SCHNEIDER SEWELL AND CO. 24 × 32

CHARLES SCHNEIDER · PHOTOGRAPHY · RARE GLASS

S138 SCHNEIDER RARE GLASS 24 × 36

G66 GROSJEAN EGG & ROSE 24 × 20

Grosjean.

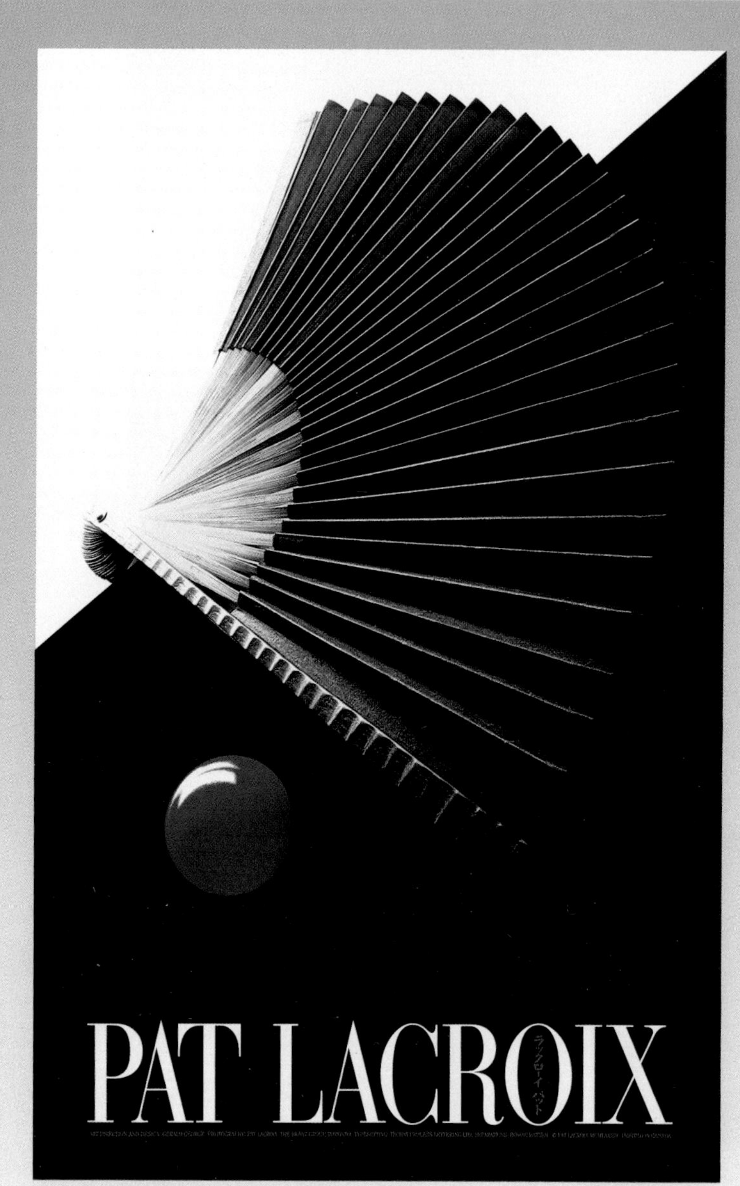
PAT LACROIX

L49 LACROIX FAN $34^1/_4 \times 21^3/_4$

Les
Chapeaux
East Wing
Editions

B81 BRESCIA LES CHAPEAUX $28^1/_8 \times 22^1/_8$

S139 SOLINSKY LAVENDER WINDOW 28 × 20

OLINSKY : COLOR

S150 SOLINSKY CHURCH WINDOW 28 × 20

SOLINSKY : COLOR

DAVID HAMILTON
POTERIES · ANCIENNES
ANTIQUITES
LES GRANGES SAINT-ANDRÉ
83350 · RAMATUELLE · 10 KM DE ST TROPEZ

H107 HAMILTON POTERIES ANCIENNES 24 × 18

Galerie
Mona

DAVID HAMILTON

15 DÉCEMBRE 1983 · 18 AVENUE MATIGNON · PARIS 8e

H106 HAMILTON ROSE STILL LIFE 24 × 18

K89 KELLEY BLUE TABLETOP 34 × 24

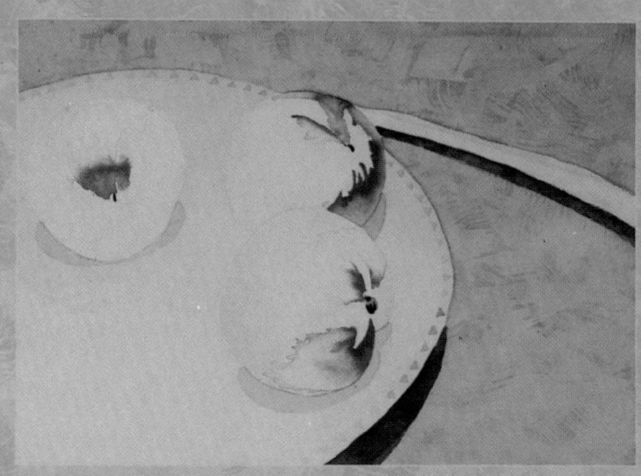
BRIAN KELLEY

POSTERS INTERNATIONAL INC.

BRIAN KELLEY
POSTERS INTERNATIONAL INC.

K88 KELLEY PINK TABLETOP 18 × 39

BRIAN KELLEY
POSTERS INTERNATIONAL INC.

K90 KELLEY CHERRIES 18 × 39

D115 DOJC WHEAT DECO 36 × 18 1/2

·YURI·DOJC·

Z7 ZELDIN STILL LIFE 39 1/4 × 31 3/4

D MASTERSON / PHOTOGRAPHY

M86 MASTERSON WINE & GLASS 20 × 30

P105 PORTER BLUE CRAYONS 20 × 16

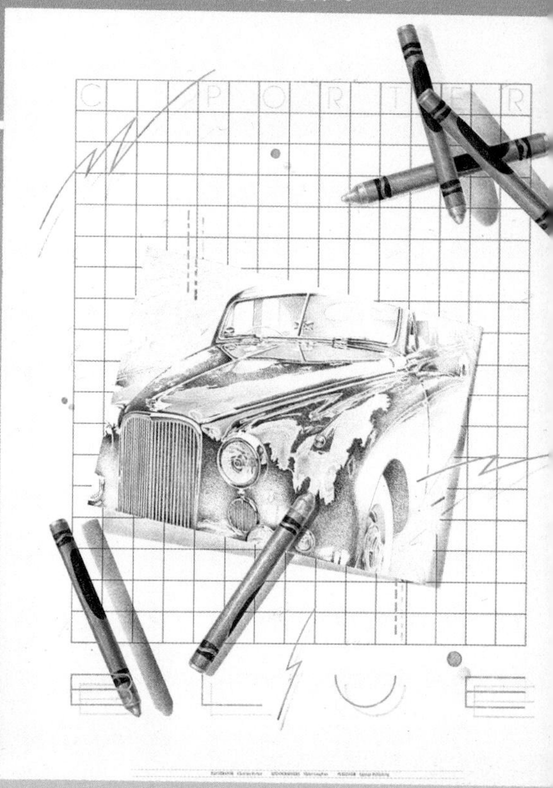
PORTER
BLUE

V11 VINCI BATHROOM SUITE 17 × 19$^{1}/_{2}$

PIERO VINCI 84
PIERO · VINCI ··· BATHROOM · SUITE
LETRATONE · AND · PANTONE · COLLAGES L'AFFICHE · ILLUSTREE · FLORENCE · ITALY

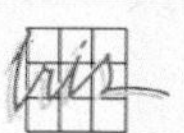
Iris

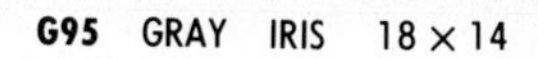

G95 GRAY IRIS 18 × 14

Carnations

G94 GRAY CARNATIONS 18 × 14

P104 PORTER RED CRAYONS 20 × 16

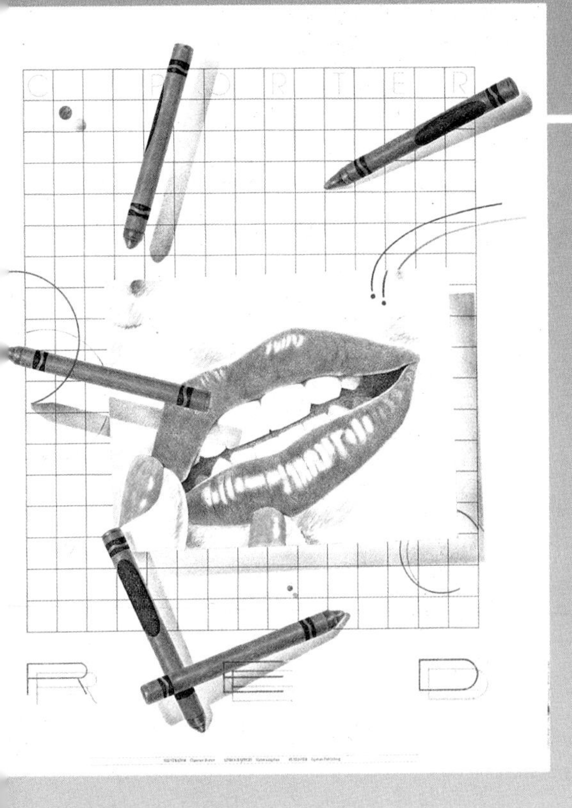
PORTER
RED

V12 VINCI BATHROOM SINK 17 × 19 1/2

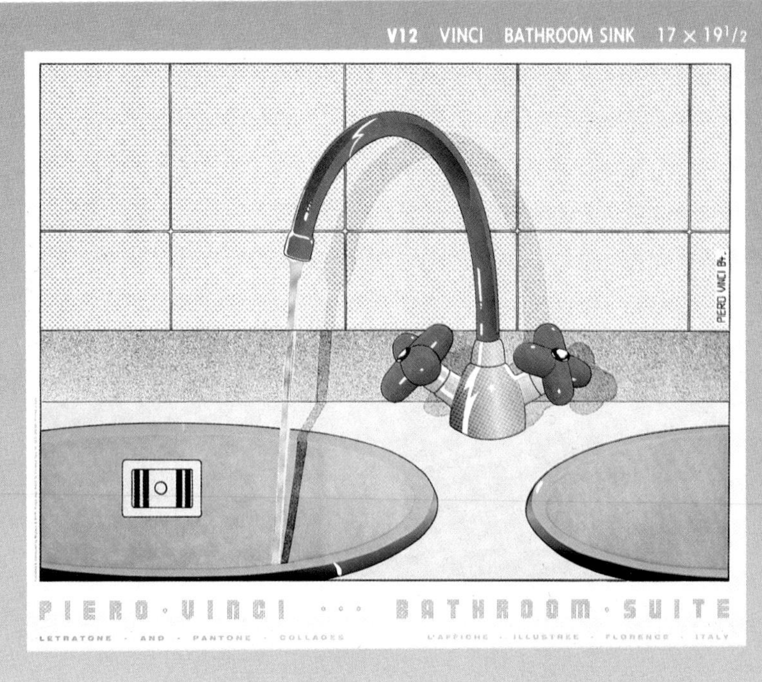
PIERO VINCI
PIERO · VINCI ··· BATHROOM · SUITE
LETRATONE · AND · PANTONE · COLLAGES
L'AFFICHE · ILLUSTREE · FLORENCE · ITALY

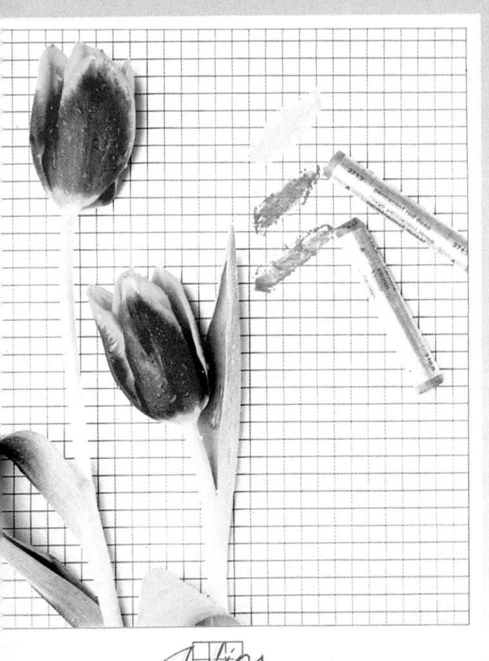
Tulips

G96 GRAY TULIPS 18 × 14

Orchids

G97 GRAY ORCHIDS 18 × 14

C75 COTA WHITE SHELL 34 × 35

ED COTA
DISCOVERY GALLERIES
SANTA MONICA · CALIFORNIA

M54 MARTIN NAUTILUS 20 × 29 1/4

KENNETH MARTIN · SEASIDE GALLERY / AUGUST 1982

34 × 12 1/2

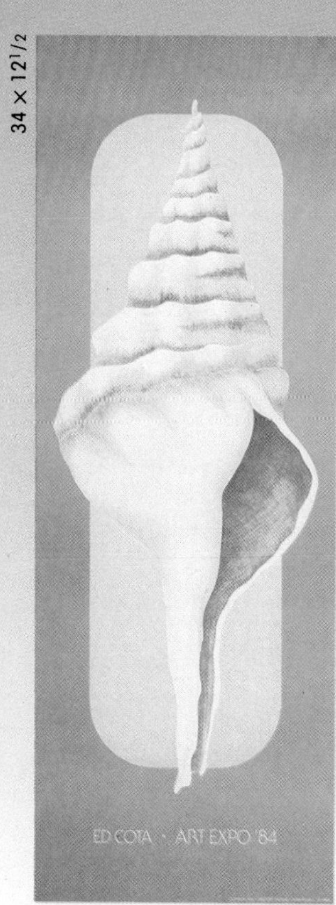
ED COTA · ART EXPO '84

C130A COTA SEA SHELL "A"

ED COTA
DISCOVERY GALLERIES CENTURY CITY · LOS ANGELES

C57 COTA CONCH SHELL 34 × 25

ED COTA · ART EXPO '84

C130B COTA SEA SHELL "B

S81 SPAFFORD NAUTILUS 34 × 25

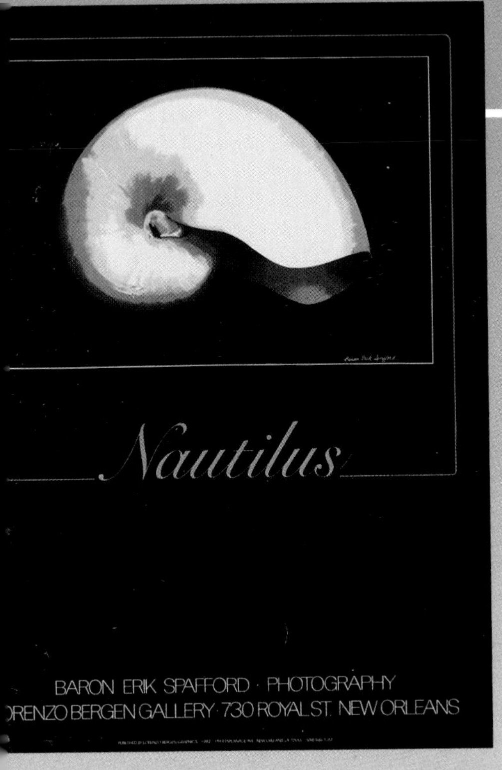
Nautilus
BARON ERIK SPAFFORD · PHOTOGRAPHY
RENZO BERGEN GALLERY · 730 ROYAL ST. NEW ORLEANS

J22 JORSTADT NAUTILUS 26 × 31

JOHN G. SHEDD
A·Q·U·A·R·I·U·M
N·A·U·T·I·L·U·S
THE OCEAN BY THE LAKE CHICAGO

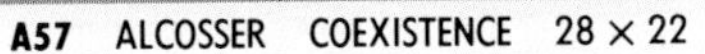
COEXISTENCE

A57 ALCOSSER COEXISTENCE 28 × 22

JAMES RANDKLEV
CHAMBERED NAUTILUS

R17 RANDKLEV SHELL 24 × 30

G76 GAETANO Z GALLERIE 36 × 24

Z·GALLERIE
· LOS ANGELES ··· SAN FRANCISCO ·

D29 DAVIS STILL LIFE $32^1/_4 \times 24^1/_4$

Richard Davis
Atelier Gallery
3039 Granville St., Vancouver, Canada

LAKE VIEW · METROPOLITAN ART GRAPHICS

S142 SHTEIMAN MIXED MEDIA $24 \times 35^3/_4$

steven r. miller
ART EXPO 1981 · SAN FRANCISCO
KRASKIN GARNER

M46 MILLER PENCILS 36 × 24

Y12 YANAI OPEN WINDOW $25^7/_8 \times 35^3/_4$

S101 SANTANDER AFRICAN VIOLETS $24^5/_8 \times 29$

narek yanai
lea r. malis, art publishers

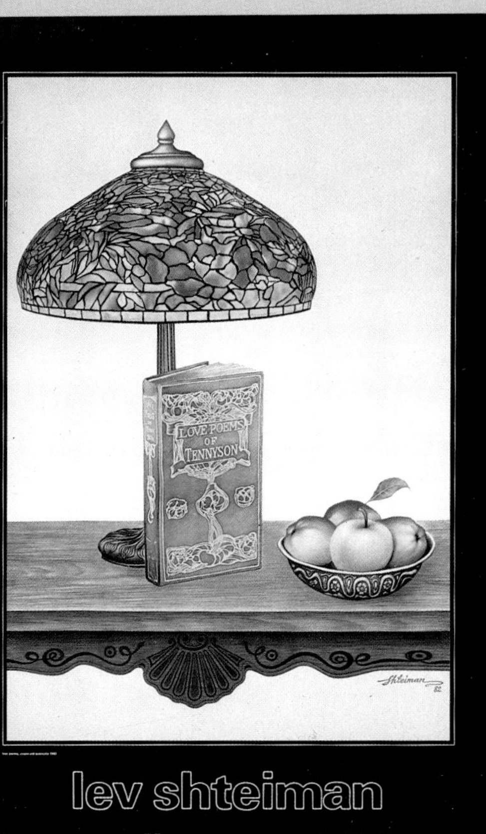
LOVE POEMS OF TENNYSON
lev shteiman
lea r. malis art publishers

S84 SHTEIMAN LOVE POEMS $38^5/_8 \times 25^3/_4$

ELLEN MAYER
FRONT LINE EDITIONS
MAY 1983

M84 MAYER TEDDY BEAR AND VASE 24×36

H127 HARTE DEJEUNER $31^{1}/_{2} \times 23$

GLYNN BOYD HARTE
L'Affiche Illustrée - Via Guelfa 14/r Via dei Servi 69/r Florence

H126 HARTE POT-AU-FEU $31^{1}/_{2} \times 23$

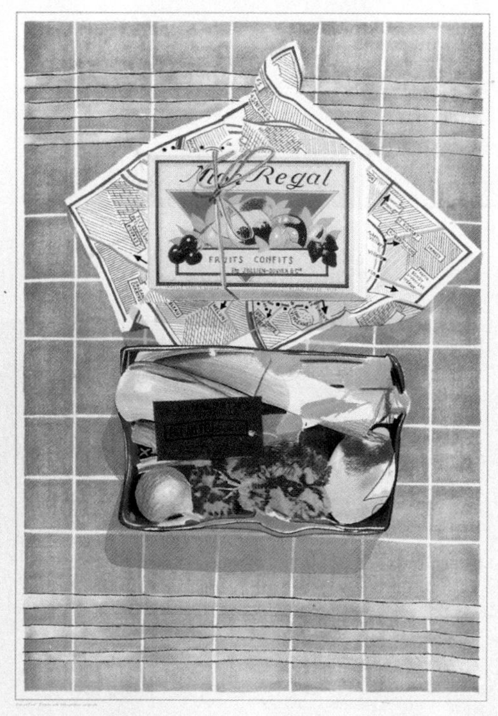
FRUITS CONFITS
Glynn Boyd Harte
L'Affiche Illustrée - Via Guelfa 14/r - Via dei Servi 69/r - Florence

L70 LEONARDO PORTAL 28 × 22

GRAPHIQUE DU JOUR / NIK LEONARDO

L72 LEONARDO PALLADIO 22 × 28

GRAPHIQUE DU JOUR / NIK LEONARDO

A R R

F106 FARR APRICOTS & SKY 23 × 23

FLORIDA
KIM WHITESIDES

W63 FLORIDA ☆ 25 × 36

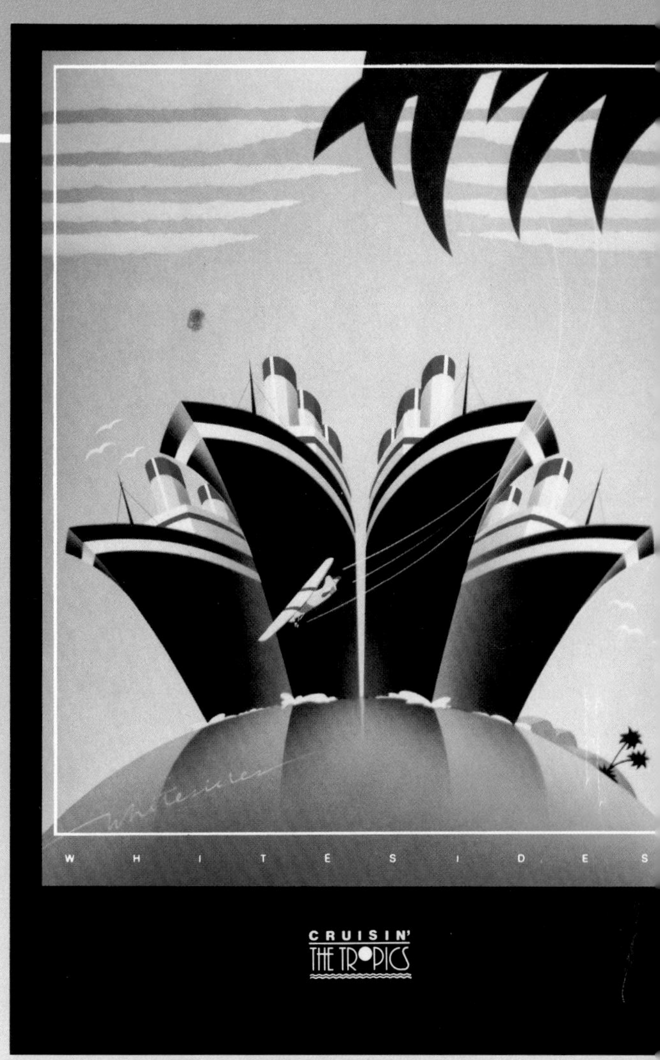
W H I T E S I D E S
CRUISIN'
THE TROPICS

W64 CRUISIN' THE TROPICS ☆ 36 × 25